Quiet Pioneering

Quiet Pioneering

Robert M. Stern and His
International Economic Legacy

Edited by
Keith E. Maskus,
Peter M. Hooper,
Edward E. Leamer, *and*
J. David Richardson

Ann Arbor
THE UNIVERSITY OF MICHIGAN PRESS

Copyright © by the University of Michigan 1997
All rights reserved
Published in the United States of America by
The University of Michigan Press
Manufactured in the United States of America
♾ Printed on acid-free paper

2000   1999   1998   1997   4   3   2   1

A CIP catalog record for this book is available from the British Library.

Library of Congress Cataloging-in-Publication Data

Quiet Pioneering : Robert M. Stern and his international economic
    legacy / Keith E. Maskus . . . [et al.].
          p.   cm. — (Studies in international economics)
    Papers presented at a festschrift conference in November, 1994.
    Includes bibliographical references and index.
    ISBN 0-472-10839-5 (alk. paper)
    1. International trade—Congresses. 2. Commercial policy—
Congresses. 3. International finance—Congresses.
4. International economic relations—Congresses. 5. Stern, Robert
Mitchell, 1927– —Congresses. I. Stern, Robert Mitchell, 1927– .
II. Maskus, Keith E. (Keith Eugene) III. Series.
HF1372.Q54 1997
382—dc21   97-37446
                                                                CIP

STUDIES IN INTERNATIONAL TRADE POLICY

Studies in International Trade Policy includes works dealing with the theory, empirical analysis, political, economic, legal relations, and evaluations of international trade policies and institutions.

General Editor: Robert M. Stern

John H. Jackson and Edwin Vermulst, Editors.
Antidumping Law and Practice: A Comparative Study

John Whalley, Editor. *Developing Countries and the Global Trading System.* Volumes 1 and 2

John Whalley, Coordinator. *The Uruguay Round and Beyond: The Final Report from the Ford Foundation Project on Developing Countries and the Global Trading System*

John S. Odell and Thomas D. Willett, Editors.
International Trade Policies: Gains from Exchange between Economics and Political Science

Jagdish Bhagwati and Hugh T. Patrick, Editors.
Aggressive Unilateralism: America's 301 Trade Policy and the World Trading System

Alan V. Deardorff and Robert M. Stern. *Computational Analysis of Global Trading Arrangements*

Ulrich Kohli. *Technology, Duality, and Foreign Trade: The GNP Function Approach to Modeling Imports and Exports*

Stephen V. Marks and Keith E. Maskus, Editors.
The Economics and Politics of World Sugar Policies

J. Michael Finger, Editor. *Antidumping: How It Works and Who Gets Hurt*

Horst Herberg and Ngo Van Long, Editors.
Trade, Welfare, and Economic Policies: Essays in Honor of Murray C. Kemp

Robert M. Stern, Editor. *The Multilateral Trading System: Analysis and Options for Change*

David Schwartzman. *The Japanese Television Cartel: A Study Based on* Matsushita v. Zenith

Barry Eichengreen.
Reconstructing Europe's Trade and Payments: The European Payments Union

Alan V. Deardorff and Robert M. Stern, Editors.
Analytical Perspectives and Negotiating Issues in the Global Trading System

Edwin Vermulst, Paul Waer, and Jacques Bourgeois, Editors.
Rules of Origin in International Trade: A Comparative Study

Alan V. Deardorff and Robert M. Stern, Editors.
The Stolper-Samuelson Theorem: A Golden Jubilee

Kent Albert Jones. *Export Restraint and the New Protectionism: The Political Economy of Discriminatory Trade Restrictions*

Alan V. Deardorff, James A. Levinsohn, and Robert M. Stern, Editors.
New Directions in Trade Theory

Robert Baldwin, Tain-Jy Chen, and Douglas Nelson. *Political Economy of U.S.–Taiwan Trade*

Bernard M. Hoekman and Petros C. Mavroidis, Editors.
Law and Policy in Public Purchasing: The WTO Agreement on Government Procurement

Danny M. Leipziger, Editor. *Lessons from East Asia*

Tamin Bayoumi. *Financial Integration and Real Activity*

Foreword

Robert M. Stern occupies a distinctive position in the international economics profession. His career is marked by a firm commitment to analyzing applied international economic problems with well-chosen and accessible techniques. He is equally versed in international economic theory and empirical methods, using both to excellent advantage in advancing our understanding of global issues. He poses difficult questions and finds insightful answers. To read a Stern paper is to savor the art of the sensible applied to hugely interesting inquiries. His work is as welcomed by governmental practitioners of international trade and financial policy as it is by his colleagues in academe.

Perhaps as impressive as Stern's research contributions has been the fact that he has mentored an extraordinarily large cadre of outstanding graduate students over the years. Many of these students have gone on to notable careers themselves. While writing in varied aspects of international economics, the work of Stern's "children" and "grandchildren" clearly is influenced by its root inspiration. It involves a passion for analyzing significant policy questions with innovative methods and a concern for developing well-reasoned solutions. From international monetary economics to strategic trade policy; from balance-of-payments theory to econometric analysis of trade patterns; from analysis of multilateral negotiations to applied-general-equilibrium modeling; Stern's stamp lies indelibly on the breadth of applied international economics.

Finally, Robert Stern is a respected research collaborator and professional colleague, as any number of prominent international economists will testify. His presence at major conferences is desired all around the world, because his presentations and commentaries are always first-rate. Meetings are often incomplete until Stern informs the participants of what the Michigan Model of World Production and Trade has to say about the topic of the day.

In recognition of these accomplishments, several former students of Robert Stern's, and many of their students, chose to honor him with a *festschrift* conference in November, 1994. The conference was organized by the editors of this volume, with substantial assistance from Alan Deardorff at the University of Michigan. Eleven papers were chosen for presentation from a large number of abstracts submitted by Stern's colleagues, former students, and their students. In selecting these papers, one main criterion was that they exemplify the Stern tradition of high-quality, applied analysis in some aspect of international trade and finance. The organizers also asked senior officials in the U.S. government and academics who are familiar with Stern and his work to provide some reflective commentary on what he has accomplished from their perspectives. Revised versions of the papers and remarks from the panel of commentators constitute this volume.

Bob Baldwin's Comments on Stern's Career

In his after-dinner tribute speech at the festschrift conference, Robert Baldwin of the University of Wisconsin mused about Stern's accomplishments in research and teaching. Following are his comments, reproduced with slight editing.

When I was asked to speak at the dinner in honor of Bob Stern, I assumed that I would be only one of several speakers. Appropriate to my personality, I supposed that I would be called on to describe in factual and rather dull terms just what Bob's many academic accomplishments have been. So it was with considerable surprise that I noted in the program that I was the only after-dinner speaker scheduled. I mentioned this to Lucetta when she was visiting Madison and she said that Bob did not want a lot of speakers.[1] I assume it was because he felt he might be somewhat uncomfortable by various speakers lavishing praise on him or relating amusing incidents in their relationships with him. So we start right out by seeing one of Bob's unique abilities, namely, the ability to shape the outcome of events without being assertive or seeming to intervene at all.

To begin, let me express what a happy and joyous occasion this is. We have come together to honor Bob Stern, not just as an economist but as a friend. In many of the *festschrifts* I have attended, exclusive attention is devoted to the professional accomplishments of the person being honored. The reason is, I think, because many of the individuals who have gained fame in their professional fields are often not the most admirable individuals at the personal level. Gaining fame is not an easy task and many individuals who succeed are rather self-centered in the sense of letting others know frequently how important and original their own writings are in winning the race to fame.

With Bob we have a completely different picture. Here is a person who has gained fame as an economist and at the same time is warmly admired as a person. I remember that Leontief always felt that one of the highest forms of praise he could give anyone was to say that he was a "straight shooter." To my mind, this description fits Bob very well. When Bob tells you what he thinks about some idea or some person, you know that is what he is telling everyone. He doesn't play games in order to make a point or to put someone down. Nor does he try to elicit some remark about how great a scholar he is. You also know that your friendship with Bob is not something he is going to use for some self-serving purpose or just as a way of meeting other people who can be beneficial to his career. It is a friendship you can count on for life and one that is going to continue to be deeply rewarding at both a personal and professional level.

Now let me turn to Bob's academic accomplishments. I knew Bob had written a large number of articles but I didn't realize just how many until I got a copy of his vitae. He has averaged over three articles a year for the last 36 years. When you add in the substantial number of books he has written, is there any wonder that he is the father of only 2 children, rather than 4, as I am? The guy was too busy writing papers and books. And, of course, his articles are in the top professional journals.

Frankly, I did not realize until I looked over his vita carefully that most of his articles in the first 5 or 6 years after he got his Ph.D. from Columbia in 1958 dealt with agricultural products. How did a city boy from Boston get interested in farm and commodity issues? For example, his first article was entitled "Changes in the Structure of World Food Exports" and the second "The Price Responsiveness of Egyptian Cotton Producers". He has two papers on Malayan rubber production and another on cocoa supply in West Africa in these early years. Now maybe he wrote on these topics because he wanted to travel abroad and undertake research in these exotic places. I don't know, but frankly I have always thought of Bob, at least in his early years, as the kind of guy whose idea of a really exciting journey was going down to Cape Cod for a couple of weeks.

I suppose his interest in commodities was due to the influence of Ragnar Nurske, with whom he studied at Columbia. However, another theory that might account for his early interest in agricultural goods is that I understand his family was in the food business and they wanted him to enter the business too. Maybe his interest in commodities while getting an MBA from Chicago in 1952 and his writings about commodities early on in this career as an economist are tied up in some complex Freudian way with his childhood connections and with his rejection of the food business as a career. But I think we can let professionals like Lucetta figure out if there is anything to that hypothesis.

In any event, we also see in those early years examples of articles on topics that we have come to expect from Bob over the years. He wrote his first papers on the elasticity of import demand as well as on the elasticity of substitution in 1962. He has written on both of these subjects periodically over his career. For example, he addressed both of these topics in the 1970 book with Ed Leamer, called *Quantitative International Economics.* We all are still greatly indebted to him for his survey of import and export demand elasticities that he published with Francis and Schumacher in 1976. He revisited the elasticities of substitution topic in 1989.

A more important topic that he started writing about early and has pursued ever since concerns empirical tests of such trade theories as the Ricardian and Heckscher-Ohlin models. His first paper dealing with the Ricardian model was in 1962, and he seemed to become interested in testing the Heckscher-Ohlin model after writing that brilliant article entitled "Testing Trade Theories," which appeared in 1975. Other topics on which he began to write in the early 1960s deal with various trade policies and institutions and with macroeconomic issues relevant for an open economy. His 1973 book, *The Balance of Payments: Theory and Economic Policy,* is a classic.

But it seems to me that the important point about Bob's research is not so much the particular topics on which he has written but the general approach that he has taken. From the beginning, Bob got it right. Somehow he realized that the period in which his career would take place was the age of empirical economics. I don't know just what the status of the computer was at the time he began his career, but he started right out by testing various hypotheses empirically. It is apparent that he appreciated early on the importance of applying sophisticated statistical techniques to gain important empirical insights. This appreciation of the importance of applying sophisticated econometrics and utilizing the new computer technology to analyze important empirical and public policy issues is what, in my mind, uniquely characterizes his career.

Further, he has passed this approach on to his students. Empirical work in trade is widely followed today but let me point out that in the 1960s and 1970s it was not. In their book on quantitative international economics, Bob Stern and Ed Leamer were way ahead of the rest of us in appreciating what was unique about research in the modern era. Theory is still important, but I am convinced that historians will look back and characterize this period as one in which empirical economics came of age and began to dominate the discipline.

A major accomplishment of Bob's research career has been the Michigan computable general equilibrium (CGE) model, which he developed along with Alan Deardorff. This is easily the most important CGE model in international economics and has had tremendous influence, not only in academic economics, but also in the policymaking field. For every major international economic policy in recent years, ranging from the Tokyo Round to the Uruguay Round and the U.S.-Canada Free Trade Agreement to NAFTA, this model has been very important in influencing what economists and policymakers think about the economic impact of the policy.

One additional benefit from the model is that it has encouraged its developers to think even more deeply about trade policies and the various institutions dealing with these policies. In my view, Stern and Deardorff have gone beyond being outstanding empirical economists and are now also wise in the ways of trade policy in a real-world setting.

Now let me move away from Bob's accomplishments through his writings and discuss another important feature of his career, namely, his ability to attract an extraordinarily talented group of graduate students. He has done this consistently over the last 30 years. One can look at the students of other trade economists, not just contemporary ones, but leading trade economists over the years, to realize how extraordinary this accomplishment is. Think of people like Taussig, Ohlin, Haberler, and Viner. They really had only a comparatively small number of top-notch students who became academics in the trade field. Other trade economists in the same age group as Bob also have not been nearly as successful as he has. For example, think about Harry Johnson, Max Kreinin, T.N. Srinavansan, Dick Cooper, Ron Jones, Anne Krueger or myself. I suppose the person who comes the closest that I can think of is Jagdish Bhagwati, but I don't think his list matches the Stern list, especially when you consider students of students.

I have always been rather envious of Bob on this point. Dave Richardson and I have had a number of good students who have gone on to distinguished academic careers but nothing like Bob has had. My claim to fame in terms of producing other economists has been achieved the old-fashioned way, namely, by procreation and arranging marriages. But one is strictly limited in the number of economists one can produce via this route.

I began to think about just how Bob might have achieved this remarkable feat. The most obvious explanation is that Bob teaches a very clear and interesting graduate trade course and thereby attracts many of the most talented individuals in any class of graduate students to take the course and become hooked on trade as a field of specialization. I am sure that when Bob does teach the graduate trade course, it is clear and interesting. The difficulty with this explanation is that he no longer teaches this course but focusses on the public affairs students. I next thought that maybe he gets these good students because he is so kind and considerate to them and thus they become attached to him and the field. He does have a kind of friendly, grandfatherly quality. Perhaps he invites them over to the house often and serves up one of his nice buffets and lets Lucetta talk to them and ease their personal problems. Well, maybe this is the case, but I rather doubt it.

Still another hypothesis I thought about is that perhaps he charms them with his unique personality. One knows of the great charm and personal magnetism of individuals like Max Corden and Jagdish Bhagwati. When Max takes you for one of his famous walks where he displays not only his brilliance but deep interest in your research, it is easy to see how students are attracted to such personalities. Well, perhaps this is the case, but let's admit it: very few of us have the charisma of a Max Corden or Jagdish Bhagwati.

So what is the secret of his success in attracting top-notch graduate students? Well, after talking to several of them, I think I've figured it out. Bob has followed what I would call the big-time football model in building up his teams of outstanding graduate students—a model he must have become familiar with over his many years here at Michigan. How has Michigan managed to build up and maintain consistently an outstanding football team? The first point to make is that its coaches don't get their players just by waiting for them to walk in and express interest in playing. The coaches go out and recruit their players. And that is what Bob seems to do. He identifies the top graduate students, not just those who have wandered into trade but those in other fields (Ed Leamer was recruited from econometrics) and goes after them to write theses in the trade area.

But how is successful recruitment done? Well, first of all you've got to have some scholarships to attract your recruits. And this is where the Stern-Deardorff research organization comes into play. These two guys have used Bob's MBA knowledge to put together a highly efficient, smooth research operation that must be the envy of many private research firms. They put out first-rate research proposals involving funding for graduate students that seem to be better than any of the rest of us can do. I know this from personal experience in competing against them for research funds. And they have found places to tap for research funds that I have never heard of. Thus, they always seem to have the funds to offer research assistantships to the top graduate students that they go after.

But, successful recruiting is much more than just having attractive scholarships. A key question in the mind of a recruit is whether the particular team he joins will be useful in helping him get into the pros after he or she completes his or her college career. And Bob is especially helpful on this point. First, while they are on the team, he makes sure that their names get around to the pros. Part of the funds he raises are used for the series of working papers that come out of the Workshop on International Economics. So a graduate student knows that if he gives a good paper in the workshop, it will appear in this series and be sent around to all the major academics and nonacademics in the trade field. It makes it much easier to get a job afterwards. Secondly, a prospective recruit sees that Bob often writes papers jointly with his students so they can rely on his name to help them get published early on after they leave. Third, Bob also uses the funds he raises to hold a large number of conferences for which he is able to attract the top trade people. He invites his former students to give papers at these conferences so they get further exposure. Bob now even has his own book series at the University of Michigan Press, so a good recruit realizes he has a possible book publishing outlet if he joins the Stern-Deardorff (and now Jim Levinsohn) team. (Fortunately, he allows some of his friends to use this publication channel.) I have always been surprised that Bob did not start his own journal and give his students still another outlet to get to the big time.

So is it any wonder that Bob has been so successful in attracting outstanding graduate students? He has built a big-time research organization that not only recruits but ensures that members of the team get the best opportunity to make the top professional ranks after they leave. None of the rest of us has come close to operating such an organization as the Michigan research machine.

So I hope I have reminded you of some of the many ways in which Bob Stern is an extraordinary individual. I have not had time to talk about a number of his other special talents, such as his administrative ability, his unflappability, or his ability to persuade you to present a paper at one of his conferences, even though you are already overcommitted. It is a pleasure to honor such an individual, and I know I speak for all present here tonight when I say how wonderful it is to know Bob and to wish him and Lucetta continued success and happiness in the rest of their professional careers and personal lives.

Editors' Addendum

To the editors of this volume, this analogy is amusing and accurate. Yet it all rests on the presumption that the football coach knows what he is doing. Robert Stern knows what the important issues are, knows how to analyze them (and even who best to do so; frequently he has steered students into particular topics based on some unexplained intuition he has regarding their individual comparative advantages), and knows better than anyone how to disseminate the analytical results. It is also important to mention that, nearly alone among his contemporaries in the profession (Baldwin being a notable exception), he understands the value of solid empirical work and passes on his passion for it, so long as it is well-grounded in theory. Perhaps that is the ultimate characteristic of a Michigan training in international economics.

For all of these reasons, the editors join the hundreds of other Stern students, and their students, in expressing our gratitude for his service to the profession. He is an outstanding mentor and an even greater colleague.

Acknowledgments

No project of this scope is manageable without the important contributions of numerous individuals. We wish to thank Mary Braun, Judith Jackson, and Tonia Short of the Institute for Public Policy Studies at the University of Michigan for their support. Jill Van Stone, Jill Holman, Rebecca Neumann, and Grace Norman of the University of Colorado were indispensable in helping to organize the conference and preparing the volume for publication. Finally, without the guidance and support of Alan Deardorff at the University of Michigan this project could not have succeeded.

NOTE

1. Lucetta Stern is Bob Stern's wife and is a noted psychologist.

Contents

Abbreviations

Abbreviations	Full Meaning
AD	Anti-Dumping
AFTA	ASEAN Free Trade Area
ALJ	Administrative Law Judge
APEC	Asian Pacific Economic Cooperation Forum
ASEAN	Association of Southeast Asian Nations
BLS	Bureau of Labor Statistics
CBI	Central Bank Independence
CGE	Computable General Equilibrium
COMTAP	Compatible Trade and Production Database
CRS	Congressional Research Service
CVD	Countervailing Duty
DOC	Department of Commerce
EBA	Extreme Bounds Analysis
EC	European Community
ECB	European Central Bank
EEC	European Economic Community
EFTA	European Free Trade Area
EMS	European Monetary System
EMU	European Monetary Union
EPG	APEC Eminent Persons Group
EPPP	Expenditure Purchasing Power Parity
ERM	Exchange Rate Mechanism
EU	European Union
FDI	Foreign Direct Investment
G-7	Group of Seven Industrial Countries
GATS	General Agreement on Trade in Services
GATT	General Agreement on Tariffs and Trade
GDP	Gross Domestic Product
GNP	Gross National Product
GPA	Government Procurement Agreement
GSP	Generalized System of Preferences
HK	Helpman-Krugman Model

HO	Heckscher-Ohlin
ICOP	International Comparison of Output and Productivity
ILAB	International Labor Affairs Bureau
IMF	International Monetary Fund
IPRs	Intellectual Property Rights
ISDB	International Sectoral Database
ISIC	International Standard Industrial Classification
ITC	International Trade Commission
ITT	Intra-Industry Trade
IV	Instrumental Variables
LDC	Less-Developed Country
MFN	Most Favored Nation
MLE	Maximum Likelihood Estimate
MTN	Multilateral Trade Negotiation
NAFTA	North American Free Trade Agreement
NTB	NonTariff Barrier
OECD	Organization for Economic Cooperation and Development
OPR	Output Price Ratio
PAC	Political Action Committee
PTA	Preferential Trading Arrangement
R&D	Research and Development
RCA	Revealed Comparative Advantage
RER	Real Exchange Rate
SDR	Special Drawing Right
SIC	Standard Industrial Classification
SII	Structural Impediment Initiative
SITC	Standard International Trade Classification
SUR	Seemingly Unrelated Regressions
TPRM	Trade Policy Review Mechanism
TRIMs	Trade-Related Investment Measures
TRIPs	Trade-Related Intellectual Property Rights
ULC	Unit Labor Costs
UN	United Nations
UNCTAD	United Nations Conference on Trade and Development
USTR	United States Trade Representative
UVR	Unit Values Ratio
VER	Voluntary Export Restraint
VIE	Voluntary Import Expansion
WTO	World Trade Organization

CHAPTER 1

Introduction: The Contributions of
Robert M. Stern

Keith E. Maskus

In his distinguished career, Robert Stern has published over 120 articles, authored seven books, and edited another 12 volumes (see appendix for selected listing). In the current age of marked specialization in international economics, Stern's work displays true breadth, covering trade theory and policy, development economics, empirical analysis, multilateral trade relations, and international monetary economics. Our purpose here is not to review all, or even many, of these contributions, but to use them to illustrate the growth of an outstanding professional life. Throughout, Stern has exhibited an extraordinary knack for being at the forefront of analyzing an emerging issue of great significance. Perhaps it is this prescience that best characterizes his career.

Robert Stern earned his Ph.D. in economics at Columbia University in 1958, supervised by Ragnar Nurkse. Nurkse invited Stern to spend two years in the Netherlands, in order to continue his research into an issue of growing importance at that time, the use of market incentives in food policies in developing countries [references 1, 2, 6 in the appendix]. A significant piece from that work was an early demonstration that cotton farmers in Egypt indeed were responsive to price variations [1], a finding that was extended to Indian jute and Malayan rubber acreage responses later [6,12] and that also led to a publication on lag specification in econometric theory [5]. These results were in some contrast to the structuralist notions prevalent in development economics in that era, which held that numerous impediments in the economy would preclude such price responsiveness. At this time, Stern also displayed what would become a life-long passion for analyzing the determinants of international trade patterns [3] and the advisability of various trade policies, in this case the issue of export subsidies for excess agricultural production [2,4]. Needless to say, this latter question has only grown in analytical interest and political influence since that time. Stern demonstrated his gratitude to his mentor by co-editing, with Gottfried Haberler, a volume of Nurkse's essays [69] that remains well worth perusing.

Stern can be quite critical of other peoples' work if it is lacking in analytical rigor or even common sense. For example, with Elliott Zupnick he issued a strongly negative appraisal of the empirical practice in the early 1960s of using unit-value price data by country to estimate cross-elasticities of import substitution from different supply sources [7]. Their contention was that market prices could not be used to infer disequilibrating price changes and quantity responses, which were themselves typically functions of unobservable shocks. This methodological issue was taken up again in a paper on devaluation effects [11]. Perhaps the best example of Stern's early insistence on reliance on firm methodological procedures was his condemnation of a proposal by a United Nations Committee of Experts to set up a special financing facility for developing countries to cover their shortfalls in export proceeds associated with volatility in commodity prices [9]. Among other criticisms, Stern pointed out that the Committee's endorsement of economic planning advocated policies that might themselves be the root cause of inadequate investment, rigid supply responses, and balance-of-payments difficulties. Instead, Stern called for more limited financial assistance that was tied to structural economic and political reform in badly distorted economies. Prescience, indeed, although it evidently required 20 years for multilateral institutions like the World Bank to be swayed fully by the wisdom of this approach.

The first half of Stern's career is perhaps best known for his studies of the determinants of trade patterns [3, 8, 13, 17, 18, 21, 28, 64]. All of these studies deserve comment, but three are classics that continue to be cited in textbooks and numerous follow-on studies each year. In 1962 Stern published "British and American Productivity and Comparative Costs in International Trade" [8], a significant reworking of earlier studies by Sir Donald MacDougall. He added figures on relative unit costs, accounting for productivity differences, in an examination of comparative export performance in several manufacturing industries of the United Kingdom and the United States in 1950 and 1959. The results were suggestive of a strong influence of relative productivity differentials on comparative advantage. It is worth noting that in this paper Stern exhibited what would become a hallmark of his research: a careful and comprehensive treatment of data inadequacies. This care became a signal of quality, not unlike a trademark, that allowed readers the luxury of taking for granted that, in analyzing various problems Stern had already worried seriously about the data. Indeed, his insistence on taking care with the data, in the clear expectation that figures should be allowed to be as informative as possible within the context of theory, continues to characterize the substantial body of empirical literature published by generations of his students.

More than any other Stern mentee, Edward Leamer took this lesson to heart. A graduate student in the late 1960s, Leamer noticed that Stern was laboring in the then-thinly populated vineyard of empirical international economics. Combining Leamer's interests in econometric methodology with Stern's command of applied international economic issues, the two collaborated on a small, classic volume, *Quantitative International Economics* [64]. The book efficiently discusses major empirical topics in both finance and trade, often presenting new econometric methods for dealing with them [see also 14, 21, 25]. It remains (25 years later) a standard reference for many international economists and the profession would benefit from an update.

Stern is coauthor, with Keith Maskus, of one of the most heavily cited studies in empirical trade determinants [28]. That study is notable for its use of a variety of state-of-the-art techniques for analyzing U.S. factor services trade, showing, among other things, that the Leontief Paradox seemed to have disappeared from the data by the early 1970s. This finding has been an important stimulus to other researchers who have analyzed the changing structure of global factor endowments and technologies over time. He also wrote an important early survey of empirical work on the determinants of trade patterns [16].

Stern's wide-ranging policy interests are evident in the breadth of his early policy analysis, ranging from structural estimation of the welfare costs of trade barriers [10], to policy surveys [15, 19, 20, 24, 27, 31], to participation in formulating an important set of recommendations (which remain the basic standards) on the presentation of the balance of payments [23]. No review of his work would be complete without mentioning two celebrated books. First, his famous text in international finance, *The Balance of Payments: Theory and Economic Policy* [65] was published in 1973 at a time of great turmoil in financial markets and instantly became a standard textbook and reference in international finance. It remains well worth consulting today. Second, three years later he published, with two graduate students, the important survey, *Price Elasticities in International Trade* [66]. For the first time, this volume gathered in one place the extant estimates of important elasticities of import demand across countries and commodities. It has been extremely widely cited as a source of parameter values for countless partial-equilibrium and general-equilibrium computations of trade policies since that time. This is yet another book that could be updated with great utility for the rest of the profession. Indeed, a later paper on substitution elasticities is now firmly on the shelf of trade economists looking for parameter estimates [38].

In the late 1970s and early 1980s came early returns on the major project to which Stern, with Alan Deardorff and later with Drusilla Brown, has devoted his efforts in the second half of his career—the renowned

Michigan Model of World Production and Trade [22, 26, 29, 30, 32, 33, 34, 35]. This was one of the first computable general-equilibrium (CGE) trade models, using matched input-output technologies from a number of countries in conjunction with a variety of estimates on primary factor substitution and consumption and trade substitution elasticities. It has proven invaluable in calculating sectoral employment effects of exchange-rate changes and of unilateral and multilateral trade liberalization. The Michigan Model is one of the more ambitious and complex CGE models used for trade analysis, involving large numbers of sectors and countries and capable of simulating numerous policy scenarios. It quickly became a standard in the field; no major conference in the last ten years on regional or multilateral trade liberalization was ever complete without a report from Stern and Deardorff on their model simulations [39, 49, 50, 53, 54, 58]. Interested readers are referred to two books in which the model and its refinements are fully explained [67,68]. One noteworthy aspect of the Michigan Model is that it has provided employment and dissertation topics for a succession of graduate students [41, 42, 43, 45, 46, 48, 52, 55]. Drusilla Brown's career, in particular, is closely linked to her important work on updating and refining the model to account for terms-of-trade effects and returns to scale.

With Drusilla Brown as co-author, Stern developed a distinct second generation of the Michigan Model, specifically designed to be appropriate for analyzing preferential trade arrangements (PTAs). The first version of this new model included only the United States, Canada, and the rest of the world and was used to quantify the effects of the U.S.-Canada Free Trade Agreement. It departed from the earlier Michigan Model by including aspects of imperfect competition, product differentiation, and economies of scale. They were thus able to incorporate the essential features of the New Trade Theory, developed by Krugman and others, into a practical modeling tool that could be used for real-world policy analysis.

Shortly thereafter, joined again also by Deardorff, Stern, and Brown expanded this model to include Mexico so as to examine the North American Free Trade Agreement. The three authors then expanded the framework further to cover eight countries, the identities of which could be aggregated and changed as the need arose by drawing upon their established database covering initially 34 countries. This Brown-Deardorff-Stern Michigan modeling framework has been applied to numerous actual and potential PTAs around the globe in the later volume [68].

The Michigan Model by no means represents the sum of Stern's recent work. He has written path-breaking papers on conceptual and measurement issues regarding nontariff barriers [36, 47] and services trade [37, 44, 51, 60, 61]. He continues to write insightful and timely reviews of trade policy issues [40, 56, 57, 59, 62, 63]. In recent years Robert Stern has become a prominent research organizer, staging important conferences at Michigan and editing the resulting volumes [70, 71, 72, 73, 74, 76]. One such project that deserves special mention is Stern and Deardorff's book honoring the fiftieth anniversary of the Stolper-Samuelson theorem [75]. This book offers a delightful mix of retrospective insights and modern theorizing and deserves to be on the shelf of all trade economists. Of course, Stern's purpose in staging that conference was to honor two truly significant figures in the trade field. With this volume, we do no less for an equally significant international economist.

The Plan of this Book

The papers in this volume were presented at the *festschrift* conference in Ann Arbor in November, 1994. The conference organizers selected them from over 35 submissions of abstracts. They represent the full range of international economic inquiry to which Stern's career has been devoted, and all were written by former students, or their students, or close colleagues. Taken together they represent a fitting and high-quality tribute.

We have organized the book into four parts. The first part comprises empirical studies of trade patterns and trade policies. In the first paper (chapter 2), Edward Leamer uses patterns of industrial specialization in OECD countries to characterize comparative advantage in goods as deriving from Ricardian or Heckscher-Ohlin influences. An extensive data analysis describes sectors and countries in terms of specialization according to these theories or combined factors.

In chapter 3, Kishore Gawande applies some original econometric sensitivity analysis to a classic Stern-type empirical question: Why are trade barriers high in some industries and low in others? Among the possible forces that might determine the level of barriers are political self-interest, political altruism, and comparative advantage. An important conclusion that Gawande draws from his study of U.S. 1983 data is that nontariff barriers against Japan appear to be driven by comparative-advantage factors while political factors are more important determinants of barriers against the European Community.

In chapter 4, John Mutti and Bernard Yeung undertake an empirical analysis of U.S. law covering imports of products that infringe American patents, trademarks, and copyrights, and how the law affects business strategy. Section 337 is discriminatory in its impact in that it does not provide foreign firms equal access to U.S. judicial procedures for purposes of defending themselves against charges of infringement. Mutti and Yeung investigate whether decisions to engage in innovation activity (R&D) are perceptibly influenced by complaint filings and case dispositions under Section 337. The outcome of an investigation, whether positive or negative from the complainant's view, has ambiguous impacts on R&D investment in theory because of conflicting impacts on the value of existing inventions and returns to further investment, along with market-structure issues. There appear to be important differences between R&D decisions of filing firms and control firms, depending on the outcome of the case, while substitution between existing and future innovations is also a critical issue.

In chapter 5, Keith Maskus and Mohan Penubarti ask whether international trade flows are influenced by differences across countries in patent regimes. They present a model in which a firm's decisions to export to various markets are ambiguously affected by variations in patent laws. Their empirical analysis demonstrates that there is a perceptibly positive, but small, impact. That is, countries with stronger patent laws attract somewhat more imports on a bilateral basis than would be expected within a particular general-equilibrium framework than do countries with weaker laws. The magnitudes of this effect are small, however.

The second part of the book is devoted to analyses of trade policies. In chapter 6, Will Martin and Joseph Francois present a new approach to evaluating trade reforms that involves setting tariff bindings (ceilings) for the first time in the context of trade negotiations, even if actual applied tariffs are not cut. The result of the bindings is to remove the upper portion of the distribution of potential tariff rates, which, in a world of uncertainty about tariffs, has a liberalizing impact that is greater than generally recognized. They apply this methodology to recent liberalization in agriculture in OECD nations and note that extensive tariff bindings under the Uruguay Round comprise potentially significant policy liberalization despite the height of the tariffs themselves.

In the subsequent chapter, Rachel McCulloch and Peter Petri discuss the static and dynamic consequences of preferential trade arrangements, or PTAs. They go beyond the traditional textbook emphasis on trade diversion and trade creation to focus on the economic implications of creating larger markets. They observe that PTAs that have succeeded, such as the European Union, have generated significant economic gains from scale economies and increased competition among producers. Moreover, these gains have proven to be far more important empirically than inefficiencies associated with trade diversion. This chapter also addresses the potential implications of PTAs for progress in multilateral trade liberalization. McCulloch and Petri's analysis of the evolution of PTAs suggests that they have tended to foster further trade liberalization both by shifting production towards more efficient, internationally minded industries and by drawing recalcitrant nonmember countries into the multilateral negotiation process.

In chapter 8, Bernard Hoekman analyzes the crucial linkages between external trade policies and internal regulatory policies for countries in the trading system. He notes that the secular reduction of trade barriers has not necessarily corresponded to an increase in market access in many countries because domestic regulatory structures have failed to allow greater contestability of local markets. It follows that national competition policies must fall even further under the purview of the World Trade Organization if international access is to translate into market competition. Hoekman notes that this process is underway with limited agreements on competition policy having been reached in the intellectual property and services components of the Uruguay Round. However, much depends on the forms of competition in each market, including the prevalence of state enterprises, which may be exempt from antitrust regulation. Hoekman cogently discusses various forms of regulatory policy that can hinder market contestability and considers prospects for further multilateral negotiations on this significant question.

In chapter 9, Wilhelm Kohler studies the effects of the formation of trading blocs on the incentives to pursue strategically motivated trade and industrial policies vis-à-vis non-members. As an example, Kohler raises the specter of "Fortress Europe," which would allow free trade among European members but, as a result of its increased collective "clout," would choose to pursue aggressive trade policy against non-members. Indeed, he argues that this risk is real, since there is a presumption that integration increases the strategic incentives faced by European governments to subsidize domestic firms.

Part 3 of the book is devoted to theoretical and empirical analyses of international financial issues. Chapter 10, by Peter Hooper and Elizabeth Vrankovich, addresses the measurement of absolute levels of unit labor costs in manufacturing (and two-digit manufacturing sectors) across major industrial countries. Movements over time in the various components of relative unit labor costs, reflecting changes in nominal exchange rates, labor compensation, and productivity, have been well documented. As the authors note, however, much less is known about the comparative absolute levels of unit labor costs. This chapter reviews various methodologies for making such calculations and extends previous efforts in this area by using expenditure-purchasing-power parities adjusted for the influences of indirect taxes and distribution margins, among other factors. The analysis concludes that in 1990 unit labor costs in the U.S. manufacturing sector were nearly 20 percent below those in Japanese manufacturing and 33 percent below those in German manufacturing. Exchange rate movements since 1990 have widened these cost differentials substantially, although cross-country differences in labor cost levels continue to vary greatly across manufacturing sub-sectors.

In chapter 11, Filip Abraham and Aileen Thompson present an empirical analysis of the prospects that a European monetary union (EMU) will generate net benefits to the economies of the member countries. They do so essentially by "surveying" the expectations of stock market investors about the economic consequences of EMU. This survey is achieved by evaluating stock market responses to various events that would have affected views about the likelihood that EMU will be realized. The events considered are the announcement of a successful negotiation of the treaty at the Maastricht Summit, the outcomes of various national referenda on the Maastricht Treaty, and the European currency crises of 1992 and 1993. The empirical results are mixed and, in general, provide little consistent evidence that stock market participants felt that improved prospects for EMU would have either significant positive or significant negative impacts on the economies of member countries. The authors note that stock market reactions during the events considered could well have reflected changes in expectations about factors other than prospects for EMU that were engendered by those events (for example, expectations about changes in monetary policy in the short run in the case of currency crises).

In chapter 12, Jay Levin considers the effects of changes in macroeconomic policy within a monetary union on the economies of member countries. His analysis is based on a three-country simulation model that includes two members of a monetary union. He finds that monetary expansion within the union causes output in both member countries to rise temporarily via declines in real interest rates and real depreciation of the union currency. Over time, prices rise and real interest rates, exchange rates, and outputs return to their original levels. Levin also finds that when one of the member countries engages in fiscal expansion, its own output rises temporarily, but output in the other member country can either rise or fall, depending upon where various behavioral parameters lie within plausible ranges. This chapter also considers the dynamic effects of the policy changes on real wages and external balances in the member countries.

The final part of the volume presents a panel discussion of Robert Stern's impacts on the profession and on policy. His contributions to academic scholarship are examined by W. Max Corden, while views of prominent U.S. policymakers are represented in papers by Geza Feketekuty, formerly of the United States Trade Representative's office, Gregory Schoepfle and Jorge Perez-Lopez of the U.S. Department of Labor, and Alfred Reifman, formerly of the Congressional Research Service.

Part One:
Empirical Trade Models

CHAPTER 2

Evidence of Ricardian and Heckscher-Ohlin Effects in OECD Specialization Patterns

Edward E. Leamer

This paper reports an analysis of value-added specialization patterns of the OECD countries in 1990.[1] The United Kingdom is the least specialized country, and Turkey is the most. Compared with other OECD countries, Turkey has an unusually large share of value added in petroleum refining. The least specialized countries generally are large and productive; they have both relatively large manufacturing sectors and also high value added per employee. Transportation equipment is the least specialized product at the two-digit SIC level of aggregation of value added data. Professional equipment is the most specialized 2-digit ISIC commodity mostly because of the dominance of the US.

The purpose of this paper is not to report facts but to attempt to disentangle Heckscher-Ohlin (HO) effects on these specialization patterns from Ricardian effects. The Heckscher-Ohlin model suggests that comparative advantage comes from relative abundance of productive resources. According to this model, all countries have access to the same technologies, and countries rich in capital or other productive resources have output mixes shifted in favor of those sectors that use the abundant resources intensively. The Ricardian model, on the other hand, suggests that comparative advantage comes from technological superiority, not from factor abundance. Countries concentrate output on those sectors in which they have a technologically conferred comparative advantage.

A useful way to contrast a Heckscher-Ohlin model from a Ricardian model is to refer to the identity that expresses the economy's overall productivity as a weighted average of the productivities in disaggregated sectors of the economy:

$$\frac{V}{E} = \sum_i \frac{V_i}{E_i} w_i$$

11

where V and E stand for value added and employment and the weights are employment shares $w_i = E_i/\Sigma_i\, E_i$. An implication of this identity is that a country with a greater overall output/labor ratio must either have labor allocations (weights) that favor the sectors with greater productivities or else the country must have relatively high sectoral productivities. A Heckscher-Ohlin model suggests that at a suitable level of disaggregation, the sectoral productivities are identical across countries and what differs is the allocation of labor across the sectors. A Ricardian model, however, allows sectoral productivities to differ across countries and allows labor to concentrate on those sectors for which the productivities are greatest. According to a Ricardian model, a country with a relatively high overall productivity does so because of relatively high productivities at the sectoral level and because of a concentration of labor on those sectors with unusually high productivity.

The empirical analysis reported herein attempts to predict 1990 OECD value-added specialization patterns using a Heckscher-Ohlin variable and a Ricardian variable. A separate regression is estimated for each two-digit ISIC aggregate industrial. The Heckscher-Ohlin variable in each equation is a characteristic of the country: the country overall value-added per worker adjusted for the composition of output. The Ricardian variable is a characteristic of the country and industry pair: the country's productivity in a sector relative to the country's productivity overall. The Ricardian variable thus identifies the sector in which the country is unusually productive.

The regression horse-race is sometimes won by the Heckscher-Ohlin variable and sometimes by the Ricardian variable. Textiles are found to be a strongly HO sector, located especially in low-wage, low-productivity countries. Petroleum refining is a strongly Ricardian sector, located in countries with especially high productivity in refining compared with other sectors, namely Turkey, New Zealand, France, and Germany. The location of production of machinery is driven by both Ricardian and HO effects. Japan is favored in machinery for both reasons—having high overall productivity (HO effect) and also having unusually high productivity in machinery (Ricardian effect). While the OECD specialization in these and other products is well explained by this simple combined Ricardian and HO model, the specialization patterns in chemicals, rubber manufactures, and iron and steel are completely unexplainable using these two simple predictors.

An OECD trade data base is not an ideal place to look for either Heckscher-Ohlin effects or Ricardian effects. The Heckscher-Ohlin effects may be minor because these OECD countries have similar factor supply ratios. The Ricardian effects may be minor because technology may be rather fluid among these OECD countries. Nonetheless, the tentative conclusion that seems appropriate from this examination of this data set is that both sector-specific technological advantages and capital abundance play a role in determining OECD specialization patterns. The success here is encouraging in terms of broader applicability since both the HO effects and the Ricardian effects may be stronger for North-South comparisons than for intra-OECD comparisons.

OECD Patterns of Specialization

The basic data are reported in table 1 and table 2. Table 1 has measures of comparative advantage by country and by commodity. Table 2 reports the corresponding labor productivities. The revealed comparative advantage numbers in table 1 indicate the extent of specialization in value added data, after correcting for country size and for commodity size. Using the notation

V_{ic} = value added in Sector i for Country c ,
$V_{i.} = \Sigma_i V_{ic}$ = total OECD value added in Sector i ,
$V_{.c} = \Sigma_c V_{ic}$ = total value added in Country c ,
$V_{..} = \Sigma_c \Sigma i V_{ic}$ = total OECD value added ,

a traditional measure of revealed comparative advantage is $[V_{ic} / V_{i.}] / [V_{.c}/V_{..}]$ which is equal to the country's share of world value-added in this sector compared with its share overall. The measure of *Revealed Comparative Advantage* used here is slightly different:

$$RCA_{ic} = \log_2 \{[V_{ic}/(V_{i.} - V_{ic})] / [(V_{.c}/(V.. - V_{.c})] \} .$$

The use of rest-of-OECD value-added instead of total OECD figures corrects for country-size effects, which limit apparent specialization patterns of large countries, particularly the United States. The base-2 logarithmic function makes the measure symmetric: an $RCA_{ic} = 1$ means that the sector is twice as large as expected after controlling for country and commodity size, while an $RCA_{ic} = -1$ means that the sector is twice as small as expected.

The revealed comparative advantage ratio equal to 1.16 in the upper left corner of table 1 indicates that Portugal has $2^{1.16} = 2.23$ times more footwear value added than would be predicted based on the size of the apparel sector and the size of Portugal. Some of the other extreme RCA figures are Portuguese and Italian footwear (2.65, 2.70), and Portuguese and Italian pottery (2.95, 3.07). In the opposite direction, Greece has a

TABLE 1. Revealed Comparative Advantage

Commodity	OECD 1990 Avg. VApw	Port 87	Tur 89	NZ 86	Gre 90	Ice 90	Spa 88	Aut 89	Den 90	Ita 89	Net 89	UK 90	Nor 90	Can 86	Fin 909	Fra 90	US 90	Ger 90	Jap 90
Wearing Apparel	30	1.16	0.89	0.84	1.48	-0.35	0.45	0.02	-0.57	1.09	-1.33	0.15	-1.93	0.42	0.00	0.43	0.36	-0.69	-0.41
Footwear	33	2.65	-0.26	1.00	2.21	-1.43	1.76	1.27	0.27	2.70	-0.66	1.21	-.56	0.39	.63	1.49	-0.63	-0.14	-0.64
Textiles	41	2.22	1.88	0.39	2.14	0.02	0.39	0.47	-0.04	1.29	-0.52	0.02	-1.00	-0.13	-0.88	0.04	-0.07	-0.35	0.21
Pottery, china	41	2.95	1.89	0.16	1.73	-0.88	1.03	0.28	0.39	3.07		1.47	-0.28	-1.37	0.35		-1.09	0.36	0.73
Leather	43	1.88	0.46	2.01	1.89	1.75	1.64	0.25	-1.80	2.10		0.09	-0.79	-0.52	-0.09	1.21	-0.37	-0.19	0.11
Wood	44	1.09	-1.18	1.60	0.34	-3.54	0.63	0.58	0.50	-0.50	-0.30	-0.27	1.66	1.62	2.02	-0.01	0.12	-0.44	0.09
Furniture	44	-0.69	-2.29	0.51	-0.39	2.03	0.28	1.35	1.10	0.55	-0.59	0.49	0.42	0.53	0.72	0.21	-0.06	0.20	-0.55
Other Manufactures	54	-2.48	-2.24	-0.19	-1.41	1.43	-0.63	-0.47	0.67	-0.46	-2.25	-0.33	-0.90	0.22	-0.83	0.31	0.13	-1.49	0.27
Fabricated Metal	58	-0.44	-0.99	0.36	-0.36	0.85	-0.06	0.38	0.37	-0.19	0.13	-0.08	-0.08	-0.02	0.22	0.33	-0.34	0.29	0.26
Plastics, nec	59	-0.52	-1.71	0.13	0.00	0.28	-0.23	-0.86	-0.10	0.13	-0.11	0.13	-0.58	-0.15	-0.95	-0.23	-0.12	0.15	0.30
Rubber	60	-0.12	0.57	0.12	-0.37		0.71	-0.09	-1.13	0.48	-0.93	0.03	-1.35	0.06	-1.43	0.16	-0.30	0.05	0.19
Printing, Publishing	67	-0.72	-2.43	0.30	-0.95	0.89	-0.29	-0.62	0.21	-0.51	0.34	0.40	0.78	0.08	0.44	-0.25	0.69	-1.82	-0.21
Food Manufactures	68	0.38	0.25	1.33	0.83	2.22	0.55	-0.17	1.13	-0.44	0.69	0.29	0.49	0.35	0.19	0.31	0.25	-0.71	-0.17
Electrical Machinery	68	-0.94	-1.39	-1.34	-1.23		-0.87	0.09	-0.96	-0.18	0.04	-0.36	-1.08	-0.97	-0.70	-0.15	-0.58	0.35	0.63
Machinery	71	-2.16	-1.55	-1.11	-2.70		-0.95	-0.31	0.09	0.25	-0.65	-0.08	-0.04	-0.80	0.11	-0.37	-0.29	0.37	0.26
Professional Equip.	74	-3.21	-3.45	-2.68	-4.15	-0.82	-2.97	-2.03	-0.19	-1.44	-2.18	-1.17	-2.44	-1.47	-1.18	-1.00	2.04	-1.18	-1.36
Glass	75	0.78	1.10	0.18	-0.68	1.02	0.66	0.89	-0.77	0.44	-0.21	-0.05	-0.61	-0.26	-0.42	0.59	-0.23	0.10	0.23
Nonmetal Minerals	76	1.08	0.83	0.21	1.53	-2.08	0.99	0.95	0.77	0.15	0.30	0.61	0.16	0.08	0.79	0.38	-0.62	-0.12	0.44
Transport	76	-1.29	-1.16	-0.95	-1.07	1.78	0.21	-1.16	-1.17	-0.04	-1.06	0.04	-0.59	0.15	-1.00	0.01	0.13	0.23	-0.06
Non-ferrous Metals	77	-1.43	.81	0.85	1.44	-1.43	0.36	0.32	-2.14	0.09		-0.37	2.05	1.28	0.03	0.51	-0.11	0.07	-0.06
Paper	83	1.24	-0.77	.55	-0.19	-1.54	-0.40	0.35	-0.29	-0.48	-0.07	-0.09	0.73	1.27	1.88	-0.42	0.67	-0.47	-0.54
Iron and Steel	85	-0.36	1.13	-2.14	-0.23	-2.74	0.20	0.99	-1.54	0.76		-0.16	-0.49	0.05	-0.15	0.03	-0.82	0.03	0.93
Misc. Pet. and Coal	109		2.34	-0.44	0.50	0.66	1.62	-0.25	2.15	0.85	0.28	0.55	1.31	0.11	1.15		1.37		-0.35
Beverages	132	0.61	0.81	0.59	1.57	-1.51	1.45	0.61	0.94	-0.42	.90	0.65	1.37	0.60	0.11	0.44	-0.18	0.44	-0.74
Other Chemicals	135	0.05	-0.02	-0.80	0.31	-1.30	0.11	-0.60	0.29	-1.05	-0.43	0.10	-1.01	0.05	-1.04	-0.13	0.30	-0.08	-0.08
Industrial Chemicals	139	-0.18	0.08	-1.22	-0.81		-0.23	-0.41	-0.18	-0.26	1.31	0.03	0.09	-0.53	-0.10	-0.51	0.04	0.34	-0.46
Tobacco	430	0.77	1.82	1.26	1.26		0.03	2.04	-0.52	-1.12	1.62	-0.47	-0.96	-0.57	-0.96	-0.84	0.79	1.15	-2.86
Petroleum Refining	437	0.25	2.95	1.10	0.24		0.12	0.02	-1.96	-1.31	0.04	-0.20	-0.46	-0.35	-0.75	1.84	-0.30	1.14	-2.19

TABLE 2. Value Added per Worker (All Figures in thousand $)

Commodity	Port 87	Tur 89	NZ 86	Gre 90	Ice 90	Spa 88	Aut 89	Den 90	Ita 89	Net 89	UK 90	Nor 90	Can 86	Fin 90	Fra 90	US 90	Ger 90	Jap 90	Commodity Factor
Wearing Apparel	6	9	10	14	21	19	18	20	27	24	23	31	20	27	41	32	41	24	0.10
Footwear	6	8	11	16	16	22	21	37	23	24	28	82	12	28	29	53	38	43	0.11
Textiles	12	13	15	23	18	26	22	11	37	0	92	36	91	26	55	46	45	42	0.13
Pottery, china	8	12	18	22	26	24	29	35	37	38	31	34	32	33	35	42	52	43	0.14
Leather	5	11	13	16	39	19	28	30	34	29	38	37	26	45	46	93	56	52	0.14
Wood	8	10	16	25	18	23	36	32	36	32	39	45	37	47	42	41	59	46	0.15
Furniture	8	12	13	20	50	27	29	38	33	37	36	42	27	42	42	51	53	62	0.15
Other Manufactures	10	23	13	24	25	22	31	28	46	0	33	34	36	57	0	48	42	43	0.16
Fabricated Metal	10	17	16	23	36	28	34	39	39	37	44	40	37	51	57	54	59	71	0.18
Plastics, nec	10	15	16	22	0	31	27	40	41	35	43	52	33	59	61	85	56	59	0.18
Rubber	13	15	17	28	25	31	35	45	47	45	49	38	43	49	58	90	76	59	0.19
Printing, Publishing	11	14	21	29	52	30	31	49	42	43	48	51	35	49	57	56	60	68	0.19
Food Manufactures	10	17	16	21	0	31	36	36	46	38	53	53	39	59	58	70	70	90	0.19
Electrical Machinery	12	18	21	29	39	42	38	27	60	44	63	46	39	52	59	67	57	83	0.20
Machinery	13	28	20	36	0	38	39	41	42	41	47	55	38	44	35	66	65	75	0.20
Professional Equip.	15	22	19	32	0	37	36	40	45	39	44	47	41	61	57	73	70	73	0.20
Glass	10	18	15	22	30	43	40	42	41	36	54	45	50	49	54	80	71	103	0.20
Nonmetal Minerals	15	26	22	26	36	46	45	40	46	49	49	54	43	51	59	71	68	121	0.22
Transport	15	28	12	50	44	34	50	63	52	0	53	94	47	66	49	77	74	144	0.24
Non-ferrous Metals	15	17	26	35	47	41	48	62	52	49	73	64	53	66	94	66	87	84	0.25
Paper	35	20	27	30	40	42	55	56	49	52	53	68	55	77	63	97	83	87	0.26
Iron and Steel	12	24	44	61	55	59	46	38	51	0	47	79	54	85	98	71	74	97	0.27
Misc. Pet. and Coal	19	40	21	39	48	47	46	86	62	48	87	72	64	67	75	169	98	211	0.31
Beverages	0	49	19	25	29	91	50	72	85	60	93	90	74	171	0	110	0	128	0.33
Other Chemicals	30	41	24	45	65	83	52	103	64	97	98	102	92	98	83	183	115	213	0.39
Industrial Chemicals	26	45	43	46	62	67	54	106	61	109	95	130	72	105	141	153	138	139	0.40
Tobacco	79	25	0	30	0	78	594	98	42	208	180	0	87	156	388	550	814	223	0.74
Petroleum Refining	78	601	238	47	0	180	123	188	88	118	512	175	95	135	705	317	855	231	1.00
Country Factor	74	100	125	129	175	177	197	208	210	214	251	254	255	269	308	354	366	377	
VA/worker (1000s)	12	22	19	27	33	36	40	43	44	48	52	53	43	57	61	76	75	80	

value of RCA of –4.15 for professional equipment with value-added only equal to $2^{-4.15} = .06\%$ of that predicted from country and commodity size. The U.S. has a strong RCA = 2.04 in professional equipment, and also an RCA >1 in miscellaneous petroleum and coal products. Oddly, the U.S. has a positive RCA = .36 in wearing apparel. Keep in mind that these RCA numbers use OECD value-added patterns as the norm, not world value-added patterns. The positive RCA for the U.S. in wearing apparel means that, in comparison with other OECD countries, the U.S. has clung to its apparel sector as the sector has moved out of the OECD into the third world. The biggest negative RCA for the U.S. is in pottery and china, with RCA = –1.09. The next is iron and steel, with RCA = –.82. Specialization in iron and steel is led by Japan, Austria, and Turkey, and will be shown below not to be well explained using either Heckscher-Ohlin or Ricardian variables.

Commodities are ordered in tables 1 and 2 by the overall OECD value added per worker. First is wearing apparel with value added per worker of $30,000 and last is petroleum refining with value added per worker of $437,000. Countries are sorted by the country factors reported in the last row of table 2. Country and commodity factors are found by regressing the logarithm of value added (V) per worker (E) on country dummies and commodity dummies:

$$\ln(V_{ic}/E_{ic}) = \alpha_i + \beta_c$$

with the normalization that $\exp(\alpha_{petrol}) = 1$. The estimated country factors $\exp(\beta_c)$ and commodity factors $\exp(\alpha_i)$ are reported in the last column and last row of table 2. They closely correlate with value added per worker across commodities and countries. The one outlier is tobacco, which has a substantial downward adjustment of $\exp(\alpha_i)$ compared with value-added per worker. This correction comes from the fact that tobacco value-added per worker is closely associated with value-added per worker in the country.

It is apparent from table 1 that some commodities and some countries have highly specialized production patterns while others are more uniformly dispersed. Industry and country specialization indices are reported in tables 3 and 4. These indices are value-added weighted averages of the absolute values of the RCA (remembering that RCA = 0 means no specialization):

$$S_i = \sum_c |RCA_{ic}| \, w_c , \qquad w_c = \sum_i V_{ic} / \sum_i \sum_c V_{ic}$$

$$s_c = \sum_i |RCA_{ic}| \, w_i , \qquad w_i = \sum_c V_{ic} / \sum_i \sum_c V_{ic}$$

TABLE 3.   Specialization Indices by Commodity

Commodity	1990 OECD Total ($b)	Value Added Share (%)	OECD 1900 Avg. VA/ Workers (1000s $)	Specialization Index/Value Added Weights
Transport	378	11.0	76	0.20
Plastics nec	102	3.0	59	0.23
Industrial Chemicals	187	5.5	139	0.26
Fabricated Metal	212	6.2	58	0.28
Textiles	93	2.7	41	0.28
Other Chemicals	187	5.5	135	0.29
Non-Ferrous Metals	48	1.4	77	0.29
Glass	29	0.8	75	0.30
Machinery	427	12.5	71	0.31
Furniture	45	1.3	44	0.31
Rubber	40	1.2	60	0.32
Wood	51	1.5	44	0.33
Food Manufacture	281	8.2	68	0.34
Non-Metal Minerals	83	2.4	76	0.45
Leather	7	0.2	43	0.47
Other Manufactures	46	1.3	54	0.49
Beverages	59	1.7	132	0.52
Electrical Machinery	381	11.1	68	0.55
Wearing Apparel	57	1.7	30	0.56
Paper	115	3.3	83	0.58
Iron and Steel	121	3.5	85	0.63
Printing, Publishing	205	6.0	67	0.69
Misc. Pet.. and Coal	7	0.2	109	0.76
Footwear	8	0.2	33	0.80
Pottery, China	8	0.2	41	0.81
Petroleum Refineries	68	2.0	437	1.04
Tobacco	43	1.3	430	1.31
Professional Equip.	106	3.1	74	1.69
Total	3428			

The cumulative distributions of RCA for the two least concentrated commodities (plastics and transportation equipment) and for the two most concentrated commodities (tobacco and professional equipment) are displayed in figure 1. The most concentrated commodity is professional equipment, mostly because the United States has an extremely large share of the market and because the low-wage developing countries in the sample are substantially underrepresented in this category. Tobacco and petroleum refining are also highly concentrated. Transportation equipment is the least concentrated commodity; next are plastics and then industrial chemicals. No country has an especially large share of plastics or transportation equipment. These products are about equally overrepre-

TABLE 4.   Specialization by Country

Country	Country Factor	Total Value Added		Specialization Index
		$ Billions	Share (%)	
UK	251	254	6.9	0.23
France	308	256	6.9	0.31
US	354	1322	35.8	0.40
Japan	377	892	24.1	0.42
Italy	210	123	3.3	0.46
Germany	366	536	14.5	0.48
Canada	255	77	2.1	0.48
Spain	177	66	1.8	0.57
Austria	137	25	0.7	0.57
Netherlands	214	40	1.1	0.59
Finland	269	26	0.7	0.61
Denmark	208	23	0.6	0.67
Norway	254	14	0.4	0.68
New Zealand	125	6	0.2	0.95
Iceland	175	1	0.0	0.99
Portugal	73	8	0.2	1.04
Greece	129	9	0.3	1.19
Turkey	100	21	0.6	1.24
Avg./Total	225	3698		

sented in a half dozen advanced countries and about equally underrepresented elsewhere.

The cumulative distributions of RCA for the two least specialized countries, the U.K. and France, and the two most specialized countries, Turkey and Greece, are illustrated in figure 2. The U.K. and France have only a few sectors with RCA's larger than one in absolute value. The French overrepresented sectors are footwear, leather and refining. The U.K. overrepresented sectors are footwear and pottery. Both are underrepresented in professional equipment. Greece and Turkey are either substantially under- or substantially over-represented in the majority of sectors.

The panels in figure 3 compare these specialization indices with total value added and with value added per worker. At the top are comparisons across commodities; at the bottom are comparisons across countries. Across commodities there is very little relationship between specialization and value-added per worker, but there appears to be some negative association between specialization and total value added in the sector. If the association were stronger, this would be a disturbing finding since it sug-

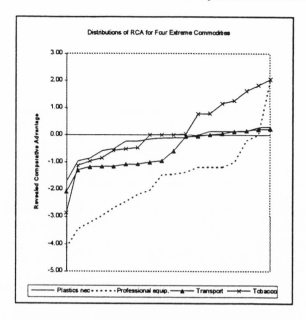

Fig. 1

gests that the results of this empirical exercise may be influenced greatly by the level of aggregation. The high value-added commodities like machinery, electrical machinery, and transportation equipment may be combinations of different products, each of which is just as specialized internationally as professional equipment.

The association between specialization and both productivity and total value added is more clear across countries, as can be seen in the displays at the bottom of figure 3. The least specialized are large countries with high value added in manufacturing and productive countries with high levels of value added in manufacturing relative to employment levels. The negative association between country size and specialization is suggestive of scale economies. The negative association between value-added per worker and specialization is suggestive of technological differences. These features of the data clearly demand more careful attention. They are reminiscent of Leamer's (1987) finding that small SMSA's (cities) in the United States have more concentrated manufacturing than large ones, even though there is little overall tendency for any industry to locate mostly in small or large SMSA's.

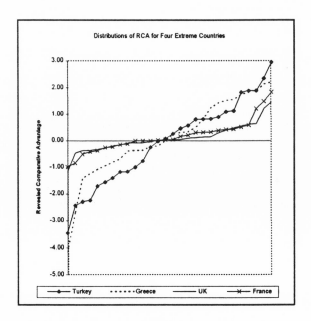

Fig. 2

Heckscher-Ohlin and Ricardian Effects in Explanation of Specialization

The explanatory variables that are suggested by the Heckscher-Ohlin model are ratios of factors, such as the ratio of capital to labor. Instead of attempting to measure capital abundance directly, I will use the estimated country factors:

$$\mathbf{HO_c} = \beta_c \,.$$

At a theoretical level, this is an uncomfortable way of representing the HO model since the theory predicts that sectoral productivities should be the same everywhere and be perfectly predictable from a set of sectoral dummy variables. If this theory were correct, there would thus be no country effect. Total value added per worker could vary across countries, but only because of differences in product mix.

There are a variety of ways that the theory could be amended to allow for the empirical fact that there is an important country effect that is highly correlated with overall productivity in manufacturing. One possibility is that the country effect measures a kind of technological superiority that is common across sectors. I prefer to interpret the country effects as a symptom of an aggregation problem. According to the HO model, at the highest level of aggregation with a single composite commodity there is a country effect since countries abundant in capital have high per capita GDP's. Countries achieve higher GDP per capita by shifting output mix in favor of the subsectors with higher productivities. Country differences in sectoral productivity due to aggregation distortions can also be present at the two-digit ISIC data used in this paper. For example, the mix of apparel products made in Germany is more capital intensive than the mix of apparel products made in Portugal. I will therefore take the estimated country effect to be an (imperfect) indicator of the country capital/labor abundance ratio.[2]

The Ricardian theory suggests that comparative advantage comes from superior technology. Table 5 reports indicators of productivity advantage. With

E_{ic} = employment in industry i in country c,
$Pic = V_{ic} / E_{ic}$ = productivity in industry i in country c,

the *Ricardian Productivity Advantage* is

$$RIC_{ic} = \log_2 \left([P_{ic}/\overline{P_{ic}}] / [P_c/\overline{P_c}] \right)$$

where

$P_c = \Sigma i V_{ic} / \Sigma_i E_{ic}$ = country c's average productivity
$\overline{P_{ic}} = \Sigma_{j \neq c} Vij / \Sigma_{j \neq c} Eij$ = industry i's average productivity, excluding country c
$\overline{P_c} = \Sigma_{j \neq c} \Sigma_i V_{ij} / \Sigma_{j \neq c} \Sigma_i E_{ij}$ = value added per worker, excluding country c

Using this index a country is said to have a Ricardian technological advantage in a sector if its productivity in that sector is high after adjusting for the commodity and country general levels of productivity.[3] According to the numbers in table 5, the United States is particularly productive in tobacco, professional instruments, and industrial chemicals, but particularly unproductive in petroleum refining and furniture. Japan has a Ricardian advantage in iron and steel, while France and Germany and the United Kingdom have a Ricardian advantage in petroleum refining. Some of these Ricardian advantages will be shown to have apparent effects on value added in the sectors but other productivity advantages do not.

Table 6 reports estimates of equations explaining the revealed com-

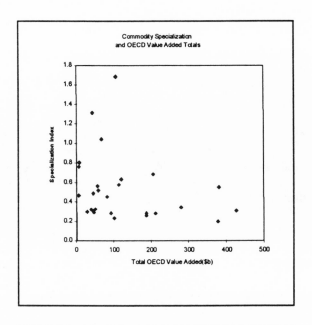

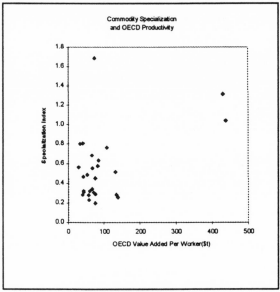

Fig. 3. Specialization Indices

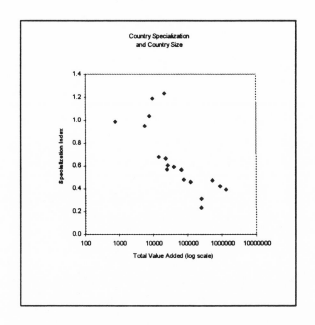

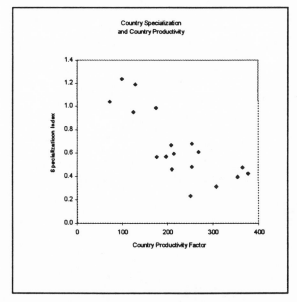

Fig. 3. Specialization Indices (continued)

TABLE 5. Ricardian Productivity Advantage

Commodity	OECD 1990 Avg. VApw	Port 87	Tur 89	NZ 86	Gre 90	Ice 90	Spa 88	Aut 89	Den 90	Ita 89	Net 89	UK 90	Nor 90	Can 86	Fin 90	Fra 90	US 90	Ger 90	Jap 90
Wearing Apparel	30	0.24	0.04	0.27	0.32	0.62	0.31	0.10	0.15	0.61	0.26	0.07	0.45	0.03	0.18	0.74	0.01	0.42	-0.59
Footwear	33	0.21	-0.20	0.41	0.34	0.08	0.46	0.27	0.88	0.27	0.22	0.16	0.17	0.18	0.08	0.02	-0.06	0.12	0.24
Textiles	41	0.24	-0.12	0.72	0.50	0.47	0.21	0.35	0.53	0.61	0.48	0.05	0.17	0.37	0.02	0.03	-0.06	0.30	-0.12
Pottery, china	41	0.44	0.80	0.40	0.61	0.40	0.03	0.35	0.17	0.85		0.08	0.16	0.64	0.79		0.16	-0.05	-0.11
Leather	43	0.75	-0.01	0.51	0.49	-0.12	0.29	-0.10	-1.21	0.50	0.05	-0.13	0.17	-0.36	-0.42	0.67	0.01	-0.01	-0.25
Wood	44	-0.12	-0.46	0.33	0.56	-0.15	-0.01	0.47	0.27	0.36	-0.03	0.31	0.44	0.38	0.43	0.20	-0.30	0.40	-0.11
Furniture	44	-0.52	-0.24	0.06	-0.05	0.93	-0.23	0.16	0.15	0.33	-0.01	0.24	0.17	-0.12	0.35	0.33	-0.46	0.31	0.07
Other Manufactures	54	-0.33	-0.52	-0.22	-0.07	1.01	-0.06	-0.05	0.23	-0.04	-0.09	-0.15	0.05	-0.38	-0.05	-0.16	-0.29	-0.12	0.07
Fabricated Metal	58	0.02	-0.04	0.06	0.03	0.44	-0.09	0.09	0.16	0.14	0.08	0.04	-0.13	0.08	0.12	0.22	-0.28	-0.05	0.18
Plastics, nec	59	0.04	-0.33	0.34	0.37	0.94	-0.05	-0.10	0.47	0.23	0.03	0.18	0.20	-0.11	0.06	0.20	-0.25	-0.04	0.07
Rubber	60	0.26	0.62	0.28	0.62		0.29	0.24	0.16	0.21	-0.11	0.08	0.29	0.01	-0.13	-0.63	0.05	0.04	0.21
Printing, Publishing	67	-0.01	-0.25	0.10	0.19	0.37	0.33	-0.01	-0.57	0.52	-0.03	0.39	-0.12	-0.20	-0.03	0.06	-0.12	-0.33	0.17
Food Manufactures	68	0.09	-0.46	-0.09	0.08	-0.30	-0.15	-0.08	0.13	0.19	-0.26	-0.03	-0.44	0.02	-0.16	-0.01	0.51	0.08	-0.51
Electrical Machinery	68	0.39	0.10	0.07	0.29		0.07	-0.07	-0.04	0.11	-0.36	-0.21	-0.12	-0.04	0.15	-0.03	0.00	-0.04	-0.05
Machinery	71	-0.22	-0.34	-0.25	-0.36		-0.23	-0.14	-0.26	0.05	-0.56	0.02	0.00	-0.16	0.06	-0.06	-0.17	-0.12	0.24
Professional Equip.	74	-0.42	-0.66	-0.41	-0.38		-0.31	-0.67	-0.16	-0.18	-0.07	-0.34	-0.08	-0.52	-0.01	-0.03	0.49	-0.54	-0.58
Glass	75	0.16	0.18	0.06	-0.13	0.06	0.20	0.10	-0.17	-0.01	-0.07	-0.17	-0.05	-0.15	-0.24	-0.15	-0.24	-0.26	0.69
Nonmetal Minerals	76	0.14	-0.44	0.34	0.25	0.44	0.04	0.17	0.44	0.17	-0.53	0.42	0.17	0.20	0.12	0.58	-0.44	0.12	-0.01
Transport	76	-0.34	-0.39	-0.42	-0.43	-0.22	0.18	-0.10	-0.12	-0.22		-0.06	-0.36	0.13	-0.32	-0.28	-0.01	-0.22	0.33
Non-ferrous Metals	77	-0.08	-0.03	1.21	1.05	0.66	0.50	0.01	-0.29	0.03	-0.18	-0.29	0.45	0.32	0.47	0.65	-0.32	-0.16	0.23
Paper	83	1.28	-0.38	0.28	-0.10	0.09	-0.06	0.19	0.17	-0.11		-0.22	0.12	0.10	0.20	-0.19	0.27	-0.10	-0.14
Iron and Steel	85	0.24	0.07	-0.58	0.61	0.17	-0.33	0.04	0.31	-0.08	-0.40	-0.26	-0.37	0.14	-0.04	-0.63	-0.34	-0.34	0.89
Misc. Pet. and Coal	109		0.44	-0.83	-0.76	-0.76	0.65	-0.37	0.13	0.25	0.38	0.25	0.15	-0.09	0.99		-0.09		0.09
Beverages	132	0.35	0.24	0.49	-0.15	0.05	0.13	-0.35	0.42	-0.32	-0.91	-0.06	0.39	0.04	-0.01	0.36	0.19	-0.01	-0.12
Other Chemicals	135	-0.29	-0.01	-0.68	-0.42	-0.36	-0.55	-0.70	0.08	-0.40	0.01	-0.22	-0.49	-0.32	-0.69	-0.69	0.39	-0.66	0.59
Industrial Chemicals	139	0.45	-0.06	-0.35	-0.24	0.03	0.26	-0.60	0.30	-0.46	0.17	-0.07	-0.04	0.34	-0.19	-0.55	0.47	-0.43	0.52
Tobacco	430	0.93	-2.04		-2.58		-0.74	2.01	-1.42	-2.10		-0.88		-0.61	-1.14	0.10	0.53	1.09	-1.23
Petroleum Refining	437	0.40	2.37	1.34	-1.88		-0.08	-0.85	-0.48	-1.51	-1.21	0.73	-0.91	-1.25	-1.38	1.09	-0.91	1.14	-1.24

TABLE 6. Combined Regressions by Commodity (R denotes Ricardian, and C denotes combined)

Commodity	OECD 1990 Avg. VApw (1000s $)	HO Slope * Range	t–value	Ricardian Slope * Range	t-value	Adj. R_2	Best Model
Textiles	41	–2.73	–4.54	–0.44	–0.81	0.53	HO
Electrical Machinery	68	1.27	2.27	–0.20	–0.32	0.34	HO
Wearing Apparel	30	–1.78	–2.42	–0.19	–0.20	0.19	HO
Pottery, china	41	–2.32	–1.92	0.15	0.15	0.17	HO
Footwear	33	–1.86	–1.72	1.41	0.99	0.12	HO
Food Manufacture	68	–0.91	–1.58	–0.29	–0.45	0.05	HO
Printing, Publishing	67	1.10	1.46	0.81	0.99	0.05	HO
Petroleum Refining	437	–0.77	–0.96	3.10	3.98	0.54	R
Furniture	44	0.34	0.50	2.54	3.11	0.38	R
Non–ferrous Metals	77	0.69	0.90	2.39	3.30	0.36	R
Glass	75	–0.47	–0.95	0.96	1.69	0.14	R
Wood	44	–0.37	–0.34	2.17	2.14	0.13	R
Other Chemicals	135	–0.14	–0.30	0.90	1.81	0.07	R
Iron and Steel	85	0.56	0.67	0.94	1.07	–0.04	R
Machinery	71	1.94	3.53	0.94	1.67	0.68	C(HO)
Non–metal Minerals	76	–1.18	–3.39	0.60	1.67	0.41	C (HO)
Leather	43	–1.14	–1.81	3.33	4.52	0.67	C (R)
Fabricated Metal	58	0.65	2.57	1.18	3.67	0.50	C (R)
Misc. Pet. and Coal	109	–1.41	–1.18	3.19	3.41	0.41	C (R)
Paper	83	0.83	1.25	2.71	3.14	0.32	C (R)
Professional Equip.	74	2.79	3.57	2.53	2.90	0.66	C
Plastics nec	59	0.80	2.28	1.30	3.06	0.40	C
Transport	76	1.14	2.13	0.87	1.57	0.39	C
Other Manufactures	54	1.52	2.07	2.54	2.64	0.39C	
Tobacco	430	–2.61	–2.55	2.25	2.15	0.35	C
Beverages	132	–0.86	–1.72	0.49	1.09	0.16	C
Industrial Chemicals	139	0.49	0.95	0.19	0.43	–0.06	??
Rubber	60	–0.33	–0.45	0.19	0.20	–0.10	??

parative advantage for each commodity with both the Heckscher-Ohlin and the Ricardian variables. The equations take the form

$$RCA_{ic} = \alpha_i + \delta_i HO_c + \theta_i RIC_{ic}$$

There is one equation for each 2-digit ISIC commodity aggregate estimated across countries. Keep in mind that both the dependent variable and the explanatory variables are logarithmic. The estimates are reported both in terms of the "economic significance" of the effect and also the "statistical significance" of the effect. The economic significance is measured by the product of the estimated coefficient times the range of the explanatory variable. The HO variable has the same range for every commodity but the Ricardian range differs by commodity. This measure of economic significance indicates by how much the predicted revealed comparative advantage changes with extreme changes in the HO variable and the Ricardian variable. Also in these tables are the traditional measures of "statistical significance": t-values and adjusted R^2s.

The commodities in table 6 are sorted into four subgroups, depending on the relative size of the t-values of the HO and Ricardian variables. First are the HO products with high t-values for the HO variable, then are the Ricardian products with high t-values for the Ricardian variable. After that are three "combined" classes, the first leaning in favor of the HO effect, the second toward the Ricardian model, and the third neutral. Last are two commodities (industrial chemicals and rubber manufactures) that defy explanation and allow only a negative adjusted R^2. Within each subgroup, commodities are ordered by the adjusted R^2. Scatter diagrams, most of which are not shown, corresponding to these simple regressions clearly indicate that many of these associations are broadly supported by the data and are not driven by one or two outliers.

The first HO commodity is textiles, with a predicted HO effect over the range of this sample equal to -2.73, meaning that the value added decreases to $2^{-2.73} = 15$ percent of its initial value as one ranges from the country at the lowest stage of development to the highest. The scatter diagram for the textiles data is in the upper-left corner of figure 4. Wearing apparel, pottery, and footwear are also strongly HO products located in countries at the lowest level of development. Comparative advantage goes the opposite direction for electrical machinery and printing and publishing, which tend to be located in the advanced countries. In this class, both footwear and printing and publishing also have fairly strong Ricardian effects.

The top Ricardian commodity is petroleum refining. Figure 4 illustrates these data in the upper-right graph. The estimate of the Ricardian coefficient times the Ricardian range for petroleum refining equals 3.10, which means that predicted value added increases by a factor of $2^{3.10} = 8.6$ as one ranges from the least to the most productive country. Furniture and wood products are also Ricardian commodities, although this may be because we have not given the HO model a fair "shake" by including softwood forests as a source of comparative advantage. Note that the iron and steel sector is placed in this Ricardian category since it has a t-value in excess of one, but the adjusted R^2 is nonetheless negative. For this category and several of the others with very low R^2s, I suspect that trade barriers and government interventions are an important part of the explanation of the OECD specialization pattern.

The adjusted R^2 exceeds 0.3 in 16 of 27 commodity aggregates. Par-

Heckscher-Ohlin Scatters

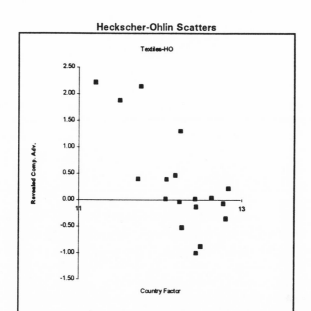

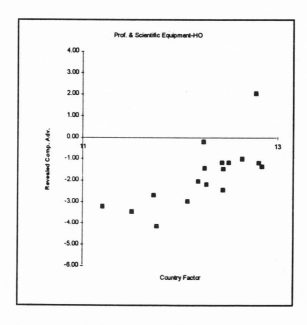

Fig. 4. Selected Scatters

Ricardian Scatters

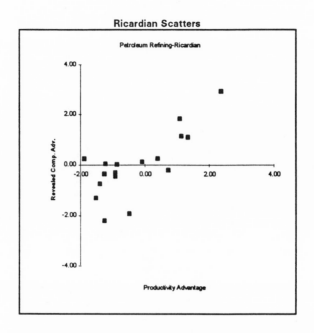

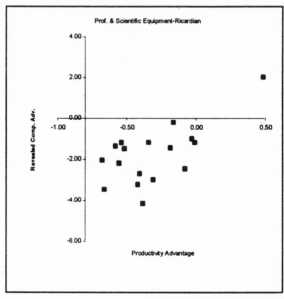

Fig. 4. Selected Scatters (continued)

ticularly good fits are obtained for professional equipment, leather products, and machinery. For 11 of the commodities the adjusted R^2's less than 0.2. Of the 16 products with adjusted R^2 exceeding 0.3, four are HO or HO-leaning, seven are Ricardian or Ricardian-leaning, and five are combined. Thus, the Ricardian model wins this contest, but keep in mind that the HO model in this race has a particularly weak representative.

Professional equipment has both HO effects and Ricardian effects. This product is over-represented in the most developed country (HO effect), which also have a productivity advantage in professional equipment (Ricardian effect). Both of these regressions are illustrated in the scatter plots in the bottom of figure 4.

The possibility of nonlinearities is explored in table 7. A multicone Heckscher-Ohlin model suggests that specialization patterns may be nonlinear, with value-added being especially high for countries in the middle of the range but not at the extremes. The possibility of nonlinearities is formally explored by including in the model a quadratic HO term. The t-values of the quadratic HO term are reported in table 7 together with the value within the HO range (from 0 to 1) at which the extreme predicted specialization occurs. Commodities are ordered by the estimated location of the extreme. Most commodities have extreme specialization estimated to be either at the lowest value of the range or at the highest value. Nonlinearities that favor countries in the middle of the range do seem to be detectable for furniture and beverages and also for tobacco, food manufactures, and printing and publishing.

Finally, table 8 reports the estimated residuals with country and commodity R^2s on the edges. Countries and commodities are sorted by their residual sum-of-squares, thus placing problem observations at the lower right. Residuals in excess of one in absolute value are listed in bold. Because of the sorting of this table, these entries are concentrated at the lower right.

Although the United States is a problem country in the sense of having a low R^2(.15), it is not a problem country in the sense of contributing to the overall lack of fit. The low R^2 of the U.S. comes from its diverse mix of products and thus the lack of variability of RCA across commodities. The United States does have an unpredictably large RCA in professional equipment, miscellaneous petroleum and coal products, tobacco, and wood products. Generally there is a strong association between country specialization and the overall fit of the model, as can be seen from figure 5. The least specialized countries are the most difficult to predict.

The problem countries in terms of additions to the overall lack of fit are Iceland, Norway and Italy. It is apparent from unreported scatter diagrams that the model would work much better if these countries were

TABLE 7.   Quadratic HO Model (Regression with Quadratic HO Term)

Commodity	OECD 1990 Avg. VA/Work (1000$)	t–value for quadratic term	Valus for HO at max
Wood	44	1.52	0.00
Textiles	41	1.30	0.00
Glass	75	1.09	0.00
Other Chemicals	135	0.93	0.00
Pottery, china	41	0.89	0.00
Misc. Pet. and Coal	109	0.71	0.00
Non–metal Mineral	76	–0.67	0.00
Rubber	60	0.64	0.00
Wearing Apparel	30	0.54	0.00
Footwear	33	0.42	0.00
Tobacco	430	–1.27	0.22
Petroleum Refining	437	–0.41	0.25
Leather	43	–1.51	0.38
Food Manufacture	68	–1.82	0.39
Beverages	132	–2.38	0.39
Furniture	44	–1.44	0.60
Printing, Publishing	67	–1.30	0.74
Non–ferrous Metals	77	–0.64	0.74
Paper	83	–0.62	0.88
Fabricated Metal	58	–1.08	0.90
Other Manufactures	54	–0.71	0.96
Electrical Machinery	68	1.44	1.00
Machinery	71	–1.15	1.00
Plastics nec	59	1.00	1.00
Transport	76	0.91	1.00
Professional Equip.	74	0.91	1.00
Iron and Steel	85	0.52	1.00
Industrial Chemical	139	0.43	1.00

removed. Iceland is so small that it has an extreme concentration of value added on leather and food manufactures (fish products). This is evident not so much by the positive numbers in table 8 as by the negative ones. Iceland has virtually no value added in wood products, footwear, or iron and steel. Norway is unusual also in this negative sense, with low value added in several industries, including footwear and wearing apparel. Italy is different with unusually high value added in textiles, wearing apparel, pottery and china, and footwear.

The problem commodities are footwear, wood, and pottery and china. Footwear value added is unusually high in Italy, the United Kingdom and France, but is low in Iceland, Norway, the Netherlands, and Turkey. Pottery and china value added is especially high in the United Kingdom and Italy, but low in Canada, New Zealand and Iceland. These

TABLE 8. Residuals for Combined Models
Countries and Commodities Sorted by Residual Sum-of-Squares

Commodity	Spa	Aus	UK	Fra	Can	US	Port	Fin	NZ	Ger	Jap	Net	Gre	Tur	Den	Ital	Nor	Ice	RSS	R2
Fabricated Metal	0.21	0.32	-0.30	-0.13	-0.17	-0.03	0.01	-0.02	0.53	0.21	-0.21	0.33	-0.16	-0.57	0.17	-0.36	0.11	0.26	1.34	0.50
Plastics nec	0.27	-0.36	0.06	-0.26	0.23	0.24	0.32	-0.77	0.40	0.28	0.31	0.16	0.23	-0.64	-0.21	0.26	-0.51	-0.22	2.34	0.40
Non-metal Minerals	0.41	0.37	0.30	-0.12	-0.34	-0.42	-0.20	0.46	-0.80	-0.23	0.43	-0.08	0.59	0.12	0.07	-0.39	-0.24	0.19	2.45	0.41
Elec. Machinery	-0.11	0.72	-0.23	0.14	-0.53	-0.39	0.61	-0.25	-0.31	0.51	0.76	0.54	-0.16	-0.18	-0.37	0.45	-0.67	0.00	3.53	0.34
Machinery	0.01	0.38	-0.33	-0.34	-0.38	-0.25	-0.15	0.12	0.30	0.30	-0.42	0.29	0.27	0.10	0.90	0.57	0.13	0.00	3.61	0.68
Transport	0.50	-0.66	0.09	0.37	0.24	0.13	0.14	-0.50	0.19	0.41	-0.45	-0.19	0.05	0.02	-0.69	0.53	-0.01	-1.38	4.31	0.39
Other Chemicals	0.52	-0.09	0.38	0.42	0.36	0.21	0.23	-0.51	-0.34	0.46	-0.28	0.22	0.62	0.66	0.34	-0.71	-0.60	-1.21	4.37	0.07
Glass	0.37	0.73	0.24	0.82	-0.09	0.13	0.27	-0.14	-0.07	0.49	-0.34	-0.17	-0.73	-0.23	-0.63	0.41	-0.54	-0.97	4.68	0.14
Beverages	0.78	0.27	0.45	-0.07	0.17	-0.52	-0.66	-0.26	-0.47	0.23	-0.87	0.18	0.89	0.66	0.19	-0.74	0.74	0.03	4.74	0.16
Industrial Chemicals	0.00	-0.06	0.11	-0.31	-0.42	0.03	0.29	0.08	-0.78	0.47	-0.50	1.53	-0.39	-0.23	0.00	0.04	0.27	-1.02	5.36	-0.06
Leather	0.56	-0.09	0.20	-0.13	-0.24	-0.49	-0.61	0.33	0.31	-0.25	0.48	0.00	0.24	0.54	-0.22	0.78	-1.41	1.36	6.36	0.67
Food manf.	0.01	-0.63	0.16	0.11	0.06	0.28	-0.59	-0.12	0.61	-0.79	-0.40	0.29	0.17	-0.70	0.76	-0.79	0.06	1.63	6.49	0.05
Rubber	0.86	0.08	0.35	0.55	0.32	0.02	-0.15	-1.14	0.20	0.38	0.50	-0.71	-0.34	0.55	-0.93	0.67	-1.13	0.00	6.54	-0.10
Textiles	-0.28	0.05	0.42	0.20	-0.11	0.28	0.08	-0.95	-0.60	0.24	0.63	-0.73	1.09	0.08	-0.27	1.12	-1.09	-0.53	6.62	0.53
Paper	-0.17	0.11	0.04	-0.27	1.05	0.00	-0.26	1.47	0.40	-0.55	-0.57	0.25	0.26	0.27	-0.52	-0.26	0.48	-1.44	7.09	0.32
Furniture	0.62	0.99	-0.13	-0.54	0.60	0.54	0.34	-0.03	0.42	-0.55	-0.89	-0.64	-0.29	-1.81	0.75	-0.12	-0.01	0.36	8.18	0.38
Professional Equip.	-0.92	0.62	-0.23	-0.51	0.42	1.16	0.61	-0.50	0.19	0.13	-0.01	0.09	-1.40	0.35	1.26	0.03	-1.51	0.00	9.68	0.66
Non-ferrous Metals	-0.26	0.42	-0.04	-0.57	0.79	0.26	-0.77	-0.71	-0.73	0.18	-0.57	0.00	0.10	1.26	-1.59	0.14	1.36	0.92	10.11	0.36
Petroleim Refining	-0.09	0.42	-0.68	1.03	0.46	0.42	-0.73	0.18	-0.31	0.38	-1.20	0.74	1.19	0.68	-1.80	-0.40	0.10	0.00	10.21	0.54
Other Manf.	0.06	0.10	-0.13	0.65	1.11	0.56	-0.51	-0.54	1.10	-1.37	0.04	-1.82	-0.40	-0.24	0.73	0.04	-0.73	0.35	10.35	0.39
Wearing Apparel	0.19	-0.15	0.61	0.84	0.52	0.82	-0.08	0.18	0.20	-0.14	0.03	-1.38	1.24	-0.03	-0.67	1.06	-1.77	-0.57	10.68	0.19
Printing, Publishing	-0.21	-0.36	-0.03	-0.35	0.31	0.63	0.21	0.50	0.79	-1.74	-0.52	0.62	-0.55	-1.53	0.85	-0.69	0.95	0.95	11.03	0.05
Misc. Pet. and Coal	-0.26	-0.26	-0.03	0.00	-0.16	1.38	0.00	-0.96	-0.04	0.00	-0.60	0.40	0.80	0.33	1.32	-0.18	0.62	-2.17	11.13	0.41
Iron and Steel	0.62	1.14	-0.02	0.44	0.05	-0.63	0.01	-0.06	-1.45	0.21	0.33	0.00	-0.29	1.49	-1.58	0.96	-0.17	-1.43	12.34	-0.04
Tobacco	-0.23	0.60	0.44	-0.63	-0.32	1.02	-1.74	-0.36	0.00	1.15	-1.67	1.22	1.39	1.27	-0.19	-0.44	0.00	0.00	14.66	0.35
Pottery, china	0.18	-0.46	1.60	0.00	-1.80	-0.97	0.77	-0.02	-1.24	0.56	0.98	0.00	0.34	0.10	-0.25	2.34	-0.63	-1.80	19.68	0.17
Wood	0.75	-0.30	-0.67	-0.21	0.99	1.02	1.25	1.30	0.92	-1.03	0.60	-0.26	-0.82	-0.23	0.06	-1.13	0.91	-3.12	21.31	0.13
Footwear	0.75	0.63	1.38	1.68	0.16	-0.18	0.95	0.59	-0.34	0.12	-0.50	-1.14	0.99	-1.06	-1.09	2.13	-1.78	-1.96	23.55	0.12
Sum of Squares	5.78	6.84	7.15	8.42	9.65	9.82	10.02	10.42	10.58	10.78	11.50	13.76	15.03	15.80	19.03	19.63	20.25	38.28		
R²	0.78	0.63	0.03	0.23	0.30	0.15	0.83	0.50	0.66	0.11	0.41	0.36	0.75	0.77	0.34	0.42	0.37	0.33		

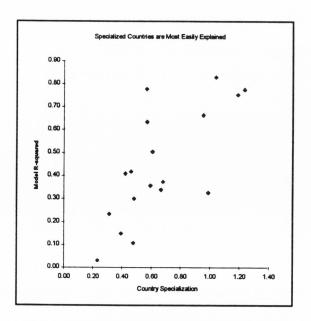

Fig. 5. Model Fit and Country Specialization Indices

findings should be no surprise to world shoppers. The question is why? What feature is excluded from the model that accounts for these large residuals? Keep in mind that since we are controlling for sectoral productivities, the Italian concentration in footwear does not come from especially productive shoemakers. It could well be that the value of the product comes not in manufacturing but in retailing. Italian shoes are not created on the shop-floor, but in the retail outlet.

Wood value added is high in the United States, Portugal, and Finland but low in Germany, Italy, and Iceland. Clearly this is a HO commodity that needs another measured resource, specifically softwood forests. It is surprising, however, that the Ricardian variable does not pick up this effect.

Concluding Remarks

The Heckscher-Ohlin theory and the Ricardian theory of international commerce traditionally have been treated as separate conceptual frameworks, but a growing body of empirical work is relying on both simultaneously and calls for an integrated theory.[4] The need for an integrated treatment is made all the more urgent by the dramatic liberalizations that have occurred in Eastern Europe, Mexico, South America, China, India and so on. These countries that formerly chose economic isolation suffered both Heckscher-Ohlin effects and Ricardian effects. They lost the exchange benefits that would have come from specialization and they also had greatly limited access to technological improvements. Integration of these formerly isolated regions will involve both technology transfer (Ricardian effects) and also increased specialization (Heckscher-Ohlin effects).

The traditional separate treatment of technological differences and factor supply differences leads to the conclusion that economic integration of these formerly isolated regions will have severe consequences for the low-skilled workers in advanced developed countries if most of the action is Heckscher-Ohlin in character, but relatively little effect if most of the action is Ricardian. A Heckscher-Ohlin framework implies great gains from exchange, but also potentially great pressures on wages of the unskilled in the advanced developed world since the effective global supply of unskilled workers has increased greatly by liberalization, with little increase in physical or human capital. A Ricardian framework is less optimistic about the economic gains to the advanced countries but more optimistic about the adjustment problems. According to the Ricardian model, the formerly isolated regions can be expected rapidly to adopt the superior technology. This technology transfer will cause wage convergence mostly from below but not from above. Integration can be accomplished with relatively little increased international trade and relatively little disruption in the advanced regions. We might expect that a combined model would lead to conclusions that fall somewhere between these extremes. However, the combined model discussed in Leamer (1995) suggests that the Ricardian technology gap creates very strong comparative advantage in the labor-intensive sector regardless of the Southern initial capital abundance. This makes the South more dependent on exports of labor-intensive manufactures in the medium run than even the Heckscher-Ohlin model suggests. Thus in a sense the Ricardian effects and the Heckscher-Ohlin effects interact to create special pressure for wage convergence from above and also special gains from specialization.

The OECD specialization patterns do seem to be driven by both Heckscher-Ohlin factor endowment differences and by Ricardian technological superiority, although the measurements here of both endowment differences and technological differences are primitive. The existence of Ricardian effects in OECD specialization patterns where technology presumably is relatively fluid suggests that technological differences have a long life and the emerging countries may not expect very rapid convergence to the productivity levels of the most advanced countries. A panel study of these productivity differences would be desirable to place these issues in firmer context.

NOTES

1. This research was supported by NSF grant SBR-9409011.

2. Kotlikoff and Leamer (1987) and Dollar, Baumol and Wolff (1988) find substantial and persistent differences in productivities across countries at the two-digit level of commodity aggregation. Bowen, Leamer and Sveikauskus (1987) and Trefler (1993,1995) make the point that the HO model works well only if factor supplies are corrected for neutral technological differences.

3. An alternative would be to find the extremes, not the averages and to define the Ricardian advantage as $RIC_{ic}^{*} = (P_{ic} / \max_c P_{ic} \max_i P_{ic}) (P..)$.

4. For example, Bowen, Leamer and Sveikauskus (1987), and Trefler (1993, 1995).

REFERENCES

Bowen, Harry P.; Leamer, Edward E.; and Sveikauskus, L. 1987. "A Multi-Country MultiFactor Test of the Factor Abundance Theory." *American Economic Review* 77:791–809.
Dollar, David; Baumol, William; and Wolff, Edward. 1988. "The Factor Price Equalization Model and Industry Labor Productivity: An Empirical Test Across Countries." In Robert Feenstra, ed., *Empirical Methods for International Trade.* Cambridge, MA: The MIT Press.
Kotlikoff, Lawrence J., and Leamer, Edward E. 1987. "Empirical Tests of Alternative Models of International Growth." In Colin Jr. Bradford and William H. Branson, eds., *Trade and Structural Change in Pacific Asia.* Chicago: University of Chicago Press.
Leamer, Edward E. 1984. *Sources of International Comparative Advantage: Theory and Evidence,* Cambridge, MA: The MIT Press.
Leamer, Edward E. 1987. "Theory and Evidence of Immigrant Enclaves." Unpublished Working Paper.
Leamer, Edward E. 1987. "Cross Section Estimation of the Effects of Trade Barriers." In Robert Feenstra, ed., *Empirical Methods for International Trade.* Cambridge, MA: The MIT Press.
Leamer, Edward E. 1987. "Paths of Development in the Three-Factor N-Good General Equilibrium Model." *Journal of Political Economy* 95:961–999.
Leamer, Edward E. 1993. "Wage Effects of a U.S.-Mexican Free Trade Agreement." In Peter M. Garber, ed., *The Mexico-U.S. Free Trade Agreement.* Cambridge, MA: The MIT Press.

Leamer, Edward E. 1995. "A Combined Ricardian and Heckscher-Ohlin Model of Comparative Advantage." Institute for Advanced Studies. Economics Series. 17:December.

Trefler, Daniel. 1993. "International Factor Price Differences: Leontief Was Right." *Journal of Political Economy* 101:961–987.

Trefler, Daniel. 1995. "The Case of the Missing Trade and Other Mysteries." *American Economic Review* 85:1029–46.

CHAPTER 3

Testing Theories of Endogenous Protection: Robust Evidence from U.S. Nontariff Barrier Data

Kishore Gawande

An econometric assessment of the validity of political-economic theories of protection involves the examination of the size and sign of coefficients on a list of variables that represent each theory. The link from the theory to the selection of representative variables is tenuous enough that a large set of specifications is possible. Conceivably, with enough experimentation, any theory can be validated. Since some is used, however well-intentioned, the standard errors reported inadequately convey the uncertainty surrounding the estimates. The method of extreme bounds analysis (EBA) described in Leamer (1982) and Polasek (1984) provides a better way of conveying uncertainty in such a setting. In this method prior beliefs are formally incorporated into the analysis, and the extreme bounds analysis is designed to expand the set of prior beliefs and observe which inferences, if any, remain unambiguous. Inferences are thus shown to be fragile or robust to a range of prior beliefs. In the area of empirical political economy, where a wide range of prior beliefs are entertained, this methodology seems apt. The method is conceptually simple and is computationally easy to use.

In the present study, the extension of EBA to the nonlinear Tobit model described in Gawande (1995) is used to study the political economy of protection using nontariff barrier (NTB) coverage data from 1983. The empirical methodology follows the pioneering study by Baldwin (1985), where variables representing quite disparate theories of political economy are collected in an econometric model. Cross-industry U.S. NTBs on imports from nine partner countries are pooled to form the data set for the econometric analysis. A separate analysis is also performed for each trade bloc. The present study incorporates Baldwin's recommendations that more direct measures of political economy models be used.

The paper proceeds as follows. In the next section, Leamer's method and its extension to the Tobit setting is explained. I then motivate the choice of regressors, and explore some features of the data. The following section enumerates two sets of priors over these regressors, one based on elasticities and another based on standardized coefficients, or Beta coefficients. The Tobit EBA is used to investigate robust inferences about the political economy of protection from both pooled data and data broken down by trade blocs. Some concluding observations are offered in the final section.

Extreme Bounds Analysis in the Tobit Model

Leamer's (1982) extreme bounds analysis (EBA) in the linear regression model makes use of the fact that the posterior mean, b^{**}, in a k-variable regression is a matrix-weighted average of the OLS estimate b and the prior mean b^* with the weights given by the inverse of the covariance matrix of OLS estimates (or their precision matrix), $\sigma^{-2}X\_X$, and a prior precision matrix V^{-1}, where V is a symmetric positive definite (s.p.d.) matrix:

$$b^{**} = E(\beta | Y, X, \sigma^2, V) = (\sigma^{-2}X'X + V^{-1})^{-1}(\sigma^{-2}X'Xb + V^{-1}b^*), \quad (1)$$

where X is $N \times k$, Y is $N \times 1$, V is $k \times k$ s.p.d., and $\sigma^2 > 0$. The assumptions behind equation (1) are: (i) Y is normally distributed with mean $X\beta$ and covariance matrix $\sigma^2 I_N$, and (ii) β is normally distributed with mean vector b^* and covariance matrix V.

The strength of EBA is that it recognizes that prior information, especially about V, is usually uncertain, and that restricting the prior covariance to a single matrix V would lead to a Bayes estimate based on a straitjacketed prior. If uncertainty about V is reflected by allowing V to be any s.p.d matrix bounded above and below, respectively, by s.p.d. matrices V^* and V_*:

$$V^* \leq V \leq V_*, \quad (2)$$

then Leamer (1982, Theorem 7) provides analytic extreme bounds for the posterior estimates as a function of the data (X, Y), OLS estimates b, prior mean b^*, and covariance bounds V^* and V_*. If for any coefficient these extreme bounds contain the value zero then inference about its value is ambiguous and it is concluded that the coefficient is very sensitive to the choice of prior. In this case the bounds can be narrowed by restricting V even further. However, this demonstrates less uncertainty and more confidence about the prior covariance.

The extension to the Tobit model of EBA is described in Gawande (1995), and essentially involves the following steps. Let the model be given by

$$Y_i = X_i'\beta + u_i, \text{ if RHS} > 0,$$
$$Y_i = 0 \text{ otherwise,} \qquad\qquad (3)$$

where $u_i \sim$ iid N$(0, \sigma^2)$, $i = 1, \ldots, N$. Split the N-vector of observations on the dependent variable Y into its observed and censored component vectors of dimension N_0 and N_1 respectively, and write $Y = (Y_1', Y_0')'$. Compute $\Theta^{MLE} \equiv (b, \hat\sigma)$ and replace the censored Y_{0i} observation by their expectation conditional on Θ^{MLE}. Let $\hat{Y} = (Y_1', \hat{Y}_0')'$ be the N-vector that replaces the vector Y. Hence wherever the extreme bounds analysis in Leamer (1982) requires the use of the k-vector $X'Y$, its Tobit counterpart employs $X'\hat{Y}$. After this redefinition the Tobit MLE, b, is equivalent to the b that appears in the expression for the posterior mean in (1). Finally, wherever the EBA in the linear model requires the weight matrix $\sigma^{-2}X'X$, its Tobit counterpart employs the negative of the Hessian evaluated at Θ^{MLE}.[1] With appropriate redefinition of the conditional expectation this method applies to top and/or bottom censoring,

Econometric Specification and Data

Here I take the view, shared by Baldwin (1990), that a trading nation's NTBs have three components—a self-interested political component that is a response to protectionist pressures which is substantially influenced by the lobbying efforts of private agents, an altruistic political component influenced by welfare-oriented motives of the government, and a retaliatory component that serves as a strategic deterrent against undesirable protectionist policies of its partners. The empirical relevance of the political components has been demonstrated, among other authors, by Caves (1976) using tariff data from the Kennedy Round, by Baldwin (1985) using tariff data during the Tokyo Round of cuts, and by Trefler (1993) using aggregate U.S. NTB data from 1983. An investigation of whether the retaliatory component is empirically relevant has been investigated in Gawande (1995).

Choice of Variables

Following Baldwin's framework, I employ the following specification in the econometric analysis:

$$N_{i,j} = \pmb{X1}_{i,j}\,\alpha_1 + \pmb{X2}_{i,j}\,\alpha_2 + \pmb{X3}_{i,j}\,\mathbf{a_3} + bN_{i,j} + \pmb{D}_j^* + \epsilon_{i,j},$$
$$\epsilon_{i,j} \sim N(0,\sigma^2),\ i=1,\dots,435,\ j=1,\dots,9. \tag{4}$$

U.S. NTBs on good i against country j, $N_{i,j}$, are determined by a self-interested political component whose variables are represented by the vector $\pmb{X1}_{i,j}$, an altruistic political component represented by $\pmb{X2}_{i,j}$, the theory of comparative costs represented by $\pmb{X3}_{i,j}$, and an offensive component, $\beta N_{i,j}^*$, designed to thwart foreign NTBs. Country-effect dummy variables are included in $\pmb{D}_j^*$. In the first set of specifications estimated, the parameters α_1, α_2, α_3, and β are assumed stable across countries, and equation (4) is estimated by pooling industry and country data. Here cross-industry data at the 4-digit SIC level of disaggregation are pooled across nine countries: Belgium, Finland, France, Germany, Italy, the Netherlands, Norway, and U.K. The errors are assumed homoskedastic across countries and goods. While previous econometric work has focused usually either on the industry dimension and, less frequently, the country dimension, an important feature here is pooling across both dimensions. Further, in order to account for possible variations in α_1, α_2, α_3, and across countries, I also estimate a second set of specifications where observations are split up by four blocs: Japan, EC, Benelux, and EFTA. In addition to overall U.S. NTBs, the study investigates the political economy of three distinct disaggregated NTBs. These are price NTBs (e.g. countervailing duties, anti-dumping duties), quantitative NTBs (e.g. quotas, VERs), and threat NTBs (e.g. price and quantity monitoring). See Leamer (1990) for a detailed taxonomy of nontariff barriers.

Cross-industry trade and manufacturing data from 1983 at the 4-digit SIC level of detail is employed in the construction of the exogenous variables in equation (4). The level of nontariff barrier protection is measured as coverage ratios, that is, the percentage of imports covered by *some* NTB. Corporate lobbying expenditures were constructed from campaign contributions over the four congressional election cycles 1977–78, 1979–80, 1981–82, and 1983–84. Data on contributions from Federal Election Commission tapes were concorded into cross-industry data using a mapping constructed from Weinberger and Greavey (1984). Other industry characteristics variables were constructed from the 1982 Census of Manufacturing and many Annual Survey of Manufactures. A description of the variables included in the empirical analysis is provided in Table 1 and details on the construction of variables, including NTB coverage ratios, are provided in the data appendix.

My choice of regressors for equation (4) is highly influenced by Baldwin's (1985) study but also includes newly constructed variables. Table 2 shows the association of regressors with the underlying theory, together with some descriptive statistics. The Special-Interest Group model associated with Olson (1965) and Pincus (1975), and subsequently formalized by Brock and Magee (1978) and Findlay and Wellisz (1982), suggests measures of special-interest pressure. The concentration ratio (CONC4) and measures of scale economies (SCALE) have traditionally been used as proxies for special-interest pressures on the assumption that protection would lead to larger gains in industries with higher concentration or scale economies. In addition to these proxies, I also employ more direct measures of pressures, such as protectionist corporate campaign contributions (PACCVA83), which I presume to be positively related to the level of protection. Corporate PAC contributions are scaled by industry value added to prevent spurious scale effects. The Adding Machine model in Caves (1976) focuses on the voting strength of the industry and suggests that number of employees (NE82) and degree of unionization (UNION) in that

TABLE 1. Descriptions of variables used in the econometric analysis

Variable	Description
$N_{i,j}$	U.S. All NTB coverage of imports of good i from partner j (Ratio)
$P_{i,j}$	U.S. Price NTB coverage of imports of good i from partner j (Ratio)
$Q_{i,j}$	U.S. Quantitative NTB coverage of imports of good i from partner j (Ratio)
$T_{i,j}$	U.S. Threat NTB coverage of imports of good i from partner j (Ratio)
$N^*_{i,j}$	Partner j's All NTB coverage of its imports of good i from the U.S. (Ratio)
PACCORP	Corporate PAC spending per firm, per election cycle, 1977-84. ($ '000)
PACCVA83	PACCORP/Value Added(1983). ($'000 /$Mn)
SCALE	Measure of industry scale: Value added per firm, 1982. ($Bn/firm)
CONC4	4-firm concentration ratio, 1982
NE82	Number of employees, 1982. (Mn. persons)
UNION	Fraction of employees unionized, 1981
REPRST	Number of states in which production is located, 1982 (scaled by 100)
LABINT82	Labor intensity: Share of labor in value added, 1982
AVEARN	Average earnings per employee, 1982. ($mn/year)
TAR	Ad Valorem tariff rate
P_UNSK	Fraction of employees classified as unskilled, 1982
NEGR82	Growth in employment, 1981-82
$M_{i,j}$/ CONS	Penetration of U.S. consumption of good i by imports from partner j
$X_{i,j}$/ CONS	U.S. exports of good i to partner j, scaled by consumption
DPEN7982	IMP/CONS(1979) å IMP/CONS(1982), IMP=Total industry imports
P_SCI	Fraction of employees classified as scientists and engineers, 1982
P_MAN	Fraction of employees classified as managerial, 1982
MELAST	Real-exchange-rate elasticity of import.
XELAST	Real-exchange-rate elasticity of exports
COUNTRY	20 2-digit SIC level dummy variables

Note: Data are for 1983 unless indicated otherwise.

industry and the industry's labor intensity (LABINT82) are all positively related to the level of NTBs.

The number of states in which production is located (REPRST) is another measure of the spread and, consequently, of voting power. Further, this model predicts that industries with a large number of unconcentrated firms are more likely to receive protection than a concentrated industry so that the level of protection is expected to be negatively associated with the concentration ratio (CONC4). The Status Quo model associated with Corden (1974), which focuses on maintaining the existing benefits of major groups, has been used by Baldwin with some success in explaining tariff cuts during the Tokyo round. This model suggests that the proportion of unskilled workers (P_UNSK) and the level of tariff pro-

TABLE 2.   Variables Representing Political Economy Theories: Expected Signs and Descriptive Statistics

Theory	Variable	Sign	Mean	Variance
Dependent variable	$N_{i,j}$		.046	.0313
	$P_{i,j}$		.028	.0201
	$Q_{i,j}$		.015	.0110
	$T_{i,j}$		.007	.0032
Retaliation;Strategic Policy.	$N^*_{i,j}$	+	.133	.0834
Special Interest,	PACCVA83	+	.045	.0039
Pressure Groups.	SCALE	+	.012	.0035
	CONC4	+, −	.383	.0425
Adding Machine.	NE82	+	.040	.0310
	UNION	+	.452	.0314
	LABINT82	+	.447	.0193
	REPRST	+	.010	.0001
Equity, Social Justice; .	AVEARN	−	.019	.0001
Status Quo	TAR	+, −	.049	.0034
	P_UNSK	+	.062	.0022
	NEGR82	å	−.054	.0194
Comparative Costs,	$M_{i,j}$/ CONS	+	.0033	.0001
Comparative Advantage	$X_{i,j}$/ CONS	−	.0022	.0001
	DPEN7982	+	.016	.0457
	P_SCI	å	.041	.0025
	P_MAN	å	.100	.0016
Other	MELAST	å	−1.020	.3212
Control Vars.	XELAST	+	1.450	.5518
	COUNTRY			
	Constant			

tection (TAR) will be positively related to the level of NTB protection. The Social Justice model that has been offered as an explanation as to why industries without much political clout such as apparel and textiles have been successful in obtaining protection suggests that industries with low average earnings (AVEARN) or high labor intensity (LABINT82) will likely obtain high levels of protection. The Special-Interest Group model and the Adding Machine model fall under the category of political models motivated by self-interest, and variables that represent them are collected in *X1*, while the Status Quo and Social Justice models fall under the category of altruistic political models and their variables are contained in *X2*.

The Comparative Cost Model of Bhagwati (1982) suggests that NTBs are positively related to import penetration ($M_{i,j}$ / CONS) and negatively to exports ($X_{i,j}$ / CONS). Since U.S. industries have been demonstrated to have a comparative advantage in skill-intensive industries, industries with a high proportion of scientists (P_SCI) and managers (P_MAN) are expected to require less protection. A large change in import penetration (DPEN7982) may be a sign of an industry that has lost its comparative advantage and hence is a candidate for protection according to this theory. Other control variables included in *X3*, in addition to the comparative cost variables, address the concerns of incorporating the effects of real exchange rates into the cross-sectional analysis. Ceglowski (1989) provides real-exchange-rate (RER) elasticities of imports and exports for 2-digit SIC industries, which vary considerably across industries. From 1981 till 1984 the U.S. experienced an extended period of RER appreciation. The rise in import penetration (and the lowering of exports) and thus protectionist pressures in industries, particularly those with a high absolute RER elasticity of imports (and/or exports), may have been due to such an appreciation. Hence the *absolute* value of both, the RER elasticity of imports (MELAST) and RER elasticity of exports (XELAST), are expected to be positively related to the level of protection during this period.[2]

The aim of using retaliatory NTBS, as opposed to employing them for purely protectionist purposes, is to deter undesirable foreign trade policy at minimum domestic cost. In a game-theoretic political economy model based on fairly real-world assumptions, Baldwin (1990) shows the existence of optimal non-negative retaliatory trade barriers. His argument is motivated by the ability of retaliatory measures to discourage special interest pressures in the foreign country that lead to the formation of the foreign trade barrier in the first place. Helleiner (1977) describes a bargaining model in which governments try to obtain the largest cuts in protection while conceding fewer cuts with the implication for bilateral NTB "negotiations" that a country will enact domestic laws to force down foreign levels of protection. Chan's (1988) model based on a Nash bargaining solution concludes that a country like the United States whose endowment patterns and tastes that are varied, rather than biased towards a single commodity, has an upper hand in trade negotiations with a country whose endowment and tastes are narrowly concentrated. Deardorff and Stern (1987) indicate instances of both unilateral retaliation as well as the offensive use of GATT antidumping laws facilitated by a relaxation of U.S. trade laws, and investigate the effects of a unilateral U.S. surcharge on imports (allowed under present U.S. trade laws). It has long been contended that tariffs and NTBs on agricultural trade among developed countries have been historically retaliatory, and it is widely suspected that antidumping laws have been used offensively by firms as strategic business tools (Prusa, 1992). Finally, Kelly et al. (1988, 123) indicate 60 cases of explicit retaliation under Section 301 of the U.S. Trade Act of 1974, of which 16 were directed against the European Community, and 8 against Japan. In order to investigate whether the structure of U.S. NTBs is retaliatory, foreign NTBs on U.S. exports, $N^*_{i,j}$ is included as an exogenous variable.

Features of the Data

In this section, I describe features of the data that have helped me form the priors I use. Tables 3a–3e depict the industrial breakdown at the 2-digit SIC level of bilateral NTBs between the U.S. and each of the nine partners. In table 3a U.S. total NTB coverage (an aggregation of price, quantitative, and threat NTBs) of imports for each 2-digit industry from each partner is computed across industries. Highly protected U.S. industries (with NTB coverage greater than 5 percent) against these partner countries are FOOD, TOBACCO, PAPER, PETROLEUM REFINING (protected by Threat NTBs as shown in table 3d) and TRANSPORT. Although the rankings of the 10 most protected industries are in broad agreement across the eight European countries, the rankings for Japan are distinctly different. TEXTILES, APPAREL, PAPER, CHEMICALS, RUBBER, LEATHER, STONE AND GLASS, FABRICATED METAL, MACHINERY, AND ELECTRICAL EQUIPMENT, can all be added to the list of industries that are heavily protected against Japanese exports. Table 3b and 3c show that price NTBs, such as countervailing duties and antidumping duties, were the chief instruments of protection except in the case of FOOD and Japanese exports of TEXTILES, APPAREL, and TRANSPORT, where quantitative NTBs, such as quotas and voluntary restraint agreements, were used.

In table 3e total NTB coverage by each partner country against U.S. exports is computed across 2-digit industries. In general, partner NTB coverages are much higher than U.S. NTB coverages. Japanese markets for all goods *except* PAPER, FABRICATED METAL, MACHINERY, FUR-NITURE, ELECTRICAL EQUIPMENT, and PRINTING are heavily protected against U.S. exports. Japanese protection often takes the more subtle forms of health and other ostensibly regulatory impediments that have the effect of discouraging imports.

The European market for FOOD, TEXTILES, APPAREL, WOOD, PAPER, and CHEMICALS are highly protected against U.S. exports. France and Italy heavily protect, in addition, their PRIMARY METAL (notably steel), ELECTRICAL EQUIPMENT, TRANSPORT, FURNI-TURE (France), RUBBER (Italy), and LEATHER (Italy) industries.

A feature of bilateral NTBs, upon comparing NTB columns in table 3a with their counterparts in table 3e is that U.S. NTBs may possess a retaliatory component, that is, the structure of U.S. NTBs may resemble the structure of Foreign NTBs because they have been put in place to dis-courage Foreign NTBs. A notable example is the high level on NTBs on both sides in FOOD. From tables 3a–3e it may be surmised that 2-digit

TABLE 3a.   U.S. Total NTB Coverage of Imports from 9 Partners Bilateral trade–weighted means by 2–digit SIC Industry Groups

SIC2	NAME	N	BLX	FIN	FRA	GER	ITA	JAP	NDL	NOR	UK
20	FOOD	46	0.194	0.313	0.482	0.415	0.431	0.082	0.348	0.169	0.571
21	TOBACCO	3	1	–	0.214	1	1	0.214	1	–	1
22	TEXTILES	30	–	–	–	–	0.004	0.905	–	–	–
23	APPAREL	30	–	–	–	0.008	0.001	0.264	0.015	–	–
24	WOOD	17	–	–	–	–	–	0.047	–	–	–
25	FURNITURE	13	–	–	–	–	–	0.068	–	–	0.004
26	PAPER	17	0.093	0.144	0.356	0.061	0.125	0.111	0.072	0.035	0.04
27	PRINTING	16	–	–	–	–	–	–	–	–	–
28	CHEMICALS	28	0.027	–	0.079	0.011	0.062	0.156	0.024	0.006	0.024
29	PETROL. REF.	3	0.841	–	0.412	0.532	0.682	0.07	0.608	0.58	0.961
30	RUBBER	5	0.001	–	0.009	0.009	0.012	0.482	0.009	–	–
31	LEATHER	9	0.018	0.007	0.057	0.02	0.05	0.213	0.022	0.003	0.012
32	STONE,GLASS	27	0.085	0.002	0.003	0.016	0.146	0.122	0.026	0.006	–
33	PRIM. METAL	25	0.009	–	0.013	0.008	0.007	0.083	0.058	–	0.005
34	FABR. METAL	36	0.017	0.058	0.033	0.035	0.034	0.219	0.031	0.023	0.035
35	MACHINERY	44	0.035	0.002	0.006	0.053	0.109	0.076	0.035	0.03	0.021
36	ELEC. EQUIP.	37	–	–	0.003	–	0.002	0.138	–	–	0.001
37	TRANSPORT	16	0.058	0.002	0.003	0.175	0.205	0.396	0.009	0.007	0.024
38	INSTRUMENTS	13	–	0.047	0.002	–	–	0.016	–	0.001	–
39	MISC.	20	0.003	0.002	0.034	0.015	0.014	0.057	0.021	0.001	0.003

Notes: All NTBs include price NTBs, quantitative NTBs, and threat NTBs; NTBs are measured as coverage ratios. Partner countries are Belgium and Luxembourg (BLX), Finland (FIN), France (FRA), Germany (GER), Italy (ITA), Japan (JAP), Netherlands (NDL), Norway (NOR), and U.K. (UK).

industries with a large number of observations are likely to influence the results more than industries with a small number of observations.

Tables 4a–4d give an industrial breakdown at the 2-digit SIC level of the means of the regressors in the estimating equation, with one table for each of the five political-economy models summarized in table 2. The Special-Interest Group variables appear in table 4a. The PACCORP (per firm PAC expenditure per election cycle during the 4 cycles during 1977–84) rankings reinforce my belief that PAC spending is an important determinant of U.S. protection levels. Many industries that are shown by table 3a to be protected in the U.S. also have a high ranking in terms of corporate PAC spending. These include PETROLEUM REFINING, TOBACCO, PAPER, and TRANSPORT. Industries that are protected against Japanese exports are shown to be highly politically active, except for FOOD, FURNITURE, TEXTILES, APPAREL, and LEATHER.[3] These industries are also ranked low in terms of the traditional measures of special-interest pressure, namely SCALE (output per firm) and CONC4 (4-firm concentration ratio). Perhaps the models of public-interest apply more readily there. The variables representing Caves' Adding Machine model are ranked in table 4b. The variables NE82 (number employed) and

Table 3b.   U.S. Price NTB Coverage of Imports from 9 Partners
Bilateral trade–weighted means by 2–digit SIC Industry Groups

SIC2	NAME	N	BLX	FIN	FRA	GER	ITA	JAP	NDL	NOR	UK
20	FOOD	46	0.093	0.231	0.371	0.301	0.408	0.077	0.264	0.076	0.501
21	TOBACCO	3	1	–	0.214	1	1	0.214	1	–	1
22	TEXTILES	30	–	–	–	–	0.003	0.048	–	–	–
23	APPAREL	30	–	–	–	–	–	–	–	–	–
24	WOOD	17	–	–	–	–	–	0.046	–	–	–
25	FURNITURE	13	–	–	–	–	–	0.067	–	–	0.004
26	PAPER	17	0.093	0.144	0.356	0.061	0.125	0.056	0.072	0.035	0.04
27	PRINTING	16	–	–	–	–	–	–	–	–	–
28	CHEMICALS	28	0.018	–	0.066	0.009	0.056	0.109	0.02	0.002	0.022
29	PETROL. REF.	3	–	–	–	–	–	–	–	–	–
30	RUBBER	5	0.001	–	0.008	–	0.005	0.475	–	–	–
31	LEATHER	9	0.018	0.007	0.057	0.02	0.05	0.213	0.022	0.003	0.012
32	STONE,GLASS	27	0.006	0.002	–	–	0.141	0.117	–	–	–
33	PRIM. METAL	25	–	–	0.002	–	–	0.06	–	–	–
34	FABR. METAL	36	–	0.026	0.006	0.002	0.002	0.161	–	–	–
35	MACHINERY	44	0.035	0.002	0.006	0.027	0.101	0.075	0.035	0.03	0.021
36	ELEC. EQUIP.	37	–	–	0.003	–	0.002	0.138	–	–	0.001
37	TRANSPORT	16	0.058	0.002	0.003	0.175	0.205	0.178	0.009	0.007	0.024
38	INSTRUMENTS	13	–	0.047	0.002	–	–	0.016	–	0.001	–
39	MISC.	20	–	–	0.001	–	0.007	0.053	0.011	–	–

REPRST (geographic dispersion) rank some protected industries high (TRANSPORT, RUBBER) and some low (FOOD, TOBACCO), so the 2-digit rankings do not indicate a clear relationship between these variables and U.S. protection. UNION (unionization) and LABINT82 (labor intensity) rankings also do not show a simple correlation with the NTB rankings in table 3a.

The variables representing the Status Quo model, AVEARN (average earnings) and TAR (ad valorem tariffs), ranked in table 4c do show some support for the theory. Industries with low average earnings, such as APPAREL, LEATHER, TEXTILES, WOOD, FURNITURE, TOBACCO, and RUBBER, have fairly high levels of protection, particularly against Japanese exports. Many of these are also the same industries that have traditionally been protected by tariffs. The Status Quo theory predicts that tariff cuts in these industries will be more than compensated by rising NTBs. However, some industries that are ranked high in terms of AVEARN are also highly protected, such as TRANSPORT. The variables representing the Social Justice model, PUNSK (proportion unskilled) and NEGR82 (employment growth) do not seem to be correlated in any evident way with NTB protection. The rankings of the Com-

**TABLE 3c. U.S. Quantity NTB Coverage of Imports from 9 Partners
Bilateral trade–weighted means, by 2–digit SIC Industry Groups**

SIC2	NAME	N	BLX	FIN	FRA	GER	ITA	JAP	NDL	NOR	UK
20	FOOD	46	0.106	0.092	0.118	0.122	0.03	0.005	0.084	0.102	0.067
21	TOBACCO	3	–	–	–	–	–	–	–	–	–
22	TEXTILES	30	–	–	–	–	0.001	0.868	–	–	–
23	APPAREL	30	–	–	–	–	–	0.261	–	–	–
24	WOOD	17	–	–	–	–	–	0.001	–	–	–
25	FURNITURE	13	–	–	–	–	–	–	–	–	–
26	PAPER	17	–	–	–	–	–	0.055	–	–	–
27	PRINTING	16	–	–	–	–	–	–	–	–	–
28	CHEMICALS	28	–	–	0.01	0.002	–	0.066	–	–	–
29	PETROL. REF.	3	–	–	–	–	–	–	–	–	–
30	RUBBER	5	–	–	–	0.004	–	0.001	–	–	–
31	LEATHER	9	–	–	–	–	–	–	–	–	–
32	STONE,GLASS	27	–	–	–	–	–	–	–	–	–
33	PRIM. METAL	25	0.009	–	0.012	0.007	0.007	–	0.058	–	0.003
34	FABR. METAL	36	0.011	–	0.013	0.008	–	–	0.002	–	0.008
35	MACHINERY	44	–	–	–	–	–	0.001	–	–	–
36	ELEC. EQUIP.	37	–	–	–	–	–	–	–	–	–
37	TRANSPORT	16	–	–	–	–	–	0.218	–	–	–
38	INSTRUMENTS	13	–	–	–	–	–	–	–	–	–
39	MISC.	20	0.002	–	0.032	0.006	–	0.001	0.004	–	0.001

parative Cost model variables in table 4d, particularly IMP/CONS (import penetration ratio), do correlate with protection for industries such as LEATHER, TEXTILES, APPAREL, STONE AND GLASS, MACHINERY, and RUBBER. However, industries like TOBACCO, FOOD, PAPER, and TRANSPORT do not seem to owe their protection to comparative costs since they rank relatively low in terms of import penetration and relatively high in terms of P_SCI (fraction of employees that are scientists and engineers) and P_MAN (fraction of employees that are managers). Their protection must be attributable to another model, such as the Special-Interest Group theory.

Empirical Results

The dependent variable, $N_{i,j}$ is measured only when it takes a positive value. Theoretically there exist arguments for export taxes and import subsidies which are negative trade barriers (Vousden 1990). With intra-industry trade in intermediate goods, which characterizes a large part of the trade among the countries in the present analysis, there is certainly the

TABLE 3d. U.S. Threat NTB Coverage of Imports from 9 Partners
Bilateral trade–weighted means, by 2–digit SIC Industry Groups

SIC2	NAME	N	BLX	FIN	FRA	GER	ITA	JAP	NDL	NOR	UK
20	FOOD	46	–	–	–	–	–	–	–	–	0.006
21	TOBACCO	3	–	–	–	–	–	–	–	–	–
22	TEXTILES	30	–	–	–	–	–	0.031	–	–	–
23	APPAREL	30	–	–	–	0.008	0.001	0.003	0.015	–	–
24	WOOD	17	–	–	–	–	–	–	–	–	–
25	FURNITURE	13	–	–	–	–	–	–	–	–	–
26	PAPER	17	–	–	–	–	–	–	–	–	–
27	PRINTING	16	–	–	–	–	–	–	–	–	–
28	CHEMICALS	28	0.008	–	0.004	–	0.006	0.041	0.003	0.004	0.002
29	PETROL. REF.	3	0.841	–	0.412	0.532	0.682	0.07	0.608	0.58	0.961
30	RUBBER	5	–	–	0.008	0.006	0.006	0.006	0.009	–	–
31	LEATHER	9	–	–	–	–	–	–	–	–	–
32	STONE,GLASS	27	0.079	0.002	0.003	0.016	0.006	0.058	0.026	0.006	–
33	PRIM. METAL	25	0.001	–	0.002	–	–	0.023	–	–	0.002
34	FABR. METAL	36	0.006	0.058	0.02	0.028	0.034	0.125	0.028	0.023	0.027
35	MACHINERY	44	–	–	–	0.026	0.063	0.022	–	–	–
36	ELEC. EQUIP.	37	–	–	–	–	–	0.048	–	–	–
37	TRANSPORT	16	–	–	–	–	0.169	–	–	–	–
38	INSTRUMENTS	13	–	–	–	–	–	–	–	–	–
39	MISC.	20	–	0.002	–	0.01	0.014	0.03	0.006	0.001	0.002

possibility of subsidizing imports. Hence the dependent variable is truncated at zero, requiring the use of a Tobit specification.[4]

Enumeration of Priors

Extreme bounds analysis is employed to investigate the robustness of the posterior estimates to reasonable departures from the priors. The EBA methodology is especially appropriate here since the variables in the empirical model are just a suggested list based on underlying theory, and incorporating the level and nature of doubt about these variables is important for making realistic inferences. The EBA here performs a sensitivity analysis over the priors.

Extreme bounds analysis is performed for the two sets of priors detailed in table 5. One set of priors, labeled PRIORS I, is enumerated in terms of elasticities, which are a convenient unit-free medium.[5] Within this set of priors, are two priors labeled *Weak* and *Informative*. Weak priors reflect skepticism (prior mean b^* set equal to zero) and great uncertainty (prior standard error set to a relatively large number) about each and

TABLE 3e. Partner NTB Coverage of Imports from U.S.
Bilateral trade–weighted means by 2–digit SIC Industry Groups

SIC2	NAME	N	BLX	FIN	FRA	GER	ITA	JAP	NDL	NOR	UK
20	FOOD	46	0.896	0.397	0.912	0.887	0.773	0.995	0.909	0.77	0.861
21	TOBACCO	3	–	–	–	–	–	1	–	–	–
22	TEXTILES	30	0.016	0.841	0.056	0.014	0.018	0.801	0.024	0.005	0.035
23	APPAREL	30	0.004	0.551	0.434	0.001	0.343	0.131	0.001	0.562	0.546
24	WOOD	17	0.276	0.027	0.324	0.146	0.178	0.592	0.389	0.002	0.352
25	FURNITURE	13	–	0.079	0.236	–	0.022	0.041	–	–	0.018
26	PAPER	17	0.099	0.045	0.177	0.422	0.705	0.07	0.107	0.031	0.483
27	PRINTING	16	–	–	0.174	–	0.099	0.023	–	–	–
28	CHEMICALS	28	0.115	0.047	0.206	0.054	0.21	0.975	0.102	0.604	0.063
29	PETROL. REF.	3	0.403	0.151	0.098	0.029	0.065	0.393	0.274	0.036	0.055
30	RUBBER	5	0.003	0.174	0.049	0.014	0.281	0.935	0.015	0.041	0.018
31	LEATHER	9	–	0.156	0.001	–	0.124	0.217	–	–	–
32	STONE,GLASS	27	0.037	0.099	0.134	0.001	0.152	0.176	0.007	–	0.01
33	PRIM. METAL	25	0.001	0.066	0.443	0.005	0.271	0.147	0.005	–	0.008
34	FABR. METAL	36	0.003	0.006	0.143	–	0.04	0.07	–	–	–
35	MACHINERY	44	–	–	0.037	–	0.077	0.055	–	–	–
36	ELEC. EQUIP.	37	0.007	–	0.306	–	0.088	0.034	–	–	0.008
37	TRANSPORT	16	–	–	0.363	–	0.085	0.263	–	–	–
38	INSTRUMENTS	13	–	–	0.052	–	0.045	0.319	–	–	–
39	MISC.	20	0.039	0.061	0.077	0.015	0.041	0.275	0.02	0.013	0.018

every coefficient, with the result that it is the data that shapes future (posterior) beliefs. This is not my set of priors but I analyze the data with it because it represents the belief of a significant fraction of the profession.

My priors are those labeled *Informative* and quantify my view of a world in which trade policy is largely influenced by special interest groups, comparative costs, and the possibility of retaliation to influence bilateral policy on trade. The features of the data summarized earlier and reinforce my prior beliefs, which I enumerate here. First, I expect the elasticity of the retaliation coefficient against each country, and hence on $N^*_{i,j}$, to be between 0 and 1 with about a 70 percent probability. This relies on Baldwin's (1990) theory that some form of retaliation does discourage foreign NTBs. Second, the share of imports in consumption is a major determinant of NTBs, especially when there are dramatic increases in import penetration over a short period. The demonstration of injury, which often precedes the granting of NTB protection in the U.S., is to a large extent based on showing a declining market share that has gone to a foreign competitor, combined with some evidence on unfair pricing. Thus, I believe the elasticity of NTBs with respect to import penetration ($M_{i,j}$ / CONS) to be between 0 and 1.5 with a probability of about 65 percent. Fourth, although

TABLE 4a.   Special-Interest Group Theory Variables
Simple Means by 2-digit SIC Industry Groups: Sorted by PACCORP

SIC2	NAME	PACCORP	Rank	PACCVA83	Rank	SCALE	Rank	CONC4	Rank
29	PETROL. REF.	75.37	1	0.028	13	0.024	3	0.298	16
21	TOBACCO	46.27	2	0.058	6	0.366	1	0.691	1
26	PAPER	42.687	3	0.069	3	0.016	6	0.385	10
36	ELEC. EQUIP.	38.901	4	0.043	8	0.011	9	0.493	3
37	TRANSPORT	37.398	5	0.024	15	0.058	2	0.550	2
38	INSTRUMENTS	35.681	6	0.03	12	0.004	14	0.396	9
28	CHEMICALS	34.646	7	0.039	10	0.017	4	0.429	7
32	STONE,GLASS	28.452	8	0.084	1	0.007	10	0.436	5
35	MACHINERY	28.027	9	0.04	9	0.005	12	0.332	13
33	PRIM. METAL	28.023	10	0.057	7	0.016	5	0.430	6
30	RUBBER	24.303	11	0.016	19	0.015	7	0.369	11
24	WOOD	22.574	12	0.066	4	0.002	20	0.217	20
34	FABR. METAL	21.701	13	0.024	16	0.005	11	0.310	14
27	PRINTING	20.958	14	0.024	17	0.002	19	0.260	19
23	APPAREL	20.837	15	0.061	5	0.002	17	0.279	17
20	FOOD	18.221	16	0.027	14	0.014	8	0.453	4
22	TEXTILES	15.101	17	0.082	2	0.004	13	0.416	8
25	FURNITURE	13.656	18	0.023	18	0.002	18	0.265	18
39	MISC.	10.954	19	0.032	11	0.003	15	0.365	12
31	LEATHER	3.521	20	0.014	20	0.003	16	0.299	15

poor export performance may affect the demand for protection, its effect is less direct than imports. Finally, I suspect that corporate campaign contributions (PACCVA83) do influence the granting of protection although I am quite uncertain about the degree of its influence. All other variables I treat as doubtful, although I am willing to let the data evidence dominate my skepticism. In deciding whether the reader's priors are closer to the weak or informative priors, note that posterior estimates (or Bayes estimates) based on the weak prior are expected to be close to the MLEs. Also, a prior standard error reflecting the degree of personal certainty about that coefficient may influence the posterior estimates of all other coefficients.

The second set of priors labelled PRIORS II are expressed in terms of another convenient unit-free medium, the standardized coefficients or Beta coefficients. The Beta coefficient on an independent variable x_i in a linear regression is the OLS estimate b_i times $sd(x_i)/sd(y)$, where $sd(.)$ denotes standard deviation. While the numbers for the prior means and standard deviations are the same for PRIORS I and PRIORS II, they are not equivalent in the mapping of their priors from the transformed ith coefficient into the coefficient β_i. But applied Bayesian analysis should recognize that the enumeration of priors is to a great degree an approxima-

TABLE 4b. Adding Machine Model Variables
Simple Means by 2-digit SIC Industry Groups: Sorted by NE82

SIC2	NAME	NE82	Rank	UNION	Rank	LABINT82	Rank	REPRST	Rank
30	RUBBER	0.136	1	0.438	12	0.463	10	0.021	1
37	TRANSPORT	0.098	2	0.509	6	0.498	4	0.013	4
27	PRINTING	0.081	3	0.313	18	0.446	12	0.015	2
36	ELEC. EQUIP.	0.052	4	0.456	11	0.436	13	0.012	6
35	MACHINERY	0.050	5	0.423	13	0.481	6	0.012	7
38	INSTRUMENTS	0.048	6	0.335	17	0.433	14	0.014	3
29	PETROL. REF.	0.046	7	0.643	2	0.300	19	0.009	14
34	FABR. METAL	0.041	8	0.470	8	0.474	8	0.011	8
23	APPAREL	0.039	9	0.466	9	0.473	9	0.009	12
26	PAPER	0.036	10	0.534	4	0.416	16	0.012	5
24	WOOD	0.034	12	0.271	20	0.545	2	0.005	18
33	PRIM. METAL	0.034	11	0.674	1	0.639	1	0.009	10
25	FURNITURE	0.034	13	0.421	14	0.488	5	0.010	9
28	CHEMICALS	0.031	14	0.415	15	0.313	18	0.009	11
20	FOOD	0.029	15	0.493	7	0.287	20	0.009	13
22	TEXTILES	0.024	16	0.284	19	0.503	3	0.005	19
32	STONE,GLASS	0.020	17	0.589	3	0.455	11	0.006	17
31	LEATHER	0.020	18	0.459	10	0.476	7	0.007	15
39	MISC.	0.019	19	0.409	16	0.426	15	0.007	16
21	TOBACCO	0.018	20	0.527	5	0.319	17	0.003	20

tion. To be exact about such mappings is to make the process of enumerating prior opinion prohibitively costly. The EBA recognizes this, and therefore focuses on the robustness of posterior estimates to variations in a prior. My use of two sets of priors explores, as a useful supplement, whether inferences are strikingly different across these two priors.[6] If the inferences are close, then it matters little whether priors are expressed in elasticities or Beta coefficients. Given this wider choice in which to express priors, it is easier for the reader to match his priors with those in table 5.

Empirical Results from the Extreme Bounds Analysis

Table 6a presents ML estimates, Bayes estimates and extreme bounds (EB) for the model with overall NTBs as the dependent variable.[7] Traditional (non-Bayesian) goodness-of-fit statistics which are provided in note 2 in the tables show that the models have an acceptably good fit for cross-sectional data at this level of disaggregation. The ML estimates in table 6a indicate that every political economy model finds some support from the data. At least one variable from the group of variables representing each theory has the expected sign and a large t-value. The model of retaliation

TABLE 4c.   Status Quo/Social Justice Model Variables
Simple Means by 2–digit SIC Industry Groups: Sorted by AVEARN

SIC2	NAME	AVEARN	Rank	TAR	Rank	P_UNSK	Rank	NEGR82	Rank
29	PETROL. REF.	0.026	1	0.024	15	0.165	1	0.032	1
37	TRANSPORT	0.025	2.5	0.015	17	0.014	20	−0.043	11
28	CHEMICALS	0.025	2.5	0.041	10	0.042	14	−0.024	8
33	PRIM. METAL	0.024	4	0.015	18	0.078	7	−0.175	20
35	MACHINERY	0.022	5	0.036	12	0.028	18	−0.075	14
26	PAPER	0.021	6.5	0.024	16	0.083	6	−0.075	15
38	INSTRUMENTS	0.021	6.5	0.061	7	0.020	19	−0.024	7
32	STONE,GLASS	0.020	9.5	0.060	8	0.122	3	−0.127	18
36	ELEC. EQUIP.	0.020	9.5	0.048	9	0.030	16	−0.062	13
34	FABR. METAL	0.020	9.5	0.028	14	0.047	12	−0.04	10
20	FOOD	0.020	9.5	0.040	11	0.127	2	−0.014	4
27	PRINTING	0.019	13	0.012	19	0.043	13	−0.016	5
21	TOBACCO	0.019	13	0.096	3	0.056	11	−0.083	16
30	RUBBER	0.019	13	0.111	2	0.089	5	−0.057	12
25	FURNITURE	0.016	15	0.011	20	0.077	8	−0.022	6
39	MISC.	0.015	16.5	0.080	6	0.029	17	0	2
24	WOOD	0.015	16.5	0.031	13	0.099	4	−0.099	17
22	TEXTILES	0.014	18	0.090	4	0.071	10	−0.03	9
31	LEATHER	0.012	19	0.080	5	0.075	9	−0.141	19
23	APPAREL	0.011	20	0.121	1	0.040	15	−0.005	3

TABLE 4d. Comparative Cost Model Variables
Simple Means by 2-digit SIC Industry Groups: Sorted by IMP/CONS=Total Imports/Consumption
EXP/CONS=Total Exports/Consumption

SIC2	NAME	IMP/CONS	Rank	EXP/CONS	Rank	DPEN7982	Rank	P_SCI	Rank	P_MAN	Rank
31	LEATHER	0.330	1	0.036	14	0.032	2	0.007	17	0.061	20
39	MISC.	0.192	2	0.059	8	0.008	9	0.007	16	0.103	10
22	TEXTILES	0.167	3	0.262	1	0.152	1	0.006	18	0.073	18
23	APPAREL	0.140	4	0.018	18	0.004	12	0.005	19	0.071	19
36	ELEC. EQUIP.	0.139	5	0.115	6	0.019	3	0.083	4	0.093	12
38	INSTRUMENTS	0.132	7	0.148	3	0.003	13	0.078	5	0.111	7
32	STONE,GLASS	0.132	6	0.057	10	0.009	8	0.020	11	0.078	16
35	MACHINERY	0.124	8	0.164	2	0.014	5	0.056	6	0.115	5
30	RUBBER	0.114	9	0.037	13	-0.018	20	0.037	9	0.083	15
33	PRIM. METAL	0.106	10	0.029	16	0.017	4	0.055	7	0.093	13
24	WOOD	0.088	11	0.030	15	-0.003	18	0.009	14	0.095	11
37	TRANSPORT	0.086	12	0.122	5	0.011	7	0.153	1	0.108	9
28	CHEMICALS	0.062	13	0.136	4	-0.001	17	0.104	3	0.133	4
26	PAPER	0.057	14	0.050	11	0.005	11	0.047	8	0.088	14
34	FABR. METAL	0.055	15	0.058	9	0.005	10	0.033	10	0.108	8
20	FOOD	0.054	16	0.080	7	-0.008	19	0.013	12	0.112	6
25	FURNITURE	0.048	17	0.022	17	0	15	0.011	13	0.077	17
21	TOBACCO	0.047	18	0.041	12	0.013	6	na	–	0.139	3
29	PETROL. REF.	0.034	19	0.011	19	0.002	14	0.106	2	0.152	2
27	PRINTING	0.010	20	0.009	20	0	16	0.008	15	0.153	1

TABLE 5. Prior Means and Standard Errors

| | PRIORS I: Elasticities | | | | PRIORS II: Beta Coefficients | | | |
| | Weak | | Informative | | Weak | | Informative | |
Variable	Mean (b^*)	Std. Error	Mean (b^*)	Std. Error	Mean (b^*)	Std. Error	Mean (b^*)	Std. Error
$N^*_{i,j}$	0	5	.5	.5	0	5	.5	.5
$M_{i,j}$/CONS	0	5	.5	1	0	5	.5	1
$X_{i,j}$/CONS	0	5	-.25	.5	0	5	-.25	.5
PACCVA83	0	5	.25	.75	0	5	.25	.75
All Other variables	0	5	0	5	0	5	0	5

Note: The priors in terms of elasticities and Beta coefficients are converted into actual units at the variable means. The prior covariance matrix $\bar{V}$ here is diagonal with the square of the prior standard errors on the diagonal.

TABLE 6a. MLE, Bayes, and Extreme Bounds Estimates
Tobit Model with Dependent Variable All U.S. NTBS

Variable	Weak Prior I			Informative Prior I			Informative Prior II		
	MLE	Bayes	$\sigma_L=1/4, \sigma_U=4$	Bayes	$\sigma_L=1/4, \sigma_U=4$	$\sigma_L=1, \sigma_U=4$	Bayes	$\sigma_L=1/4, \&_U=4$	$\sigma_L=1, \sigma_U=4$
$N^*_{i,j}$	.337**	.340**	[.296, .389]	.324**	[.123, .465]	[.307, .353]	.341**	[.260, .446]	[.330, .348]
PACCVA83	1.332**	1.234**	[.494, 1.455]	1.123**	[-.194, 1.899]	[1.062, 1.379]	1.229**	[.346, 1.645]	[1.205, 1.349]
SCALE	.079	.122	[.009, .478]	.123	[-.017, .493]	[.072, .133]	.122	[.009, .485]	[.076, .128]
CONC4	-.037	-.008	[-.194, .252]	.001	[-.206, .277]	[-.049, .016]	-.008	[-.199, .252]	[-.048, .005]
NE82	1.047**	1.008**	[.238, 1.588]	1.025**	[.202, 1.650]	[.956, 1.114]	1.009**	[.967, 2.069]	[1.788, 1.922]
UNION	-.136	-.132	[-.348, .111]	-.126	[-.360, .133]	[-.159, -.602]	-.131	[-.350, .114]	[-.157, -.109]
LABINT82	-1.286**	-1.183**	[-1.48, -.380]	-1.166**	[-1.520, .329]	[-1.309, -1.134]	-1.182**	[-1.486, -.371]	[-1.303, -1.158]
REPRST	6.110*	6.078*	[-2.47, 12.71]	5.538*	[-4.318, 13.25]	[4.745, 6.861]	6.057*	[-2.630, 13.04]	[5.298, 6.867]
AVEARN	20.42**	18.01**	[-1.618, 27.92]	17.51**	[-2.963, 28.72]	[16.49, 21.22]	17.98**	[-1.760, 28.10]	[17.09, 21.13]
TAR	1.909**	1.810**	[.978, 2.068]	1.794**	[.938, 2.111]	[1.769, 1.927]	1.808**	[.967, 2.069]	[1.788, 1.922]
P_UNSK	.417	.447	[-.263, 1.178]	.501	[-.271, 1.438]	[.358, .566]	.446	[-.310, 1.190]	[.354, .510]
NEGR82	.141	.146	[.070, .248]	.149	[.069, .262]	[.134, .157]	.146	[.069, .249]	[.134, .153]
$M_{i,j}/CONS$	4.427**	4.241**	[2.645, 4.801]	4.016**	[.340, 6.984]	[3.780, 4.631]	4.258**	[1.607, 6.423]	[4.102, 4.571]
$X_{i,j}/CONS$	-19.44**	-18.74**	[-22.04, -11.17]	-16.31**	[-33.50, 6.49]	[-21.11, -14.40]	-18.59**	[-30.34, -3.16]	[-20.43, -17.52]
DPEN7982	.039	.039	[.012, .067]	.041	[.004, .080]	[.035, .045]	.039	[.010, .069]	[.036, .042]
P_SCI	-1.056**	-.961**	[-1.454, -.067]	-.902**	[-1.575, -.018]	[-1.116, -.905]	-.963**	[-1.485, -.056]	[-1.089, -.923]
P_MAN	.249	.316	[-.998, 1.625]	.322	[-1.082, 1.726]	[.110, .466]	.316	[-1.013, 1.635]	[.130, .439]
MELAST	.190**	.187**	[.111, .235]	.183**	[.059, .236]	[.179, .194]	.187**	[.111, .237]	[.182, .194]
XELAST	.055**	.052**	[-.010, .090]	.052**	[-.012, .096]	[.048, .060]	.052**	[-.011, .090]	[.049, .059]
COUNTRY	Note 4	Note 4	Note 4	Note 4	Note 4	Note 4	Note 4	Note 4	Note 4

Notes: 1. N=3915, k=28, Degree of truncation=84.3%. Four-digit SIC level cross-industry data are pooled across 9 countries. 2. Measures of fit: Likelihood-ratio statistic=685.62, Maddala's R^2=.160, McFadden's R^2=.213, Cragg-Uhler's R^2=286. 3. ** and * indicate, respectively, that $|t| > 1.98$ and $|t| > 1.66$. 4. All country dummies (COUNTRY) have negative MLE's and Bayes estimates, with t-values in excess of 2. Weak priors and informative priors ($\&_L$=1/4) lead to strictly negative intervals. With informative priors ($\&_L$=1/4), only the dummies for BLX, FIN, NOR have strictly negative intervals.

is clearly supported, and the retaliation coefficient on $N_{L\gamma}^*$ is both statistically and economically significant, somewhat surprisingly so if one's priors are represented by those labeled Weak in table 5. The Special-Interest Group model finds strong support in the significant estimate on corporate PAC spending (PACCVA83). This variable provides clear-cut and direct inference about special interest groups rather than the indirect inference through the coefficient on the industry concentration ratio (CONC4).

The Adding Machine model finds support from the estimate on number employed (NE82) and on the geographic spread of firms within an industry (REPRST), validating Caves' (1976) theory that voting power in terms of numbers is an important determinant of whether an industry receives protection. However the unexpected sign on labor intensity (LABINT82) is evidence against this model, and this finding is hard to rationalize. The data provide mixed inferences about models of political altruism. Though the positive ML estimate on average earnings (AVEARN) does not support the Status Quo model of Corden, the positive coefficient on ad valorem tariffs (TAR) indicates that the same industries that were earlier protected by tariffs now receive NTB protection, thus undermining the multilateral cuts from the Tokyo round and preserving the status quo. The Status Quo model predicts that to prevent damage to industries from a sudden removal of protection for the most highly protected before the Tokyo round implementations, these industries would be supported in some alternative way. The results show that NTBs filled the gap in protection left by the Tokyo round tariff cuts.

The Social Justice model does not receive support from the data. Although the coefficient on the proportion unskilled (P_UNSK) is positive, it has a low t value. Perhaps the labor intensity variable (LABINT82), earlier attributed to the Adding Machine model, is more representative of the Social Justice model and the negative coefficient is evidence against it. The model of comparative costs is strongly supported by the data. Bilateral imports and exports ($M_{i,j}$/CONS, $X_{i,j}$/CONS) have the expected signs and high t-values. Industries with high skill levels measured by the proportion of scientists and engineers (P_SCI) do not receive protection largely because, as past empirical studies have shown (Maskus, 1985), the U.S. has a comparative advantage in the production of skill-intensive goods.

The Bayes estimates from the weak priors in PRIORS I are close to the ML estimates. Although the posterior t-values from the Bayes estimates are close to those from the ML estimates, it is important to note that the t-values for ML estimates allow only asymptotic inferences while those for Bayes estimates allow exact small-sample inferences. The Bayes estimates from informative PRIOR I (based on elasticities) are also close to the ML estimates, with one exception (CONC4). I take this to imply that the data evidence is strong relative to my prior information, and also that my prior information is not in conflict with the information in the data.

While the Bayes estimates are based on one, possibly narrow, set of priors, I wish to investigate whether the same inferences may be drawn for a wider range of priors. There are two reasons that motivate such a sensitivity analysis. One is that I would like to investigate the robustness of the posterior estimates to non-local changes in the prior in order to incorporate a range of valid beliefs. The second, and possibly more important, reason is that it is not a costless task to describe precisely one's subjective beliefs. Indeed in many cases, beliefs are themselves fuzzy and imprecise and probably characterized as belonging "somewhere in a set" of beliefs. The sensitivity of the posterior estimates to changes in both priors are computed as extreme bounds (EB) where the prior covariance, V, is allowed to vary freely as $1/4\bar{V} \le V \le 4\bar{V}$. In tables 6a the EBs in bold face do not contain zero and are thus robust to such non-local variations in the prior covariance.

The inferences from the EB intervals based on the weak priors is similar to those from the Bayes estimates. The model of retaliation, the Special-Interest Group model, the Adding Machine model, the Status Quo model, and the model of comparative costs each have some validity, and the bold intervals show that inferences about the validity of each model are in agreement with a fairly wide set of beliefs.[8]

The EB intervals based on the informative PRIOR I have fewer posterior estimates that are robust to variations in the prior. Inferences about the Special-Interest Group model are no longer robust to variations in the prior covariance in the range $1/4\bar{V} \le V \le 4\bar{V}$. This is surprising since my strongest beliefs *are* about the validity of the Olson-Stigler theories of pressure-group behavior and the model of political self-interest of Brock and Magee (1978). It is probably the case that some prior covariances in the set $1/4\bar{V} \le V \le 4\bar{V}$ are in conflict with the data evidence, leading to greater uncertainty about the posterior, which is then reflected in posterior intervals that contains zero for PACCVA83, and SCALE. Is there a narrower set of priors over which the inferences *are* robust? It may be sensible to narrow the set of priors under consideration. For this reason I have presented EB intervals for the informative priors where the prior covariance is allowed to vary in the narrower region $\bar{V} \le V \le 4\bar{V}$, that is, where $\sigma_L=1$, $\sigma_U=4$. All posterior estimates in table 6a are shown to be robust to variations in the prior covariance within this region, with the exception of the coefficient on the concentration ratio (CONC4). This is a significant exception, since the concentration ratio has been mainly used in earlier studies of ad valorem tariffs to infer about the validity of the Special-Interest theory. Clearly inferences about nontariff barriers based on the concentration ratio are rather fragile.

The inferences from the Bayes estimates using informative PRIOR II (based on Beta coefficients) are very close to those based on informative PRIOR I. The extreme bounds from PRIOR II are narrower and more robust to variations in the priors for both, the $\sigma_L = 1/4$, $\sigma_U = 4$ case (notably the Special-Interest Group variables) and the $\sigma_L = 1$, $\sigma_U = 4$ case. From the point of view of posterior inferences, therefore, PRIORS I and II are similar enough that it makes little difference here whether the priors are specified using elasticities or Beta coefficients.

Evidence about the political economy of price NTBs is presented in table 6b. Bayes estimates based on the weak prior validate the theory of retaliation, which is not surprising given the recent studies about antidumping duties by Prusa (1992), and Herander and Schwartz (1984). The Special-Interest Group model receives strong support, and this time the concentration ratio is statistically and economically significant. Since Price NTBs are closest in nature to ad valorem tariffs, this finding reconciles with similar findings in earlier studies of ad valorem tariffs. Inferences about other theories from the Bayes estimates based on both weak and both informative priors in table 6b are similar to the inferences from table 6a about overall NTBs. The EB intervals where $1/4\bar{V} \le V \le 4\bar{V}$ show the Bayes estimates to be fragile. With informative PRIOR I the only robust inference that may be drawn is about the validity of the Status Quo model from the positive interval for the posterior estimate on the tariff rate (TAR). If robust estimates are to be found, we clearly need to narrow the range of priors. When the prior covariance is allowed to vary in the region $\bar{V} \le V \le 4\bar{V}$ the EB intervals indicate clear support for the model of retaliation, the Special-Interest Group model, the Adding Machine model, the Status Quo model, and the theory of comparative costs. With informative PRIOR II, however, even if the priors are allowed to vary in the wider region $1/4\bar{V} \le V \le 4\bar{V}$, robust inferences can be made in favor of the Special-Interest Group model, the Status Quo model (from the EBs of TAR), and the Comparative Cost model. For the narrower region $\bar{V} \le V \le 4\bar{V}$ the Adding Machine model also becomes a contender.

The determinants of quantitative NTBs are quite different from factors that determine price NTBs, as shown by the estimates in table 6c. The Bayes estimates show no support for the Special-Interest Group model. The Adding Machine model is somewhat validated by the strength of the Bayes estimate on industry employment (NE82), but the estimates on unionization (UNION) and labor intensity (LABINT82) run counter to the model's predictions. The Bayes estimates point to variables representing the Status Quo model (TAR, P_UNSK) and the model of comparative

TABLE 6b. MLE, Bayes, and Extreme Bounds Estimates.
Tobit Model with Dependent Variable Price NTBS

Variable	Weak Prior I MLE	Weak Prior I Bayes	Weak Prior I EB: $\sigma_L=1/4, \sigma_U=4$	Informative Prior I Bayes	Informative Prior I EB: $\sigma_L=1/4, \sigma_U=4$	Informative Prior I EB: $\sigma_L=1, \sigma_U=4$	Informative Prior II Bayes	Informative Prior II EB: $\sigma_L=1/4, \sigma_U=4$	Informative Prior II EB: $\sigma_L=1, \sigma_U=4$
$N^*_{i,j}$	.323**	.327**	[.204, .416]	.280**	[-.038, .507]	[.236, .363]	.330**	[.182, .483]	[.307, .347]
PACCVA83	1.095**	.852**	[-.210, 1.49]	.646**	[-.969, 2.18]	[.427, 1.270]	.853**	[.368, 1.794]	[.781, 1.17]
SCALE	.062	.194	[-.073, .808]	.186	[-.113, .822]	[.041, .216]	.193	[-.072, .822]	[.054, .212]
CONC4	.220**	.261**	[-.202, .575]	.270**	[-.221, .596]	[.163, .333]	.261**	[-.210, .577]	[.167, .318]
NE82	1.086**	.924**	[-.550, 2.083]	.948**	[-.624, 2.133]	[.776, 1.247]	.923**	[-.565, 2.097]	[.785, 1.210]
UNION	.035	.023	[-.431, .441]	.022	[-.452, .461]	[-.059, .115]	.023	[-.438, .444]	[-.049, .106]
LABINT82	-1.367**	1.046**	[-1.693, .078]	-1.033**	[-1.739, .116]	[-1.425, -.945]	-1.046**	[-1.706, .086]	[-1.407, -.979]
REPRST	4.312	4.382	[-12.16, 17.33]	3.470	[-13.34, 18.20]	[1.783, 6.923]	4.409	[-12.19, 17.83]	[1.909, 6.842]
AVEARN	16.41**	11.16**	[-13.63, 30.75]	10.85**	[-14.61, 31.85]	[7.287, 19.47]	11.19**	[13.84, 31.05]	[8.053, 19.10]
TAR	1.748**	1.458**	[.067, 2.077]	1.463**	[.047, 2.169]	[1.372, 1.815]	1.458**	[.042, 2.079]	[1.392, 1.791]
P_UNSK	.140	.248	[-1.275, 1.623]	.395	[-1.275, 1.922]	[-.030, .589]	.240	[-1.359, 1.608]	[-.045, .435]
NEGR82	-.006	.035	[-.166, .291]	.038	[-.171, .325]	[-.026, .062]	.034	[-.172, .294]	[-.024, .055]
$M_{i,j}$/CONS	4.818**	4.289**	[1.640, 5.803]	4.102**	[-1.870, 9.624]	[3.439, 5.416]	4.371**	[.474, 8.136]	[4.057, 5.098]
$X_{i,j}$/CONS	-4.692	-3.848	[-12.93, 6.145]	-3.229	[-29.57, 22.00]	[-11.267, 3.528]	-4.284	[-25.07, 13.91]	[-7.466, -1.463]
DPEN7982	.008	.006	[-.056, .064]	.011	[-.074, .080]	[-.006, .025]	.006	[-.063, .066]	[-.003, .017]
P_SCI	-.390	-.261	[-1.420, .926]	-.253	[-1.548, .989]	[-.559, -.071]	-.258	[-1.434, .972]	[-.531, -.106]
P_MAN	-.563	-.304	[-2.709, 2.018]	-.263	[-2.784, 2.175]	[-.948, .153]	-.304	[-2.736, 2.046]	[-.922, -.081]
MELAST	.208**	.194**	[.033, .283]	.187**	[.022, .285]	[.173, .220]	.194**	[.034, .287]	[.180, .220]
XELAST	.011	.004	[-.109, .103]	.006	[-.111, .112]	[-.011, .027]	.004	[-.111, .104]	[-.010, .024]
COUNTRY	Note 3	Note 3	Note 3	Note 3	Note 3	Note 3	Note 3	Note 3	Note 3

Notes: 1. $N=3915$, $k=28$, Degree of truncation=89.6%. 2. Measures of Fit: Likelihood-ratio statistic=507.5. Maddala's R^2=.122, McFadden's R^2=.209, Cragg-Uhler's R^2=.263. 3. All country dummies (COUNTRY) have negative MLE's and Bayes estimates, with *t*-values in excess of 2. Informative priors ($\sigma_L=1/4$) lead to strictly negative intervals. With weak and informative priors ($\sigma_L=1$) the intervals all contain 0.

TABLE 6c. MLE, Bayes, and Extreme Bounds Estimates
Tobit Model with Dependent Variable Quantitative NTBS

Variable	Weak Prior I			Informative Prior I			Informative Prior II		
	MLE	Bayes	EB: $\sigma_L=1/4$, $\sigma_U=4$	Bayes	EB: $\sigma_L=1/4$, $\sigma_U=4$	EB: $\sigma_L=1$, $\sigma_U=4$	Bayes	EB: $\sigma_L=1/4$, $\sigma_U=4$	EB: $\sigma_L=1$, $\sigma_U=4$
$N_{i,j}$	.411**	.397**	**[.069, .589]**	.193**	[-.196, .632]	**[.078, .482]**	.400**	**[.082, .652]**	**[.330, .478]**
PACCVA83	.430	-.036	[-2.373, 2.412]	-.037	[-2.604, 2.955]	[-1.366, 1.687]	.011*	[-2.392, 2.768]	[-.676, 1.037]
SCALE	-1.549	.469	[-6.532, 5.674]	.829	[-6.592, 6.120]	[-2.343, 2.183]	.497	[-6.620, 5.703]	[-2.319, 1.700]
CONC4	.111	.046	[-.860, .933]	.052	[-.883, .967]	[-.315, .494]	.043	[-.874, .936]	[-.282, .445]
NE82	1.617**	1.292**	[-1.907, 3.722]	1.283**	[-2.023, 3.824]	**[.442, 2.470]**	1.296**	[-1.925, 3.759]	**[1.537, 2.358]**
UNION	-.336**	-.220*	[-1.164, .783]	-.191**	[-1.178, .832]	[-.705, .217]	-.212	[-1.175, .790]	[-.686, .147]
LABINT82	-.656**	-.353**	[-1.691, 1.001]	-.401**	[-1.721, 1.026]	[-1.219, .198]	-.354**	[-1.704, 1.011]	[-1.129, .156]
REPRST	6.742	.209	[-26.31, 30.39]	-.274	[-27.26, 30.98]	[-9.211, 14.13]	.291	[-26.5, 30.72]	[-7.102, 13.15]
AVEARN	22.98**	1.809	[-32.62, 48.93]	1.569	[-34.36, 49.76]	[-14.12, 32.09]	1.723	[-33.07, 49.2]	[-11.34, 30.45]
TAR	1.783**	.864**	[-.980, 2.650]	.959**	[-1.030, 2.750]	**[.614, 1.949]**	.858**	[-1.031, 2.636]	**[.641, 1.827]**
P_UNSK	1.860**	.912*	[-2.328, 3.983]	1.302**	[-2.328, 4.250]	**[.274, 2.807]**	.896*	[-2.402, 3.982]	**[.241, 2.391]**
NEGR82	.626**	.500**	[-.066, .974]	.495**	[-.107, .990]	**[.351, .748]**	.496**	[-.090, .971]	**[.402, .095]**
$M_{i,j}$/CONS	4.900**	2.636	[-5.391, 9.641]	1.295	[-11.36, 16.66]	[-2.274, 7.432]	2.599**	[-7.203, 13.65]	**[1.080, 6.079]**
$X_{i,j}$/CONS	-31.10**	-20.95**	[-62.37, 21.71]	-3.788	[-59.4, 37.0]	[-39.81, 15.50]	-18.43**	[-71.4, 32.2]	**[-41.31, -5.98]**
DPEN7982	.055	.057	[-.064, .173]	.053	[-.084, .178]	[-.002, .110]	.056	[-.072, .173]	**[.014, .097]**
P_SCI	-4.121**	-2.560**	[-7.226, 2.553]	-2.860**	[-7.517, 2.597]	**[-5.307, -1.508]**	-2.623**	[-7.313, 2.570]	**[-4.881, -1.589]**
P_MAN	2.861**	.851*	[-3.040, 5.438]	.793**	[-3.213, 5.562]	[-.420, 3.750]	.833*	[-3.093, 5.463]	[-.158, 3.593]
MELAST	-.004	.060	[-.283, .322]	.059	[-.295, .332]	[-.096, .165]	.059	[-.285, .325]	[-.081, .152]
XELAST	.169**	.070**	[-.125, .275]	.073**	[-.131, .284]	**[.033, .195]**	.070**	[-.128, .277]	**[.040, .185]**
COUNTRY	Note 3	Note 3	Note 3	Note 3	Note 3	Note 3	Note 3	Note 3	Note 3

Notes: 1. $N=3915$, $k=28$. Degree of truncation=94.4%. 2. Measures of Fit: Likelihood-ratio statistic=446.5, Maddala's R^2=.282, Cragg-Uhler's R^2=.325. 3. All country dummies (COUNTRY) have negative MLE's and Bayes estimates, with t-values in excess of 2. Informative priors ($\sigma_L=1$) lead to strictly negative intervals. With weak and informative priors ($\sigma_L=1/4$) the intervals all contain 0.

costs ($M_{i,j}$/CONS, $X_{i,j}$/CONS, P_SCI) as the main factors determining quantitative NTBs. The EB intervals, however, show only the retaliation coefficient to be robust to variations in the prior for $1/4\bar{V} \leq V \leq 4\bar{V}$. When the prior covariance is allowed to vary as $\bar{V} \leq V \leq 4\bar{V}$, the EB intervals for both informative priors indicate robust support for the models of retaliation, the Adding Machine model, the Status Quo model, and the model of Comparative Costs. For quantitative NTBs the Special-Interest Group model (EB intervals contain zero) and the Social Justice model (opposite signs on NEGR82, LABINT82) are neither supported by the Bayes estimates, nor are they shown to be robust to changes in the prior.

Since the pooled econometric models do not convey the effects of any distinct bilateral or country-specific unilateral U.S. trade policy, an analysis by trade bloc is reported in tables 7a–7c. Table 7a presents a view of the political economy of overall U.S. NTBs, separately by trade blocs. Bayesian results are based on both my informative prior from table 5, and only those EB intervals (with $\sigma_L = 1$, $\sigma_U = 4$) are reported that are strictly negative or positive. Of note is the strikingly similar posterior bounds from both priors.[9] There are many similarities in the determinants of overall U.S. NTBs on trade with Japan, compared with those on trade with the four EC countries, France, Germany, Italy, and U.K. The structure of U.S. NTBs is shown to be retaliatory against Japan and the EC4. Clearly, special interests matter in determining NTBs against Japan and the EC4. Corporate PAC spending has high t values and its EB interval is positive and quite narrow, indicating robustness. Scale economies are protected. The Adding Machine model is also validated as an important underlying force behind U.S. NTBs against Japan and the EC4 (the counter-intuitive coefficient on LABINT82 and UNION notwithstanding). Evidence on the validity of the Status Quo model is mixed. While the strong positive coefficient on the tariff rate (TAR) would seem to validate the model, the signs on average earnings (AVEARN), and proportion unskilled (P_UNSK) run counter to the theory. The Social Justice model does not seem to play a role in determining NTBs on trade with Japan and the EC4. LABINT82, P_UNSK, and employment growth (NEGR82) all have signs that run counter to that theory. The model of comparative costs is also strongly validated by both sets of results, with the important difference that industries with a high level of managerial skill (P_MAN) were not protected from imports from Japan, which is not surprising, but were, surprisingly, protected from European imports. The control variables real-exchange-rate elasticity of imports and exports (MELAST, XELAST) have the correct sign for Japan but MELAST is positive for the EC4 indicating that the overvaluation of the dollar during this period did not greatly increase the need for NTBs due to the increased imports. The pos-

TABLE 7a. MLE, Bayes, and Extreme Bounds Estimates
Tobit Model with Dependent Variable All U.S. NTBS

Variable	JAPAN MLE	JAPAN Prior I $\sigma_L=1,\sigma_U=4$	JAPAN Prior II $\sigma_L=1,\sigma_U=4$	EC4 (FRA, GER, ITA, UK) MLE	EC4 Prior I $\sigma_L=1,\sigma_U=4$	EC4 Prior II $\sigma_L=1,\sigma_U=4$	BENELUX (BLX, NDL) MLE	BENELUX Prior I $\sigma_L=1,\sigma_U=4$	BENELUX Prior II $\sigma_L=1,\sigma_U=4$	EFTA2 (FIN, NOR) MLE	EFTA2 Prior I $\sigma_L=1,\sigma_U=4$	EFTA2 Prior II $\sigma_L=1,\sigma_U=4$
$N^*_{i,j}$	.412**	.345, .430	.390, .431	.352**	.300, .379	.337, .370	.617**	.479, .657	.560, .659	.176*		.109, .409
PACCVA83	1.091**	.884, 1.191	.978, 1.162	1.044**	.603, 1.174	.826, 1.094	1.270**	.330, 1.511	.819, 1.370	1.497*		
SCALE	.795*	.761, .839	.764, .816	.164	.150, .263	.156, .254	.336	.267, .569	.320, .558	−1.767*		−1.739, −.082
CONC4	.005			.028			−.049			−.338*		
NE82	.249	.214, .471	.204, .403	.790*	.643, .909	.654, .885	.548	.265, .898	.280, .828	3.117**	.258, 3.446	.501, 3.461
UNION	−.008			−.115	−.164, −.056	−.163, −.066	−.078			.013		
LABINT82	−.122	−.245, −.079	−.221, −.084	−1.330**	−1.38, −1.089	−1.373, −1.112	−.917**	−1.128, −.50	−1.014, −.549	−2.745**		−2.382, −.368
REPRST	7.38*	4.690, 7.780	5.413, 7.865	7.886	5.439, 9.167	6.204, 9.140	9.974*	3.986, 12.49	5.656, 12.39	−10.74*		
AVEARN	18.11**	12.85, 19.00	13.41, 18.65	18.42**	12.21, 20.04	12.84, 19.95	20.07**	5.656, 22.90	7.036, 22.20	23.95*		
TAR	2.811**	2.618, 2.829	2.628, 2.892	1.431**	1.196, 1.475	1.213, 1.465	1.422**	.803, 1.477	.874, 1.455	1.672*		
P_UNSK	−2.274**	−2.435, 2.080	−2.437, −2.280	.652*	.523, .913	.510, .826	.165			−.470		
NEGR82	.226**	.203, .234	.204, .230	.097	.082, .129	.083, .125	.019			−.047		
$M_{i,j}/$CONS	3.639**	2.778, 3.949	3.246, 3.886	3.411	1.588, 4.614	2.527, 3.918	34.60*	14.03, 49.71	28.30, 41.9	475.5**	144, 494	285, 475
$X_{i,j}/$CONS	10.78*	−13.7, −5.34	−12.78, −8.83	−12.72**	−16.5, −5.23	−14.27, −9.65	−12.50*	−17.70, −5.594	−17.70, −5.594	−210.9*		
DPEN7982	.141*	.134, .145	.136, .144	−.013	−.021, −.001	−.019, −.006	.038	.009, .060	.014, .049	−.003		
P_SCI	−1.303*	−1.38, −1.137	−1.358, −1.184	−.898*	−.993, −.670	−.964, −.688	−1.267*	−1.454, −.64	−1.382, −.700	−1.442		
P_MAN	−1.583*	−1.924, −1.42	−1.906, −1.490	.807*	.480, 1.159	.503, 1.131	.483			−1.557*		
NEGR82	.226**	.203, .234	.204, .230	.097	.082, .129	.083, .125	.019			−.047		
$M_{i,j}/$CONS	3.639**	2.778, 3.949	3.246, 3.886	3.411	1.588, 4.614	2.527, 3.918	34.60*	14.03, 49.71	28.30, 41.9	475.5**	144, 494	285, 475
$X_{i,j}/$CONS	10.78*	−13.7, −5.34	−12.78, −8.83	−12.72**	−16.5, −5.23	−14.27, −9.65	−12.50*	−17.70, −5.594	−17.70, −5.594	−210.9*		
DPEN7982	.141*	.134, .145	.136, .144	−.013	−.021, −.001	−.019, −.006	.038	.009, .060	.014, .049	−.003		
P_SCI	−1.303*	−1.38, −1.137	−1.358, −1.184	−.898*	−.993, −.670	−.964, −.688	−1.267*	−1.454, −.64	−1.382, −.700	−1.442		
P_MAN	−1.583*	−1.924, −1.42	−1.906, −1.490	.807*	.480, 1.159	.503, 1.131	.483			−1.557*		
MELAST	−.148**	−.154, −.117	−.148, −.117	.229**	.210, .237	.214, .238	.283**	.233, .303	.246, .304	.284**	.051, .343	.077, .349
XELAST	.185**	.171, .187	.173, .186	.001			−.017			−.015		
Constant	.983**	−.990, −.739	−.982, −.756	Note 2	Note 2	Note 2	Note 2	Note 2	Note 2	Note 2	Note 2	Note 2
k		20			23			21			21	
R^2	{.274, .262, .388}			{.176, .234, .312}			{−.215, .323, .408}			{.118, .239, .288}		
Truncation	66.9%			83.8%			86.0%			92.4%		

Notes: 1. R^2's reported are {Maddala's R^2, McFadden's R^2, Cragg-Uhler's R^2}. 2. Country dummies within each bloc are negative for each model with |t| > 2. EB intervals for the dummies are strictly negative.

TABLE 7b. MLE, Bayes, and Extreme Bounds Estimates
Tobit Model with Dependent Variable Price NTBS

Variable	JAPAN			EC4 (FRA, GER, ITA, UK)			BENELUX (BLX, NDL)			EFTA2 (FIN, NOR)		
	MLE	Prior I	Prior II	MLE	Prior I	Prior II	MLE	Prior I	Prior II	MLE	Prior I	Prior II
		$\sigma_L=1, \sigma_U=4$	$\sigma_L=1, \sigma_U=4$		$\sigma_L=1, \sigma_U=4$	$\sigma_L=1, \sigma_U=4$		$s_L=1, s_U=4$	$s_L=1, s_U=4$		$\sigma_L=1, \sigma_U=4$ $\sigma_L=1, \sigma_U=4$	$\sigma_L=1, \sigma_U=4$
$N^*_{i,j}$	.454**	.192, .424	.354, .465	.328**	.167, .401	.283, .366	.329**	.101, .476	.261, .637	.394**		.192, .631
PACCVA83	.035			1.251**	.101, 1.571	.637, 1.362	1.153*		.146, 1.378	1.370*		
SCALE	.592*	.518, .690	.538, .651	.111	.073, .407	.091, .398	.084	.267, .569	.081, .725	-1.671*		
CONC4	.248*	.082, .288	.129, .280	.233*	.113, .411	.116, .394	.250*			.101		
NE82	.108			1.228**	.631, 1.507	.639, 1.470	.523			3.734**		
UNION	.009			-.003			.069			.651*		
LABINT82	.180			-1.67*	-1.759,-.911	-1.751,-.953	-1.276**	-1.483,-.235	-1.468,-.260	-2.833**		
REPRST	5.919		1.827, 7.138	4.823			9.905*			-13.49*		
AVEARN	8.090		.423, 10.47	17.61**	.825, 22.88	2.669, 22.7	14.49*			11.32		
TAR	.990*	.458, 1.033	.540, .987	2.004**	1.264, 2.100	1.286, 2.078	1.988**	.624, 2.005	.657, 1.988	1.261*		
P_UNSK	-1.310*	-1.379,-.512	-1.495,-1.010	.118			-.144				-1.201	
NEGR82	-.013		-.059,-.003	.038			-.090			.077		
$M_{i,j}/$ CONS	3.130*	.954, 3.540	2.245, 3.476	3.888		1.374, 5.017	5.218			579.8**	274, 549	
$X_{i,j}/$ CONS	1.416			-6.934		-12.91,-.313	7.473			1.034		
DPEN7982	-.088	-.092,-.047	-.092,-.065	.034	.004, .063	.008, .051	.043			.091		
P_SCI	-1.078*	-1.114,-.430	-1.123,-.698	.136			-.971*			-1.056		
P_MAN	-2.461*	-2.611,-1.213	-2.743,-1.845	-.354			.095			.991		
MELAST	.065	.023, .094	.049, .097	.244**	.179, .266	.187, .268	.254**	.139, .296	.147, .296	.221*		
XELAST	.001			.012			-.017			.001		
Constant	-.604*	-.623,-.060		Note 1	Note 1		Note 1	Note 1		Note 1		
k	20			23			21	21		21		
R^2	{.122, .148, .208}			{.137, .227, .287}			{.144, .276, .334}			{.109, .276, .318}		
Truncation	79.5%			89.3%			90.5%			94.5%		

Note: 1. Country dummies are negative for each model with |t| > 2. EB intervals for the dummies all contain zero.

TABLE 7c. MLE, Bayes, and Extreme Bounds Estimates
Tobit Model with Dependent Variable Quantitative NTBS

Variable	JAPAN			EC4 (FRA, GER, ITA, UK)			BENELUX (BLX, NDL)			EFTA2 (FIN, NOR)		
	MLE	Prior I	Prior II	MLE	Prior I	Prior II	MLE	Prior I	Prior II	MLE	Prior I	Prior II
		$\sigma_L=1, \sigma_U=4$	$\sigma_L=1, \sigma_U=4$		$\sigma_L=1, \sigma_U=4$	$\sigma_L=1, \sigma_U=4$		$\sigma_L=1, \sigma_U=4$	$\sigma_L=1, \sigma_U=4$		$\sigma_L=1, \sigma_U=4$	$\sigma_L=1, \sigma_U=4$
$N^*_{i,j}$	.442**	.137, .490	.334, .484	.492**	.025, .493	.334, .529	.763**	.012, .497	.267, .637	.085		−.696, −.159
PACCVA83	.760*		.365, 1.122	−.215			−2.121			−1.307		
SCALE	.371	.116, .555	.130, .457	−6.156**			−11.34**			−99.85**		
CONC4	.344*	.054, .458	.076, .430	.285*			−.055			1.183*		
NE82	.382	.185, 1.383	.158, 1.187	1.138*			1.250*			28.48**		
UNION	.140			−.326*			−.577*			1.869		
LABINT82	.057			−.323*			−.420			−4.887**		
REPRST	8.767*	1.961, 2.747	2.001, 2.706	9.662*			14.33*			−111.53**		
AVEARN	4.516			32.53**			54.73**			79.61*		
TAR	2.715**			.517			.596			3.706**		
P_UNSK	−3.587**	−4.111, −2.336	−4.085, −2.967	2.153**			2.982**			6.670**		
NEGR82	.482*	.305, .497	.323, .479	.581**		.218, .646	−.264			1.326*		
$M_{i,j}/$CONS	1.463		−18.73, −2.871	2.736			74.41*			1362.7**		
$X_{i,j}/$CONS	−8.601			−9.361			1.734			−1592.1		
DPEN7982	.125*	.091, .143	.099, .138	−.141			.164			−.416		
P_SCI	−1.213*	−1.797, −.238	−1.629, −.451	−5.208**	−5.592, −.703	−5.169, −.092	−5.055**			−79.99**		
P_MAN	−.480		−1.950, −.139	3.596**			4.502**			.094		
MELAST	−.415*	−.421, −.182	−.401, −.187	.047			.127*			1.343**		
XELAST	.239**	.163, .245	.172, .244	.048*			.254**			1.992**		
Constant	−1.657**	−1.585, −.420	−1.543, −.485	Note 1			Note 1			Note 1		
k	20			23			23			21		
R^2	{.340, .469, .578}			{.112, .312, .352}			{.153, .507, .548}			{.144, .908, .909}		
Truncation	82.8%			94.5%			95.6%			98.7%		

Note: 1. Country dummies are negative for each model with |t| > 2. EB intervals for the dummies all contain zero.

sibly large amount of intra-industry trade with the EC4 may explain this surprising result.

Tables 7b and 7c indicate that for NTBs disaggregated by type, their political economic determinants differ, sometime considerably, across trading partners. Table 7b shows that while comparative costs are important determinants of U.S. price NTBs on imports from Japan, this is not the case for the EC4 countries, probably on account of the large volume of two-way trade. While the Adding Machine model is applicable for price NTBs on imports from the EC4, this is not shown to be true of Japan. Special interest pressure in the form of PAC spending is not successful at obtaining Price NTBs on imports from Japan, but it is successful in doing so against the EC4.

Table 7c shows that four of the five political economy theories (save for the Social Justice model) contribute to explaining quantitative NTBs on imports from Japan, but only the model of retaliation is applicable to such NTBs on imports from the EC4. This is a puzzle that needs to be theoretically and empirically resolved, and is left as an avenue for future research. While studies that explore the choice of the type of instrument used for trade protection exist, as surveyed by Vousden (1990), most are theoretical and few have emphasized intra-industry trade as a key factor. The differences in the results for Japan and the EC4 seem to be driven by the difference in the pattern of U.S. trade with these two blocs. The trade-weighted intra-industry trade (IIT) average in 1983, where intra-industry trade is measured as (Exports + Imports)/|Exports − Imports|, was 1.80 with Japan, 5.13 with France, 10.53 with Germany, 4.70 with Italy, and 7.36 with U.K. Indeed, across most 2-digit commodities, U.S. trade with the EC4 countries clearly possesses a greater degree of two-way trade than with Japan. Further, the IIT measure for U.S-Japan trade is below the value of 2 in many industries, implying that trade with Japan may be better characterized as inter-industry, Heckscher-Ohlin trade.

Summary and Conclusion

Leamer's (1982) sensitivity analysis of posterior estimates to variations in the prior is here extended to the Tobit model. This Tobit extreme bounds analysis (EBA) is used to test the validity of a set of theoretical models explaining protection. These include the political economy models of political self-interest, political altruism, and models based on comparative advantage. U.S. NTB coverage data from 1983 is pooled across 435 SIC 4-digit industries and nine developed countries. The posterior estimates from the pooled runs, based on both a weak prior that lets the data dominate the inferences and my set of prior beliefs about the model parameters, show that each model of protection has some validity. The posterior estimates of coefficients on variables representing each theory have the expected signs, with the exception of the Social Justice model of political altruism. Further, the Tobit extreme bounds analysis indicate that the posterior estimates are fairly robust to reasonably wide deviations around the prior means. The inferences are similar, but more sensitive to, variations in the priors when NTBs are disaggregated into price NTBs and quantitative NTBs. An analysis disaggregated by trade blocs shows that the determinants of protection from Japanese imports are fundamentally different from the determinants of protection from EC imports. The main reason for this seems to be that the trade with the EC is largely intra-industry trade while trade with Japan can be characterized as Heckscher-Ohlin inter-industry trade. Hence, comparative advantage factors dominate the pattern of quantitative NTB protection with Japan, while political factors appear to be responsible for the pattern of price NTB protection with EC countries.

Data Appendix

Aggregation and Measurement of NTBs

The data for this study are from an UNCTAD and World Bank project on nontariff barriers to trade. They inventory 50 types of tariff and nontariff barriers employed by the U.S. and other countries in 1983 that can be broadly classified into price-oriented NTBs (e.g. anti-dumping, countervailing duties), quantitative NTBs (e.g. quotas, VERs), and threats (e.g. price and quality monitoring). The following example of aggregation from the raw data at the 5,500 product tariff-line (TSUSA) to the 4-digit SIC level is instructive. The data consist of a binary indicator, I_{nip}, of the presence or absence of an NTB of type n on tariff-line product i against trading partner p (exporter to the U.S.). Bilateral imports, M_{ip}, and ad valorem tariffs are available at this level of disaggregation. Since no industry data is available at the tariff-line level, the aggregation of NTBs is necessary in order to combine NTB data with industry data for the analysis in the paper. For this purpose imports, M_{ip}, are the weights used. To aggregate to the 4-digit SIC level let G_j be the set of tariff-line products that feed into the 4-digit SIC product j. A coverage ratio for an NTB of type n on good j against trading partner p, CR_{njk}, is defined as

$$CR_{njp} = \sum_{i \in G_j} \frac{M_{ip}}{\sum_{i \in G_j} M_{ip}} \cdot I_{nip} = \sum_{i \in G_j} W_{ip} I_{nip}$$

In words, a coverage ratio is the proportion of imports subject to an NTB. In the paper, NTBs are aggregated across all types *n* to obtain an overall NTB coverage ratio. This is the measure of NTBs employed here and also by Leamer (1990) and Trefler (1993).

Other Variables

The sample accounts for over 97% of manufacturing sales. In the following COMTAP refers to the *Compatible Trade and Production Database, 1968–86,* CM refers to the 1982 *Census of Manufactures,* ASM to the 1983 *Annual Survey of Manufactures,* and CPS refers to the 1983 *Current Population Survey.*

For countries other than the United States, bilateral and total trade and production (the latter required to obtain domestic consumption) were constructed using 1983 figures from COMTAP. These data are at the ISIC level, which was concorded into the SITC (Revision 1) level and then into the 4-digit SIC level. For the U.S., bilateral and total (across all partners) imports and exports is aggregated up from tariff-line data.

Political Action Committee (PAC) campaign contribution data are from the Federal Election Commission (FEC) tapes for the election cycles 1977–78, 1979–80, 1981–82, and 1983–84. Since PACs are associated with individual firms, the variable PACCORP was constructed as follows. Using COMPUSTAT tapes, firms were classified into 3- or 4-digit SIC industries. Where firm coverage was incomplete in COMPUSTAT, I classified PACs into 2-digit SIC industries using Weinberger and Greavey (1984) and replicated this at the 4-digit level. The problem is that the classification of PACs to SIC industries is one-to-many since most firms are multi-product firms. Hence *total* PAC spending by an industry by simply summing would erroneously inflate the measure of PAC spending for some industries and understate it for others. Hence PACCORP is measured as spending per firm (the one-to-many classification is correctly averaged).

Value added is from ASM. REPRST is constructed from the *Geographic Area Series* of the CM. Earnings and employment (for AVEARN, LABINT82) are also from ASM, as are capital stock figures. NE82 and CONC4 are taken from CM. The division of workers by skill class (used for P_SCI, P_MAN, P_UNSK) is from CPS. UNION is from Kokkenberg and Sockell (1985). MELAST and XELAST are replicated from the 2-digit results in Ceglowski (1989).

NOTES

1. If, instead, $\hat{\sigma}^{-2}(X'X)^{-1}$ or $\sigma_{OLS}^{-2}(X'X)^{-1}$ is used (where σ_{OLS}^{-2} is estimated using equation (7)), the precision matrix of the ML estimates is overstated and the posterior t-values become incorrect. Further, neither $\hat{\sigma}_{OLS}^{-2}(X'X)^{-1}$ nor $\sigma_{OLS}^{-2}(X'X)^{-1}$ are consistent estimates of the precision matrix.

2. The variable MELAST is measured as a negative number. Hence the coefficient of MELAST is expected to be negative.

3. Since the variable PACCORP may also be measuring industry or firm "size", to prevent spurious scale effects the variable PACCVA83 (PACCORP/industry value added) is used in the regression analysis.

4. The single equation Tobit employed here may be seen as a first approximation to the more appropriate simultaneous Tobit as in Trefler (1993). An EBA for that model is under development.

5. Prior elasticities are converted into priors on actual coefficients at the variable means.

6. Since I am fairly comfortable with both sets of (informative) priors, strikingly different inferences would be discomforting, and if I needed to make a decision based on the posterior estimates from each set of priors I would need to explicitly provide weights for each set.

7. All estimation was done using GAUSS v. 2.1. Fowles' EBA software package (see Shiba, 1992) was modified to compute the Tobit extreme bounds.

8. They are, however, not in agreement with the much wider set of beliefs where the prior covariance matrix is free to vary, that is, when the prior covariance can be any positive definite matrix. In that case, all intervals contain zero.

9. The Bayes estimates are not reported to prevent cluttering, but are qualitatively not very different from the MLEs that are reported.

REFERENCES

Amemiya, Takeshi. 1985. *Advanced Econometrics.* Cambridge, MA: Harvard University Press.

Baldwin, Richard E. 1990. "Optimal Tariff Retaliation Rules." In Ronald W. Jones and Anne O. Krueger, eds., *The Political Economy of International Trade: Essays in Honor of Robert E. Baldwin.* Cambridge, MA: Basil Blackwell, pp. 108–121.

Baldwin, Robert E. 1984. "Trade Policies in Developed Countries." In Ronald Jones and Peter Kenen, eds., *Handbook of International Economics* Vol.1. New York: North-Holland, pp. 571–619.

Baldwin, Robert E. 1985. *The Political Economy of U.S. Import Policy.* Cambridge, MA: MIT Press.

Bhagwati, Jagdish. 1982., ed., *Import Competition and Response.* Chicago: University of Chicago Press.

Brock, William P. and Magee, Stephen P. 1978. "The Economics of Special Interest Politics: The Case of Tariffs." *American Economic Review* 68:246–50.

Caves, Richard E. 1976. "Economic Models of Political Choice: Canada's Tariff Structure." *Canadian Journal of Economics* 9, pp. 278–300.

Ceglowski, Janet. 1989. "Dollar Depreciation and U.S. Industry Performance." *Journal of International Money and Finance* 8:233–251.

Chan, Kenneth S. 1988. "Trade Negotiations in a Nash Bargaining Model." *Journal of International Economics* 25, pp. 353–363.

Corden, W. Max. 1974. *Trade Policy and Welfare.* Oxford: Oxford University Press.

Deardorff, Alan V., and Stern, Robert M. 1987. "Tariffs and Defensive Response." *International Economic Journal* 1:1–23.

Findlay, Ronald and Wellisz, Stanislaw. 1982. "Endogenous Tariffs and the Political Economy of Trade Restrictions and Welfare." In Jagdish Bhagwati, ed., *Import Competition and Response.* Chicago: University of Chicago Press.

Gawande, Kishore. 1995. "Are U.S. Nontariff Barriers Retaliatory? An Application of Extreme Bounds Analysis in the Tobit Model." *Review of Economics and Statistics* 77:677–688.

Helleiner, Gerald K. 1977. "The Political Economy of Canada's Tariff Structure: An Alternative Model." *Canadian Journal of Economics* 10:318–326.

Herander, Mark G., and Schwartz, J. Brad. 1984. "An Empirical Test of the Impact of the Threat of U.S. Trade Policy: The Case of Antidumping Duties." Southern Economic Journal 51:59–79.

Kelly, Margaret; Kirmani, Naheed; Xafa, Miranda; Boonekamp,Clemens; and Winglee, Peter. 1988. "Issues and Developments in International Trade Policy." IMF Occasional Papers Series, no. 63.

Kokkenberg, Edward C., and Sockell, Donna R. 1985. "Union Membership in the United States, 1973–1981." *Industrial and Labor Relations Review* 38: 497–543.

Leamer, Edward E. 1982. "Sets of Posterior Means With Bounded Variance Priors." *Econometrica* 50:725–736.

Leamer, Edward E. 1990. "The Structure and Effects of Tariff and Nontariff Barriers in 1983." In Ronald W. Jones and Anne O. Krueger, eds., *The Political Economy of International Trade: Essays in Honor of Robert E. Baldwin.* Cambridge, MA: Basil Blackwell. pp. 224–260.

Maskus, Keith. 1985. "A Test of the Heckscher-Ohlin-Vanek Theorem: The Leontief Commonplace. *Journal of International Economics* 19:201–212.

Olson, Mancur. 1965. *The Logic of Collective Action.* Cambridge, MA: Harvard University Press.

Pincus, Jonathan J. 1975. "Pressure Groups and the Pattern of Tariffs." *Journal of Political Economy* 83:757–778.

Polasek, Wolfgang. 1984. "Multivariate Regression Systems." In Joseph B. Kadane, ed., *Robustness of Bayesian Analyses.* Amsterdam:Elsevier Science. pp. 231–309.

Prusa, Thomas J. 1992. "Why Are So Many Antidumping Petitions Withdrawn?" *Journal of International Economics* 33:1–20.

Shiba, Tsunemasa. 1992. "MICRO-EBA: Leamer's Extreme Bounds Analysis on Gauss." *Journal of Applied Econometrics* 7:101–103.

Trefler, Daniel. 1993. "Trade Liberalization and the Theory of Endogenous Protection: An Econometric Study of U.S. Import Policy." *Journal of Political Economy* 101:138–160.

Vousden, Neil. 1990. *The Economics of Trade Protection.* Cambridge, UK: Cambridge University Press.

Weinberger, Marvin I, and Greavey, David U. 1984. *The PAC Directory: A Complete Guide to Political Action Committees.* Cambridge: Ballinger.

CHAPTER 4

Section 337 and the Protection of Intellectual Property in the U.S.: The Impact on R&D Spending

John Mutti and Bernard Yeung

The protection of intellectual property rights is an important ingredient in the success of market economies. If existing intellectual property is not adequately protected, firms lose profits and sales in the short run and may be less inclined to innovate in the long run. Over time, productivity gains and the introduction of new products will slow down. In the international arena, the recent trend is to increase the protection to intellectual property rights. Under the 1994 Uruguay Round Agreement reached by GATT members, countries agreed to establish minimal standards of intellectual property protection. The United States was particularly interested in these provisions, which when eventually phased in will provide twenty years of protection for patents, including pharmaceuticals, and up to fifty years for copyrights, including computer programs. Protection for trademarks, service marks, and semiconductor chip mask works also is specified.

However, one part of the U.S. regime to protect intellectual property, Section 337 of the Tariff Act of 1930, was declared incompatible with the GATT in 1989. Changes in U.S. practice were incorporated into the GATT enabling legislation that Congress passed in December 1994, but the extent to which these changes alter the way Section 337 functions will not be clear for several years. Nevertheless, analysis of Section 337 in its pre-1994 form provides useful insights into the way government policy may affect private efforts to innovate.

Mutti and Yeung (1996) previously examined what types of firms bring Section 337 cases and considered how the disposition of those cases affects the profitability and efforts to innovate of both filing firms and peer firms in the same industry. Based on publicly available firm-level information, they found that Section 337 is used by firms with substantial intellectual properties and that positive outcomes allow filing firms to avoid large declines in profitability that otherwise occur with infringement. They did not, however, find any relationship between firm characteristics and Section 337 rulings.

The role of Section 337 in promoting efforts to innovate is not clear. Mutti and Yeung did not find any significant impact of Section 337 rulings on R&D spending or advertising by filing firms or by peers as a group. The current paper pursues that topic using a somewhat different framework that considers the response of individual peer firms.

The disposition of a Section 337 case may influence a firm's effort to innovate in several ways, including effects on current and future profitability and on the intensity of ongoing R&D patent races. Because these influences are often opposite in sign and have uneven impacts on individual firms, the absence of a discernible effect on aggregate R&D in the affected industry is not surprising. Attention to individual firms within this control group may reveal that important changes occur even when industry aggregate measures do not.

We are able to identify a small role that changes in profitability play in firm R&D expenditures. A more substantial impact from Section 337 rulings, however, comes via the effect on ongoing R&D patent races. We do not find that positive dispositions stimulate filing firms to increase R&D spending. Instead, R&D intensity decreases among control firms, and the differences in R&D spending among control firms become compressed. In negative disposition cases, the Section 337 ruling appears to reinvigorate the R&D patent race in the sense that leaders in the race spend more and followers spend less on R&D. Also, average R&D intensity appears to increase in R&D-intensive industries. However, the set of results for negative cases is not as robust as the set for positive cases.

In the next section, we discuss briefly Section 337 procedures and practices. In the third section, we discuss the impact of Section 337 on firm R&D spending, in order to motivate the empirical specification we employ. In the fourth section, we describe the data set, relevant data transformations, and our actual empirical procedures. We report our results in the fifth section, which is followed by our conclusions.

Section 337 Provisions

Section 337 allows holders of U.S. patents, copyrights, and trademarks to challenge the infringement of their property rights by imports. Over the period 1974 to 1988, however, complainants had to demonstrate that the infringement occurred and caused injury to an efficiently-run U.S. industry. After U.S. legislative changes adopted in 1988, this link to domestic production was weakened, and for patent cases complainants now need only demonstrate that infringement occurs. In 1988 a GATT panel report also found that several provisions of Section 337 violated GATT Article III, which specifies that imports are to receive treatment no less favorable than for domestic goods. The GATT Council adopted that report in 1989. A U.S. attempt to bring Section 337 into compliance with GATT standards was delayed until the U.S. Congress adopted enabling legislation in December 1994 to accept the Uruguay Round agreements.

Changes were made in 1994. The tight 12-month time limit that applied to a standard Section 337 proceeding heard by the International Trade Commission (ITC) was dropped, a change that formally eliminates a difference between Section 337 and Federal District Court action in domestic infringement cases. Similarly, respondents in Section 337 proceedings now have the right to raise counterclaims, although those are shifted to Federal District Court for adjudication. Complainants still can choose the venue in which they file a case, and they still can seek remedies from both the ITC and the Federal District Court., but respondents need not defend simultaneously in both fora. The record from an ITC case is to be admitted into subsequent Federal District Court proceedings. The scope of general exclusion orders issued against importers in the case of a violation is to be limited to violating importers, unless difficulties of enforcement require a broader approach. These changes respond to the majority of the procedural objections raised by the GATT panel report, although they do maintain Section 337 as a judicial procedure separate from Federal District Court.[1]

Regardless of the details of these modifications, insights regarding the past operation of Section 337 are likely to be useful in interpreting its future influence. Also, Section 337 still differs in important ways from other unfair trade laws, both with respect to procedure and with respect to available remedies. For example, antidumping and subsidy cases involve a two-stage procedure, with the U.S. Department of Commerce (DOC) determining the extent of dumping or foreign subsidization, and the ITC determining whether the domestic industry has been injured. If the ITC rules that injury has occurred, importers must post a bond equivalent to the dumping or subsidy margin found by the DOC, and this remedy is imposed automatically without Presidential review. Although that standard procedure indicates one successful outcome for domestic complainants, Prusa (1992) notes an alternative scenario relevant in the surprisingly high proportion of AD cases that are withdrawn but nevertheless benefit those who file. Prusa shows that complainants do nearly as well in withdrawn cases as when AD duties are imposed. On theoretical grounds he suggests that both the complainant and the foreign producer may become better off from an agreement that allows them to cooperate and reach a collusive solution that dominates competitive outcomes.

By way of contrast, Section 337 cases are handled entirely by the ITC. The full commission, however, often plays a small role in the actual proceedings. The discovery process occurs before an Administrative Law Judge (ALJ). The ALJ hears all the arguments, recommends to the Commission whether a violation has occurred, and if so, indicates what remedy should be applied. The Commission may affirm or modify the recommendation of the ALJ. The ITC decision then goes to the President for review. That latter provision may appear to inject more political influence into a Section 337 proceeding than occurs in dumping or subsidy cases. That inference would overstate the role of the President and understate the buffering influence that occurs because the proceedings are held before an ALJ who will apply rules of evidence similar to a Federal District Court.

Also, the advantages of withdrawal noted by Prusa in the case of dumping petitions are somewhat different in Section 337 proceedings. Whereas both the domestic and foreign producer may gain from collusion in a dumping case, note that when a U.S. patent is granted, its owner already has been given monopoly power. While a filing firm can withdraw a case, as in the dumping case scenario traced by Prusa, that strategy is unlikely to re-establish a patent holder's monopoly power. That is, an outcome that rests on market collusion involves sharing market power, not restoring it to the patent holder.

Of course, a filing firm may seek a settlement agreement with the respondent before the ITC reaches a final decision. Such a strategy may be attractive when the validity or scope of the patent infringement claim made by a firm is uncertain, or when rapid resolution of a claim is more desirable than a protracted legal battle (as when a valid patent or innovation may shortly be superseded by others). In such situations a firm is less likely to be concerned that its willingness to settle rather than seek a final ruling will encourage infringement by others. A settlement agreement usually involves the respondent paying the patent holder royalties in exchange for the right to continue importing the product in question, but in any event the ITC must agree that the agreement is in the public interest. Alternatively, the ITC may issue a consent order, which involves conditions similar to a settlement agreement but calls for the ITC to take action if the respondent violates the conditions of the order.

If a case is pursued to a final ruling, the ITC may find that a violation of Section 337 has occurred. The ITC may issue an exclusion order that bans the importation of the infringing product and also may issue a cease and desist order that bars the sale of infringing goods already imported. If a firm seeks to recover damages for past infringement, however, it must file a case in Federal District Court. From 1974–89 roughly one-third of Section 337 cases ended in no violation or dismissal, 40 percent were resolved by a settlement agreement or consent order, and in the remainder the ITC ruled that violations had occurred.

While trade remedies adopted in antidumping and subsidy cases often shift resources to non-competitive industries and firms (e.g. Crandall 1987, Lenway et al. 1996), Section 337 appears somewhat different. Using publicly available firm-level information, Mutti and Yeung (1996) report that complaining firms are typically larger, produce a more diverse range of products, have invested more in intangibles and are not less profitable than their peer firms. A complaining firm suffers a substantial loss in sales and profits if no violation is found in its Section 337 case.

Section 337 Dispositions and Firm R&D

The fundamental reason for protecting intellectual property rights is to stimulate efforts to innovate. In earlier work we found no systematic or statistically significant effect of a Section 337 ruling on average R&D spending, even though a negative ruling had a pronounced adverse effect on the filing firm's profitability. That average R&D spending was not affected is not too surprising, however, because a Section 337 ruling has multiple effects on a firm's incentive to innovate, and many of these effects act in the opposite direction. Also, these effects are not uniform across firms. Therefore, we should not expect the net change in *industry* R&D spending after a Section 337 ruling to reveal much about R&D incentives. Here, we focus on how different firms within the affected industry respond.

The most straightforward influence of a Section 337 ruling on a firm's R&D spending is via its impact on a firm's internal liquidity. Hall (1992) shows empirically that investment in R&D is constrained by a firm's internal cash flow. If a positive Section 337 ruling reduces the competitive pressure on a filing firm and increases its profits, that will have a positive influence on the filing firm's R&D spending. Conversely, if a negative ruling decreases a filing firm's profits, it decreases the firm's R&D spending. For firms in the same industry as the product in which a Section 337 case is filed, we also expect that when a Section 337 ruling increases (decreases) the profits of peers, their R&D spending will rise (fall), ceteris paribus. We refer to this effect as the *liquidity effect.*

How a Section 337 ruling affects the current profitability of peer firms cannot be predicted a priori. A positive ruling may reduce foreign competition for products similar to the good produced by the filing firm, and thereby raise peer profitability. A positive ruling, however, may reduce peer profitability when those producers use the underlying product or its foreign substitute as intermediate inputs. In order words, the same ruling may lead to a positive liquidity effect for some firms and a negative liquidity effect for others, even though both types of firms are assigned to the same SIC industry.[2]

A Section 337 ruling also affects a firm's R&D spending via its impact on the profitability of future innovations and on the competitive threat from R&D by others, two channels suggested in Beath et al (1989). With respect to the profitability of future innovation, a positive ruling signals that infringers will be punished and property rights will be enforced; it should then reduce the probability of infringement by foreign and possibly also domestic producers. By reducing the likelihood of infringement, a positive ruling increases the profit an innovator can appropriate. A positive *appropriation effect* increases the value of innovation (Spence 1984).[3] Experimental results obtained by Isaac and Reynolds (1988, 664) show that average R&D spending is consistently greater under full appropriability than under partial appropriability.

There also is a *substitution effect* associated with a Section 337 ruling. Stronger protection of property rights increases the value of existing innovations. To the extent that a new innovation is a substitute for old ones, a ruling that increases the value of existing innovations reduces the net value of new innovation and may then reduce the incentive to carry out more R&D. Therefore, because of this substitution effect, even if a positive disposition increases a firm's current profits, it does not automatically increase R&D spending. On the other hand, a complementary effect of the opposite sign also can occur. An increase in the value of existing innovations due to a favorable Section 337 ruling can increase the value of future complementary innovations, even if the protection of future property rights is not perceived to be affected.

In the discussion below we refer to the substitution effect as net of the complementary effect. Note that the substitution effect and the liquidity effect are opposite in sign but are both based on the impact of a Section 337 ruling on the profit of a firm's existing intellectual assets. Both the liquidity effect and the substitution effect will be firm specific. Also note that the appropriation effect and the substitution effect may work in opposite directions. In the case of a filing firm, for example, a positive ruling induces the firm to increase its R&D spending via the appropriation effect while the same ruling may induce the firm to reduce its R&D spending via the substitution effect.

Another consideration is that strengthening the protection of current patents may make further innovations more costly and less profitable for other firms. Limiting access to ideas and technology will retard the research progress of others. Such a negative impact arises for peer firms that use the intellectual property involved in a Section 337 case as an intermediate input for further innovation. Also, the future profit from further innovation will be adversely affected if the new innovation is complementary with the protected good. For example, stronger protection for standard memory chips in the semiconductor industry may reduce the payoff to the development of more specialized microprocessors. We shall refer to the influence of greater protection of one innovation on the costs and benefits of other innovations as the *cost-benefit effect*. In the case of a positive (negative) ruling, this cost-benefit effect should reduce (increase) the R&D spending of a firm that uses the protected product as an input for its own innovative effort or of a firm that produces new innovations that are complementary with the protected good. The cost-benefit effect has non-uniform impacts on R&D spending even for firms in the same industry.

A Section 337 ruling may also change the competitive R&D threat a firm faces. It is well known in the R&D-patent-race literature that a firm's R&D effort depends on its position in the R&D patent race (Park 1987, Grossman and Shapiro 1987, and Aoki 1991). Upon an increase in the payoff to the winner of the race, a leading firm will increase its R&D effort while a follower will reduce its effort. These reactions will be more pronounced the greater the gap between leaders and followers in the race. Hence, if a Section 337 ruling increases the profit incentive to innovate and thus intensifies the R&D race, we expect the leading innovators to increase their efforts and followers to cut back theirs. Conversely, if a disposition decreases the profit incentive to innovate and thus reduces the intensity of the R&D race, we expect the leading innovator to slow down its innovation effort. The followers may then be stimulated to increase their innovative efforts because the distance between the leader and followers is reduced. We call this effect the *competitive-position effect*.

In summary, how a Section 337 ruling changes firm level innovative efforts depends on the extent the ruling changes: (i) the internal liquidity constraint of a firm (the liquidity effect), (ii) the value of existing intellectual properties (the substitution and complementary effects), (iii) the appropriability of future R&D results (the appropriation effect), and (iv) the costs and benefits of further innovations that are dependent on the protected innovation (the cost-benefit effect). Furthermore, each firm's reaction to these changes depends on a firm's position in the on-going R&D patent race (the competitive-position effect).

Note that both the magnitude and the reactions to these various changes are firm specific. As a consequence, the net impact of a Section 337 ruling varies both in sign and in magnitude across firms in the same industry. Therefore, there is little reason to expect a stable industry-wide change in R&D spending in response to a Section 337 ruling. Furthermore, simply observing that no change in industry-wide R&D occurs misses important distinctions that may be drawn with respect to the intensity of R&D competition within the industry. R&D leaders may increase their spending while followers cut back. To capture the possible importance of these effects on R&D spending, we focus on the response of individual firms, not the industry as a whole, to gain a better understanding of the consequences of Section 337 rulings.

Data and Empirical Specification

Our data set is identical to Mutti and Yeung (1996). We begin by considering all cases filed with the International Trade Commission since 1976 and up to 1988, which were all filed under the legal guidelines of the Trade Act of 1974 and before the 1988 amendments. Of all 262 cases, we are able to identify 92 cases which were filed by US parent firms or subsidiaries of the US parent firms included in various Compustat data tapes, which are our sources of firm level data. Firms included in the various Compustat data tapes are all publicly traded, listed on New York Stock Exchange, the American Stock Exchange, or are traded over the counter. Excluded filing firms are generally privately held firms, many of which are small. While some of these excluded firms may carry out extensive R&D programs, R&D spending in the private sector is in the main funded by larger publicly-traded firms. Hence, although our sample is biased, it does focus on firms whose R&D behavior is of considerable importance.

Our intention is to investigate the impact of Section 337 rulings on R&D spending by filing firms and by peer firms most directly affected by Section 337 rulings. The control group is composed of firms whose primary line of business is the same as the product in which a Section 337 case is filed. We exclude cases for which we are unable to identify five firms who list the relevant three-digit SIC category as their primary line of business. Our resultant sample contains 67 cases filed over the period from 1977 to 1988. These firms represent 27 different three-digit industries and 518 control firms are drawn from them. Because multiple cases occur in some industries, the experience of the same control firm may be relevant in two different time intervals.

We investigate separately the impact of Section 337 rulings on R&D spending by filing firms and by control firms. We expect Section 337 rulings to have a more direct impact on the filing firms whose intellectual property is infringed by imports. Furthermore, filing firms are more likely to be dependent on technological leadership and protection of property rights because they spend significantly more on R&D than control firms, as reported by Mutti and Yeung.

We are concerned that any relationship observed between a Section 337 ruling and the change in firm spending on R&D may instead capture an ex ante relationship between firm characteristics and subsequent spending on R&D, independent of any Section 337 ruling. Although this possibility cannot be conclusively rejected, Mutti and Yeung note that firm characteristics fail to predict Section 337 rulings, and therefore rulings are not simply a proxy for firm characteristics.

It would be ideal to use a regression framework to decompose the net change in firm R&D spending into the relevant Section 337 influences, including the liquidity effect, the substitution effect, the appropriation effect, the cost-benefit effect, and the competitive-position effect. However, we are not able to develop independent measures of each of these effects. It is not straightforward to infer the individual effects from any observed aggregate effect either. For example, suppose the liquidity and net of substitution and complementary effects can be represented adequately by estimated innovations in profits. Can the appropriation effect be inferred by comparing successful Section 337 cases to unsuccessful ones? If the appropriation effect were the only omitted effect, such an interpretation might be warranted. Unfortunately, that is not the case, since the cost-benefit effect and the competitive-position effect also are relevant. Measuring the cost-benefit effect requires very detailed information on firm operations and intellectual property, which is not available in Compustat. Lastly, while it is possible to proxy for the competitive-position effect, the influence of Section 337 on firm R&D spending is dependent on the expected change in the intensity of the ongoing R&D patent race, and modelling the way expectations are formed is an imprecise process that depends upon some of the same factors already mentioned.

We have to settle, therefore, for a less ambitious approach that does not allow separate inferences about each of the channels identified above. Our framework instead can be regarded as a reduced form representation where several factors contribute to the estimated coefficients of a common set of exogenous variables that we can measure. In this reduced form equation one exogenous variable captures the impact of Section 337 on R&D spending via changes in current profits. Other exogenous variables reveal how changes in the intensity of on-going R&D patent races are affected by Section 337 dispositions and thereby influence firm R&D spending.

Consider the following regression specification for firm i in industry j:

$$DRDI_{ij} = a + b_1 * IPROF_{ij} + b_2 * CRDP_{ij} + b_3 * IRDI_{.j} + b_4 * Z_{ij.}$$

Variables are defined as follows:

$DRDI_{ij}$ represents a firm's change in R&D intensity,

$IPROF_{ij}$ represents the change, or innovation, in a firm's profit due to a Section 337 ruling,

$CRDP_{ij}$ indicates a firm's competitive position in an on-going R&D-patent-race,

$IRDI_{j}$ represents industry R&D intensity, and

Z_{ij} represents other control variables.

Consider the empirical representation of these variables and our expectations regarding the coefficient estimates:

$DRDI_{ij}$

We measure the firm-level change in R&D intensity by the change in the firm's R&D expenditure per dollar of assets. To mitigate the impact of transitory changes, the variable is constructed as the difference between two three-year averages: $(R\&D/A_d + R\&D/A_{d+1} + R\&D/A_{d+2}) - (R\&D/A_d + R\&D/A_{d-1} + R\&D/A_{d-2})$, where d is the disposition year.

$IPROF_{ij}$

Both the liquidity and substitution effects depend upon the change in profits due to a Section 337 ruling, which we calculate as the actual change in profits minus the change in profits expected before the Section 337 ruling is made. To obtain expected profits for each firm, we regress its current profits on its own past profits for the time period prior to the disposition and then use that model to predict profits in the absence of a Section 337 ruling. The innovation, or difference between observed and predicted profits, is by definition unrelated to the past trend in profits. We then scale the innovation by total assets to mitigate any size effect. From the prior discussion of the liquidity and the substitution effects, a positive estimate of b_1 indicates that the liquidity effect dominates. If b_1 is negative, the substitution effect dominates.

$CRDP_{ij}$

The firm's competitive position in an on-going R&D patent race is captured by a firm's R&D/Assets minus the corresponding industry's size-weighted average R&D/Assets prior to the Section 337 disposition. To reduce the influence of transitory factors, we calculate these ratios over the three years prior to the disposition. The value of this variable will be greater for R&D leaders who have spent more on R&D per dollar of assets than the industry average. If a Section 337 ruling increases the intensity of an R&D patent race, we expect that to impact on R&D leaders more than R&D followers. In this case, b_2 is positive. Conversely, if a Section 337 ruling decreases the intensity of an R&D-patent-race, R&D spending by leaders will decline more than for followers. Indeed, the followers may see that as a chance to catch-up in the race and increase their R&D spending. In this case, b_2 is negative.

$IRDI_{.j}$

The industry R&D intensity is captured by an industry's size-weighted average R&D/Assets prior to the Section 337 disposition. Again, to mitigate the influence of transitory factors, the variable is constructed by averaging the industry's size-weighted average R&D/Assets over the three years prior to the disposition.[4] If a Section 337 ruling increases the intensity of an on-going R&D race by making a patent more valuable, this effect is likely to be greater in industries where R&D spending is higher. Levin et al. (1987) identify U.S. industries where high-level R&D managers regard patents as an effective means of protecting innovations. To the extent that these industries are also those that engage in more R&D per dollar of assets, we expect b_3 to be positive. Conversely, if a Section 337 ruling decreases the intensity of an R&D patent race, we expect the resultant firm-level decrease in R&D spending to be more pronounced the more R&D-intensive the industry is. In this case, b_3 is negative, a result we expect when b_2 also is negative.

Z_{ij}

Our control variables include both industry dummies and a proxy for the change in industry R&D intensity unrelated to Section 337 rulings. Including the industry dummies is a way to eliminate the influence of factors that affect all firms in the same industry but vary across industries, such as news about the latest scientific discoveries or shifts in demand conditions. On the other hand, if these distinctions are relatively unimportant across industries, then the industry dummies may instead capture the influence of Section 337 rulings that we hope $CRDP_{ij}$ and $IRDI_{.j}$ will reflect.

Another control variable we include is a measure of the change in an industry's R&D intensity unrelated to Section 337 rulings. We have tried two approaches. The first is to use the change in the industry's R&D/Assets that occurred between the year of the Section 337 disposition and two years prior. The other is to use an instrumental variable approach to project the expected change in industry R&D in the absence of a Section

337 ruling. To implement that approach we regress the actual change in an industry's R&D/Assets, potentially an endogenous variable, on industry average ratios calculated over the prior three years for (sales / employment) and for (sales / total dollars of physical capital). From this first stage regression we obtain the predicted value of the change in industry R&D, which we use as an instrumental variable in the equation to explain the firm's R&D response. Both approaches lead to similar results, and therefore we report estimates obtained by the first approach because of its simplicity.

Results

Filing Firms

We first examine the impact for filing firms of Section 337 rulings on R&D spending per dollar of total assets. The upper panel in table 1 reports average values of the dependent and independent variables. Numbers in the left panel are for cases with positive outcomes and those in the right panel are for cases with negative rulings.

On average, the filing firms increase their R&D intensity (average DRDI) by .27 cents per dollar of total assets upon a positive Section 337 ruling. Upon a negative ruling, the filing firms increase their R&D intensity by .17 cents per dollar of total assets. Thus, the filing firms facing a negative decision seem to increase their R&D intensity less than those facing a positive decision. A comparison of the first and the third row of numbers reveals that filing firms facing a negative decision also seem to have reduced their R&D relative to the industry average change, while the opposite is true for those facing a positive decision. However, none of these comparisons is statistically significant.[5]

Results from the regression as specified in equation 1 without industry dummies are reported in the mid-panel of table 1. Those with industry dummies are reported in the bottom panel. The test for heteroskedasticity based on White's (1980) Chi-square statistic is insignificant. We therefore report the OLS standard errors. All specifications indicate that the only significant variable is the profit innovation variable (IPROF). The variable is negative and significant, indicating that a profit increase will decrease R&D spending; that is, the substitution effect dominates the liquidity effect. Notice that since filing firms on average suffer from a profit decrease in a negative decision, a negative decision should stimulate rather than dampen a filing firm's R&D spending. The economic significance of the substitution effect is non-trivial for filing firms facing a negative decision. We approximate an independent variable's economic significance by

TABLE 1. Analysis of R&D Responses by Filing Firm

Mean Values

	Positive Disposition	Negative Disposition
R&D Response (DRDI)	.0027*	.0017
	(.0012)	(.0025)
Industry R&D (IRDI)	.0431*	.0368*
	(.0043)	(.0050)
Industry R&D past change (Z)	.0016	.0024**
	(.0007)*	(.0016)
Firm's Relative R&D (CRDP)	.00367	.0056
	(.0046)	(.0069)
Actual Minus Predicted Profit (IPROF)	−.0069	−.0708
	(.0080)	(.0650)
	47 firms	20 firms

Regression Analysis

	Positive Disposition Coefficient	Economic Effect	Negative Disposition Coefficient	Economic Effect
Intercept	.0018	.0018	−.0031	−.0031
	(.0022)		(.0028)	
Industry R&D (IRDI)	.0064	.0003	.0709	.0026
	(.0462)		(.0749)	
Industry R&D past change (Z)	.1397	.0002	−.2197	−.0005
	(.2466)		(.2549)	
Firm's Relative R&D (CRDP)	.0212	.0001	.0740	.0004
	(.0402)		(.0480)	
Actual Minus Predicted Profit (IPROF)	−.0480*	.0003	−.0325	.0023
	(.0219)		(.0056)	
	df = 42		df = 15	

Regression Analysis—Controlling for SIC

	Positive Disposition Coefficient	Economic Effect	Negative Disposition Coefficient	Economic Effect
Industry R&D (IRDI)	.0100	.0004	.0977	.0036
	(.1544)		(.0652)	
Industry R&D past change (Z)	.6743	.0011	−.0649	−.0011
	(.4374)		(.2749)	
Firm's Relative R&D (CRDP)	−.0825	−.0003	.1540	.0008
	(.0780)		(.0895)	
Actual Minus Predicted Profit (IPROF)	−.1164*	.0008	−.0335*	.0024
		(.0419)		(.0055)
	df = 18		df = 3	

* denotes significance at the 5 percent level
** denotes significance at the 10 percent level

the product of its mean and its regression coefficient. These products are reported in the mid- and bottom panels next to each regression coefficient.

For filing firms that receive a negative ruling we find the coefficient for their competitive position in the R&D race is positive and significant at the 10 percent level based on a 1-tailed test. The observation weakly suggests that a negative decision actually stimulates R&D spending, causing leaders (followers) to increase (decrease) their R&D intensity. The variable accounts for about 25 percent to 50 percent of the observed change in R&D/assets.[6]

The lack of significance of most explanatory variables suggests that the filing firm's change in R&D spending is not strongly related to Section 337 decisions. We check this possibility by pooling the observations and use a Section 337 dummy, 1 for positive decisions and 0 for negative decisions, to form cross terms with the independent variables. If a positive and a negative Section 337 decision affect a filing firm's R&D spending differently, the cross-term coefficient should be significant, indicating that the Section 337 ruling changes a firm's response to the independent variables. All these cross-terms are insignificant. Due to the unexceptional nature of these results we do not report them individually.

In summary, for filing firms the substitution effect dominates the liquidity effect no matter what the Section 337 decision is. Thus, although a negative Section 337 decision may reduce a filing firm's profit, it increases rather than decreases the filing firm's R&D spending. A negative decision appears to increase the intensity of the R&D patent race for the industry in which the filing firm operates. To the extent that filing firms are usually R&D spending leaders, a negative decision again increases rather than dampens a filing firm's R&D spending. In general, however, our regression results are too weak to allow any strong interpretation of how a Section 337 decision influences a filing firm's R&D spending.

Control Firms

We also conduct regression analyses on firms in the same industries in which Section 337 cases are filed. The results are reported in table 2. Numbers in the left panel are from control firms in industries with positive Section 337 outcomes while those in the right panel are from control firms in industries with negative Section 337 rulings. Again, the top panel reports variable means, the middle panel the regression as specified in equation 1 without industry dummies, and the bottom panel the regression with industry dummies. In the middle panel, we report heteroskedastic-consistent estimates for coefficient standard errors because White's Chi-square test for heteroskedasticity is significant. In the bottom panel, we report

TABLE 2. Analysis of R&D Responses by Control Firms

Mean Values

	Positive Disposition	Negative Disposition
R&D Response (DRDI)	.0018*	.0046*
	(.0010)	(.0013)
Industry R&D (IRDI)	.0582*	.0447*
	(.0011)	(.0013)
Industry R&D past change (Z)	.0042*	.0041
	(.0002)	(.0003)
Firm's Relative R&D (CRDP)	−.0139*	−.0014
	(.0023)	(.0019)
Actual Minus Predicted Profit (IPROF)	.0061	.0012
	(.0107)	(.0109)
	644 firms	274 firms

Regression Analysis

	Positive Disposition Coefficient	Economic Effect	Negative Disposition Coefficient	Economic Effect
Intercept	.0039*	.0039	−.0011	−.0011
	(.0016)		(.0016)	
Industry R&D (IRDI)	−.1070**	−.0062	.1328*	.0059
	(.0713)		(.0511)	
Industry R&D past change (Z)	.5052**	.0021	−.0213	−.0001
	(.2713)		(.0876)	
Firm's Relative R&D (CRDP)	−.1391**	.0019	.0884	−.0001
	(.0838)		(.0846)	
Actual Minus Predicted Profit (IPROF)	.0103*	.0001	−.0013	0
	(.0010)		(.0087)	
	df = 639		df = 269	

Regression Analysis—Controlling for SIC

	Positive Disposition Coefficient	Economic Effect	Negative Disposition Coefficient	Economic Effect
Industry R&D (IRDI)	−.5591*	−.0325	−.2525	−.0113
	(.3424)		(.3822)	
Industry R&D past change (Z)	.2165	.0009	−.0621	−.0003
	(.2817)		(.2782)	
Firm's Relative R&D (CRDP)	−.1730*	.0024	.8000**	−.0001
	(.0168)		(.2424)	
Actual Minus Predicted Profit (IPROF)	.0096*	.0001	−.0022	0
	(.0033)		(.0070)	
	df = 605		df = 258	

* denotes significance at the 5 percent level
** denotes significance at the 10 percent level

OLS estimates for coefficient standard errors because the Chi-square test is insignificant.

The upper panel reveals that control firms in industries that experience a negative Section 337 ruling seem on average to have increased their R&D spending more than those that experience a positive Section 337 ruling. The former increase their R&D spending by .46 cents per dollar of total assets while the latter increase by only .18 cents. Moreover, the latter group seems to have reduced its rate of increase in R&D spending, as suggested by a comparison of the first and the third rows.

The most interesting observation from the regression results is that a positive Section 337 ruling appears to reduce the intensity of R&D patent races and to compress differences in R&D spending between industry leaders and followers. On the other hand, a negative Section 337 ruling may have intensified R&D patent races, stimulating R&D leaders to increase their R&D intensity while reducing the R&D intensity of followers.

That interpretation is suggested by the regression coefficients for CRDP, which is the difference between a firm's R&D intensity and the industry average intensity. In the case of firms in industries facing a positive Section 337 ruling, the coefficient is negative and significant, both in the regressions with and without industry dummies (middle and bottom panel). The result means that industry leaders in R&D spending will decrease their R&D intensity while followers will do the opposite. Notice also that the coefficient for IRDI is negative and significant. Thus, in the case of industries facing a positive Section 337 ruling, the higher the past industry R&D intensity, the lower the current change in firm-level R&D intensity. The economic magnitude of the dampening effect, as captured by the estimated regression coefficient times the average value of the independent variable, appears to be an important part of the firms' R&D response.

In the case of industries facing a negative Section 337 ruling, the coefficient for CRDP is positive but insignificant in the regression without industry dummies. When industry dummies are introduced, the coefficient remains positive and becomes significant. This represents a weak sign that a negative Section 337 ruling may have invigorated R&D intensity, in the sense that leaders in R&D spending will further increase their R&D intensity while followers do the opposite. The regression coefficient for the past industry R&D intensity variable (IRDI) is positive and significant in the regression with no industry dummies. It becomes negative and quite insignificant when industry dummies are introduced. Whether the firm level R&D response is greater in industries with greater R&D intensity is therefore unclear. This mixed result also is evident from the economic effects reported in the final column; in the middle panel, the effect is 0.0058

(= 0.0059 – 0.0001), while in the bottom panel it is –0.0114 (= –0.0113 – 0.0001).

One possible interpretation of these results is that Section 337 does not affect firm R&D spending via the appropriation effect. That is, a positive Section 337 ruling may not be perceived as adding much to a firm's ability to earn higher profits from future innovation, and therefore it may stimulate R&D spending very little. Instead, Section 337 may have an important effect on the current profitability of intellectual properties late in their product life cycle, and a stronger pattern of enforcement may be important in prolonging the life of these existing innovations.

To verify more explicitly how Section 337 rulings affect marginal choices to expand R&D spending, we pooled the two groups of control firms and re-ran the regression by introducing cross terms formed from the independent variables and a dummy indicating a positive Section 337 ruling. If the cross terms are significantly different from zero, the Section 337 outcome appears to explain part of the firm's R&D response. The results are reported in table 3. The cross-terms are reported in the left columns and the base case coefficients for firms in industries that face a negative Section 337 ruling are reported in the right columns. Results from the regression without industry dummies are reported in the first panel and those from the regression with industry dummies are reported in the second panel. The standard errors in the top panel are heteroskedastic-consistent estimates. In the bottom panel, the standard errors are OLS.

The cross-terms for IRDI and CRDP are negative and significant in the top panel while the base case coefficients are positive. The magnitude of the cross-term coefficients is greater than the respective base case coefficients. The results confirm the pattern observed in the regressions for the two separate groups: a positive Section 337 ruling will result in a smaller R&D response by firms in industries that are more R&D intensive (the negative IRDI coefficient) and by firms that are industry leaders in R&D performance (the negative CRDP coefficient). A sharper distinction appears in the bottom-panel, where we find that the CRDP variable is positive and significant while the cross term is negative and significant. Again, the magnitude of the cross-term coefficients is greater than the base case coefficients. Thus, in industries facing a positive Section 337 decision, R&D leaders appear to decrease their R&D intensity while followers increase theirs. In industries facing a negative decision, the opposite is true.

Robustness

We attempt to check the robustness of our results, particularly those reported in tables 2 and 3. We are concerned that our results may be

TABLE 3.   Analysis of R&D Responses by Control Firms, Pooled Data Regression Analysis

	Positive Disposition Coefficient	Economic Effect	Negative Disposition Coefficient	Economic Effect
Intercept		.0023	.0023*	.0023
			(.0012)	
Industry R&D (IRDI)	–.1495*	–.0049	.0658**	.0029
	(.0558)		(.0419)	
Industry R&D past change (Z)	.4704**	.0014	.0039	0
	(.2732)		(.0890)	
Firm's Relative R&D (CRDP)	–.2381*	.0019	.0994	–.0001
	(.1208)		(.0843)	
Actual Minus Predicted Profit	.0113	.0001	–.0010	0
(IPROF)	(.0142)		(.0089)	
		df=909		

Analysis of R&D Responses by Control Firms Regression Analysis—Controlling for SIC

	Positive Disposition Coefficient	Economic Effect	Negative Disposition Coefficient	Economic Effect
Industry R&D (IRDI)	–.0309		–.5362	
	(.0527)		(.1959)	
Industry R&D past change (Z)	.3909		–.0880	
	(.3606)		(.2810)	
Firm's Relative R&D (CRDP)	–.2454*		.0735**	
	(.0481)		(.0452)	
Actual Minus Predicted Profit	.0125		–.0028	
(IPROF)	(.0082)		(.0075)	
		df = 884		

* denotes significance at the 5 percent level
** denotes significance at the 10 percent level

affected by macroeconomic effects. If R&D spending is influenced by cyclical or secular macroeconomic factors, and if dispositions of Section 337 rulings vary systematically over time, our results may be spurious. For example, we are concerned that more negative rulings might occur later in the period and coincide with a secular decline in R&D effort entirely unrelated to Section 337. To test this possibility, we first examine whether there is any time pattern in the Section 337 dispositions in our sample; the null hypothesis of no variation over time cannot be rejected. We also re-estimate our results in the following way. We first regress all variables onto a set of year by year dummies. We then reestimate our behavioral models using the residuals from the time-dummy regressions. The procedure should filter out any time trend factors that are invariant across industries. The results obtained are very similar to those reported, and the significance level of the coefficient estimates even rises slightly.

Collinearity among the independent variables may affect our results. Examination of the correlation matrix for our set of variables suggests that one possible way to reduce collinearity would be to omit the past industry R&D intensity variable (IRDI). Doing so does not alter the importance of the competitive-position effect.

The significance of our results in table 3 may be attributable to the larger sample size available. As Leamer (1978) indicates, classical t-tests are more likely to indicate regression coefficients are significant when samples are large. Indeed, table 1 based on the small sample of filing firms gives much less precise estimates than table 2 based on the large sample of control firms.

We address this possibility in two ways. First, Leamer (1978, 114) suggests a sample-size-adjusted measure of the relevant F-statistic to test whether a coefficient differs significantly from zero.[7] Making that adjustment still shows that the R&D-patent-race effects of Section 337 rulings are statistically significant. Second, we repeat our regression analysis by choosing randomly 30 percent of the firms in the pooled control firm group and estimate the same regressions for this smaller sample, focusing particularly on the results reported in table 3. In thirteen of twenty cases we find that the crossterm for CRDP is negative and significant. The probability of observing such results is 6.6×10^{-13} if the null hypothesis that the coefficient is zero actually is true and if the coefficients of the crossterms obtained are independent of one another. Our results do not appear to be attributable simply to sample size.

Another way to check the robustness of our results is to introduce additional observations from later years. We originally use only cases filed between 1976 and 1988 to avoid cases after the 1988 change in legislation. On incorporating an additional two years, the results for industries facing positive dispositions are not changed. But, the results for the industries facing negative Section 337 decisions become less significant. There are several possible interpretations. First, the suggestion above that negative Section 337 decisions reinvigorate the R&D patent race may not be robust. Second, there is a detectable general decline in R&D spending in our sample after 1988. If the decline is more extensive for R&D-intensive industries and for R&D leaders, it will strengthen the regression results reported for the industries facing positive Section 337 rulings but will weaken the results reported for industries facing negative Section 337 rulings. Third, the legislative change in 1988 may have altered the stimulative effect on R&D of a negative Section 337 decision.

We are puzzled by the finding that a negative Section 337 disposition seems to reinvigorate the R&D patent race while a positive disposition reduces the intensity of the R&D patent race. A possible interpretation of this result is that it arises from the offsetting influence of the appropriation effect and the cost-benefit effect. That is, stronger enforcement of property rights will increase the perceived appropriability of successful innovation, but such a property rights regime may make other innovation more costly and less profitable. The result suggests that in positive disposition cases, the positive appropriation effect is overwhelmed by the negative cost-benefit effect (further innovation is made more costly and less profitable). On the other hand, in the negative disposition cases, the negative appropriation effect is overwhelmed by the positive cost-benefit effect (further innovation is made less costly and more profitable). If this interpretation is correct, we would expect our results to differ if we partitioned our sample into two groups, one composed of industries where the ability to appropriate the benefits from innovation is more dependent on patent protection, and one where industries rely on other strategies to gain the benefits from innovation.

Levin et al. (1987) present survey evidence from 650 high-level R&D managers representing 130 different lines of business who rank the importance of patent protection in determining the appropriability of R&D results. Industries in our sample that report an above-average importance of patent protection are inorganic chemicals, organic chemicals, pharmaceuticals, plastic materials and products, semiconductors, auto parts and medical equipment. We refer to this group as L1 and the group composed of our remaining industries as L0. We expect that in the L1 group the magnitude of the appropriation effect will be stronger than in L0 industries. That is, a positive disposition in L1 industries will lead to a stronger positive appropriation effect than in L0 industries. On the other hand, a negative disposition in L1 industries will lead to a stronger negative appropriation effect than in L0 industries. Thus, in the case of positive rulings, the regression coefficient for CRDP will be greater in L1 industries than in L0 industries, while the opposite is true in the case of negative rulings.

That speculation is borne out. In the positive cases, while the coefficient of the CRDP variable still is negative, the coefficient is smaller in magnitude in the L1 industries, suggesting that the positive appropriation effect is stronger in L1 industries. In the negative cases, the CRDP coefficient still is positive in L0 industries, but it is negative in L1 industries, suggesting that the appropriation effect dominates the offsetting cost change effects. The latter difference is statistically significant at the 10 percent level.

In summary, our analysis suggests that a Section 337 ruling indeed alters the intensity of the R&D patent race among firms in the affected industry. In particular, a positive Section 337 ruling appears to dampen the intensity of an R&D patent race and to induce R&D spending leaders to cut back their R&D intensity while R&D spending followers may do the opposite. We find somewhat weaker evidence that a negative Section 337 ruling may invigorate a R&D patent race. Tests for the robustness of these results suggests that inferences drawn from the positive case outcomes are fairly reliable but those from the negative case outcomes are less so. A possible explanation for the lack of precision in the negative case results is suggested by partitioning the firms into one group where patents are an important form of intellectual property protection and another group where other strategies are relied upon to provide protection. In the former group the appropriation effect appears to dominate the cost-benefit effect, while in the latter group the reverse is true; if all firms are considered together, these offsetting factors yield no predictable relationship.

Conclusion

Section 337 has an uncertain and uneven influence on firm R&D spending, both for filing firms and peers in the same industry. We cannot identify empirically each of the separate influences that are relevant on theoretical grounds, and instead we must use a reduced form equation that only allows us to infer indirectly the determinants of firm R&D responses. Some of our results are counterintuitive. For instance, a Section 337 ruling does not have a predictable effect on the R&D spending of the filing firm, which we might expect to be most directly affected. Among control firms a positive ruling does not appear to cause the efforts of R&D leaders (who have a revealed comparative advantage in R&D) to expand more than for followers; rather the opposite pattern is observed. This reduced intensity of R&D efforts raises more general questions over the justification for Section 337 from the perspective of national and world welfare. Does Section 337 promote new innovation or does is provide an opportunity to keep foreign competition at bay and to promote domestic collusion?

The absence of an R&D response may be due to the aggregation of dissimilar firms and products under the same SIC heading declared by the parent firm, or the affected product may be too small a share of the firm's total activity to influence its overall R&D program. Nevertheless, those aggregation problems were not so severe in our prior analysis to prevent us from observing a clear link between Section 337 rulings and profitability. Thus, Section 337 indeed may be important in protecting existing innovations, but the potential effect of Section 337 rulings on the costs and future profitability of additional innovation appears to have little influence on the marginal valuation of ongoing R&D efforts.

NOTES

1. The GATT panel decision did not evaluate whether in a particular case (or cases) U.S. procedures applicable in the ITC and Federal District Court actually imposed a heavier burden on imports accused of infringement than would be faced by domestic infringers. Rather, the ruling was based on the possibility that imports could be treated less favorably given the different legal provisions available.

2. Mutti and Yeung (1996) find that a positive Section 337 ruling tends to reduce the profits of peer firms in importing industries but has no predictable impact on the net profits of peer firms in exporting industries.

3. Spence (1984) finds that an increase in the utilization of a firm's R&D by competitors reduces its incentive to invest in R&D. One would expect that an increase in property rights protection reduces this possibility and thus increases a firm's incentive to invest in R&D.

4. One reasonable alternative to capture an industry's R&D intensity is to include in the size-weighted industry average R&D/Assets only firms which incur positive R&D spending. Both alternatives generate similar results.

5. 5 Additional inferences that can be drawn from table 1 are consistent with findings reported in Mutti and Yeung (1996): filing firms on average spend more on R&D (row 4) and in the case of a negative decision filing firms suffer unexpectedly large losses (row 5).

6. The 25 percent is obtained as .0004/.0017, the value from the fourth row in the right middle panel divided by the value from the first row in the right top panel. The 50 percent is obtained as .0008/.0017, the fourth row in the right bottom panel over the first row in the right top panel.

7. Leamer's adjustment requires that the F statistic exceed the expression $[(T - k)/p] \times [T^{p/T} - 1]$, where T is the number of observations, k the number of coefficients estimated and p the number of restrictions tested. Based on this measure, coefficient estimates reported in Table 3 should exceed a critical value of 2.60 rather than 1.96 to indicate statistical significance at the 5 percent probability level. The t-statistic of the competitive-position cross term far exceeds this threshhold.

REFERENCES

Aoki, Reiko. 1991. "R&D Competition for Product Innovation: An Endless Race." *American Economic Review* 81:252–256.

Beath, John; Katsoulacos, Yannis; and Ulph, David. 1989. "Strategic R&D Policy." *Economic Journal* 99:74–83.

Beath, John; Katsoulacos, Yannis; and Ulph, David. 1989. "The Game-Theoretic

Analysis of Innovation: a Survey." *Bulletin of Economic Research* 41:163–184.

Crandall, Robert W. 1987. "The Effects of U.S. Trade Protection for Autos and Steel." *Brookings Papers on Economic Activity* 1:272–288.

Grossman, Gene M., and Shapiro, Carl. 1987. "Dynamic R&D Competition." *Economic Journal* 97:372–387.

Hall, Bronwyn. 1992. "Investment and Research and Development at the Firm Level: Does the Source of Financing matter?" NBER working paper 4096.

Isaac, R. Mark, and Reynolds, Stanley S. 1988. "Appropriability and Market Structure in a Stochastic Invention Model." *Quarterly Journal of Economics* 103:647–671.

Leamer, Edward. 1978. *Specification Searches, Ad Hoc Inference with Nonexperimental Data.* New York: John Wiley and Sons.

Lee, Tom K., and Wilde, Louis L. 1980. "Market Structure and Innovation: A Reformulation." *Quarterly Journal of Economics* 94:429–36.

Lenway, Stephanie; Morck, Randall; and Yeung, Bernard. 1996. "Rent Seeking and Protectionism in the American Steel Industry: An Empirical Analysis." *Economic Journal* 106:410–421.

Levin, Richard C. 1988. "Appropriability, R&D Spending, and Technological Performance." *American Economic Review* 78:424–428.

Levin, Richard C.; Klevorick, Alvin; Nelson, R.; and Winter, S. 1987. "Appropriating the Returns from Industrial Research and Development." *Brookings Paper on Economic Activity: Special Issue on Microeconomies* 3:783–821.

Mutti, John, and Yeung, Bernard. 1996. "Section 337 and the Protection of Intellectual Property in the United States: The Complainants and the Impact." *Review of Economics and Statistics* 78:510–20.

Park, J. 1987. "Dynamic Patent Races with Risky Choices." *Management Science* 33:1563–1571.

Prusa, Thomas. 1992. "Why Are So Many Antidumping Petitions Withdrawn?" *Journal of International Economics* 33:1–20.

Spence, A. Michael. 1984. "Cost Reduction, Competition and Industry Performance." *Econometrica* 52:101–21.

White, Hal. 1980. "A Heteroskedasticity-consistent Covariance Matrix Estimator and a Direct Test for Heteroskedasticity." *Econometrica* 48:817–838.

CHAPTER 5

Patents and International Trade: An Empirical Study

Keith E. Maskus and Mohan Penubarti

International disputes over patent rights are now common.[1] The United States employs a special provision in the Omnibus Trade Act of 1988 to attack the problem of weak foreign protection for U.S. products and technologies. This approach has top priority for undertaking bilateral negotiations and potential trade retaliation. The European Union has struggled with its efforts to harmonize patent laws as part of the establishment of the unified market in 1993. Numerous developing economies have undertaken significant reforms in their patent regimes since 1986, not only because of foreign pressure but also because of the belief that foreign firms interested in investing in those countries would be impressed by the changes. Patents, and intellectual property rights (IPRs) more generally, were a major issue in the negotiations covering NAFTA and the Uruguay Round.

It is important to study the linkages between trade and patents. Patent protection directly affects growth through incentives for innovation. Returns to innovation could be influenced by differences in international patent laws through affecting decisions of firms to trade with, or invest in, different markets. In turn, the international structure of patent laws could be an additional factor in the relationship between trade and growth (Grossman and Helpman 1991; Segerstrom et al. 1990).

Despite the practical and conceptual importance of this issue, there is virtually no evidence on international patent protection as a determinant of trade. In the context of the Uruguay Round, this was particularly odd since the issue perforce was framed rather narrowly, at least in principle. Specifically, the GATT could be used for the negotiation of patent standards and policy disciplines only to the extent that different patent regimes tended to distort trade flows. Simply put, the GATT is relevant only if IPRs are "trade-related".

In this study we provide systematic evidence as to whether different patent laws affect bilateral trade flows. We consider only the positive ques-

95

tion of how the importing country's patents help determine the international distribution of bilateral trade. In this sense, the approach is a small part of the larger normative questions concerning patents, trade, and growth. For example, we cannot calculate the effects of differing patent laws on profits and the inducements to innovation and growth. However, these partial results should help us understand the sensitivity of trade decisions to patents. If there are significant impacts at this level, pursuing additional specifications in the broader sense will be important.

The spirit of our analysis is in keeping with much of Bob Stern's career-long approach of applying empirical methods to thorny economic problems in international trade. It is appropriate in some contexts to think of varying levels of protection for IPRs as a mixed set of nontariff barriers to trade, calling for careful measurement of their impacts, as Stern has done in other settings.

We begin in the next section by specifying a simple model in which a dominant exporting firm competes with a fringe industry in a particular market. The fringe industry is capable of imitating the dominant firm's production process and producing competing goods. A marginal change in patent laws is considered, which operates through costs of both the firm and the fringe industry. The model shows that the optimal response of such a firm could be either to increase or decrease its exports to that country because of the tradeoff between enhanced market power and greater market size. For instance, if a country engineers a marginal strengthening of its patent law, thereby raising imitation costs, the dominant exporting firm now faces a steeper demand curve and an enhanced market power. Therefore, it operates more monopolistically, exporting less to the local market. But the demand curve is also higher, inducing the dominant firm to supply more exports to the local market. This ambiguous response holds also in a wide range of imperfectly competitive market structures. Thus, the impact of patent laws on trade is an empirical issue.

Accordingly, in the third section we develop an econometric model of bilateral trade flows. The model is based on a reduced-form version of the Helpman-Krugman gross exports equations extended by variables measuring preferences, trade distortions, and patent protection in importers. In the fourth section, estimates are presented that strongly indicate that different patent laws influence trade. Within the group of large developing economies, with which most of the trade disputes over IPRs have come, stronger patent laws attract significantly larger-than-expected flows of exports from the OECD economies. This is also true in the small developing economies in our data set, though the effect is somewhat weaker. Thus, patents are indeed "trade-related," a finding on which we make further remarks in the final section. However, the calculated impacts on actual trade volumes are relatively small.

A Model of Trade Under Localized Patent Protection

Consider the problem of identifying the impacts of patent laws on the level of international trade. This is a difficult problem empirically for numerous reasons (Maskus 1990) . First, the strength of patents will be embedded in the prices at which goods are traded and it is impossible to separate these price effects from other components of pricing behavior. Second, decisions by firms owning a new product or process to export to a particular market are codetermined with decisions to service markets through licensing or foreign direct investment (FDI; see, for example, Horstmann and Markusen 1987). Third, the essence of patents is to create market power in the distribution of new goods and technologies, implying that there will be some flexibility in the choice of market structure for analysis. Fourth, there is an important dynamic element to trade if firms find that exporting to economies with strong patent laws raises their global profits and induces additional R&D efforts. Thus, it would be difficult to specify a satisfactory counterfactual experiment in which global harmonization of patents would be expected to raise or lower trade in a computable manner.

By placing structure on the problem, however, it is possible to assess the effects of marginal changes in international patent laws on current decisions to export. Patent laws vary markedly across countries in terms of length and breadth of coverage, products that are excluded from patentability, and provisions for issuing compulsory licenses. Moreover, enforcement of existing laws differs widely.[2] Thus, a firm making export decisions across different markets faces an array of effective levels of patent protection. If the firm takes this array into account, trade will be "distorted" in the sense that policy parameters will influence its international distribution. Note that this is an unusual definition of "distortion" in that there is no clear standard for defining global optimality against which to assess the trade impacts.

For a model to be useful in this context, it must capture a number of relevant market characteristics. First, low levels of patent protection do not generally deprive innovative firms completely of market power because the act of imitation by local firms is costly. On the other hand, strong patent laws do not generally create a full monopoly on a new product, either because enforcement against infringement may be limited or because legitimate substitute products are likely to be on the market.[3] In this context, a model with a dominant foreign firm facing a local competitive fringe is appealing, as has been argued elsewhere (Feinberg and Rous-slang 1990; Maskus 1990). Second, exporting firms should be able to distinguish among potential markets with varying patent regimes in terms of profit-maximizing trade levels. Such markets would be distinguished by size of the economy and the competitiveness of the local imitating sector. Also important would be differences across countries in traditional trade barriers to the product in question. In order to allow separate pricing decisions in each market, it is convenient to assume that sufficiently high trade barriers or transport costs exist for effective market segmentation, allowing the exporting firm to price-discriminate.

Small Importing Country

A simple, partial-equilibrium model that works well in this context is presented in figure 1.[4] The first panel depicts the market in a small importing country with limited capacity for local imitation. The country is "small" in the sense that the dominant firm is willing to export the good to it at a constant marginal cost of $c_0 + t$, where t is a specific tariff imposed by the importer. More specifically, the market is so small that the dominant firm does not choose to undertake any particular efforts to disguise, or mask, its product's characteristics in order to deter local imitators, as it might do in larger markets (see below). The most appropriate interpretation of c_0 is that it represents the world price of this good as charged by the dominant exporter.

Total demand in this market is given by D, with associated marginal revenue MR . There is a local competitive fringe industry with a positively sloped supply curve (not shown) emanating from point α. The intercept α indicates the ability of the local sector to imitate a new product or adapt a new technology to its own production. The higher is α the less is this ability, which depends, *inter alia,* on local endowments of skills and the technical specifications of the product or process. In figure 1a, the country is assumed to incur relatively high costs in imitation (specifically, $a >$ $c_0 + t$), reflecting a scarcity of imitative skills. We assume that, *ceteris paribus,* α rises as patent laws become stronger. Once the product or process has been imitated, it can be produced or used by the competitive fringe along a supply curve with slope β. This parameter reflects rising marginal costs, part of which occur to avoid detection by the patent authorities. We assume that stronger and better-enforced local patent laws raise b as well.

By virtue of imitation, the supply of the fringe industry may be considered infringement, to which the dominant firm must respond. In figure 1a, the dominant firm faces the residual demand curve D_F and associated marginal revenue MR_F, against which it maximizes profits. Thus, in the initial situation, the firm chooses to export Q_F units of the good to this market rather than the monopolistic level Q_M. Thus, the effect of weak patent laws in small countries is to establish local competition that induces the foreign firm to export a greater quantity and charge a lower domestic price than it would under full patent protection.

Now suppose that this country engineers a marginal strengthening in its patent law (alternatively, imagine a second importing country with identical characteristics except that it has a somewhat stronger patent law). The effect of this change is to raise α (higher imitation costs)[5] or β or both. Suppose β rises for a given α. Then the new residual demand curve (not shown) will be steeper than D_F, leading to a steeper MR curve that cuts $c_0 + t$ between points M and F. Accordingly, the dominant firm chooses to export *less* to the market with stronger patents, an effect that works monotonically as β rises to infinity.[6] By virtue of stronger and better-enforced patents, the dominant firm finds its market power enhanced and it operates more monopolistically, so long as α exceeds $c_0 + t$.

Now suppose α rises for a given β. This results in a parallel upward shift in the residual demand curve, expanding the market for the dominant firm. In figure 1a, line D_S indicates this larger residual demand, which, in this case, induces the dominant firm to supply more exports to the local market. Note that this effect relies on the absence of a kink in the MR_S schedule near point S. Clearly, as α increases and D_S shifts up the market reverts increasingly to monopoly control by the dominant firm as there will be a kink in the MR curve below the intersection of the residual demand curve and the total demand curve. Thus, there is only an *initial* expansion of exports before the monopolist begins to cut trade and this may not happen at all if α is high. In general, the impact is ambiguous, depending on relative shifts in α and β. It may well be, however, that in low-income developing countries, with limited and high-cost imitative capacity, foreign firms may choose to act markedly more monopolistically in the event of stronger domestic patents.

Two final observations are in order from figure 1a. First, because trade barriers will affect the monopolist's trade decisions, it is important to incorporate them into any empirical exercise of this sort. In the diagram, a relatively low tariff on this product ensures that a exceeds the marginal cost of exporting, $c_0 + t$. So long as the market operates to the southeast of point H , the size of the tariff will not change the direction of impacts of stronger patents. However, if the tariff is high enough to shift equilibria into the region northwest of point H, a stronger patent law would induce *greater* exports into the market. Thus, the impact of patent laws is not independent of the trade regime itself. Note that the form of the trade bar-

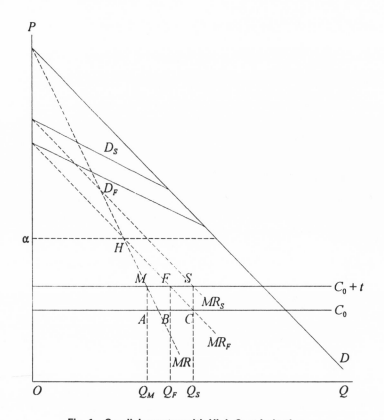

Fig. 1a. Small Importer with High-Cost Imitation

rier is also important. For example, to the southeast of point H if a quota limits imports to the initial tariff-equivalent level Q_F, the dominant firm could cut imports if desired but could not raise them, eliminating the potential market-expansion effect.

Second, and key for the ensuing empirical analysis, it is important to assess the impacts of stronger patents on the *value* of exports, since this is the variable on which data most readily exist. Because the predicted effect on quantity is uncertain, it is not clear what would happen to the value of exports at domestic prices.[7] In any event, international trade valued at internal prices is difficult to measure. Rather, we focus on the value of exports at *world* price, or c_0 in figure 1a. Clearly, because this price is fixed, if the market-power effect dominates the value of trade will fall.

Consider a brief formalization of this model in linear terms. Let total

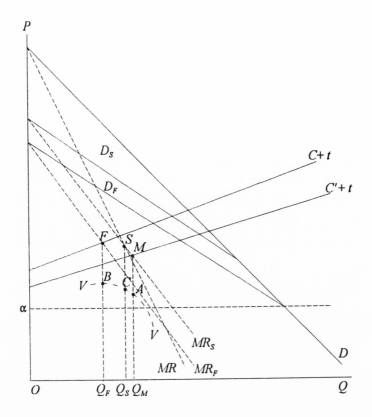

Fig. 1b. Large Importer with Low-Cost Imitation

demand be given by $P = a - bQ$ and infringing supply by $P = \alpha + \beta Q_D$, where Q_D is domestic output. Then the dominant firm faces a residual demand curve given by $P = \gamma - \theta Q_F$, where $\gamma = (\beta a + ab) / (\beta + b)$ and $q = b\beta / (\beta + b)$. The firm maximizes profits given by

$$\pi = \gamma Q_F - \theta Q_F^2 - (c_0 + t) Q_F \tag{1}$$

First-order conditions for this problem may be solved to yield:

$$Q_F = [\beta a + \alpha b - (\beta + b)(c_0 + t)]/2\beta b \tag{2}$$

In the model, α and β are rising functions of some variable I, which indexes the strength of the patent laws and enforcement. Thus, we can take the total derivatives of (2) and (3) to find the effects of changing I on the dominant firm's exports and local price:

$$P_F = [\,\beta a + \alpha b - (\beta + b)(c_0 + t)\,]/2(\beta + b) \tag{4}$$

where the prime indicates a derivative with respect to I. The impact on quantity of exports is ambiguous, with the first term indicating the positive market-expansion

$$dQ_F/dI = \alpha'/2\beta - \beta'[\,\alpha - (c_0 + t)\,]/2\beta^2 \tag{5}$$

effect and the second term the negative (if $a > c_0 + t$) market-power effect. The impact on price is unambiguously positive, because a is required to exceed α for there to be any infringing industry in the first place. As suggested earlier, a sufficient rise in the tariff could reverse the quantity effects of stronger patent protection.

Large Importing Country

The situation is more complicated when the importing country is large enough to affect the dominant firm's costs, as depicted in panel 1b. Here, the importer is large in two senses. First, and traditionally, the dominant firm experiences a rising marginal cost of supplying this market because it is a perceptible proportion of the firm's global sales. We assume that a change in patent laws does not affect the slope of the MC curve on this account alone. Second, the local imitating fringe industry has a strong imitative capacity, reflected in a low value for a (specifically, $a < c + t$ in the relevant range), and presents a genuine competitive threat. Thus, the dominant firm may expend resources in making the product or technology harder to imitate. Examples include the copy protection of software, the use of special materials, and the employment of local services to deter imitation through private enforcement of intellectual property rights.[8] It may be reasonable to suppose that this task both shifts the marginal cost curve of exporting up and increases its slope. The shift in the curve would represent how much the firm believes the initial unit of exports needs to be protected in order to safeguard proprietary information. In that sense it would reflect a "country-specific" need to disguise the technical basis of the product. The rise in the slope, or addition to marginal costs as more is sold, would reflect the possibility that greater presence of the foreign product in the domestic market could make it easier to imitate. Thus, there may be a need for rising private enforcement expenditures as exports expand. In turn, a strengthening of local patent laws would shift the marginal cost curve down and/or reduce its slope. As before, it would also shift up the infringing supply curve and/or make it steeper.

These ideas are depicted in figure 1b. The provision of complete patent protection would shift the dominant firm's marginal cost curve down from $c + t$ to $c' + t$. Because α is less than marginal costs plus tariff, the initial, cum- infringement equilibrium at F involves lower imports than would the monopolistic outcome at M. However, the monopoly level of sales is also larger due to the reduction in costs the dominant firm experiences from a fully protective patent law. Tracing through the effects of a marginal strengthening of patents, consider first a rise in β for a given α. The new marginal revenue curve (not shown) would hit some intermediate $c + t$ curve in the region bounded by point F and M. Thus, imports would expand and domestic price would rise. On the other hand, a rise in α for a given β would shift out the MR curve to MR_S, inducing an expansion of imports to level Q_S, which could be larger or smaller than the monopoly level, so long as there is no kink in MR_S in the relevant region. Thus, the level of trade could rise monotonically toward the monopoly level or it could rise and then fall. It depends on the relative shifts in α and β, plus the induced changes in marginal costs for the dominant firm. In fact, the latter impact could make the prediction for domestic price ambiguous for marginal changes in patent laws.

Again, we note the importance of trade barriers in determining these effects. Here, if the tariff is sufficiently low that α exceeds marginal exporting costs, a stronger patent law would be more likely to restrict the quantity of imports.

Finally, note the implications for the value of imports at *world* prices, which now vary with the patent law. The locations at which marginal cost curves, exclusive of tariffs, intersect the vertical lines below points F, S, and M (see points B, C, and A) would indicate the associated prices.[9] Thus, to determine whether the value of imports rises or falls, we would need to know the elasticity of the curve VV. Analytical solutions to this problem have signs that depend on relationships among various parameters, rendering this an empirical problem. Basically, curve VV is more elastic the more marginal costs of the dominant firm are reduced by stronger patents and the greater the rise in α relative to the rise in β.

To get a flavor for the analytical ambiguity, consider the formal economic problem. In this case the dominant firm needs to maximize the following profit function:

$$\pi = \gamma Q_F - \theta Q_F^2 - \int_0^{Q_F} (c_0 + \sigma Q_F + t) \, dQ_F \tag{6}$$

where σ is the slope of the marginal cost curve. The first-order conditions from this problem may be solved to yield:

$$Q_F = (\gamma - c_0 - t)/(2\theta + \sigma) \tag{7}$$

$$P_F = [\gamma\theta + \theta\sigma + \theta(c_0 + t)]/(2\theta + \sigma) \tag{8}$$

The total derivatives of these expressions with respect to a change in patents (I) are complicated, nonlinear equations that cannot generally be signed.

This indeterminacy in the effects of patents on trade flows exists in a wide range of imperfectly competitive, static market structures beyond the simple Stackelberg model presented here. For example, it carries over in Cournot duopoly models with identical goods (Maskus and Eby-Konan 1994; Taylor 1993). Moreover, if we think of patents as product-specific tariffs in a monopolistic competition model there are few unambiguous predictions about their effects on trade (Flam and Helpman 1987; Brown 1991).

An Empirical Model of Trade Under Patents and Trade Distortions

These simple models have demonstrated that no clear prediction may be made in static models about the direction of trade that may emerge in a world of varying patent regimes. Much depends on local cost conditions and the reactions of foreign firms, which are necessarily imperfectly competitive if they receive patent protection or have some other form of cost or information advantage. Thus, a clear picture can emerge only from empirical work. In this paper we opt for an econometric approach to this question based on actual trade flows.

Our model has established that bilateral imports by industry depend on characteristics of residual demand in the importing country, the marginal cost structure of the dominant (exporting) firm, trade distortions, and the strength of patents. However, it is not generally possible for available data to identify such market parameters as marginal export costs and marginal costs from either avoiding detection or enforcing property rights against infringement. Thus, a direct approach is impractical.

A Reduced-Form Approach

A suitable alternative approach is to rely on an augmented version of the Helpman-Krugman (1985) gross exports equation. As recently discussed by Harrigan (1993), the model may be used as a basis for a flexible examination of bilateral trade flows. It is important to estimate trade equations that follow from a general-equilibrium theory, for failure to embed the relevant patent and tariff effects in such a model makes interpreting coefficients ad hoc and questionable.[10]

In this approach, the estimated equations are reduced–form expressions. The model predicts that under free trade, bilateral exports are proportional to the exporting country's sectoral outputs, where the factor of proportionality is the exporting country's share in global expenditure. These variables are jointly endogenous and a regression of exports on exporter outputs is invalid. However, even in the absence of factor price equalization, the HK theory suggests that there will be a strong correlation between exporter output patterns and factor endowments. Accordingly, exporter endowments serve well as instruments for output levels in explaining bilateral exports.

The HK model assumes strongly that tastes are identical and homothetic, implying that each nation imports a proportion of every product that equals its proportion in world GNP. This assumption is false, which mandates allowing for unequal expenditure shares by sector across importers. We accomplish this in three ways. First, we estimate constant terms for each product across countries, allowing for "home market preference" (Harrigan 1993) plus intercept terms for large and small developing-country importers. Second, we add importer per capita GNP to the trade equations, taking it to be exogenous to sectoral imports. Third, we include interaction terms between our measures of patent strength and the market-size dummy variables.

We consider trade barriers to be exogenous and place them directly into the reduced-form exports equation. Two measures of trade restrictions are employed: the average tariff rate and the black-market exchange premium for each importing nation. However, the index of patent strength we use is subject to measurement error and potential endogeneity. Thus, we develop a first-stage instrumental variables equation to correct the international measure of patent laws.

Collecting these ideas, the reduced-form econometric model is specified as follows.

$$\log (x_{ijk}) = \gamma_i + \gamma_{is}D_S + \gamma_{iL}D_L + \gamma_{iQ}\log (Q_{ik}^{*}) + \gamma_{iY}\log (Y_j) + \gamma_{it}\log (1+t_j)$$
$$+ \gamma_{ib}\log (1+b_j) + \gamma_{iI}I_j^{*} + \gamma_{iIS}I_j^{*}D_S + \gamma_{iIL}I_j^{*}D_L + u_{ijk} \, . \tag{9}$$

Here, x_{ijk} is bilateral sectoral exports in sector i to country j, divided by aggregate expenditure in the importer j. Q_{ik}^{*} is sectoral exporter output predicted from the first-stage endowments equations and Y_j is importer per-capita income. The variables t_j and b_j are trade-distortions (tariff revenues as a proportion of dutiable imports and percentage black-market premia, respectively) in the importing country and I^*_j is the IV-corrected index of patent strength by importing country. Asterisks denote predicted variables from the first-stage estimation.

Data Sources and Construction of Variables

Equations (9) are estimated for each of the several manufacturing sectors across a set of countries using 1984 data. Data on sectoral trade and output are taken from the OECD's Compatible Trade and Production (COMTAP) data base. The data base, organized by the three-digit ISIC classification, includes outputs in OECD nations plus bilateral trade of the OECD countries among themselves and with most countries in the rest of the world. Thus, trade and output figures are consistent, which is a difficult task using data from other published sources (Maskus 1991). Exporters in our model must be limited to the 22 OECD member countries because of limitations in output data. Note, however, that the OECD countries may be expected to provide the overwhelming share of exporters in goods subject to patent protection.

Data on factor endowments and outputs in 1984 were assembled for the OECD nations plus another 25 developing countries, with outputs for the latter nations taken from United Nations, *Industrial Statistics Yearbook, Volume II.* Five factor endowments are included in the output equations. The first is a measure of the real net national capital stock in millions of US dollars. Investment deflators were taken from Summers and Heston (1988) and capital formation and exchange rates were from the *International Financial Statistics* of the International Monetary Fund. The second and third endowments are the skilled and unskilled labor forces in thousands, as reported in the *Yearbook of Labour Statistics* of the International Labour Organization. Skilled labor is defined as occupational categories 0/1 and 2 and low-skilled labor as all other categories. The fourth endowment is the sum of two types of land areas: LAND1, the area of arable land and land under permanent crops or permanent pasture and LAND2, the area of forests and woodland, both measured in thousands of hectares. These figures come from the *Production Yearbook* of the Food and Agricultural Organization. The final "factor" is the cif- fob factor reported for each country by the IMF. It is a measure of the transport costs costs involved in aggregate commerce with each country.

Total expenditure in each importer is measured as GNP less the current-account imbalance. These figures and per capita GNP in 1984 are from The World Bank, *World Tables*. As noted earlier, the effects of patent laws on trade could vary depending on whether the importing country is a high-income developed economy, a large developing economy, or a small developing economy. Thus, we split our sample into three groups: H, L, and S. The 19 high-income countries include the major OECD exporters plus Switzerland. Large developing countries include Greece, Portugal, Turkey, and Yugoslavia among the OECD nations and 18 others. This group is defined as developing nations with a GDP greater than $18 billion, which includes both larger poor countries, such as India, and smaller upper-middle income countries, such as Singapore. The final group of 31 nations is small developing countries, such as Ecuador, which have both low per capita incomes and small aggregate GDP figures.

Measuring the extent and effects of trade barriers in particular industries across nations is highly problematic. It is difficult to aggregate tariff-line data into meaningful measures on an ISIC basis and to do so on a bilateral basis. Further, tariffs are often of limited consequence in relation to nontariff barriers, particularly in developing economies. Even if there were a published list of sectoral nontariff barriers in developing countries, determining their true restrictiveness is complicated and uncertain (Leamer 1992; Lee and Swagel 1994). We employ two national measures of trade impediments. The first is tariff revenue as a percentage of dutiable imports, compiled from International Monetary Fund, *Government Finance Statistics Yearbook*. Though problems with this variable as a measure of trade impedance are well-known, it seems to concur well with casual beliefs about protection rankings across countries. The second is the black-market exchange-rate premium discussed by Levine and Renelt (1992). It is a measure of the aggregate "openness" to trade of each importing country, in the sense that a higher premium indicates a more heavily distorted economy.

Turning finally to patents, there may be sectoral differences in effective duration or protection. However, in principle patent laws are applied uniformly to all sectors within each nation. Thus, we use an indicator of relative strength of patent laws across countries in 1984. Such an index has been developed recently by Rapp and Rozek (1990). Based on surveys of business and government officials and an examination of patent laws and their enforcement, the index provides a discrete ranking from zero to five of effective patent strength, with five indicating full conformity with minimum standards espoused by the U. S. Chamber of Commerce Intellectual Property Task Force (1987). A zero score pertains to countries with effectively no patent law.

Since the index is subjective, potential for measurement error exists. For instance, several poor countries have strong laws because they were

British colonies and modeled their systems on the United Kingdom Patents Act. However, enforcement problems reduce the effective strength of patents there. Moreover, a potential endogeneity problem exists in that levels of economic development and trade flows may influence legislation and enforcement. To deal with these problems we adopt an instrumental variables approach to correcting the raw patent index. The instruments include four indicators of the level of economic development in 1965, dummy variables for former British and French colonies, and general measures of intellectual property protection. These variables should be highly correlated with patent strength yet uncorrelated with the second-stage regression error terms. The instruments were taken from World Bank, *World Development Report, 1988,* and Siebeck (1990). Results of this IV regression are available on request. We use the predicted patent index as the continuous variable I^* in the reduced-form import regressions.

We note an interesting relationship between the corrected patents index and per-capita GNP (see the Appendix table). A simple regression of I^* on log of Y results in a strong positive relationship, though it appears not to be linear. Countries with high or low income levels have patent indexes above the regression line, while those in the middle tend to have indexes below the line. On this evidence it seems that effective patent laws differ across countries for reasons other than simply differences in economic status.

Estimation Results

We report in table 1 coefficient estimates on the patent variables from the reduced- form imports equations.[11] The significance levels of the estimates are based on the White heteroskedasticity-consistent standard errors. We report first the regression for all 28 sectors pooled, allowing for sectoral intercept dummies.[12] Significance levels are indicated by the superscripts "*" (99 percent level) and "**" (95 percent level).

The positive coefficient on the patent index is highly significant. Thus, across all sectors and countries a stronger effective patent law does attract greater bilateral imports, holding constant other trade determinants. This result is markedly stronger in both the small and large developing economies, as suggested by the significantly positive coefficients on the patent interaction variables. Coefficient sums (on the patent variable plus the relevant interaction term) that are significantly greater than zero are indicated by the superscript "+". Accordingly, in the pooled sample there is substantial indication that stronger patents induce more trade across all nations, with this effect being particularly pronounced in the developing

TABLE 1. Patent Coefficients from Pooled and Sectoral Imports Equations

Sector	I^*	I^*D_S	I^*D_L	n	R^2
Pooled	0.18*	0.14*+	0.50*+	39153	0.47
A Priori Most Patent–Sensitive Sectors					
Petroleum and Coal Products	−0.36	0.79*+	0.77*+	1196	0.26
Food Products	0.13	0.03	0.74*+	1514	0.20
Professional Goods	−0.06	0.26+	0.57*+	1466	0.58
Metal Products	0.12	0.23+	0.58*+	1508	0.49
Electrical Machinery	0.00	0.29+	0.53*+	1498	0.53
Plastic Products	0.27	0.05+	0.49*+	1443	0.49
Other Chemical Products	0.11	−0.06	0.38**+	1494	0.45
Pharmaceuticals	−0.10	0.35**+	0.47*+	653	0.33
Machinery, nec	0.09	0.18+	0.35***+	1515	0.55
Industrial Chemicals	−0.07	0.39**+	0.23	1490	0.45
Pooled	0.03	0.23*+	0.51*+	13124	0.52
A Priori Least Patent–Sensitive Sectors					
Leather Products	0.19	0.28+	0.95*+	1286	0.36
Wearing Apparel	0.40*+	−0.28+	0.95*+	1286	0.36
Footwear	0.21	0.34+	0.64*+	1212	0.25
Rubber Products	0.22	0.10+	0.39***+	1425	0.49
Printing and Publishing	0.37**	−0.10+	0.31+	1441	0.43
Transport Equipment	0.19	0.03	0.21+	1472	0.53
Nonferrous Metals	0.56*	−0.44	0.02+	1397	0.30
Beverages	0.79*	−0.26+	−0.09+	1377	0.23
Iron and Steel	0.42**	−0.29	−0.12+	1430	0.39
Pooled	0.38*	−0.05+	0.33*+	12466	0.43
Other Sectors					
Tobacco Products	−0.67*	1.14*+	1.55*+	984	0.27
Textiles	0.11	0.28+	0.91*+	1487	0.41
Wood Products	0.01	0.14	0.85*+	1387	0.24
Furniture	0.39*	0.15+	0.68*+	1369	0.43
Other Manufactures	0.28	0.03+	0.63*+	1464	0.51
Paper and Products	0.14	0.24+	0.54***+	1419	0.30
Glass and Products	0.33	0.02+	0.48*+	1412	0.35
Nonmetal Products	0.24	0.18+	0.47***+	1407	0.36
Pottery and China	0.21	0.30+	0.45*+	1353	0.39
Petroleum Refining	0.36	0.01	0.09+	1281	0.24
Pooled	0.14*	0.23*+	0.66*+	13563	0.40

countries. It seems that intellectual property rights are indeed "trade-related."

Clearly such effects could vary across industries. The remainder of table 1 provides estimates for each ISIC 3-digit industry, classified into three groups. One might expect the first nine (ignore pharmaceuticals for now) industries to be especially sensitive to international differences in patent laws. This group incorporates sectors with U.S. R&D programs that seem most dependent on the likelihood of receiving American patents (Mansfield 1986; Levin, 1987) and those U.S. sectors that claim the greatest damages of all kinds from limited foreign intellectual property protection in a government survey (U.S. International Trade Commission 1988). The second is a set of nine industries one might expect to have the least sensitivity, based on the same subjective criteria. The third contains the remaining manufacturing industries.

Two qualifications about these groups must be kept in mind. First, at this level of aggregation patents could influence economic decisions in all sectors. We would not necessarily expect no effect of patents on trade, even in sectors such as nonferrous metals and wearing apparel, because their classifications contain commodities that are subject to substantial technological changes and process improvements. A more sensible hypothesis is that imports of the most patent-sensitive group are more positively affected than are those of the least patent-sensitive group on average.

The second qualification could overturn this hypothesis. As our model showed, the theoretical reaction of firms to changes in patent regimes is ambiguous. In patent-sensitive sectors the market-expansion effect could well be offset by the market-power effect, resulting in an insignificant patent coefficient. Sectors are arrayed within each group by the size of the coefficient on the patent interaction with the large-country index, because the policies of the large developing countries covering intellectual property rights have been of greatest policy focus.

The variable I^* captures international differences in strength of patent laws. The coefficients measure the average effect of patent laws on bilateral imports across all trading partners. This effect could be negative or positive in principle. In the a priori most patent-sensitive sectors all coefficients are virtually zero, indicating an insignificant influence overall. However, in the second set all coefficients are positive and five of them are significant. It seems, therefore, that bilateral trade flows are more affected by patent regulations in sectors with presumably less sensitivity (in terms of their R&D efforts) to patent availability. This finding is consistent with the notion that trade reductions through the exercise of market power are more prevalent in patent-sensitive sectors than in patent-insensitive sectors.[13] Further, FDI might be more significant in the patent-sensitive sectors as we have discussed. Bayard (1994), for example, noted that in 1985 U.S. pharmaceutical firms had investments of some $700 million in Brazil, a nation often criticized for its weak patent protection, accounting for $600 million in sales there. At the same time, U.S. exports of drugs and medicines to Brazil by these firms came to only $50 million.[14]

Finally, for the other sectors (those with presumably intermediate patent sensitivity) the patent coefficients were largely positive though insignificant, with one significantly positively case (furniture) and one significantly negative case (tobacco products). Coefficients on the interaction terms measure the additional impact of protection in small and large developing importers relative to the average effect. Here, the highest sensitivity to patents comes in the most patent-sensitive sectors. In the small nations, the coefficients on I^*D_S are significantly positive for petroleum and coal products and industrial chemicals. None of these coefficients is significant in the least patent-sensitive group and one case, tobacco products, is significantly positive in the intermediate group.

For the large importers, the effect of stronger patents is clearly positive in all but one case in both the most patent-sensitive group (ignoring pharmaceuticals) and the intermediate group, and in four of nine cases in the least patent-sensitive group. In addition, the coefficients for the large nations are nearly always markedly higher than the coefficients for the small nations.

These conclusions are fortified by looking at the coefficient sums, which are not shown, on I^* and $I^* D_S$ and on I^* and $I^* D_L$. In 22 of 28 sectors this sum is significantly positive in the small group and in all but one case it is significant in the large group. In the pooled regressions within each group, these sums are also significantly greater than zero. Note that the coefficient sums are lowest in the a priori most patent-responsive group, again indicating that market-power effects most restrain trade in this group.[15]

We mentioned the possibility that these aggregate-industry results may disguise different impacts in subcategories. For instance, it is perhaps surprising that the "other chemical products" industry has an insignificant coefficient overall and in small nations, because it contains drugs and medicines, the prototypical patent-sensitive sector. To investigate this question, we matched bilateral trade data in pharmaceuticals with output data for the 4-digit drugs sector.[16] The resulting regression, given in table 1, suggests that patents are in fact a significantly positive determinant of trade flows into both small and large developing countries.

Overall, our results support the hypothesis that stronger patent laws incent higher bilateral trade flows. Further, this result is found across nearly all manufacturing industries. We note that the finding is robust in several dimensions.[17] First, gravity regressions generate similar outcomes. Second, all our equations are consistent with the HK model. Third, though we have corrected for measurement error in the patent index, the results are the same when we use the uncorrected patent index. Finally, use of alternative measures of trade openness does not alter the patent results materially (Penubarti 1994).

We conclude by comparing the elasticities of trade with respect to changes in patents by calculating them at the average patent index for each country set. These elasticities are roughly equivalent in concept to the elasticity of curve VV in figure 1b, the difference being that exports are scaled by expenditure in the regression estimates. Formulas for their computation are $\eta_I = {}_I I^*$ for the full sample, $\eta_{IS} = \gamma_{IS} D_S I^* + \eta_I$ for the small economies, and $\eta_{IL} = \gamma_{IL} D_L I^* + \eta_I$ for the large economies, where the D's are dummy variables incorporating all 72 observations. Taking all countries together there is little responsiveness of trade flows to variations in patent laws.[18] However, the elasticities are clearly positive in both the small and large developing countries. The effects are uniformly significant in the large group. At the same time, all of these elasticities are less than 0.1 in absolute value, suggesting that trade flows, while influenced by patent laws, are not particularly responsive to variations in IPRs regimes.

It is possible to calculate the implied increases in exports across these country groups for each sector by assuming (strongly) that increases in patent strength have no effect on national expenditure levels, leaving the increase in exports-to-expenditure ratios to be taken up by trade. We do this in table 2 for reasonable guesses about the new patent strengths that would ensue in the event of implementation and phase-in of the Uruguay Round intellectual property agreement. Across the small developing economies perhaps $3.4 billion, or about 0.02 percent of their GNP, in extra imports might result, concentrated on transport equipment, machinery, and industrial chemicals. Across the large developing economies perhaps $10.6 billion, or about 0.01 percent of their GNP, in extra imports might be induced, with food products and textiles added to the prior list of sectors. While these figures are relatively small in relation to global trade in manufactures (some $819 billion in 1984), particular international firms in certain sectors would find the enhanced business worthwhile.

Concluding Remarks

Our theory suggests that exporting firms with a choice of export markets may find their decisions influenced by the effectiveness of local patent laws. However, there is an important tradeoff between the market power generated by local patents and the expanded market size and

TABLE 2. Implied Increases in Total Imports by Sector into Developing Countries from Strengthening Patent Laws (millions of dollars)

Sector	Small LDCs	Large LDCs
Food Products	71.2	926.4
Beverages	67.5	140.6
Tobacco Products	25.4	75.9
Textiles	171.3	713.0
Apparel	94.5	468.5
Leather and Products	33.1	127.8
Footwear	58.0	143.7
Wood Products	29.5	255.6
Furniture and Fixtures	49.1	157.6
Paper and Products	154.7	460.0
Printing and Publishing	24.6	102.2
Industrial Chemicals	383.0	332.2
Other Chemical Products	18.4	271.5
Pharmaceuticals	56.9	142.6
Petroleum Refining	197.6	391.8
Petroleum and Coal Products	19.6	29.8
Rubber Products	42.0	127.5
Plastic Products, nec	31.7	114.5
Pottery and China Products	19.8	41.6
Glass and Products	27.9	104.4
Nonmetal Products, nec	48.1	130.4
Iron and Steel	78.3	271.5
Nonferrous Metals	38.1	330.1
Metal Products	126.1	403.8
Industrial Machinery	488.0	1269.8
Electrical Machinery	361.2	1082.4
Transport Equipment	530.3	1610.0
Professional Goods	80.8	360.3
Other Manufactures	70.0	323.7
Total (in dollar value)	3378.0	10637.0
Total (as percentage of GDP)	0.02	0.01

Note: This table assumes national expenditure levels remain unchanged after patent law changes. Assumptions on patent law changes include a 12% increase in I* for small countries (from 2.68 to 3.00) and (separately) a 22% increase in I* for large countries (from 2.86 to 3.50).

lower marginal exporting costs that could result. This question is ultimately empirical.

Our results clearly point to the view that exporting firms discriminate in their sales across export markets, accounting for local patent laws. While the average impact across all economies is small, firms increase activity in developing countries with stronger patents, both when those markets are relatively small and when they are large and have strong imitative potential. We conclude that the trade flows of manufactures exporters in OECD nations favor (relative to expected levels of trade) developing countries with stronger patents. In short, differences in international patent regimes detectably affect international trade. However, the actual trade flows that would be generated by a strengthening of global patent laws are relatively small.

Appendix

Countries and Basic Data

Country	Symbol	Type	Patent Index	Est. Patent Index	Income in U.S. dollars
Argentina	ARG	L	1	2.50	2230
Australia	AUS	H	4	4.64	11740
Austria	AUT	H	4	4.37	9140
Benin	BEN	S	2	3.15	270
Burkina Faso	BFO	S	2	3.06	160
Belgium	BLX	H	5	4.53	8610
Bangladesh	BNG	S	2	2.05	130
Bolivia	BOL	S	1	1.05	540
Brazil	BRA	L	1	2.08	1720
Canada	CAN	H	4	5.03	13280
Cameroon	CAO	S	2	2.96	800
Chile	CHL	S	2	1.75	1700
Colombia	COL	L	2	1.51	1390
Costa Rica	COS	S	3	2.88	1190
Denmark	DNK	H	5	4.37	11170
Dominican Rep.	DOM	S	2	3.19	970
Ecuador	ECU	S	1	2.37	1150
Egypt	EGY	L	2	2.75	720
El Salvador	SAL	S	3	2.46	710
Ethiopia	ETH	S	0	0.98	110
Finland	FIN	H	4	4.33	10770
France	FRA	H	5	4.84	9760
Germany	DEU	H	5	4.54	11130
Great Britain	GBR	H	5	5.18	8570
Ghana	GHA	S	4	2.45	350
Greece	GRC	L	4	2.63	3770
Guatemala	GUA	S	3	2.35	1160
Hong Kong	HKO	L	3	4.68	6330
Hungary	HUN	L	3	2.91	2100
India	IND	L	1	2.28	260
Indonesia	ISN	L	0	1.68	540
Ireland	EIR	H	4	4.49	4970
Israel	ISR	L	5	4.88	5060
Italy	ITA	H	5	4.30	6420
Jamaica	JAM	S	3	3.21	1150
Jordon	JOR	S	4	3.03	1570

Countries and Basic Data — *Continued*

Country	Symbol	Type	Patent Index	Est. Patent Index	Income in U.S. dollars
Japan	JPN	H	4	4.44	10630
Kenya	KEN	S	4	3.39	310
Korea	ROK	L	3	3.56	2110
Liberia	LBR	S	4	2.14	470
Malaysia	MAL	L	3	3.22	1980
Mauritius	MAS	S	4	2.80	1090
Malawi	MAW	S	4	3.11	180
Mexico	MEX	L	2	2.28	2040
Mali	MLI	S	2	2.01	140
Morocco	MOR	S	4	2.29	670
Nigeria	NIG	L	4	3.27	730
Norway	NOR	H	4	3.39	13940
Netherlands	NTH	H	5	4.34	9520
New Zealand	NZL	H	4	4.50	7730
Oman	OMA	S	0	0.90	6490
Pakistan	PAK	L	3	2.18	380
Panama	PAN	S	2	2.65	1980
Paraguay	PAR	S	1	1.56	1240
Peru	PER	S	1	1.33	1000
Philippines	PHI	L	4	3.14	660
Portugal	PRT	L	3	2.76	1970
South Africa	SAF	L	5	4.02	2340
Sierra Leone	SIE	S	4	3.10	310
Singapore	SIN	L	4	3.65	7260
Spain	ESP	H	4	2.71	4440
Sri Lanka	SRI	S	4	3.83	360
Sweden	SWE	H	5	4.80	11860
Switzerland	SWZ	H	5	4.85	16330
Syria	SYR	S	2	1.96	1620
Thailand	THI	L	1	1.65	860
Turkey	TKY	L	1	1.92	1160
Togo	TOG	S	2	2.95	250
Tunisia	TUN	S	3	2.41	1270
Uganda	UGA	S	4	3.41	230
Uruguay	URU	S	3	2.50	1980
United States	USA	H	5	5.32	15390
Venezuela	VEN	L	2	1.82	3410
Yugoslavia	YUG	L	2	2.68	2120
Zaire	ZAI	S	4	1.88	140
Zambia	ZAM	S	3	3.48	470
Zimbabwe	RHO	S	4	3.97	760

NOTES

1. This research was supported by NSF grant SBR-9410625.

2. Indeed, enforcement may be so stringent that it acts as a barrier to trade, which was an issue in the Uruguay Round negotiations.

3. See Gadbaw and Richards (1988) for a discussion of the latter point and some data concerning pharmaceuticals markets in major developing countries.

4. A drawback of this model is that it assumes equal quality levels for imported and local goods, which is at odds with cases in which imitative goods are of lower quality. Allowing for different quality would not change the central message of the analysis, however.

5. A stronger patent law could not raise the cost of imitating a product that has already been imitated, unless there is some element of detection avoidance in fixed costs. Again, a cleaner interpretation is that the firm is considering its sales in two otherwise identical countries with marginally different patent laws.

6. This is true in the linear case presented here. All that is required analytically is that the residual demand curve become less elastic in the neighborhood of the solution, which would generally be true.

7. This statement may be too strong in the small-country case, for if the market-power effect dominates the lower quality and higher price resulting from stronger patents, together with the requirement that the dominant firm operate in an elastic portion of its demand curve, it would ensure the value of exports falls. However, price rises unambiguously in any case, so it is possible that export value at internal prices could rise.

8. See Taylor (1993) for an analysis of this issue in the context of a North-South duopoly model. Private expenditures by foreign firms on local enforcement of their IPRs are common in the major industrializing countries.

9. If a change in patent law had no impact on $c + t$, then rising imports would raise marginal costs along a given line, worsening the terms of trade as in the usual story. We ignore here considerations of the optimal tariff.

10. An acceptable alternative strategy would be to estimate gravity models in which consumers have a taste for variety and there are country-specific product varieties for technological reasons. We have estimated gravity equations and the results are consistent with those we report for the HK model.

11. Detailed results are reported in Maskus and Penubarti (1995). To summarize them, the coefficient on exporter output was near unity in each sector, consistent with the HK model. Per capita GNP had insignificant effects on imports in most cases, suggesting homothetic preferences. Both the tariff rate and the black-market premium had significantly negative coefficients, suggesting that trade restrictions do reduce bilateral imports, consistent with Harrigan's (1993) results. There were also market-specific demand effects, as evidenced by significant coefficients on the country group dummies.

12. Coefficients of the industry dummies were highly significant.

13. Perhaps our patent index serves also as a measure of copyright and trademark laws. In the low-patent-sensitivity set there are some industries, such as bev-

erages, printing and publishing, and apparel, that could be responsive to these property rights.

14. Further evidence from U.S. Department of Commerce (1992) is consistent with this view. In electrical machinery, industrial machinery, and chemicals host-country·sales of U.S. foreign affiliates in 1989, divided by local GDP, exceed twice those for all sectors on average. The number of affiliates per parent was greatest in chemicals and even greater in the subcategory drugs.

15. Standard F-tests reject the hypothesis of joint equality of these patent and interaction- variable coefficients in each group.

16. Production data are from COMTAP and the trade figures are from the United Nations *Commodity Trade Statistics* volumes.

17. See Maskus and Penubarti (1995).

18. The detailed elasticity estimates are not reported here.

REFERENCES

Bayard, Thomas O., and Elliott, Kimberly A. 1994. *Reciprocity and Retaliation in U.S. Trade Policy.* Washington, D.C.: Institute for International Economics.

Brown, Drusilla. 1991. "Tariffs and Capacity Utilization by Monopolistically Competitive Firms." *Journal of International Economics* 30:371–381.

Feinberg, Robert, and Rousslang, Donald. 1990. "The Economic Effects of Intellectual Property Rights Infringement." *Journal of Business* 63:79–90.

Flam, Harry, and Helpman, Elhanan. 1987. "Industrial Policy under Monopolistic Competition." *Journal of International Economics* 22:79–102.

Gadbaw, R. Michael, and Richards, Timothy J. 1988. *Intellectual Property Rights: Global Consensus, Global Conflict?* Boulder: Westview Press.

Grossman, Gene M., and Helpman, Elhanan. 1991. *Innovation and Growth in the Global Economy.* Cambridge, MA: The MIT Press.

Harrigan, James. 1993. "OECD Imports and Trade Barriers in 1983." *Journal of International Economics* 35:91–111.

Horstmann, Ignatius, and Markusen, James. 1987. "Licensing versus Direct Foreign Investment: A Model of Internalization by the Multinational Enterprise." *Canadian Journal of Economics* 20:464–481.

Leamer, Edward. 1992. "The Structure and Effects of Tariffs and Nontariff Barriers in 1983." In Ronald Jones and Anne O. Krueger, eds., *The Political Economy of International Trade.* Basil Blackwell.

Lee, Jae-Woo, and Swagel, Philip. 1994. "Trade Barriers and Trade Flows across Countries and Industries." Manuscript.

Levin, Richard C.; Klevorick, Alvin K.; Nelson, Richard R.; and Winter, Sydney G. 1987. "Appropriating the Returns from Industrial R&D." *Brookings Papers on Economic Activity* 3:783–820.

Levine, Ross, and Renelt, David. 1992. "A Sensitivity Analysis of Cross-Country Growth Regressions." *American Economic Review* 82:942–963.

Mansfield, Edwin. 1986. "Patents and Innovation: An Empirical Study." *Management Science* 32:173–81.

Maskus, Keith E. 1990. "Normative Concerns in the International Protection of Intellectual Property Rights." *The World Economy* 13:387–409.

Maskus, Keith E. 1991. "Comparing International Trade Data and Product and National Characteristics Data for the Analysis of Trade Models." In Peter Hooper and J. D. Richardson, eds., *International Economic Transactions: Issues in Measurement and Empirical Research.* Chicago: University of Chicago Press.

Maskus, Keith E., and Eby-Konan, Denise. 1994. "Trade-Related Intellectual Property Rights: Issues and Exploratory Results." In A. V. Deardorff and R. M. Stern, eds., *Analytical and Negotiating Issues in the Global Trading System.* Ann Arbor: University of Michigan Press.

Maskus, Keith E., and Penubarti, Mohan. 1995. "How Trade-Related are Intellectual Property Rights?" *Journal of International Economics* 39:227–248.

Penubarti, Mohan. 1994. *Market Openness and U.S. Japan Trade Conflict.* Ph.D. Thesis. University of Colorado.

Rapp, Richard, and Rozek, Richard. 1990. "Benefits and Costs of Intellectual Property Protection in Developing Countries." Working paper No. 3. National Economic Research Associates, Inc.

Segerstrom, Paul S.; Anant, T.C.A.; and Dinopoulos, Elias. 1990. "A Schumpeterian Model of the Product Life Cycle." *American Economic Review* 80:1077–1091.

Siebeck, Wolgang E. 1990. *Strengthening Protection of Intellectual Property in Developing Countries: A Survey of the Literature.* Washington, D.C.: World Bank.

Summers, Robert, and Heston, Alan. 1988. "A New Set of International Comparisons of Real Product and Price Levels: Estimates for 130 Countries, 1950–1985." *Review of Income and Wealth* 34:1–25.

Taylor, M. Scott. 1993. "TRIPS, Trade, and Technology Transfer." *Canadian Journal of Economics* 26:625–638.

U.S. Department of Commerce. 1987. Guidelines for the Protection and Enforcement of Intellectual Property Rights. Technical Report, Washington, D.C.

U.S. Department of Commerce. 1992. *U.S. Direct Investment Abroad: 1989 Benchmark Survey, Final Results.* Washington, D.C.: Government Printing Office.

U.S. International Trade Commission. 1988. *Foreign Protection of Intellectual Property Rights and the Effect on U.S. Industry and Trade.* Washington, D.C.: Government Printing Office.

WIPO. 1988. Background Reading Material on Intellectual Property. Technical Report. World Intellectual Property Organization, Geneva.

Part Two:
Trade Policy Analysis

CHAPTER 6

Bindings and Rules as Trade Liberalization

Will Martin and Joseph Francois

A key feature of Bob Stern's long and distinguished career has been a focus on measuring the effects of trade policies on economic performance. In much of this work, protection has been treated as exogenously determined. However, he has clearly long realized that protection is determined by the interaction of competing political pressures. His important 1987 volume (Stern 1987), for example, was largely devoted to understanding the determinants of protection and exploring the nature of rules that could reduce the magnitude and costs of protection.

Once we recognize protection as endogenous, and rules as a means to tame (but never fully domesticate) the destructive forces of protectionism, it becomes clear that we can no longer treat protection as a purely exogenous influence on the economic system. Only after a particular form of protection has been tamed very thoroughly, and over a very long time, does it become reasonable to treat it as safely under control and responding one-for-one to agreed tariff reductions. This condition was clearly satisfied for manufacturing sector protection in the industrial countries during the Tokyo Round, the seventh GATT round to focus on this type of protection. With protection reduced vastly below its initial levels, and the protectionist instinct seemingly tamed, it was reasonable for Deardorff and Stern (1986) to assume that the agreed reductions would be translated one-for-one into actual reductions.

The events of the 1980s have borne out Tennyson's warning "The vow that binds too strictly snaps itself," as tariffs on manufactured goods have become augmented by an array of protectionist devices such as antidumping and voluntary export restraints (VERs). Even for tariffs bound at low levels, it now seems optimistic to assume that an agreed tariff reduction will be translated into an equal reduction in protection. Dealing with these more pernicious forms of protection requires more rules, in addition to the basic GATT rule that countries will not increase their tariffs above agreed, bound levels.

A key feature of the Uruguay Round agreement is a substantial increase in the use of bindings, particularly in the developing countries that participated actively in the GATT for the first time. In developing countries, the percentage of industrial tariff lines subject to bound tariffs increased from 22 to 72, while the percentage of agricultural tariff lines subject to bindings increased from 18 to 100 (GATT 1994a, 7). In developed countries, a high proportion of industrial goods was already covered by bound tariffs. However, enormous progress was made on agricultural goods, where the coverage of tariff bindings increased from 58 to 100 percent (GATT 1994a, 9).

The introduction of a binding on a previously unbound tariff has long been recognized by the GATT as liberalization. This is clearly true when the tariff binding is at the applied rate, because such a binding rules out increases in the applied rate—increases that experience suggests are very common with unbound tariffs.[1] Even when bindings are offered at rates above the currently applied rate, these bindings have some liberalizing effect by ruling out increases in tariffs to even higher levels. Much of the discussion of tariff bindings has identified their advantages in terms of increased market security, which might seem to refer to a reduction in the variability of protection, its second moment about the mean. In this paper, we emphasize the impact of a binding on the mean of the distribution of protection, its first moment. In a related paper, we consider the effects of tariff bindings on the cost of protection, taking into account both first and second moments (Francois and Martin 1995).

Formal modeling of trade liberalization has tended to focus on situations where liberalization takes the form of a reduction in a bound tariff rate which is also the applied tariff rate. For analyses focusing on liberalization under the Tokyo Round, this approach was reasonable since liberalization efforts focused upon industrial goods in the developed countries and virtually all of these goods were already covered by bindings at the applied tariff rate. In this situation, it seems reasonable to represent the reduction in the bound rate as an equal reduction in the effective, applied tariff rate. This conventional procedure has been carried over to most of the *ex ante* evaluations of trade liberalization under the Uruguay Round (e.g. Nguyen, Perroni and Wigle 1993; Goldin, Knudsen and van der Mensbrugghe 1993; Brandão and Martin 1993; and Francois, McDonald, and Norsdtröm 1993).

When trade liberalization occurs through the introduction of a tariff binding, this approach is likely to be misleading. When, for example, the binding is introduced at the current applied tariff rate, it would suggest that no liberalization has taken place. When the binding is introduced above the current applied rate, it would imply that protection has actually increased. Because a binding imposes an upper limit on the rate of protection where none previously existed, this seems an inappropriate conclusion.

Another important feature of the Uruguay Round has been the reform of the rules under which trade policy decisions are taken. Important reforms have taken place under safeguards, where gray-area measures such as VERs have been abolished and other safeguard measures have been brought under stronger disciplines. The multi-fiber arrangement, which applied rates of protection varying across time and across suppliers, is to be phased out. Procedures for the imposition of anti-dumping duties are also to be reformed.

To date, analyses of the implications of trade reforms have tended to focus on the relatively easily quantifiable market access provisions, and to ignore the implications of changes in the rules, which are widely held to be at least as important. In this paper, we outline a general approach that we feel offers considerable promise of allowing the benefits of new bindings, reductions in existing bindings, and improvements in the rules of the trading system to be evaluated.

In the next section of the paper, we outline the basis for our treatment of protection as stochastic, rather than deterministic, phenomenon. Then, we discuss some of the bindings and rule changes introduced as trade liberalization measures under the Uruguay Round.

The Stochastic Nature of Protection

Complementing basic theoretical insights on the impact of trade policies on production, trade, and the distribution of income is an active literature emphasizing that the economic interaction between trade policy and the distribution of the gains or losses from trade, when viewed in a political economy context, implies that protection is endogenously determined, and follows a stochastic process.[2] In part, the emphasis of the political economy literature is placed on explaining why we observe a given level of protection. A logical extension involves modifying the measurement of "protection," in terms of its observed level for the purposes of quantitative analysis, to reflect not just an observed incidence of protection, but rather the impact of expectations about future protection, including the threat, likely magnitude, and likely duration of future actions.[3]

Ronald Findlay (1987) provided a very useful diagrammatic summary of the wide range of models of protection as resulting from the interaction of a supply for protection and a demand for protection. In this general framework, protection rates depend upon a set of influences which are themselves random, so that the positions of the supply and demand curves vary over time. As long as the model captures the underlying structure of protection its parameters will be constant over time, and hence amenable to analysis.

One class of structural model designed to explain changes in protection across industries and over time is based upon the work of Olson (1965) and Stigler (1974). It focuses on factors such as the structure of the industry, its costs of organization, and its success as a special interest group. Another set of explanations surveyed by Dornbusch and Frankel (1987) emphasises the role of macroeconomic shocks. Another set of models considers in more depth the nature of the political decision making system that generates protection decisions (Magee and Young 1987) and introduces shocks from random political outcomes. Yet another approach emphasizes the role of past and present shocks to import levels. Finally, the choice of protective instrument will both reflect the preferences of decision makers regarding the volatility of protection (Falvey and Lloyd 1991), and induce an additional random element into the behavior of protection.

Anderson (1978, 1980) draws on the theoretical work of Olson and Stigler to explain differences in protection levels across industries in terms of a range of predetermined variables, including the number of firms, the size of the industry, whether the industry is export or import oriented, the labor intensity of the production process, and its geographical concentration, which influences its political clout. While most of the structural variables in models of this type are likely to change relatively slowly, the estimated models have important stochastic residuals. Gawande's (1997) analysis of endogenous protection in this volume incorporates structural determinants suggested by the special interest model, together with related variables suggested by Caves' (1976) Adding Machine model.

Dornbusch and Frankel (1987) offer models of protectionist pressures based on highly variable macroeconomic influences, such as the real exchange rate, the real interest rate and the rate of unemployment. Other evidence linking protection to unemployment and recessions is provided by Ray (1987), Hanson (1990), and Bohara and Kaempfer (1991). The variables that generate changes in protection in these models are random, and are augmented by other random influences not captured in the models.

We know that tariff levels are positively correlated with import levels (Leamer 1988), which in turn are variable and subject to swings in exchange rates and macroeconomic conditions.[4] In terms of quotas, Bhagwati and Srinivasan (1976) offer a theoretical example where the level of imports in one period determines the probability of an import quota in the next. The threat of such protection reduces the (optimal) incentives for export from the point of view of the exporting country. One can imagine the level of import penetration, in various permutations of such a framework, as depending on exchange rate swings, the business cycle, or a number of other factors. The more recent theoretical literature (Baldwin 1989; Magee, Brock and Young 1989; and Hillman 1982) also links protection, in its various guises, with increased import penetration. In particular, increased penetration leads to intensified lobbying for protection. Trefler (1993) offers evidence that the application of NTBs in the United States is correlated with changes in the level of import penetration. In Trefler's results, it is changing (i.e. variable) market conditions, and not the level of import penetration per se, that leads to protection. He also finds that, when the level of trade protection is treated as endogenous, the trade impact of protection is 10 times as large as that obtained from treating trade protection as exogenous.

The political mechanisms highlighted in the models emphasizing the political lobbying process (see, for example, Magee, Brock and Young 1989) introduce another source of randomness into the determination of protection policies. Voters supporting particular politicians because of their stance on particular trade policy issues are frequently disappointed and, on occasions, voter retribution introduces an additional source of variability into the trade policy process.

Randomness of protection is particularly marked in monitoring and administering protection. Winters (1994) finds that import surveillance, in the case of the European Union, can have a dampening effect on trade. Tollefsen (1994) notes that, as a group, VERs and monitoring mechanisms are the most common form of NTB protection applied in the industrial countries. Both are a common outcome of threatened or suspended antidumping and countervailing duty actions. While EU antidumping (AD) cases are more frequently settled by price undertakings and associated monitoring mechanisms (Hindley 1990), U.S. practice in this area can take a similar tack, as evidenced by the U.S. export restraint arrangements on bearings from Japan and uranium from the republics of the former Soviet Union. Hindley postulates that, given the administrative uncertainly inherent in the U.S. system, there is an incentive for exporters to the United States to raise their price on products not covered by antidumping duties, simply to reduce the probability of an investigation. Similar incentives exist to accept "voluntary" restraint arrangements under the threat of AD actions. In addition to administrative uncertainty, Feinberg (1989) links findings of dumping to swings in exchange rates, while Feinberg and Hirsch (1989) relate such findings in downstream industries to the imposition of protection in upstream sectors.

Finally, under the U.S. system of administrative reviews and revision to dumping duties, existing dumping orders themselves serve as a type of monitoring mechanism. This mechanism may have a significant effect, even when bonding requirements are for duties below one percent. Boltuck, Francois, and Kaplan (1990) offer empirical evidence related to the outcome of administrative reviews. Because dumping duties in the United States are collected as bonds, with the actual duty rates determined long after the actual entry of imports, the variance in the duty-inclusive price of imports subject to bonding requirements can be quite large. Palmeter makes the point this way:

> The uncertainties connected with this system can have a chilling effect on trade. Although the exporter would seem to have the opportunity to change its pricing practices to avoid future determinations of dumping, this is never easy, if it is ever possible, particularly because Commerce is permitted to change its methodology from one investigation or review to another, and does so. Moreover, although it is the foreign seller's home market and export prices that determine whether dumping is occurring, it is the importer who pays the duty, and the importer essentially is powerless to know—much less to affect—either the home market price of the exporter or the costs on which adjustments to that price will be based. Thus any company that imports merchandise from an exporter subject to a dumping order is acquiring an open-ended contingent liability. . . . Even a minuscule dumping margin can put an entire import trade at enormous risk. (Palmeter 1990, 80)

As Vousden (1990, 70) explains, particular forms of protection may be chosen because of their impacts on the variance of domestic incomes. Under some circumstances, a quota may reduce the variability of domestic income relative to the situation with a tariff. The widespread popularity of policies that set domestic target policies for agricultural goods and bridge the gap between this price and world prices with a variable import levy or an export subsidy can probably be explained in the same way. Once such instruments have been selected, they can induce substantial variation in rates of protection. While there are some "menu" costs involved in changing the protection rates where protection is provided by tariffs, these do not exist when non-tariff barriers are used. With fixed quotas, for example, shocks to either the domestic or the world market result in changes in the rate of protection.

An Approach to Measuring the Liberalizing Effects of Tariff Bindings

To analyze the effects of a tariff binding, we represent the effects of trade distortions in a particular market in terms of their tariff equivalents. This tariff equivalent is the result of a set of interacting pressures from interest groups within the country, from interactions between the country and its trading partners through the GATT, and other international trading arrangements such as regional trade agreements. While the diversity of political economy models discussed in the previous section makes us reluctant to specify a single, unique model, it does lead us to conclude that tariff equivalents will be stochastic. Tariff equivalents will vary in response to changes in the underlying determinants of protection, which are themselves stochastic, and to idiosyncratic factors such as the personality and ideology of the ministers responsible for trade policy, and prevailing beliefs about the role of trade in economic performance.

Given the distributions of the factors determining the level of protection, it seems reasonable to represent the level of protection for a particular commodity as a random variable, rather than as a constant. The distribution of one such variable is represented by the stylized curve in figure 1. This distribution implies that the rate of protection on a particular commodity is likely to be near its mean level, and that tariff rates much higher or lower than this value are considerably less likely. We assume that the expected level of the tariff over time is μ_0 in the absence of any constraint, such as a binding, on the tariff rate applied. The introduction of a tariff binding at B rules out all tariff rates above B. If the underlying probability distribution does not change, then all of the probability mass formerly associated with applied tariffs equal to or above B is mapped onto tariff rate B. The resulting distribution of tariffs is a winsorized distribution consisting of a truncated distribution of tariff rates up to the binding, and a "spike" at the bound rate, B. With the binding, the expected rate of protection will decline to a point like μ_1, and its variability will decrease. The effect of a binding at any given level above μ_0 on the mean of the protection process will be greater the larger is the variance of the protection process. Letting τ denote the tariff rate, we have

$$\mu_1 \quad = \quad \int_0^B \tau f(\tau) \, d\tau \quad + \quad \int_B^\infty B f(\tau) \, d\tau \tag{1}$$

The effect of a tariff binding on the mean of the protection rate can be evaluated by calculating the expected tariff rate in the presence of a binding and comparing it with the mean of the underlying distribution. Using the approach of Martin and Urban (1984), this can be done with the formulation in equation (1), where $\mu 1$ is the mean of the new distribution where tariffs are constrained by the binding, and f is the density function of the tariff rate.[5]

Because B is a constant, equation (1) may be simplified to:

$$\mu_1 = \int_0^B \tau f(\tau) \, d\tau + B \left(1 - F(B)\right) \tag{2}$$

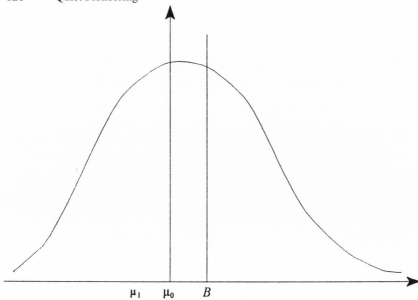

Fig. 1. The distribution of tariffs and the effect of a tariff binding

where $F(\tau)$ is the distribution (cumulative density) function of the tariff rate.

If we assume the distribution of the tariff rate can be approximated by a normal distribution, then the mean of the tariff can be expressed in normalized form μ_z as:

$$\mu_z = -\frac{1}{\sqrt{2\pi}}e^{-1/2(Z^*)^2} + Z^*(1 - F(Z^*)) \qquad (3)$$

where $Z = (\tau - \mu_0)/\sigma_0$ is the normalized tariff rate, defined by calculating the deviation of the tariff rate from its mean and dividing by σ_0, the variance of the original distribution, and $Z^* = (B - \mu_0)/\sigma_0$ is the value of the normalized variable at the bound rate.

Equation (3) yields a simple expression for the long run mean of the tariff following the introduction of a binding:

$$\mu_1 = \mu_0 - \sigma\frac{1}{\sqrt{2\pi}}e^{-1/2(Z^*)^2} + (B - \mu_0)(1 - F(Z^*)) \qquad (4)$$

From the structure of the problem, it is clear that I must be less than the mean of the unbound tariff, μ_0. The relationship between the mean subject to binding (μ_1), and the unbound mean (μ_0) is a nonlinear one, implying that the expected tariff cannot change one-for-one with the binding, as is frequently assumed. To explore this relationship further, it is useful to differentiate (4) with respect to B to obtain:

$$\frac{\partial \mu_1}{\partial B} = (1 - F(Z')) \tag{5}$$

This formulation makes it clear that a bound tariff rate well below the initial mean has the largest impact on the expected future mean tariff rate; for B well below μ_0, F(Z*) will be close to zero and so μ_1 will decline one-for-one with reductions in the tariff binding. At higher bound rates, the effect of a reduction in the tariff binding will be less than unity. For very high values of B, F(Z*) will be approximately unity, and so marginal changes in the binding will have essentially no effect on the long run expected value of the tariff.

A typical, operational approach to assessing the liberalizing effects of the introduction of a new binding, or a reduction in an existing binding above the applied rate, is to take the marginal impact of the binding to be zero if the final binding is below the initial applied rate, and to be unity if it is above the initial applied rate. This can be seen as an approximation to the true marginal impact depicted in figure 2. If we take the initial applied rate as a proxy for the mean of the underlying distribution, then this approach is depicted using the dashed lines in figure 3.[6] Under this assumption, it is clear that the conventional approach completely ignores the effect of tariff bindings above the mean. Less obviously, it tends to overstate the marginal impact of reductions in bindings occurring at or below the initial applied rate.

Qualitative Impacts of Changes in Rules under the Uruguay Round

If governments can be expected to exercise a number of different policy instruments when providing protection, then the GATT can be viewed as a rules-based system designed, in large part, to limit these instruments through rules-based disciplines. Hence, tariffs are limited by MFN requirements, as well as by tariff bindings. The application of certain quotas is limited, or even prohibited, by the Uruguay Round Agreements. Contingent protection, through fair trade and safeguard actions, is in theory limited by related GATT disciplines as well. Other rules apply to

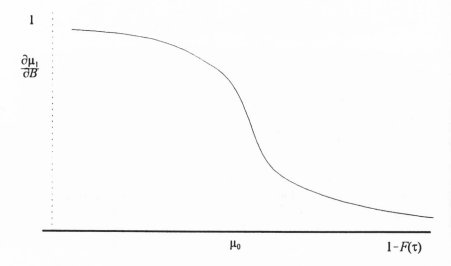

Fig. 2. The impact of a change in a binding on the mean tariff

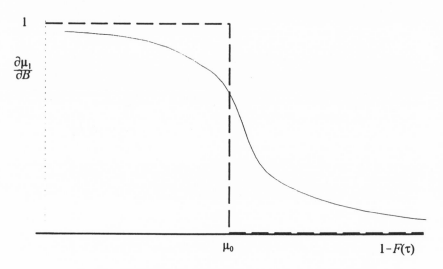

Fig. 3. Estimated impacts of bindings under different assumptions

balance-of-payments actions, licensing requirements, and trade-related investment measures. For the first time, market-access bindings have also been entered for the service sectors.

Tariff Bindings

The most obvious limitation on tariff instruments is the tariff binding. If an observed tariff could be unilaterally raised at will, any liberalization would have to be weighed against the probability of backsliding. An exporting firm may be reluctant to pursue new markets, even given a tariff cut, if the treatment afforded to products it intends to export is expected to be short-lived, or if it is otherwise uncertain. Beyond the expected tariff level, the fact that the national government might subsequently raise a tariff also creates uncertainty. By binding tariffs, the range of the tariff is limited by the binding, reducing its expected value. Bindings themselves are considered to be so important that countries agreeing to bind previously unbound tariffs are given "negotiating credit" for the decision. This is true even if the tariff is bound at a level above the currently applied level.

Other Bindings

Tariff levels are not the only commitments that can be bound. In addition to tariffs or other measures affecting trade in industrial products, the schedules of commitments made by members of the World Trade Organization (WTO) cover measures affecting trade in agricultural products and services. For industrial products, these bindings generally take the form of maximum or ceiling rates for the tariffs applied to the products listed in the schedule. For agricultural products, commitments include bindings on duties applied to imported products, as well as commitments on subsidies granted to exported products or to volumes exported with the aid of subsidies, and on internal support to agricultural producers. In the case of services, where obstacles to trade generally do not involve border measures, countries have bound the level of market access and national treatment for sectors listed in their respective schedules, meaning that no new measures affecting entry and operation in the market may be imposed with respect to the four possible modes of supplying a service (cross-border, consumption abroad, commercial presence, and movement of personnel).

Quotas, "Voluntary" Restraints, and Other Safeguards

Two provisions of the Final Act involve the phase-out of quantitative restrictions. The Agreement on Textiles and Clothing covers quotas administered under the MFA, while the Safeguards Agreement covers both measures taken pursuant to Article XIX of the General Agreement, and the so called "gray-area" measures taken outside the Agreement. The Agreement on Balance-of-Payments Provisions should also reduce the number of quantitative restrictions in the medium term. It requires the announcement of schedules for the timely removal of restrictive measures. In addition, parties implementing new measures are committed to using "price-based measures" wherever possible, and to avoiding the imposition of new quantitative restrictions unless, in a critical balance-of-payments situation, price-based measures cannot arrest a sharp deterioration in the payments situation. Here again, the introduction of rules may have the effect of reducing expected protection.

The Multi-fiber Arrangement (MFA) currently has 44 participants, eight of which are considered to be importers. Of these, Austria, Canada, the European Community, Finland, Norway and the United States apply restrictions under the MFA, while Japan and Switzerland do not. Even though they do not currently impose quotas, the act of monitoring by Japan and Switzerland, arguably, sends a signal of willingness to intervene under certain market conditions. Other participants in the MFA are described as exporters. Most of these are subject to bilateral restraint agreements. Estimates based on 1990 data suggest that approximately 11 percent of world trade in textiles and 35 percent of world trade in clothing, were subject to bilateral restraint agreements negotiated under the MFA. This arrangement is scheduled to be phased out over a 10 year period.

To ensure that the MFA phaseout is credible, meaning that the expected protection of textiles and clothing production will actually be reduced, it is necessary to limit the remaining set of available instruments as well. Tariff bindings accomplish part of this, as does the limitation on industrial quotas. The Uruguay Round Agreement on Safeguards establishes an explicit prohibition on gray area measures. In theory, this includes the introduction of new quotas under Article XIX, though only time will tell what form actual implementation follows.

The Agreement on Safeguards limits the application of safeguard actions. It provides for the termination of measures taken pursuant to Article XIX of the General Agreement not later than eight years after the date on which they were first applied or five years after the date of entry into force of the Agreement establishing the WTO, whichever comes later. It also sets out commitments on the phase-out of measures not conforming with the provisions of this Article. The Agreement covers voluntary export restraints, orderly marketing arrangements, or any other similar measures on the export or the import side. These measures are to be brought into conformity with the Agreement or phased out within four years after the entry into force of the agreement establishing the WTO. (Each WTO member is allowed to keep one specific measure in force until the end of 1999, subject to the agreement of the exporting country in question.)

The Agreement regarding the application of Article XIX also applies a "sunset clause" to all Article XIX safeguard actions and sets out requirements for safeguard investigations. This includes public notice for hearings and other appropriate means for interested parties to present evidence, including on the issue of whether a safeguard measure would be in the public interest. Generally, the duration of a measure should not exceed four years, though it can be extended up to a maximum of eight years under certain conditions.[7] Any measure imposed for a period greater than one year should be progressively liberalized during its lifetime. MFN treatment is also encouraged (though not required). In principle, safeguard measures have to be applied to imports from all sources. However, it would be possible for the importing country to apply the measure selectively, if it can demonstrate that imports from certain contracting parties had increased disproportionately in relation to the total increase, and that such a departure is justified and equitable to all suppliers. The duration of a selective safeguard measure must not exceed four years.

If they prove workable (meaning that they are enforceable through dispute settlement proceedings), all of these measures should constrain the range of safeguard-related instruments of protection, and should therefore reduce the expected value of protection in the process. For example, the Sunset clause reduces the duration of certain incidents of protection, while a whole set of instruments has been prohibited or eliminated, relating to quantitative measures. The public interest clause can also be perceived as limiting the probability that safeguard actions will be taken.

Dumping and Countervailing Duties

One of the most important sources of contingent protection, at least in North America and Europe, has been in the application of AD and countervailing (CVD) rules. For example, the share of U.S. imports affected by dumping and countervailing duty orders rose from 0.4 percent in 1988 to 1.3 percent by the end of fiscal year 1992 (excluding recent steel actions and suspension agreements). Such duties often range above 75 percent. In the case of steel, the expiration of the steel VERs in March 1992 has been following by a series of dumping cases.[8] Almost all of the countries formerly subject to VERs are now covered instead by dumping duties.

The processes for assessing whether dumping has occurred and for levying antidumping duties highlight the importance of stochastic protection and the use of rules to control its impact. Dumping is typically defined as selling products below a "fair value" reference price. The actual calculations are made by comparing individual sales over the period of investigation with an average reference price. This reference price may be a home market price, or alternatively a "constructed value" based on cost. Consider an example where market conditions are stochastic, but where average selling prices are equal to the reference average price. The distribution of the difference between selling prices and the average reference price is presented in figure 4. When comparing all prices to an average price, the dumping margin (and resulting duty) would be zero. However, in practice, sales above fair value are assumed to be at fair value. Essentially, the whole right hand side of the distribution in figure 4 is stacked onto the vertical axis, creating a winsorized distribution of estimated dumping margins like that depicted in figure 2. The result is that, even where the true price difference is zero, the calculated average is in fact some number like μ_1. The magnitude of the assessed dumping margin will increase with the variability of individual selling prices. Boltuck, Francois, and Kaplan (1990) demonstrate that, under the current U.S. averaging rule, average dumping margins approximate the standard deviation of price in the absence of actual dumping. In practice, the expected duty will also depend on the probability that an investigation will be initiated, and the probability of a positive injury finding.

It has been argued that the Agreement on Implementation of Article VI (Anti-Dumping) clarifies many aspects of the rules governing the application of anti-dumping measures. In particular, the revised Agreement provides for more detailed rules for determining whether a product is being dumped, clearer criteria for determining whether dumped imports are causing injury to a domestic industry, better defined procedures for AD investigations, and for the implementation and duration of AD measures. There is a new provision under which anti-dumping measures expire five years after the date of imposition, unless it is determined that dumping and injury would be likely to continue or recur if the measures were terminated. Another new provision requires the immediate termination of an anti-dumping investigation in cases where the authorities determine that the margin of dumping is *de minimis* or that the volume of dumped imports is negligible. The new Agreement also clarifies the role of dispute settlement panels in this area. Similar modifications have also been introduced in the area of countervailing duties.

Clarification of rules does not, in itself, guarantee a reduction in expected protection. For example, the averaging rule discussed above creates findings of dumping even where no dumping occurs. Clarification of

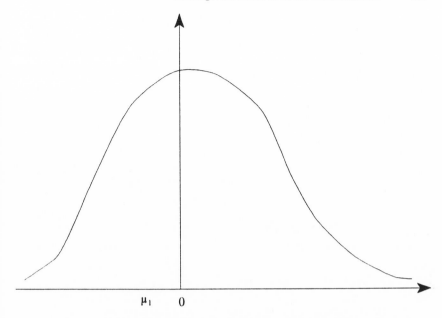

μ_1 0

Fig. 4. Random prices and estimated dumping margin

these particular procedures has not helped. New rules and rules clarification can raise or lower expected protection. However, where rules explicitly close loopholes, or otherwise limit the application of protection instruments, we would expect them to lower the expected rate of protection. Therefore, the sunset clause, as in the case of Article XIX, should lower the expected value of protection through AD and CVD use. The same is true of *de minimus* standards as well. The credibility of such rule changes, however, also hinges on effective dispute settlement.

Instrument Portfolios and Instrument Switching

As the preceding discussion makes clear, there is a broad array of instruments available to governments to limit imports (or exports) and to otherwise intervene in trade. One interpretation of the role of the GATT is that it seeks to restrict the application of these instruments through rules-based disciplines. However, the continued success of this endeavour hinges on the coverage of the rules keeping up with the development and application of new instruments. As gray area measures have demonstrated, this is not a simple task.

A related issue concerns the availability of a portfolio of instruments. Limiting the application of one set of instruments, such as VERs, may simply lead to the application of alternative instruments. For example, U.S. steel quotas lapsed in March 1992 and were followed by a series of dumping cases. The first set of cases involved flat-rolled steel products. The application of AD duties and CVDs to a broader set of steel producers and products is likely. The outcome of the flat-rolled cases is illustrated in the appendix table. 17 countries covered by the steel VERs, half of these are now covered by AD duties and/or CVDs. For this reason, we would expect that an assessment of the impact limiting a particular trade policy instrument, such as steel VERS, through the application of rules, should in principle take into account the availability of alternative instruments and limitations on those instruments. As long as the degree of substitutability between instruments is not perfect, limiting a particular instrument should in itself be trade liberalizing. However, the extent of liberalization will hinge on the possibilities for substitution toward other instruments. We do not, in this paper, try to address formally the role of instrument switching. We do, however, feel it is a potentially important factor in assessing expected protection and merits further exploration.

A Quantitative Application to Agricultural Bindings

The agricultural agreement of the Uruguay Round presents a particularly interesting set of challenges. Under this agreement, developed countries are required to establish tariff bindings with a protective effect equal to the combined effects of tariffs and nontariff barriers in a base period (1986–88) and to subsequently reduce them by at least 15 percent. Developing countries had the option to set their tariff bindings even higher through the use of ceiling bindings (Ingco 1994). Because the procedures used to estimate the protective effects of nontariff barriers allowed considerable scope for discretion, it appears that many of the new tariff bindings in developed and developing countries will be set above their levels in the reference period.[9]

In this situation, simple approaches to evaluating the liberalizing effect of the agriculture agreement are likely to underestimate its benefits. If the tariff bindings are simply compared with the previously applied rates of protection, it may even appear that the agreement has resulted in an increase in protection.

The approach taken in our application is to estimate the mean and variance of the underlying distribution of protection, and to evaluate the mean of the modified distribution using equation (4). Comparison of this mean with the mean of the data during the sample period provides an initial indication of the extent of liberalization. We use data calculated by the OECD for the annual *ad valorem* equivalents of agricultural trade barriers in OECD countries (OECD 1994) made available on diskette by the OECD Agricultural Directorate. These data are available over the period 1979–93, providing a sample large enough to make a rough estimate of the standard deviation of protection for each commodity under the policy regime applying during this period. For illustrative purposes, our calculations are based on the assumption that the average rate of protection over the 1979–93 period would continue to apply in the future in the absence of a tariff binding.[10]

In the procedure we use in this initial, illustrative application, we take the world price of the good as exogenous to each individual country, and the rate of protection as distributed independently of this world price. In a short-run context of sticky internal prices, it is clear that the protection rate is not completely independent of the world price on a year-to-year basis. In fact, once the domestic price is set for a season under arrangements such as the European Union's variable levy system, the protection rate and the world price are perfectly negatively correlated. Over the longer term, however, there is evidence that domestic prices tend to follow world prices of agricultural products, except for a randomly determined margin term which includes the effects of protection policy (Mundlak and Larson 1992). Mundlak and Larson also provide evidence that the elasticity of price transmission is very close to unity, implying that domestic prices move proportionately with world prices in the long run.

As an additional check on the robustness of our results, we calculated the correlation between the world price and the protection rate using our sample. In general, these correlations were very small, suggesting that the lack of independence between the world price and the protection rate would not significantly affect the estimate of the variance. Had the correlations been significant, we could have adjusted our procedures to obtain an estimate of the variance of the protection rate conditional on our projection of the world price.[11]

We assume that the moments of the process generating the distribution of protection remain constant after the introduction of bindings. That is, we assume that the fundamental determinants of the supply of and demand for protection do not change because of the introduction of tariff bindings, and that basically the same instruments continue to be used to determine the rate of protection below the constraint imposed by the binding. In some important cases, such as EU agricultural policy, it appears that the same general instruments for border protection will continue in effect subject to the constraint imposed by the GATT tariff bindings (Josling and Tangermann 1994). Even if the specific instruments utilized do change, it seems reasonable to assume, as a general rule, that protection will still vary in similar ways, since the fundamental stochastic determinants of protection remain in place.

Importantly, we assume that the mean of the distribution of protection rates will not merely be increased to compensate for the introduction of a policy binding. While possible, such a reaction would seem to require more knowledge of the system, and a greater degree of coordination between suppliers and demanders of protection than is likely. If individual industries were able to counter GATT rules so easily, then presumably they could block the entire GATT process of protection reduction, an assumption that flies in the face of the enormous success experienced by the GATT in lowering protection rates on manufactured goods imported by industrial countries. We provide an illustrative application of the measure for three important agricultural commodities (wheat, sugar, and beef) in seven OECD countries for which *ad valorem measures* of the final tariff bindings resulting from the Uruguay Round are available from Ingco (1995, 1994 and personal communication). In most cases, the tariff commitments have been made in specific terms, and these *ad valorem* equivalents have been calculated using 1989–93 average prices as an indicator of likely future prices. We discuss all of the protection measures in terms of import protection, even for exporting countries, since import restrictions are an essential backstop for export subsidy programs.

Some results for liberalization of border protection to wheat are presented in table 1. The first column of the table shows the average rate of protection, estimated by the OECD, for the longest available period. These estimates are intended to provide an indication of the underlying mean of the process generating protection to the wheat industry in the absence of effective trading rules. The second column contains estimates of the standard deviation of protection over the same period, and is intended to represent the standard deviation of the underlying distribution of protection into the future. The third column shows the protection rate in the three-year period on which tariff bindings were to be based, 1986–88. The final level of tariff bindings following tariffication and agreed reductions are presented in the fourth column. The final column of the table contains estimates of the mean tariff in the presence of the final binding.

The results presented in table 1 highlight the very substantial variation across regions and across time in the rates of border protection applying to wheat. Also evident in the Table is the generally much higher level of protection in the 1986–88 period, the base period for the tariffication calculations, than the more representative 1979–93 period. Despite the height of protection in the 1986–88 base period, it is clear that the bound rates will remain higher than the base in several countries. This does not imply that the Uruguay Round "liberalization" actually resulted in increases in protection rates. When we look at the mean protection rates in the final column of the table, it is clear that even these generally high bindings can be expected to lead to some liberalization in particular markets. This liberalization is particularly important in Japan, where the average rate of protection declines 287 percentage points from the 1979–93 average.

In some of the cases considered for wheat, the naive approach of treating a tariff binding as causing a reduction in protection only when it results in a tariff rate below the previous long run average tariff rate would provide a reasonable approximation. In the EU, however, average protection is reduced by five percentage points even though the final binding is well above the average tariff rate. Moreover, the enormously high binding offered by Norway has almost no impact on the average rate of protection. In terms of protection *levels*, the binding provides a reasonable indication of the post-Uruguay Round rate of protection only in Japan, where the binding is so far below the previously applied tariff rate that virtually all of the probability density is collected at the binding, and in Australia, where the tariff is bound at zero. In the USA and most other countries, the average rate of protection would be substantially overestimated if the binding alone were used to represent the new level of protection.

The estimates of the impact of sugar market liberalization in table 2 present a somewhat more diverse pattern than the results for wheat. The EU's binding, at 152 percent causes a reduction of 31 percent in its average protection because the variability of sugar protection is so large. The binding offered by the USA, at 91 percent, causes the average protection rate to fall by 32 percent, despite being only seven percent below the previous average rate of protection. In Japan, the binding itself virtually determines

TABLE 1.   Effects of Bindings on Import Protection for Wheat

	Average 1979-93 %	Standard Deviation %	Average 1986-88 %	Final Binding %	Mean w/ Binding %
EU	56	37	103	82	51
USA	12	14	20	4	1
Japan	438	153	651	152	151
Canada	22	18	30	58	22
Norway	170	126	266	495	170
Australia	0	1	1	0	0
Turkey	13	29	36	200	13

the expected rate of protection. In this case, the binding is so far to the left of the underlying mean rate of protection that virtually all of the probability mass is collected at the bound rate. The bindings offered by Canada, Norway, Australia and Turkey are all too high to reduce the average rate of protection significantly.

The case of beef is interesting because the standard deviation of protection is much lower for this commodity than for wheat or sugar. In part because of this, and in part because of the setting of the protection rates, the bindings above the average tariff rate offered by all countries but Japan and Australia do not have a substantial liberalizing effect in any of the cases considered. In Japan, the binding is below the average rate of protection and has a magnified impact on the mean rate of protection. Even though the binding is fifteen percentage points below the underlying mean rate, the mean with the binding is 18 percentage points below the underlying mean. In terms of figure 3, it is clear that this liberalization is occurring in a region of the distribution where the marginal impact of liberalization is particularly large.

From the results presented in tables 1 to 3, it appears that the extent of reduction in average agricultural protection rates implied by the Uruguay Round was relatively small in many cases because of the high settings of the bindings offered. The reduction in the cost of protection resulting from these bindings is in some cases very significant because the high rates of protection ruled out by the bindings are the most costly (Francois and Martin 1995). Even though the extent of liberalization under the Uruguay Round appears to have been disappointing for many commodities (Hathaway and Ingco 1995), the introduction of the framework of a rules-based system may still be important in providing the basis for substantial progress in future negotiations. Such negotiations are scheduled to

TABLE 2.   Effects of Bindings on Protection for Sugar

	Average 1979-93 %	Standard Deviation %	Average 1986-88 %	Final Binding %	Mean w/ Binding %
EU	149	80	259	152	118
USA	98	70	131	91	66
Japan	227	74	274	58	58
Canada	8	3	11	35	8
Norway	0	0	0	211	0
Australia	7	7	12	52	7
Turkey	17	30	12	150	17

begin even before the end of the phase in period for the Round cuts, and hence future gains might be achievable within a realistic time frame.

To provide an indication of whether the cut in protection of the general magnitude which has been achieved in past rounds of trade negotiations would provide a substantial degree of liberalization, the estimates presented in figures 1 to 3 were recalculated assuming a 36 percent reduction in the *ad valorem* equivalent of the post- Uruguay Round bindings. The impacts on average rates of protection are given in table 4. For each commodity, the first column presents the expected final rates of protection given in tables 1 to 3. The second column shows the rates of protection which would apply following a subsequent 36 percent reduction in the tariff binding resulting from a future "Stern" Round of tariff negotiations.[12]

From the results presented in table 4, it appears that a subsequent Round of negotiations building on the Uruguay Round would have the potential to bring about substantial reductions in the average protection

TABLE 3. Effects of Bindings on Protection for Beef

	Average 1979-93 %	Standard Deviation %	Average 1986-88 %	Final Binding %	Mean w/ Binding %
EU	84	16	90	125	84
USA	2	2	3	31	2
Japan	54	21	87	39	36
Canada	2	2	2	38	2
Norway	146	25	145	405	146
Australia	0	0	0	0	0
Turkey	28	29	−4	250	28

TABLE 4. Expected Average Protection Following a 36 Percent Reduction from Uruguay Rounds Level

	Wheat		Sugar		Beef	
	Post-Uruguay	Post-Stern	Post-Uruguay	Post-Stern	Post-Uruguay	Post-Stern
EU	51	26	118	85	84	80
USA	1	0	66	46	2	2
Japan	151	96	58	37	36	24
Canada	21	10	8	7	2	2
Norway	170	83	0	0	146	146
Australia	0	0	7	6	0	0
Turkey	13	0	17	17	28	28

rates applying on most of the commodities covered. For wheat, a 36 percent reduction in post-Uruguay Round bindings would bring about substantial reductions in the average rate of protection for all countries except Australia, which is now bound at a zero tariff. Some marked reductions would occur in Canada and Norway where bindings provided under the Uruguay Round provided very little liberalization. Over the range relevant to post-Uruguay Round liberalization, reductions in bindings are particularly effective because they take place in a relatively dense part of the distribution associated with positive rates of protection.

For sugar, the Uruguay Round has also resulted in rates of protection which are located in relatively dense portions of the distribution of protection. As a result, subsequent reductions in tariff bindings result in quite substantial reductions in average rates of protection in most of the countries considered.

For beef, most of the bindings are sufficiently far above the average rate of protection that changes in the binding have relatively little impact on the expected value of the distribution except in Japan, where a further reduction in the average rate of protection would be expected. This result is due in part to the fact that the standard deviation of protection for this commodity is relatively low, so that there is little probability associated with rates of protection as high as the bindings offered on this commodity. For commodities like this, achieving substantial liberalization may require either larger future reductions in protection, or several subsequent Rounds.

Conclusion

Key features of the Uruguay Round agreement are the introduction of tariff bindings on a wide range of previously unconstrained commodities and substantial reforms in the trading rules. We provide a general framework for evaluating the consequences of these measures and apply this framework to the important problem of evaluating the effects of introducing tariff bindings on three major agricultural products.

The theory of endogenous protection provides an explanation for the variations in protection rates which are observed in the real world. Given varying rates of protection, tariff bindings have a liberalizing impact even if they are set above the average rate of protection. This is because they restrict the range of the distribution and accumulate some of its probability mass at a lower rate of protection than was previously the case. In the increasingly important area of anti-dumping, current rules imply positive rates of protection for a similar reason. Part of the probability mass, that associated with positive estimated dumping margins, is accumulated at a zero estimated dumping margin. With only negative (i.e. dumped) and zero margins included in the sample, the rules followed must lead, on average, to findings that products are dumped, and hence to the imposition of dumping duties.

Once the stochastic nature of protection is acknowledged, it becomes possible to analyze the consequences of the introduction of tariff bindings and other changes in rules in a manner analogous to the traditional market-access instruments. We illustrate this with a relatively straightforward procedure for evaluating the consequences of introducing and then changing tariff bindings.

From the empirical examples provided, it appears that the degree of liberalization achieved was reasonably modest for the three commodities considered. The exception to this pattern was Japan, where sizable reductions in protection were achieved from very high initial levels. The analysis suggests that the Uruguay Round may have been more successful in establishing a foundation from which subsequent rounds of negotiations could achieve more substantial reductions in average rates of protection.

Appendix

The Expiration of Steel VERs and the Imposition of Antidumping and Countervailing Duties

Country	VER on Exports of Certain Steel Products 1984-92	Antidumping Duty Orders on Certain Flat-Rolled Steel Products 1993	Countervailing Orders on Certain Flat-Rolled Steel Products 1993
Australia	yes	yes	no
Austria	yes	no	no
Brazil	yes	yes	yes
China	yes	no	no
Czechoslovakia	yes	no	no
EC	yes	yes	yes
Finland	yes	yes	no
GDR	yes	no	no
Hungary	yes	no	no
Japan	yes	no	no
Korea, Rep. of	yes	yes	yes
Mexico	yes	yes	yes
Poland	yes	yes	no
Romania	yes	yes	no
Trinidad and Tobago	yes	no	no
Venezuela	yes	no	no
Yugoslavia	yes	no	no

NOTES

1. Even Chile, which has reduced its tariff rates enormously over the past 20 years has had episodes of substantial tariff increases around a marked downward trend in protection rates (Dean, Desai and Riedel 1993).

2. See the reviews in Nelson (1994) and Rodrik (1994).

3. Ideally, as the theoretical and empirical literature suggests, where possible we should try to explicitly model the endogeneity of protection in applied models. Instead of modeling particular processes, however, one could instead focus on expectations about protection, based on evidence of the pattern of protection across regimes, products, and sectors. In reduced form, the associated moments could be linked to the factors emphasized in the empirical literature.

4. The round of trade activism in trade-sensitive sectors in the United States in the mid 1980s, during a period with a soaring dollar and massive capital inflows, could be characterized as one of microeconomic triage for macroeconomic imbalances. Demand for protection can be responsive to swings in conditions well beyond those related to the immediate workings of particular sectors and their respective agents.

5. Alternative approaches have been suggested by Fraser (1988) who derived the mean price by mixing the two distributions, and by Bardsley and Cashin (1990), who applied option pricing theory.

6. This would be the case if the tariff followed a random walk.

7. Safeguard measures are not applicable to a product from a developing country (i) if the share of the developing country in the imports of the product concerned does not exceed 3 percent, and (ii) if developing countries with less than 3 percent import shares collectively account for no more than 9 percent of total imports of the product concerned.

8. GATT (1994b).

9. The tariff equivalents were generally to be calculated at the 4-digit level of the Harmonized System, while tariffs are applied at the individual national tariff line level, which may involve 10 or 12 digits.

10. This assumption is clearly important. If protection rates are increasing, then this assumption may understate the degree of liberalization which has been achieved. Importantly, we also assume that the balance between those seeking and resisting protection will be unchanged by the presence of a binding. If, however, both parties are fully rational in their understanding of the system, it is possible that the suppliers and demanders of protection would understand that a higher level of protection during unbound periods is required to achieve any given level of average protection. In this super-rational case, our results may overstate the degree of liberalization actually achieved.

11. Given a predicted value for the world price, the conditional variance of the protection rate is: $\sigma^2_{\tau/\rho} = \sigma^2_{\tau}(1 - \rho^2)$ where $ is the correlation between the world price and the protection rate (Freund and Walpole 1980). If the mean over the forecast period were expected to deviate from its underlying mean, an adjustment to the conditional mean of the distribution of protection would also be required before the impact of the binding on protection could be evaluated.

12. Here we assume a reversion to the earlier GATT practice of naming its negotiating Rounds after a distinguished individual (e.g. the Dillon Round, or the
Kennedy Round), rather than on a geographic basis.

REFERENCES

Anderson, Kym. 1978. "On Why Rates of Assistance Differ between Australia's
Rural Industries." *Australian Journal of Agricultural Economics* 22:99–114.
Anderson, Kym. 1980. "The Political Market for Government Assistance to Aus-
tralian Manufacturing Industries." *Economic Record* 56:132–44.
Baldwin, Robert E. 1989. "The Political Economy of Free Trade." *Journal of Eco-
nomic Perspectives* 3:119–135.
Bardsley, Peter, and Cashin, Paul. 1990. "Underwriting Assistance to the Aus-
tralian Wheat Industry—An Application of Option Pricing Theory." *Aus-
tralian Journal of Agricultural Economics* 34:212–222.
Bhagwati, Jagdish N., and Srinivasan, T.N. 1976. "Optimal Trade Policy and
Compensation Under Endogenous Uncertainty." *Journal of International
Economics* 101:1–31.
Bohara, Alok K., and Kaempfer, William H. 1991. "A Test of Tariff Endogeneity
in the United States." *American Economic Review* 81:952–960.
Boltuck, Richard; Francois, Joseph F.; and Kaplan, Scott. 1990. "The Economic
Implications of the Administration of the U.S. Unfair Trade Laws." In R.
Boltuck and R. Litan, eds., *Down in the Dumps.* Brookings: Washington DC.
Brandão, Antonio, and Martin, Will. 1993. "Implications of Agricultural Trade
Liberalization for the Developing Countries." *Agricultural Economics*
8:313–43.
Caves, Richard E. 1976. "Economic Models of Political Choice: Canada's Tariff
Structure." *Canadian Journal of Economics* 9:278–300.
Dean, Judith; Desai, Seema; and Riedel, James. 1993. Trade Policy Reform in
Developing Countries. Johns Hopkins University, Manuscript.
Deardorff, Alan, and Stern, Robert M. 1986. *The Michigan Model of World Pro-
duction and Trade.* Cambridge: MIT Press.
Dornbusch, Rudiger, and Frankel, Jeffrey. 1987. "Macroeconomics and Protec-
tion." In R. M. Stern, ed., *US Trade Policies in a Changing World Economy.*
Cambridge: MIT Press.
Falvey, Rodney, and Lloyd, Peter. 1991. "Uncertainty and the Choice of Protec-
tive Instrument." *Oxford Economic Papers* 43:463–78.
Feinberg, Robert. 1989. "Exchange Rates and 'Unfair Trade." *Review of Econom-
ics and Statistics* 71:704–07.
Feinberg, Robert, and Hirsch, Barry. 1989. "Industry Rent Seeking and the Filing
of 'Unfair Trade' Complaints." *International Journal of Industrial Organiza-
tion* 7:325–40.
Findlay, Ronald. 1987. "Comment on Deardorff and Stern," in R.M. Stern, ed.,
U.S. Trade Policies in a Changing World Economy. Cambridge: MIT Press.

Fraser, R. W. 1988. "A Method for Evaluating Supply Response to Price Under-writing." *Australian Journal of Agricultural Economics* 32:22–36.

Francois, Joseph, and Martin, Will. 1995. "Multilateral Trade Rules and the Expected Cost of Protection." Discussion Paper, Centre for Economic Policy Research.

Francois, Joseph; McDonald, Bradley; and Nordström, Hakan. 1993. "Economy-wide Effects of the Uruguay Round." Uruguay Round background paper, General Agreement on Tariffs and Trade, Geneva.

Freund, J., and Walpole, R.E. 1980. *Mathematical Statistics: Third Edition.* New Jersey: Prentice Hall.

GATT. 1994a. *News of the Uruguay Round of Multilateral Trade Negotiations,* April.

GATT. 1994b. *Trade Policy Review: United States.* General Agreement on Tariffs and Trade, Geneva.

Gawande, Kishore. 1997. "Testing Theories of Endogenous Protection: Robust Evidence from US Nontariff Barrier Data." in this volume.

Goldin, Ian; Knudsen, O.; and van der Mensbrugghe, Dominique. 1993. *Trade Liberalisation: Global Economic Implications.* Paris and Washington: OECD and the World Bank.

Hanson, J.M. 1990. "Taxation and the Political Economy of the Tariff." *International Organization* 44:527–552.

Hathaway, Dale, and Ingco, Melinda. 1995. "Agricultural liberalization and the Uruguay Round" in W. Martin and L.A. Winters, eds., *The Uruguay Round and Developing Countries.* Cambridge: Cambridge University Press.

Hillman, Arye L. 1982. "Declining Industries and Political-Support Protectionist Motives." *American Economic Review* 72:1180–1197.

Hindley, Brian. 1990. "Comment: The Economic Implications of the Administration of the U.S. Unfair Trade Laws." In R. Boltuck and R. Litan, eds., *Down in the Dumps.* Washington, D.C.: Brookings.

Ingco, Melinda. 1994. "How Much Trade Liberalization was Achieved under the Uruguay Round?" World Bank, manuscript.

Ingco, Melinda. 1995. "Agricultural Trade Liberalization in the Uruguay Round: One Step Forward, One Step Back." Supplementary Paper for the World Bank Conference on the Uruguay Round and the Developing Economies, January.

Josling, Timothy, and Tangermann, Stephan. 1994. "Tariffication in the Uruguay Round Agreement on Agriculture." Paper presented to the symposium on "World Agriculture in a Post-GATT Environment," Saskatoon, Saskatchewan.

Leamer, Edward. 1988. "Cross-Sectional Estimation of the Effects of Trade Barriers." In R.C. Feenstra, ed., *Empirical Methods for International Trade.* Cambridge: MIT Press.

Magee, Stephen P., and Young, Leslie. 1987. "Endogenous Protection in the United States, 1900–1984." in R.M. Stern, ed., *US Trade Policies in a Changing World Economy.* Cambridge: MIT Press.

Magee, Stephen P.; Brock, William A.; and Young, Leslie. 1989. *Black Hole Tariffs and Endogenous Policy Theory.* New York: Cambridge University Press.

Martin, Will, and Urban, P. 1984. "Modelling Producer Response under Support Price and Stabilisation Schemes." Paper presented to the 28th Annual conference of the Australian Agricultural Economics Society, Sydney.

Mundlak, Yair, and Larson, Donald. 1992. "On the Transmission of World Agricultural Prices." *World Bank Economic Review* 6:399–422.

Nelson, Douglas. 1994. "The Political Economy of U.S. Automobile Protection." NBER working paper no. 4746.

Nguyen, Trien T.; Perroni, Carlo; and Wigle, Randall. 1993. "An Evaluation of the Draft Final Act of the Uruguay Round." *Economic Journal* 103:1540–1558.

OECD. 1994. *Monitoring and Outlook on Agricultural Policies, Markets and Trade.* Paris, OECD.

Olson, Mancur. 1965. *The Logic of Collective Action.* Cambridge: Harvard University Press.

Palmeter, N. David. 1990. "The Antidumping Law: A Legal and Administrative Nontariff Barrier." In R. Boltuck and R. Litan, eds., *Down in the Dumps.* Washington, D.C.: Brookings.

Preeg, Ernest. 1994. "Traders in a Brave New World: The Uruguay Round and the Future of the International Trading System." Center for Strategic and International Studies, Washington D.C., manuscript.

Ray, Edward J. 1981. "The Determinants of Tariff and Non-Tariff Trade Restrictions in the United States." *Journal of Political Economy* 89:105–121.

Rodrik, Dani. 1994. "What Does the Political Economy Literature on Trade Policy (Not) Tell Us That We Ought to Know?" CEPR discussion paper 1039.

Stern, R. M., ed. 1987. *US Trade Policies in a Changing World Economy.* Cambridge: MIT Press.

Stigler, George. 1974. "Free Riders and Collective Action." *Bell Journal of Economics and Management Science* 5:359–65.

Tollefsen, T.C. 1994. "An Analysis of Barriers to Trade and Implementation of NTBs in the Haaland/Norman CGE Model." Foundation for Research in Economics and Business Administration, Norwegian School of Economics and Business Administration, working paper no. 13/1994.

Trefler, Daniel. 1993. "Trade Liberalization and the Theory of Endogenous Protection: An Econometric Study of U.S. Import Policy." *Journal of Political Economy* 101:138–160.

Vousden, Neil. 1990. *The Economics of Trade Protection.* Cambridge: Cambridge University Press.

Winters, L. Alan. 1994. "Import Surveillance as a Strategic Trade Policy." In P. Krugman and A. Smith, eds., *Empirical Studies of Strategic Trade Policy* Chicago: University of Chicago Press.

CHAPTER 7

Alternative Paths toward Open Global Markets

Rachel McCulloch and Peter A. Petri

Although the principle of nondiscrimination is central to the General Agreement on Tariffs and Trade (GATT), the potential complementarity between multilateral and discriminatory approaches to trade liberalization was acknowledged in the GATT system from its earliest days and has been carried over into the World Trade Organization (WTO) created by the Uruguay Round agreement. Notwithstanding Article I's requirement of most-favored-nation (MFN) treatment among GATT signatories, the original Agreement and subsequent amendments left room for a variety of exceptions, most notably Article XXIV's exception in favor of customs unions and free-trade areas.

The GATT system's own growth and evolution has been paralleled by the growth and evolution of what is now the European Union (EU), the most important and most durable preferential trading arrangement (PTA) in modern history. However, far from opting out of the GATT process, the expanding EU has continued to play a central role in multilateral negotiations on trade. Elsewhere regionalism has also been on the upswing, but most of the new regional groupings, in contrast to many formed and disbanded in earlier decades, are outward-looking, explicitly aimed at supplementing and possibly facilitating further multilateral liberalization. Even as blocs grow and proliferate, new countries continue to seek admittance to the WTO.

Recent events underscore that many countries do not choose *between* multilateral and regional liberalization but, rather, choose some of each. Since trade liberalization is better seen as an ongoing process rather than a once-and-for-always change in policy, a mixed strategy can sometimes expedite progress in multilateral negotiations. While writers close to the political process often cite this potential complementarity (Sapir 1990; Hormats 1994), most of the economics literature on preferential trading

149

arrangements implicitly assumes that any new situation represents members' revised, yet then final, policy choice.

This paper develops two themes often neglected by academic economists. The first section addresses what we call the non-Vinerian static consequences of preferential liberalization. While the traditional literature has stressed the economic implications of discrimination among trading partners, we emphasize the economic implications of creating larger markets. The second section addresses the dynamics of preferential arrangements. Specifically, we are interested in the implications of such agreements—and of their effects on the economic structure of members and non-members—for domestic political support of further liberalization, for the behavior of left-out countries, and for the potential compatibility or even complementarity of preferential and nondiscriminatory liberalization approaches. A final section draws conclusions for policy and future research.

The Economics of Preferential Trading

The introduction of a European trading bloc, first as an idea and later as a reality, spawned a large literature on the economic consequences of preferential trading. In that literature, one contribution remains preeminent for its impact on subsequent analysis: Jacob Viner's (1950) insight that discriminatory liberalization of trade could reduce productive efficiency and welfare not only among excluded countries but also for the participants themselves.

Before Viner, economists interpreted even discriminatory liberalization as a move *toward* free trade and therefore necessarily welfare-improving in the same way as free trade itself. As Gottfried Haberler wrote in 1936, "Customs unions are always to be welcomed . . . the economic advantage of customs union can be proved by the Theory of Comparative Cost."[1] Viner's analysis swept away this simple presumption.

The Viner Paradigm

Any formal theory necessarily focuses on some features of a complex reality and ignores others—sometimes features that are considered less important, but more often aspects that are harder to capture within a simple framework. The Vinerian tradition emphasizes the discriminatory character of a PTA. As Viner showed and others elaborated in greater generality, preferential liberalization has two opposing effects on economic efficiency—trade diversion and trade creation—and therefore an ambiguous net effect.

Viner's analysis was the first formal contribution to what was subsequently termed the general theory of second best (Lipsey and Lancaster 1956–57). This line of inquiry had an important corollary: even if a particular free-trade area was efficiency-improving, it would necessarily be dominated by an arrangement with only partial preferences toward partners, i.e., a reduced rather than zero tariff. Harry Johnson's (1962) classic exposition of customs-union theory thus observes that " . . . quite irrationally, international convention condemns preferential systems except when the degree of preference is 100 percent. . . ." This comment is a product of its times—the heyday of the Vinerian analysis and second-best fine tuning of policy.

In the 1990s, the standard textbook treatment of free-trade areas and customs unions still begins and often ends with Viner's ambiguous assessment. The emphasis is appropriate for some applications—for example, trade blocs involving small developing economies with similar factor endowments. Many such free-trade areas and customs unions were negotiated in the 1960s and 1970s, as newly independent countries looked to trade blocs as a means of establishing a viable manufacturing sector (de la Torre and Kelly 1992).[2] By rationalizing bloc production (i.e., limiting the bloc to just one steel mill, one auto plant, one refinery) members hoped to achieve lower unit costs. However, the resulting markets were still very small, and the blocs lacked an effective political mechanism for closing capacity in the protected modern industries or even restraining new entry.[3] Policy makers soon realized that the high cost of trade diversion was unlikely to be offset by gains from economies of scale, and most of these blocs were never fully implemented.

The Vinerian perspective may be less relevant, however, to the larger blocs, often of more advanced countries, that have been implemented or proposed in recent years in Europe, North America, and Asia. Noneconomists seem largely unworried by the possibility that an unchanged or even reduced common tariff wall facing nonmembers could promote welfare-lowering trade diversion. When the potential for trade diversion is clearly apparent, as with Asian exporters under the North American Free Trade Agreement (NAFTA), the issue is seen more as one of equity or political friction than of economic efficiency.[4] The heated public debate over NAFTA in fall 1993 was notable for the lack of mention of trade diversion on either side; to noneconomists, the benefits (and costs) of selective free trade look very much like the benefits of MFN free trade.

This brief overview of regional trading arrangements suggests a self-selection process in the formation of blocs. Those that would be seriously affected by trade diversion typically fail to get off the ground because the implementation of the PTA is soon recognized to involve large costs without obvious benefits. Those that are implemented, in turn, appear to be driven primarily by considerations other than the trade creation and trade diversion central to Vinerian theory.

Market Size and Its Consequences

What the Vinerian tradition omits is the most important practical consequence of a PTA, namely, the creation of a larger market.[5] The importance of market-size effects was recognized early on in Balassa's (1967) assessment of the "Common Market of the Six." Finding that both trade-creation and trade-diversion effects were modest in size, Balassa argued that the real benefits resulted from scale economies and increased innovation: "It is apparent that these dynamic effects far outweigh in importance the static effects of trade liberalization." Balassa also concluded that formation of the Common Market had attracted substantial direct investment, especially from the United States: "The enlargement of national markets through integration appears to have been a more important inducement for U.S. investments than tariff discrimination. The widening of markets open to individual producers has created possibilities for exploiting economies of scale. . . ."

Until the 1980s, issues relating to market size and market power were largely absent from the theoretical literature in international trade. Recent modeling innovations have brought welfare effects associated with economies of scale and strategic firm behavior under conditions of market power to the forefront of theoretical studies. These new insights into the role of market size affect the analysis of PTAs in several distinct ways. Here we enumerate some of the more important effects, including mechanisms that improve productive efficiency and mechanisms that alter the structure of producer competition.[6]

Scale Economies at the Firm Level

Identifiable scale economies usually have their source in an indivisibility of equipment or up-front effort (e.g., research and development). An industry operating within a small market may have per-unit production costs in excess of those in larger markets for no reason other than the difference in volume of output. This situation can lead to the appearance of "false comparative advantage"—a country has higher (average) costs even though potential costs are the same in both markets. Indeed, the cost *structure* may actually be more favorable in the apparent high-cost country. Thus, what may appear as diversion of trade to an inefficient partner need not be inefficient at all if the partner is thereby transformed from a low- to an efficient-scale producer by the PTA.

External Economies

Benefits from external economies (spillovers) may also increase with the size of the market. External economies within an industry may take the form of increased availability of specialized inputs or services (a positive externality affecting all firms), or of know-how or even proprietary technical information that moves from one firm to another through a shared pool of workers. The propensity of firms (and especially smaller firms) in a given industry to cluster geographically even when lower-cost locations are available suggests that benefits from localized externalities are large enough to offset various possible costs.

Competition

Larger markets also improve efficiency by promoting interfirm rivalry. Scale economies act as a barrier to entry and thus enforce the market position of incumbent firms. When a market can support only a few firms, or just one, governments often opt for regulation of prices and profits or even outright nationalization. While no theoretical proposition shows that market outcomes are invariably preferable, the record is eloquent on this subject.

Strategic Competition

Newer trade models incorporating scale economies and imperfect competition provide a theoretical rationale for trade interventions designed to assure access to large markets for a country's scale-dependent activities. By enlarging the scope of its own markets, a PTA makes it less likely that any firm within its area will be denied access to markets sufficiently large to achieve economies of scale. In other words, a PTA may obviate one argument in support of "strategic" trade policies. Although we do not believe that empirical conditions often justify such interventions, it seems that PTAs can provide governments with a relatively benign outlet for strategic policy urges, whether or not these urges are justified.

Innovation

Firms engaged in research and development must weigh the up-front costs of projects against the revenue flow to be generated by the innovative product or process. Other things equal, a larger market translates into a larger potential revenue flow and, hence, more innovative activity.[7] To be sure, innovative firms can also extend their markets via exports, direct investment, or licensing. However, the costs of marketing and legal protection of proprietary knowledge may rise outside of integrated markets, The United States, for most of the postwar period the world's largest market, has also been the world's leading site for innovation.

Direct Investment

PTAs are often seen as a device for attracting direct investment or avoiding the loss of investment to other regions. Investment is assumed to be attracted by larger markets and by improved access to low-cost components produced in the enlarged economic area. While increased direct investment is almost universally regarded by policy makers as a benefit, theoretical analysis suggests that the welfare consequences of such capital inflows are complex. It is well known that a capital inflow can exacerbate the nation's welfare loss from protection if the import-competing sector is capital-intensive. The loss occurs because foreign capital earns a rate of return that exceeds the value of its marginal product at world prices, i.e., the payment to additional (foreign) capital exceeds its contribution (Brecher and Diaz-Alejandro 1977; Bhagwati and Brecher 1980).

This argument is weakened if taxes reduce net payments to foreign capital, or if protection takes the form of quotas, voluntary export restraints, or other nontariff barriers. Moreover, the usual result is derived in the context of a model with two homogenous goods and two homogeneous factors. If, as is typical in direct investment, investing firms produce differentiated products that could not otherwise be produced in the PTA area, or use capital that embodies proprietary technology, then inward investment may reduce rather than increase the cost of protection.

A simple argument shows that allowing for direct investment can strengthen the static case for PTAs if barriers are high enough to prevent trade in the relevant good. Deardorff and Stern (1994) use a two-good Ricardian model to show that all the gains from MFN free trade can sometimes also be obtained from autarkic trading blocs. Of course, if the composition of the blocs is random, or at least not determined on the basis of potential gains from trade alone, the expected level of welfare is lower. Even so, to the extent that the reason for cost differences lies in technological differences, direct investment and associated technology transfer could transform the "wrong" trading partners into the right ones.

Allowing for direct investment may likewise modify Krugman's (1991) pessimistic conclusion that a world assembled into a few blocs may minimize global welfare. This much-discussed theoretical result is derived from a model in which each country produces its own distinctive good and each good enters utility functions symmetrically. As Deardorff and Stern

(1994) observe, these assumptions stack the theoretical deck against welfare-enhancing blocs; any bloc regardless of size or composition necessarily causes trade diversion because each potential trading partner has something unique to offer.[8] However, direct investment can provide an alternative means of gaining access to a given country's distinctive product. In the absence of scale economies, direct investment (or technology transfer in another form) can be a perfect substitute for trade in the country-specific products. If scale is important to either the investment decision or the production process, blocs can enhance welfare simply by increasing market size.

Empirical Evidence

Some of the market-size effects we have discussed have been estimated empirically. Any discussion of this literature must begin with work of Robert Stern and his colleagues at the University of Michigan. This work has moved from broad assessments of the Tokyo Round to influential analyses of the NAFTA agreement. Stern and his colleagues have brought a new level of quantitative sophistication to the analysis of trading arrangements and have been also in the forefront of assessing the importance of non-Vinerian effects. For example, Brown and Stern (1987) clearly specify those modeling issues that affect the scale of benefits: whether Canada should be treated as a small country, whether traded products should be treated as differentiated, whether Canadian firms have unexploited scale economies, and the likely responsiveness of direct investment flows.

The Brown and Stern paper raises central issues about the relationship between theoretical assumptions and the magnitude of estimated PTA effects. In his discussion of the paper, Harris (1987) concludes that the reason Brown and Stern's welfare effects are small even with scale effects is that they use the "Armington assumption"—that each country's goods are imperfect substitutes for goods produced elsewhere. In another comment, Petri (1987) calculates that the gains from non-Vinerian effects, if experienced throughout the tradable goods sectors of PTA economies, could be orders of magnitude larger than those attributed to trade creation.

Recent analyses of PTAs have suggest that very sizeable gains may be possible if non-Vinerian economic consequences are fully included. Baldwin (1989) has estimated large benefits from the Europe 1992 agreements by considering several factors that accelerate the growth rate (such as increased investment and productivity gains). Martin, Petri, and Yanagashima (1994) also find very substantial gains for an APEC-based free trade area—on the order of $100 billion per year—assuming that scale and productivity-growth-enhancing effects are included.

The Dynamics of Preferential Trade Areas

Although the evidence on the life-cycle of PTAs is thin, some patterns do emerge.[9] Initially, there is often great uncertainty associated with the implementation of preferential agreements. Once implementation uncertainty is resolved, pressures quickly develop to take on new members. Blocs tend to resist these pressures by setting time limits before expanding membership, but in the end they do tend to grow (Baldwin 1993).

In their external policies, blocs worry a great deal about "sensitive" industries which are often those benefiting from trade diversion. But they do not, as a rule, oppose global liberalization. Indeed, blocs often develop initiatives that favor new types of internal and even multilateral liberalization. The battle over agriculture that delayed completion of the Uruguay Round has tended to overshadow European support for several GATT rounds, and European innovations in extending liberalization to include "deep" regulatory and financial issues (Lawrence 1991).

In analyzing the impact of a PTA, therefore, one should not stop with the arrangement's immediate effects on trade barriers and trade patterns. A PTA broadly changes the payoffs to policy choices both within and outside the trading area. Over time, the cumulative effect of these changes on the size and composition of a bloc, on its policies toward protectionism, and on the behavior of outside countries, could easily outweigh the agreement's direct consequences.

Below we examine two types of effects. The first is the dynamics of bloc membership: will a bloc really come to life by implementing its agreements, will it grow by adding new members, and will it induce the development of competing blocs? The second is the dynamics of the bloc's trade policies: will the bloc exploit its market power by raising barriers, will its members move toward liberal multilateral policies to control the costs of trade diversion, and will the bloc induce more or less protection in other countries and blocs?

The dynamics of membership and policy are closely related, since the decision to expand raises many of the same issues as the decision to reduce third-country barriers multilaterally. Nevertheless, there are sufficient differences between these processes to warrant separate discussion.

Membership Dynamics Inside Blocs

In the course of its evolution, a typical PTA gradually enlarges its membership by bringing in increasingly diverse partners. In the case of Europe, the Six became Nine in 1973. Greece joined in 1981 and Spain and Portugal in 1986. These last three, with economies quite different from the original Six, brought with them opportunities for trade flows along stronger lines of comparative advantage. The U.S.-Canada agreement, similarly, led to the inclusion of Mexico and possibly other Latin American countries. The Association of South East Asian Nations (ASEAN) grew in size and economic diversity with the accession of Vietnam in 1995; membership for Laos, Myanmar, and Cambodia is receiving serious consideration also. These examples suggest that the dynamics of blocs favor increasingly diverse membership; the development of a trading bloc appears to change the balance of producer interests in ways that promote the eventual admission of members who were previously "too competitive" to be admitted.

A very simple model formalizes this insight. Suppose that each country's trade policies are decided by producer interests, which in turn are based on ownership of sector-specific assets (including both human and non-human capital). Then the desirability of a trade agreement will depend on the balance of interests between those industries that benefit and those that are harmed. If trade is liberalized multilaterally starting from a high initial protection level, then only a few industries will benefit (those in which a country has comparative advantage) and many will be harmed (those in which it does not).

In this kind of model, full MFN liberalization is not supported by the median voter. However, a free-trade area may be supported if it retains sufficient third-country barriers to allow some less-than-globally-competitive industries to survive and even to benefit from preferential access to regional markets. In effect, trade diversion helps to expand the range of industries that benefit from the agreement, thus making some liberalization possible.

Consider the case in which Country 1 starts from autarky, with 1/6th of demand and production in each of six sectors labelled a through f. Country 1's costs (in labor units) vary relative to costs in Country 2 and the rest of the world (w) across the six sectors as follows:

Product a: $c_1 < c_2 < c_w$
Product b: $c_1 < c_w < c_2$
Product c: $c_2 < c_1 < c_w$
Product d: $c_2 < c_w < c_1$
Product e: $c_w < c_1 < c_2$
Product f: $c_w < c_2 < c_1$

Suppose costs are constant. If free trade is established and the rest of the world is large, Country 1 will shift all its resources into producing goods a and b and will import goods c through f. If assets are sector-specific in the short run, only one-third of the industries will support this policy.

Alternatively, suppose that Country 1 maintains high third-country barriers and forms a preferential trade bloc with Country 2, which starts from a similar position of autarky. Now Country 1 will produce goods a, b, and e, while importing c, d, and f; half of the industrialists will be ready to support the deal. Assuming some consumer gains, or some trade with the partner before the agreement, the free-trade area will pass. A similar argument ensures passage in Country 2.

Once in place, the bloc will force each country's industrial structure to shift toward its more-efficient sectors. Each will now produce goods in which it is at least regionally competitive, and each will give up industries in which it is regionally uncompetitive. These structural shifts will be reinforced if any non-Vinerian scale effects are important and help to improve the efficiency of various industries within the PTA.

Starting from the post-bloc industrial configuration, even MFN liberalization will now have a good chance at passing. Once the PTA is established, two-thirds of each country's industries (a and b in Country 1—the industries that are globally as well as regionally competitive) will benefit from complete liberalization. Only those few industries that survived due to trade diversion will be harmed. The numerous industries that were regionally uncompetitive before the PTA have been eliminated by the formation of the bloc.

In this example, the bloc provides a transition between autarky and free trade. It "divides and conquers" the opposition to free trade by allowing the temporary survival of industries that are regionally but not globally competitive. Put another way, it allows a two-step adjustment of resource allocation. The two-step process in effect ignores the expectations of voters contemplating step one about the consequences of their actions for their eventual fate following step two. Of course, smart voters might see through this game and realize that governments will abandon their commitment to the PTA once the economy becomes more competitive. Industries that might have supported the agreement only because of benefits from trade diversion might not do so if they realize that they too will later be sacrificed. But they might: if the expected tenure of the PTA is long enough and discount rates are high enough, even temporary gains could be sufficient to elicit their support. More precisely, if owners of specific and highly durable factors to be sacrificed in the second step have perfect foresight, they will support formation of a PTA only if the discount rate is sufficiently high. As a practical matter, given the high degree of uncertainty about the overall business environment even a few years into the future, it seems reasonable to expect owners to act in their short-run interest, as the example suggests.[10]

The strategy has elements in common with strategies to liberalize trade by freeing a relatively small number of sectors at a time (World Bank 1991). The opposition is defeated sector by sector, with a majority favoring each step. Doing this via trading blocs has a distinct advantage: by ensuring access to new markets, blocs offer substantial visible benefits to the tradable industries that survive.[11]

Trade diversion plays an interesting role in our model. It is the payoff from the PTA that creates political support for liberalization. In this vein, the promise of preferential access to Mexican markets, very small compared to world markets, appears to have helped build political support in the United States for NAFTA, although the same degree of enthusiasm was harder to generate for the more abstract yet potentially more important provisions of the Uruguay Round.

Membership Dynamics Outside Blocs

Countries outside a bloc may suffer from trade diversion as well as missing out on the benefits associated with participation in a larger market. These factors will induce outsiders to seek bloc membership. Strong external interest in membership has been a characteristic of the European Community since its inception, and the membership jockeying typical of blocs has also enveloped NAFTA and APEC.[12] APEC quickly absorbed three Chinas, Mexico, and Chile, and then decided to call a moratorium on new members in order to fend off increasing pressures from Russia, South America, and South Asia.

The attractiveness of membership in a bloc is further intensified if other parallel blocs begin to gain membership, raising the possibility that a country will be excluded from open trading relationships altogether. The power of this dynamic was evident within Europe, where countries that initially resisted the pull of the EEC eventually joined. It is now also evident worldwide, as several groups of countries are proposing new blocs in order to have something to join. Even if an economy favors a particular bloc (e.g., the EEC rather than the European Free Trade Area (EFTA)), it will often make sense to join a less-desirable bloc rather than be left outside of all agreements. The emergence of blocs may push some countries into taking sides even when their economic stakes argue for a global strategy. A recent example is the 1996 decision by free-trade-minded Chile to affiliate with its Southern Cone neighbors in the Mercosur trading bloc after negotiations regarding Chile's NAFTA membership slowed to a crawl.

Taken together, these forces favor the expansion of blocs. To be sure, there will be opposition to bloc expansion from industries that were initially bribed into a PTA through diversion gains. But there are strong pressures for expansion from countries outside blocs, and possibly from increasingly efficient sectors within blocs. Once blocs take hold, these forces are likely to accelerate. So the consolidation of the world into blocs seems probable, although there may be some overlap among blocs, and their number remains unclear.

Policy Dynamics Inside Blocs

An important element in the theoretical case against trading blocs (e.g., Krugman 1991, Bhagwati 1992) is that large blocs will tend to exploit their market power by increasing protection. The empirical evidence on this issue is mixed. On one hand, blocs are often justified by their supporters as a way to provide regional firms with "market preserves" needed to develop competitive advantages, or at least for countervailing such advantages already available to foreign firms. On the other hand, the actual experiences of the European Union and ASEAN seem to suggest that blocs become increasingly liberal over time.

Internally, an expanding and increasingly diverse EU has eliminated not only trade restrictions but also barriers to cross-border movements of capital and labor. It is now striving for harmonization of national economic and social policies. Externally, the EU has erected no major new trade barriers with nonpartners (trade with nonpartners has continued to expand) and has remained an active participant in GATT negotiations. Lawrence (1991) in fact suggests that as a consequence of its internal liberalization, the EU has been more open to multilateral liberalization than would have been expected of its more protectionist members, notably France and Italy, if acting on their own. Moreover, the harmonization undertaken in Europe for internal purposes has benefitted firms in nonmember countries by promoting the integration of smaller markets into a single large and lucrative one.

What explains the difference between dire theoretical predictions of models such as Krugman (1991) and the more benign actual experience? To begin with, it is important to highlight the theoretical features of Krugman's model that underlie its conclusions. Krugman uses a Cournot framework, in which each bloc sets its tariffs non-cooperatively. In this context, the high tariffs selected reduce welfare for all participants, i.e., a "prisoner's dilemma"-type solution is obtained. This result is very sensitive to the modeling framework: large blocs are able to bypass the irrational results of a Cournot solution by negotiating Pareto-preferred solutions, especially if they see the bargaining process as an indefinitely repeated game.[13]

In addition, Krugman's model assumes that a single decision maker is manipulating a common external barrier for all countries in the bloc in order to take advantage of the bloc's market power. Today's integration agreements, however, are increasingly free trade areas (FTAs), which allow each participant to control its own barriers toward third countries. Also, trade policies are increasingly understood to reflect an aggregation of special interests, and not the choices of a single decision maker. These modifications dramatically change how bloc formation affects trade policies toward third countries.

In an FTA, the incentives of each participating country are quite different from those of the area as a whole. Specifically, each country has reason to reduce barriers that protect a regional partner's less-than-globally-competitive products. This mechanism was identified earlier as a possible engine for the enlargement of a bloc; it provides even stronger incentives for reducing third-country barriers. When each member's protection toward non-members is politically endogenous, formation of an FTA will cause external barriers to fall, thus reducing the potential for a welfare loss through trade diversion (Richardson 1993).[14]

The shifting structure of production interests will also work toward lowering each PTA member's barriers toward third countries. As the PTA's economic structure shifts toward globally competitive industries, exposing the economy to integration with the global economy becomes increasingly attractive. In addition, the economy's *globally* competitive interests—which now make up a relatively large share of the economy—will be concerned not just with the interests of its own bloc, but also with maintaining ties to third countries through global liberalization. This may mean trying to stop the proliferation of blocs, and adopting especially liberal external policies. Paradoxically, regional markets could strengthen some companies enough to make them advocates for global liberalization.

A possible example of this dynamic is provided by the ASEAN free trade area, AFTA. While ASEAN has had preferential trade measures on the books since the mid-1970s, it was not until the liberalization and foreign direct investment wave of the late 1980s that a serious PTA became feasible. Policy makers in ASEAN now see the expansion of their regional market as a means for strengthening local firms on the way toward general liberalization, and also as a mechanism for committing to liberalization through international agreements.

To be sure, interests favoring protection do survive in PTAs, but even then their influence may be diminished. De Melo and Panagariya (1992) note that protectionist interests can be diluted due to the expansion of the size of the political decision-making entity. In their terms, the influence of any one interest group will be diminished, since the group will have less influence on the area's decisions than on the decisions of its own country. Such dilution may mean that a larger area is less constrained by lobbying than a smaller area, as confirmed by the relatively liberal position of national vs. state and local governments in the United States. However, this conclusion is likely to depend sensitively on the mode of joint decision-making (e.g., majority voting versus consensus), as well as the opportunities for explicit or implicit side-payments among members though transfers or issue linkage.

Policy Dynamics Outside Blocs

Integration schemes also change the policy incentives facing outside countries. An important aspect is the coercive power of a large bloc: third countries may go further out of their way to accommodate a bloc or to avoid confrontations with it. If the prospect of trade diversion is sufficiently threatening to countries outside a bloc, then they may be willing to join international agreements that limit a bloc's internal advantage by reducing barriers worldwide. The commitment to free-trade agreements in North America in the 1980s—the concept itself had been discussed for at least a century before the Canada-United States Free Trade Agreement was signed in 1988—was motivated in part by the perception in Washington that the multilateral liberalization process had stalled. By opening up bilateral talks with Canada and other potential partners, the United States hoped to increase enthusiasm in Europe for a new GATT round.

The possibility that blocs can "ratchet up" the pace of global liberalization was made explicit by U.S. Special Trade Representative William Brock in his 1984 announcement of plans to negotiate bilateral agreements with U.S. trading partners including Israel and Canada. C. Fred Bergsten (1994) has made the same argument in favor of plans to convert APEC into a regional trading area. In Bergsten's view, the meeting of 15 APEC leaders in Seattle in 1993 played an important role in motivating European concessions in the waning days of the Uruguay Round. As chair of the APEC Eminent Persons Group (EPG), Bergsten incorporated the idea of a ratchet effect into the EPG's report calling for regional liberalization (APEC Eminent Persons Group 1993).

The EPG plan was initially a conditional MFN strategy: it proposed participation to any country willing to accept the terms of the agreement. This is, in effect, an automatically expanding FTA. However, the conditional MFN feature raised controversy as some Asian countries interpreted the strategy as an effort by the United States (and perhaps Japan) to build a bloc which they could dominate. The final EPG compromise suggested that each country could determine whether the concessions it offered would be restricted regionally or extended to all outside partners on an MFN basis.

A ratchet effect may provide an additional dynamic argument in favor of blocs. But much could go wrong on the way. For example, some outside countries might be tempted to build countervailing blocs in order to improve their negotiating positions with an emerging bloc. This motive looms large in the thinking of Prime Minister Mahathir of Malaysia, who has proposed an East Asian Economic Group (eventually Caucus) to offset the bargaining leverage of Europe and NAFTA. As already noted, it is unclear whether a system of large blocs makes it easier or harder to achieve global liberalization. The case for a ratchet effect is not entirely compelling.

Moreover, if a country is left out of blocs and fails either to join one or to promote multilateral liberalization, internal changes may begin to work against liberal trade policies. As its export markets shrink through trade diversion, the country may be forced toward an autarkic production structure with greater weight on inefficient industries. With potential gains from trade thus reduced, the country might begin to increase its own protection.[15] Over time, any resulting growth of the country's nontraded or protected interests will increase political opposition to liberalization. In practice, however, it is hard to identify an example of a country that has moved toward autarkic policies during the recent period of PTA formation.

Thus, there is at least the potential for formation of a bloc to push nonmember countries into countervailing blocs or toward greater self-reliance. These unfavorable dynamics may be offset to some extent by a ratchet effect, such as greater MFN concessions by others. But these are surely risky benefits because the countervailing leverage and structural shifts in outside countries may also make them tougher negotiators and more reluctant to reach a mutually beneficial agreement, as in Krugman's tariff-optimizing solutions.

Managing Bloc Dynamics

Since the dynamic effects of PTAs are critical in judging their effects, design features that affect the dynamics may be more important than those that determine static effects. It may be possible to develop rules that increase the likelihood that a bloc will make positive contributions to global liberalization. Several recent threads in the literature offer such approaches.

The first set of approaches is suggested by Kemp and Wan's (1976) theoretical demonstration that the external barriers of a bloc can always be adjusted to leave trade with third countries unchanged—i.e., to rule out trade diversion—while allowing net gains for members.[16] Variants of a no-trade-diversion rule have been proposed as alternatives or supplements to Article XXIV of the GATT, which restricts PTAs principally through the requirement that countries must fully eliminate internal barriers (Bhagwati 1992).[17]

Minimum diversion is not, however, synonymous with best dynamics. If trade diversion is critical for the adoption of a particular PTA, as a source of necessary political support, and if the PTA represents an essential step in the transformation of a country's industrial structure, then the no-trade-diversion criterion misses the point. Indeed, diversion may well be an incentive for subsequent liberalization in the PTA context.

A second set of approaches focuses on establishing mechanisms for the long-term liberalization of a PTA from the beginning. Conditional MFN proposals that arose in APEC illustrate several such options. Inclusion in a PTA can be made contingent on concessions, or it can be offered on an MFN basis initially, under the threat that the concessions will be withdrawn if reciprocal concessions aren't forthcoming by a specified time. The latter alternative may well end up in an MFN outcome if the adjustment costs of returning to a pre-concession industrial structure are high.

A third approach is "open regionalism," which is a strategy for integrating economies through coordinated MFN agreements rather than formal FTAs or customs unions (see World Bank 1994 for East Asia). In some contexts, MFN concessions can benefit a group of trade partners almost as much as a preferential agreement. The APEC trading area, for example, has nearly 70 percent intraregional trade. The share of benefits accruing to regional partners can be increased further by focusing concessions on products in which the region has a competitive advantage (Elek 1994; Martin, Petri, and Yanagashima 1994).

The "open regionalism" strategy offers many of the advantages of a preferential approach without its inherent drawbacks. MFN agreements can achieve partial reductions of regional barriers without violating the GATT, leading to a richer menu of liberalization solutions. Regional targeting of MFN liberalization offsets leakage of benefits to nonregional free riders, yet the likelihood of welfare-reducing trade diversion is less than with a formal PTA.[18]

Conclusion

Although theoretical analysis has often highlighted the potential dangers of preferential trading, actual experience with PTAs has not been unfavorable. Early PTAs designed for the wrong reason—to support industrialization outside of their members' comparative advantage—never really got off the ground. Operational PTAs, on the other hand, have often grown to include more members and have proved reasonably cooperative in international negotiations. In short, regional and global liberalization have not proven to be mutually exclusive.

Operational PTAs also do not appear to be as inefficient and welfare-threatening as textbook analysis suggests. Rather, PTAs seem to generate a wide range of non-Vinerian benefits associated with increased market size. These effects range from various enhanced scale economies to increased competition among producers. Interestingly, these effects are virtually always favorable to a PTA. Since the earliest analyses of the European Community, these phenomena have proven to be much more important empirically than Vinerian effects, and recent estimates suggest that they can represent significant percentages of world output.

In addition, the relatively benign behavior and evolution of PTAs suggests positive underlying political dynamics. One way to understand this dynamic is to recognize that increased intraregional trade tends to shift the production structure in each PTA member toward its most efficient and internationally minded industries. This is especially true if the non-Vinerian scale effects are important. If producers play a dominant role in determining PTA policies, then such structural shifts can explain why PTAs are, over time, willing to undertake multilateral liberalization programs that might not have been politically feasible for their individual country members earlier.

If PTAs are better than Vinerian analysis suggests, then new approaches are required to judge their welfare implications. Such analysis needs to place more emphasis on scale and competition and less on static efficiency. Even more important may be the evolution of a PTA's membership and third-country policies. Some trade diversion may be very beneficial, for example, if it draws a recalcitrant country into the liberalization process. Moreover, diversion is likely to be eroded over time if each partner later adjusts external tariffs independently. Given the strong political and economic momentum behind PTAs, it will be important for economic analysis to focus on these difficult but important issues.

NOTES

1. Saxonhouse (1994) offers this quotation as an example of the pre-Viner conventional wisdom among international economists.

2. One-way preferential trade arrangements were also created between industrial

and less- developed countries (LDCs) under the heading of the Generalized System of Preferences. As with inward-oriented LDC trading blocs, the rationale was to allow LDC enterprises to enjoy the benefits of a larger market. In Vinerian terms, any trade effect of such plans is usually pure trade diversion. This is because preferential access under GSP is typically limited to industries and countries that are not already highly competitive internationally.

3. Subsequent theoretical analysis of production with scale economies shows one economic source of the endless political wrangling: even under free trade, the equilibrium structure of production and the associated division of gains from trade are not unique. See, for example, Helpman and Krugman (1985).

4. Moreover, part of apparent trade diversion from a new or expanded PTA may actually represent the reversal of previous trade diversion (Wonnacott 1994). NAFTA eroded the Caribbean nations' own preferential access to the U.S. market under the Caribbean Basin Economic Recovery Act. The resulting substitution of Mexican for Caribbean products is diversion reversal rather than classic trade diversion.

5. Viner (1950) himself raised the possibility of scale economies for plants or firms, only to dismiss them as unlikely to be quantitatively important. Corden's (1972) theoretical analysis also focuses on economies at the plant or firm level. His subsequent survey of the normative theory of international trade (Corden 1984) observes that scale economies "do not find a place in orthodox customs union theory" even though "exploitation of scale economies is an important motive for customs unions—or proposals for unions. . . ."

6. In the economics literature, the Vinerian effects of PTAs are termed static and those related to market size termed dynamic. Here we use "static" to refer to effects from a once-and-for-always PTA and reserve "dynamic" to describe consequences of PTAs for further liberalization.

7. But other things may not be equal. Market size also increases competition, i.e., decreases concentration, and some empirical studies have shown a positive link between industry concentration and innovation.

8. A similar criticism of the Krugman approach is made by Srinivasan (1993) in the context of a Ricardian model with a continuum of goods.

9. Fieleke (1992) provides a more detailed look at the record worldwide; for Asia, see Iboshi, Plummer, and Naya (1994).

10. In our example, votes are based on ownership of sector-specific assets and hence reflect short-run interests. Given this assumption, the example demonstrates one mechanism by which a free-trade agreement can enhance prospects for multilateral liberalization. However, the assumption that voters act on short-run interests may be key. Levy (1994) considers the case in which voters perceive only their long-run interests and take no account of losses during the adjustment process. In a model with two factors and differentiated products, Levy shows that adoption of bilateral free trade can sometimes undermine political support for further multilateral liberalization.

11. The product-by-product approach offers a more abstract benefit to competitive industries: liberalization will tend to depreciate the economy's real exchange rate, thereby increasing the competitiveness of domestic producers. The literature

on liberalization in developing countries frequently observes that these benefits are more difficult to sell to voters than direct benefits from expanding export markets or providing export-oriented incentives.

12. The Asia Pacific Economic Cooperation (APEC) forum, an association of eighteen East Asian and North American countries plus Chile, has committed itself to "free trade and investment in the region" by 2020. How these ambitious objectives will be pursued, and whether APEC will move toward a free trade area or toward liberalization on an MFN basis, are unclear. APEC is perhaps the most diverse of all potential economic blocs and will face difficult problems in reconciling differences in the economic systems of its members.

13. Some have argued that the consolidation of the world around three major economic powers, i.e., the United States, Europe, and Japan, could actually facilitate liberalization by enhancing the manageability of the multilateral negotiation process.

14. This mechanism suggests only that no member will lose through trade diversion. However, as discussed below, Kemp and Wan (1976) show that external barriers can be adjusted to ensure also that no outside country loses.

15. To an excluded country, trade diversion shows up as a deterioration in its terms of trade. The optimal policy remains free trade. However, because the gains from trade are reduced, the political viability of a liberal trade policy may be undermined.

16. Redistribution among members may be required to ensure that no country's welfare falls.

17. Based on simulations of a computational model of customs union formation, Haveman (1994) concludes that even vigorous enforcement of current GATT guidelines would be sufficient to eliminate the possibility of welfare losses to excluded countries.

18. Diversion is not entirely eliminated. If two products A and B are close substitutes in demand but produced in different countries, an MFN liberalization program that eliminates barriers on A but maintains them on B will tend to divert trade even though both commodities are MFN-protected. Indeed, every economy's protection structure already incorporates some partner preferences due to differences in protection across products originating in different regions.

REFERENCES

APEC Eminent Persons Group. 1993. *A Vision for APEC,* report of the Eminent Persons Group to APEC ministers, October.

Balassa, Bela. 1967. *Trade Liberalization among Industrial Countries.* New York: Council on Foreign Relations.

Baldwin, Richard E. 1989. "Growth Effects of 1992." *Economic Policy* 9:247–282.

Baldwin, Richard E. 1993. "A Domino Theory of Regionalism." *CEPR Discussion Paper* 857.

Bergsten, C. Fred. 1994. "APEC: The Bogor Declaration and the Path Ahead." Washington, DC: Institute for International Economics, December.

Bhagwati, Jagdish N. 1992. "Regionalism versus Multilateralism." *The World Economy* 15:535–55.

Bhagwati, Jagdish N., and Brecher, Richard A. 1980. "National Welfare in an Open Economy in the Presence of Foreign-Owned Factors of Production." *Journal of International Economics* 10:103–15.

Brecher, Richard A., and Diaz Alejandro, Carlos F. 1977. "Tariffs, Foreign Capital, and Immiserizing Growth." *Journal of International Economics* 7:317–22.

Brown, Drusilla K., and Stern, Robert M. 1987. "A Modeling Perspective." In Robert M. Stern, Philip H. Trezise, and John Walley, eds., *Perspectives on a U.S.-Canadian Free Trade Agreement.* Washington, DC: Brookings.

Corden, W.M. 1972. "Economies of Scale and Customs Union Theory." *Journal of Political Economy* 80:465–75.

Corden, W.M. 1984. "The Normative Theory of International Trade." In Ronald W. Jones and Peter B. Kenen, eds., *Handbook of International Economics, Volume 1.* Amsterdam: North-Holland.

Deardorff, Alan V., and Stern, Robert M. 1994. "Multilateral Trade Negotiations and Preferential Trading Arrangements." In Alan V. Deardorff and Robert M. Stern, eds., *Analytical and Negotiating Issues in the Global Trading System.* Ann Arbor: University of Michigan Press.

de la Torre, Augusto, and Kelly, Margaret R. 1992. "Regional Trade Arrangements." International Monetary Fund Occasional Paper #93, March.

de Melo, Jaime, and Panagariya, Arvind. 1992. "The New Regionalism." *Finance and Development* 29:47–30.

Elek, Andrew. 1994. "Trade Policy Options for the Asia Pacific region in the 1990s: the Potential of Open Regionalism." In Ross Garnaut and Peter Drysdale, eds., *Asia Pacific Regionalism.* Pymble, NSW, Australia: Harper Educational Press.

Fieleke, Norman S. 1991. "One Trading World, or Many: The Issue of Regional Trading Blocs." *New England Economic Review* May/June.

Haberler, Gottfried. 1936. *Theory of International Trade with Applications to Commercial Policy.* London: Macmillan.

Harris, Richard. 1987. "Comments on "Drusilla K. Brown and Robert M. Stern, 'A Modeling Perspective.'" In Robert M. Stern, Philip H. Trezise, and John Walley, eds., *Perspectives on a U.S.-Canadian Free Trade Agreement.* Washington, DC: Brookings.

Haveman, Jon D. 1994. "Some Welfare Effects of Sequential Customs Union Formation." Purdue University, December.

Helpman, Elhanan, and Krugman, Paul R. 1985. *Market Structure and Foreign Trade.* Cambridge, MA: MIT Press.

Hormats, Robert D. 1994. "Making Regionalism Safe." *Foreign Affairs,* March/April.

Iboshi, Pearl Imada, Plummer Michael G., and Naya, Seiji Finch, eds. 1994. *Building Blocs of U.S.-ASEAN Economic Cooperation.* Honolulu: East-West Center.

Johnson, Harry G. 1962. "The Economic Theory of Customs Union." In *Money, Trade and Economic Growth.* Cambridge, MA: Harvard University Press.

Kemp, M.C., and Wan, Henry. 1976. "An Elementary Proposition Concerning the Formation of Customs Unions." *Journal of International Economics* 6:95–8.

Krugman, Paul. 1991. "The Move Toward Free Trade Zones." *Review* Federal Reserve Bank of Kansas City, December.

Lawrence, Robert Z. 1991. "Emerging Regional Arrangements:Building Blocks or Stumbling Blocks." In Richard O'Brien, ed., *Finance and the International Economy:* 5. Oxford: Oxford University Press.

Levy, Philip I. 1994. "A Political-Economic Analysis of Free Trade Agreements."Yale University, September.

Lipsey, R.G., and Lancaster, K.J. 1956–57. "The General Theory of Second Best." *Review of Economic Studies*XXIV:63. Page numbers.

Martin, Will; Petri, Peter A.; and Yanagashima, Koji. 1994. "Charting the Pacific: Empirical Consequences of Liberalization Alternatives." *International Trade Journal* 8:447–82.

Petri, Peter. 1987. "Comments on "Drusilla K. Brown and Robert M. Stern, 'A Modeling Perspective.'" In Robert M. Stern, Philip H. Trezise, and John Walley, eds., *Perspectives on a U.S.-Canadian Free Trade Agreement.* Washington, DC: Brookings.

Richardson, Martin. 1993. "Endogenous Protection and Trade Diversion." *Journal of International Economics* 34:309–24.

Sapir, Andre. 1990. "Does 1992 come before or after 1990? On Regional Versus Multilateral Integration." In Ronald W. Jones and Anne O. Krueger, eds., *The Political Economy of International Trade.* Cambridge, MA: Basil Blackwell.

Saxonhouse, Gary R. 1994. "Trading Blocs and East Asia." In Ross Garnaut and Peter Drysdale, eds., *Asia Pacific Regionalism.* Pymble, NSW Australia: Harper Educational Publishers.

Srinivasan, T.N. 1993. "Discussion." In Jaime de Melo and Arvind Panagariya, eds., *New_ Dimensions in Regional Integration.* Cambridge: Cambridge University Press.

Viner, Jacob. 1950. *The Customs Union Issue.* New York: Carnegie Endowment for International Peace.

Wonnacott, Ronald J. 1994. "Trade Diversion, Diversion Reversal and Investment Redirection: Some Missing Elements in Customs Union Theory." Working Paper No. 9401C, Centre for the Study of International Economic Relations, University of Western Ontario, October.

World Bank. 1991. *World Development Report 1991.* New York: Oxford University Press.

World Bank. 1994. *East Asia's Trade and Investment: Regional and Global Gains from Liberalization.* Washington: World Bank.

CHAPTER 8

Focal Points and Multilateral Negotiations on the Contestability of Markets

Bernard Hoekman

The GATT was created in 1947 by governments with a clear vision of the cooperation that was needed to foster economic growth and post-war reconstruction. It proved a very successful trade liberalizing instrument. As of the 1970s, trade barriers in the form of tariffs and quotas had declined significantly in importance, and governments came to be confronted increasingly with the trade-distorting aspects of domestic policies. To use Robert Baldwin's analogy, trade liberalization can be likened to the draining of a swamp: as the water level (average tariff level) falls due to successful pumping efforts, rocks, stumps and all manner of other obstacles (NTBs) emerge (Baldwin 1970). GATT proved very able to drain the swamp. It was much less successful in clearing the drained land (eliminating NTBs), and keeping the water from flooding back (contingent protection). Dealing with the tree stumps and rocks was difficult in large part because reciprocal exchange became more difficult. The issue linkages and side-payments required to establish multilateral disciplines on regulatory regimes greatly complicated progress.

A basic tenet of the GATT has always been regulatory competition. Negotiations focused on reducing trade barriers and extending and enforcing the concept of nondiscrimination. National treatment, MFN, and tariff bindings establish the conditions of competition for individual products. Governments remain free, however, to pursue domestic regulatory policies. Mounting opposition to the consequences of regulatory competition has led to ever greater emphasis on "market access." There are two dimensions to market access. The first concerns a government's *external* trade policy stance. This has been the traditional domain of GATT. Given the success in lowering trade barriers in OECD countries in particular, this has to a great extent become an issue of the use of contingent protection (anti-dumping, safeguards) and the consequent uncertainty associated with the variability of the market access conditions that apply at any point in time. The second dimension pertains to the *internal* barriers to entry by foreign firms in a particular market. This includes regulation (or the absence thereof) of private business practices, government support for industries, public procurement policies, regulations affecting services sectors and foreign direct investment policies. A key challenge for the multilateral trading system—the WTO—is to ensure that market access-centered concerns are translated into greater contestability of markets. Market access has been a major issue pushing competition policy onto the multilateral negotiating agenda. However, competition policy covers only a part of the market access waterfront. Issue areas that are of greater relevance arguably include government procurement policies, services regulations, investment policies, and contingent protection.

GATT made good progress in liberalizing trade in part because the tariff was a transparent and unambiguous trade restricting instrument. It provided a clear focal point for reciprocal negotiations. The market access issues that have become increasingly prominent in the last decade do not provide such a clear focal point. To overcome internal political constraints to enhancing the contestability of markets, the creation of analogous focal points could prove very helpful, especially with respect to services and procurement markets. The challenge is to construct them. Bob Stern has played a prominent role in establishing, clarifying and quantifying the impact of many of the non-tariff policies that came to be addressed in the GATT (Deardorff and Stern 1985, 1986, 1987, 1990). Indeed, he was among the first to identify the need for analysis and data collection in the area of services (Stern 1985) and to evaluate the GATT rules that were negotiated on non-tariff measures, including government procurement (Stern et al. 1986). Data collection and compilation are crucial to enhance the understanding of issues that are on the table, identify possible focal points and develop political consensus (Stern 1994).

The paper is organized as follows. The next section starts with a discussion of the potential role of competition policy per se in multilateral attempts to increase the contestability of markets. The following section explores what could be done unilaterally by a government to address some of the market access issues that have been raised in multilateral discussions. The paper then asks how achieving greater contestability could be facilitated by multilateral negotiations, emphasizing the need for common focal points. Attention is limited to services, procurement, and antidumping, three of the more important market access issues that are on the multilateral trade negotiation (MTN) agenda. A final section concludes.

Competition Policy and Contestability

Calls for the multilateral trading system to be extended to cover competition (antitrust) policies reflect concerns that policies—or the lack of policies—in this area can effectively restrict access to markets, even if overt trade barriers are low, thus granting exporters located in these markets an "unfair" advantage. The importance attached to competition policy enforcement by the U.S. as a necessary condition for "effective" access to the Japanese market was illustrated in the Structural Impediments Initiative (SII) talks. Competition policy disciplines figure prominently in the Treaty of Rome establishing the European Economic Community (EEC), the European Economic Area agreement between the European Union (EU) and the European Free Trade Agreement (EFTA) states, and in the Association agreements negotiated between the EU and the Central and Eastern European countries. Given bilateral and regional testing of the waters, moving on to the multilateral level appears to be an obvious next step.

This has already taken place to some extent. Three of the new agreements that were negotiated in the Uruguay round, those on Trade-related Investment Measures (TRIMs), Trade-related Intellectual Property Rights (TRIPs), and the General Agreement on Trade in Services (GATS) contain provisions on, or related to, competition policy. In the TRIMs agreement references to competition policy are limited to a call to consider the need for possible disciplines in this area in the future. Explicit provisions exist in the TRIPs agreement for the application of competition law to intellectual property protection. Governments are allowed to take measures to control anti-competitive practices in contractual licenses that adversely affect trade and may impede the transfer and dissemination of technology. Member countries may specify licensing practices or conditions in their laws that can constitute an "abuse of intellectual property rights having an adverse effect on competition in the relevant market" (Article 40:2).

The GATS contains two provisions that address competition policy issues: Article VIII (Monopolies and Exclusive Services Providers) and Article IX (Business Practices). Monopoly or oligopoly suppliers of services may not abuse their market power to nullify MFN or specific market access or national treatment commitments relating to activities that fall *outside* the scope of their exclusive rights. As regards business practices of service suppliers that have *not* been granted monopoly or exclusive rights, Members are obliged, on request, to enter into consultations with a view to eliminating business practices that are claimed to restrict trade in services.

The Member addressed "shall accord full and sympathetic consideration to such a request and shall cooperate through the supply of publicly available nonconfidential information of relevance to the matter in question." There is no requirement to act, only an obligation to provide information. It is therefore unclear how a restrictive practice is to be eliminated, or what constitutes a restrictive business practice. Indeed, Members remain free not to apply competition law and policy to services.

The focus of *national* competition laws is on competition, reflecting the belief—which is extensively supported by empirical evidence—that vigorous competition is frequently the best way to enhance economic efficiency.[1] Governments pursue *trade* policies for a variety of reasons, including as a means to raise revenue, to protect specific industries (whether "infant," "senile" or other), to shift the terms of trade, to attain certain foreign policy or security goals, or simply to restrict the consumption of specific goods. Whatever the underlying objective, by restricting competition in product markets trade policy is generally inconsistent with the objectives underlying competition policy. The way this inconsistency is frequently put is that competition law aims at protecting *competition* (the competitive process, and thus economic efficiency), while trade policy aims at protecting *competitors* (or factors of production). While a policy of trade *liberalization* is generally consistent with the objectives of competition law, it is important to distinguish trade policy in general from attempts to reduce trade barriers.[2]

The objective of trade policy officials in putting competition policy enforcement on the MTN agenda has to do with the realization of their "legitimate expectations" (to use GATT terminology) associated with negotiated trade barrier reductions (i.e., private practices that nullify or impair concessions). The perceived problem is that firms may engage in business practices that prevent the market access benefits of negotiated trade liberalization from being realized and the governments concerned tolerate these alleged practices. The actual state of competition in a particular market is of secondary importance, and may not be of concern at all. The term market access itself illustrates the potential for ambiguity regarding the objectives of trade negotiators. Access is not necessarily equivalent to more competition, nor is the state of competition per se a factor determining if there are market access restrictions. To take an example, if a market is extremely competitive, access will be difficult no matter what the public policy stance vis-à-vis foreign firms. If there are fixed costs of entry, or significant exit costs, access may be impossible. It has been argued that many Japanese markets are so competitive that long-run profit margins are simply too low to attract foreign competition.[3] Whatever the case may be for a particular market, the state of competition should be an important factor when determining whether market access is restricted. US-Japan talks, Section 301 negotiations, the NAFTA and the GATS all illustrate that the market access sought by negotiators is not necessarily driven by a lack of competition. Instead, the focus of attention is on foreign market share, the trend growth in this share and its level compared to import penetration in other countries.[4]

It is revealing that competition authorities employ rather different terminology and concepts in this regard than trade negotiators. The key concepts that are analogous to market access are barriers to entry and contestability of markets. Another difference is that in the competition policy context the focus of analysis is the "relevant market:" markets are not defined solely in spatial (geographical) terms but also in product terms (based on substitution criteria). The definition of the relevant market and the magnitude of barriers to entry are much vaguer (arbitrary) in the trade-market access context.[5] In short, there is substantial potential tension between the notion of market access and competition policy-based criteria of the contestability of markets. This paper takes the view that it is the latter that should be the focus of negotiations. Limiting attention to competition policy narrowly construed, the regulation of private business practices—is clearly too restrictive an approach in this connection. The EU illustrates that in the multilateral trade context competition policy disciplines must be defined broadly to ensure contestability. In the case of the EU, competition policy disciplines pertain to private firms, public monopolies, state-owned enterprises, and governments. The latter are restricted in their ability to subsidize firms located in their territory insofar as this affects trade between Member States, in their procurement practices, and in their ability to prevent inward investment. What matters in the EU context are the conditions of competition broadly defined.

Identifying and Rank-ordering Barriers to Market Access

There are a variety of policies that may limit the ability of a foreign firm to contest a particular market. These include trade policies (tariffs, quotas, contingent protection), restrictions on foreign direct investment (outright prohibitions or non-national treatment), discriminatory public procurement policies, subsidy practices, and regulatory regimes (competition law and enforcement and policies pertaining to the service sector). Negotiators need to rank-order these issues in importance before attempting multilateral cooperation. A lack of regulation of private business practices is unlikely to be among the most significant contestability problems raised in the trade context. This is not to deny that (differences in) competition policies can distort trade. But on average many such

problems are likely to be relatively minor, so that multilateral cooperation will have limited payoffs (although political benefits may exceed the
economic value of an agreement). As important, on a number of "bread
and butter" competition issues the costs of attaining agreement may be
high as the impact of particular policies may be unclear. Examples
include the scope of exemptions, rules regarding the abuse of a dominant
position, and the treatment of vertical relationships and strategic
alliances.[6] Negotiating multilateral disciplines in such areas is likely to be
fraught with difficulty.

Graham and Richardson (1994) have compiled a typology of issues
and criteria for a possible global competition policy agenda. Four criteria
are distinguished: (1) economic clarity (i.e., how clear are economic theory
and practice regarding the normative prescriptions); (2) feasibility of convergence; (3) the likely efficiency gains from convergence towards best
practice; and (4) the likely gains associated with a negotiated agreement in
terms of reducing disputes between nations. They identify only three clear
cases where the potential gains in terms of efficiency and conflict reduction
are high: predation, voluntary import expansion agreements (VIEs), and
antidumping. However, the probability of convergence is considered to be
low for predation and antidumping and indeterminate for VIEs. Graham
and Richardson do not mention either government procurement or services in their typology, although they do have a category called "other
related issues." Here the economics are also clear—there is a need for contestability—and the efficiency and diplomatic gains are high. The feasibility of convergence is not very high, but perhaps higher than for predation
or antidumping. Both issues have been quite prominent in market access
discussions. Both are of greater economic significance than competition
policy issues per se. The question facing negotiators then is how best to
deal with the underlying contestability problems.

Normative Considerations

Services and public procurement markets are often characterized by a lack
of competition, while antidumping is in most cases about reducing competition. Both theory and experience increasingly suggest that placing greater
reliance on contestability of service and procurement markets and constraining the use of antidumping would enhance economic welfare. The
purpose of what follows is briefly to elaborate this point, by identifying
possible modalities to achieve this goal. The next section discusses the
potential role for multilateral cooperation in inducing governments to
allow greater contestability of markets.

Services

There is no consensus as to what constitutes the appropriate regulatory regime for many service sectors. However, many governments concluded during the 1980s that there was too much regulation and not enough competition. At the same time, changes in technology allowed greater competition in many service activities (transport, communications, distribution, financial services), facilitating entry and arbitrage. Two broad categories of services can be distinguished. First are natural monopolies such as utilities, and infrastructure services, such as telecoms. Second are services where regulation has been justified on the basis of asymmetric information, such as medical services. As illustrated by privatization programs around the globe, many services can be provided more efficiently by private firms than public entities that are sheltered from competition. Whether for regulated monopolies or self-regulated associations, greater competition can be introduced for both types of services by allowing entry or the threat of entry.

Greater competition requires the mobilization of *domestic* constituencies that will benefit from liberalization of service markets. In the GATT context these have tended to be exporters. In the services context exporting interests will frequently not be there. Matters are compounded by the fact that certain industries are effectively cartelized. The group with the most to gain from liberalization of service markets are consumers, including both firms and households. Without active involvement of consumer groups, far-reaching opening of service markets is less likely to occur. As is well known, the main question here is how to overcome the free rider and public good problems that reduce individual incentives to lobby against protection. Solutions include increasing the amount of information available to consumers, active consultation of consumer organizations by the government, and granting consumer organizations statutory rights in the policy formation process.

Whatever the policy stance regarding privatization of state monopolies and allowing greater competition in services more generally, insufficient attention is paid in many countries to identifying the costs and benefits of the policies that are pursued, whether or not this includes discriminating against foreign providers. In many countries very little information exists regarding the costs of regulatory regimes. Without such information mobilization of consumers is doomed from the start. Such information can be generated through the creation of independent bodies that are given the task to evaluate existing and proposed policies (as has been done in Australia, for example), and by giving multilateral bodies such as the WTO Secretariat the task to analyze the effects of a Member's policies on domestic and foreign welfare. Such initiatives are to be supported, but will not be defended at length here, (Spriggs 1991). An option that is less often discussed is to give the competition authorities a mandate to focus not only on the welfare effects of business practices, but also on those generated by government policies. Doing so would not only encourage competition, but help constrain governments in seeking—or acceding to requests for—VIE agreements. The same applies to the incentive to *create* market access restrictions for negotiating purposes, an option that can be pursued under the GATS given the positive list approach taken by negotiators to determine the Agreement's sectoral coverage (Hoekman, 1995). Subjecting market access commitments—whether MTN-based or bilateral—to the scrutiny of competition authorities may help move the process of liberalization along and prevent its capture.

Procurement

Government procurement in many countries discriminates in favor of local suppliers by providing for price preferences or local content (offset) requirements for foreign suppliers. Discrimination may be informal, selective, or single-tendering procedures under which a government directly approaches a specific (usually domestic) firm for a bid. The costs of noncompetitive procurement can be very high. Good practices in procurement are well-known and involve the introduction of competition into the public purchasing process. The presumption is that international competitive bidding is the best policy once contract size is large enough to justify the transaction costs. The general effect of discriminatory government procurement policies is to protect domestic industries. As a result, they are often considered to be analogous to a tariff, especially when expressed as in terms of a price preference (Deardorff and Stern 1985). However, as emphasized by McAfee and McMillan (1989), much depends in this connection on the market structure of the industry and the type of good involved. In principle, nondiscriminatory procurement policies may not be optimal. Procurement costs may be lowered by pursuing price preferences *if* domestic firms have a competitive disadvantage in producing the product, *and* only a limited number of firms (foreign and domestic) bid for the contract. In the absence of a preference policy, in such a context foreign firms may exploit their cost advantage by bidding just below what they expect domestic firms to bid, which will be substantially higher than their actual cost. A price preference policy will force foreign firms to lower their bids, as it increases the effective competition from domestic firms. While the preference policy entails that the lowest bidder is not necessarily awarded the contract, thus implying higher costs to the government, on average the bids made by firms with a cost advantage may be lower than otherwise. Of course, if domestic firms do not have a cost disadvantage, no preferential policy should be pursued.

Arguments for preferences only hold in a small numbers setting. If enough foreign and domestic firms are invited to bid, competition between them should ensure that the market price is paid. In practice discriminatory government policies can be expected to be more costly than a national treatment policy, especially when no competitive tendering is sought or there is an absolute preference for domestic suppliers. Indeed, if foreign firms are excluded from bidding for contract procurement, costs are likely to rise significantly. Without going into the advantages and disadvantages of specific decision rules in this connection, what is relevant here is that criteria used in the enforcement of competition policy can be used to determine when to discriminate. As market structure is crucial, and at the focus of competition enforcement, a competition office could be given the task to ascertain if the conditions calling for discrimination have been met in individual cases. The point is that reliance on a general rule of thumb (e.g., international competitive bidding for all contracts above $300,000) may not be appropriate. But, to diverge from this principle, information and analysis are needed. For a price preference scheme to reduce average procurement costs it is necessary to obtain information on price-cost margins and market structure.

As is the case regarding the costs and benefits of regulatory regimes for services, very little is known about the way that goods and services are procured by most governments, the share of contracts that are awarded to foreign suppliers, and the conditions that are imposed in terms of local content or price preferences. A transparency body could make an even greater contribution to policy formation and evaluation if it were also given the mandate to monitor the economy-wide impact of procurement policies and practices. As with the other areas—contingent trade and services policies—a competition authority or analogous body could be given this task.

Anti-dumping

The protectionist biases that are inherent in the application of anti-dumping are well known. The best policy in this respect is clear: do not use it. The problem is how to wean domestic industries away from this form of "insurance." One option that has been suggested is to subject anti-dumping to competition scrutiny, shifting the focus of investigations from injury to competitors (the domestic industry producing the like product) to injury to competition (the economy of the importing country as a whole). In principle, no contingent protection should be granted by a government if this would have a substantially negative impact on competition (e.g., strengthen market power or dominance). A competition authority could determine whether price discrimination or selling below cost is anti-competitive, and whether the imposition of antidumping duties will lead to an excessive reduction in competition on the domestic market. Rules of thumb could also be introduced such that petitions could not be made if concentration ratios are high.[7]

Contestability and Multilateral Negotiations

A common denominator underlying market access discussions on services, procurement, and antidumping is that in all three cases state intervention is an important source of the perceived restrictions on the contestability of domestic markets. Unilateral introduction and enforcement of competition policies can clearly be beneficial from a national welfare viewpoint. A problem is that the domestic political economy may be such as to restrain the feasibility of adoption or enforcement. Another problem is that what is beneficial to the implementing country may be detrimental to the interests of another. Efforts by trading partners to address the resulting externalities through attempts to harmonize competition policies are likely doomed to fail. Focusing on quantitative market access commitments is very much a second-best policy, as it can lead to well known problems including sectoral reciprocity, managed trade, collusion between firms, and a hollowing out of the MFN principle.[8] Use of a tariff-like focal point could help offset these problems by improving the information available to agents and negotiators on the (opportunity) costs of the status quo and the contestability of markets. Without such data domestic groups with an interest in change may not have an incentive to mobilize and support market opening. The challenge facing policymakers is to identify linkages in MTNs that can help induce governments to adopt a more competition-friendly approach in instances where they are reluctant to do so unilaterally.

The WTO Government Procurement Agreement (GPA) and the GATS follow GATT in that they rely on reciprocally negotiated market access commitments to enhance the contestability of the relevant markets. The GPA does so by scheduling lists of entities that are subject to the national treatment and MFN principles in their procurement. The greater access that is offered is conditional, in that it formally applies only to other signatories. The GATS has explicit market access commitments, defined in a negative manner (i.e., members promise not to use certain quota-like instruments for specific sectors). In the case of both the GPA and the

GATS, no use was made of price-based focal points, or comparable "continuous" indicators of the coverage of country commitments. In the procurement area, the focal point is entity coverage, whereas in the services area it is sectoral coverage and the magnitude of derogations by scheduled sector. In both areas greater transparency as regards the factors and policies that restrict the contestability of markets could prove beneficial in progressing towards further liberalization.[9]

Services

State intervention is a major factor restricting the contestability of many service markets. This may be the result of monopoly provision, a reflection of the regulatory regime pertaining to specific activities, or a tolerance for competition-reducing self-regulation by service providers. The extension and enforcement of competition laws to services could in principle enhance the contestability of many service markets, as many activities tend to be beyond the reach of the competition authorities, be it de facto or de jure. Although negotiations could involve an attempt to agree to subject specific services to the reach of antitrust, different jurisdictions have different ideas on competition law and enforcement, and it is not clear a priori what effect differences in substantive rules or enforcement mechanisms have on the state of competition.[10] Rather than discussing the specifics of competition rules, it might be more fruitful to pursue an indirect approach, seeking to agree to employ competition-friendlier instruments of regulation.

The key is to ensure that markets become more contestable, allowing efficient, lower cost providers to compete with incumbents, or threaten to do so. The problem that was confronted by negotiators was that national treatment is often not enough in the service context, given the domestic entry barriers that may be imposed or tolerated by governments. It was for that reason that a market access article was introduced into the GATS. This prohibits in principle the use of policies that limit the number of service suppliers allowed or the value of transactions, assets or the quantity of service output, restrict the type of legal entity through which a service supplier is permitted to supply a service (e.g., branches vs. subsidiaries for banking), or constrain the foreign equity shareholding in a firm. Many of these restrictions will apply to both domestic and foreign firms. The distinction between market access restrictions and national treatment violations made in the GATS is not necessarily very relevant from a contestability viewpoint. Both non-national treatment of foreign providers and more generally applied market access restrictions (in the NAFTA or GATS sense) will have the effect of raising profit margins for incumbents (abstracting for the moment from price regulation). Although the objective of MTNs should presumably be to reduce these margins, little is known about their size (although indirect evidence can be obtained from opposition to liberalization in a particular activity). The challenge is to replace the current GATS approach (i.e., national treatment and market access commitments-cum-restrictions for four modes of supply on a sector-by-sector basis) with a more transparent focal point.

Deardorff (1994) has suggested that tariffication could be an answer. Deardorff suggests that negotiators should agree to full national treatment for all services, subject to the caveat that each country is allowed to levy taxes—perhaps prohibitive—on foreign providers. These taxes would be scheduled, and become the focal point for future liberalization efforts. The current structure of the GATS implies that one element of the equation would be to tariffy existing discriminatory contestability restrictions and another to tariffy nondiscriminatory barriers. An obvious way to achieve the latter is to auction them off periodically. This would appear most appropriate for regulated monopolies and for self-regulated industries where there is a *numerus fixus* constraint on new entry (e.g., certain professions). Another possibility for tariffying nondiscriminatory entry restrictions is to exchange price reduction commitments, based on comparisons of prices charged by a supplier in a market with the average of several of the lowest cost suppliers of the service concerned. Multilateral scrutiny of pricing policies could be sought, with an agreement to extend the WTO's dispute settlement mechanism to the pricing practices of monopolies or exclusive service suppliers.

Tariffication of discriminatory measures—those violating national treatment—appears to be straightforward in principle, as each government can simply set a tax rate. In practice, however, difficulties may arise in determining the nationality of firms, and in constraining opportunistic behavior. A problem is the choice of criteria to determine origin. The rules should be very clear in this connection. Note that a tax-based approach to generalizing national treatment will have the effect of acting as a TRIM: as any origin rule will require some degree of local ownership, there will be a bias towards establishment as a mode of contesting a market. This weakens the economic case for tariffication. It can also be noted that in many instances policy towards foreign providers currently may be consistent with national treatment, but countries have avoided scheduling (binding) this state of affairs.[11] To the extent that entry is free, and the applied policy is liberal, efforts should be made to avoid supplanting the situation by high taxes on foreign providers. If the status quo is relatively liberal, this should be reflected in the tax rates that are imposed. Thus, not only should established foreign firms be grandfathered from any tariffication if they are presently granted national treatment, no tariffication should be permitted in such sectors. If this cannot be achieved it further weakens the argument for tariffication.

While the case for tariffication per se is weak, it could nonetheless be very fruitful in enhancing transparency and in providing a focal point. The process of tariffication can greatly expand the amount of information regarding potential market opportunities for service providers. Rather than being used as an explicit focal point for negotiations, the calculation of tariff equivalents and price-cost margins can do much to identify those policies and sectors where negotiations should focus. This is a pressing need for further progress to be feasible on opening markets through multilateral exchange. But the greatest impact may be in domestic political markets. Once the costs of maintaining policies that restrict the contestability of markets are recognized, the scope for greater competition may be significantly enhanced, as those who bear the burden of the status quo are given an incentive to support change.

Most of the benefits of greater competition in services accrue to consumers, who face well known constraints in organizing an effective pro-competition lobby. Although the increase in transparency regarding the protective effect of government-mandated or tolerated entry restrictions in service activities that is implied by tariffication may well generate greater incentives by consumers to organize opposition, the problem is getting there. There may be sufficient export interests, however, that would gain from tariffication. Domestic potential providers of regulated services may also have an interest in supporting approaches that make regulated foreign markets contestable and more transparent. A reference to the experience obtained in agreeing to the Trade Policy Review Mechanism (TPRM) is appropriate here. Although most countries did not have much desire to subject themselves to a transparency-based review of their trade policies, the benefit of obtaining information on trading partners outweighed the perceived cost of being subjected to review as well. The result of the agreement to create the TPRM has been that domestic groups (and the Ministry of Finance) in each country have access to a substantial amount of information regarding the trade policy stance that is pursued, and can more easily compare this with policies applied by other countries. A problem with the TPRM exercise is that to be effective, the data generated must enter into the domestic political debate in the country concerned. If not used by domestic interest groups, the transparency function is limited to an intra-government audience. One way to make the TPRM reports more interesting for domestic groups would be to increase their analytical content, with particular emphasis on quantification of the redistributional impact of maintained policies. This has been resisted by WTO Members.

In principle, private parties could undertake such an analysis using TPRM-generated data, but for this to be possible, the TPRM reports would ideally generate the requisite data, especially on tariff-equivalents of non-tariff measures. Currently, this is not the case, and private parties do not even have access to the integrated database on tariffs and trade used by the TPRM staff. With the expansion of the TPRM mandate to services under the WTO, reports will have to cover the service sector in depth. Thus, a methodological framework will have to be established in any event, ideally one that allows for cross-country comparisons. The development of a tariffication-type approach to quantifying or ranking the economic impact of service sector policies could therefore be supported by WTO Members. Clearly this will entail a lot of work and it is not obvious how to construct a useful indicator or index. Nevertheless such research should be supported by countries seeking the liberalization of markets. A start could be made by building on the research that was undertaken in the run-up to the Single European Act in the mid-1980s.

Procurement

The GATT Agreement on Government Procurement was initially negotiated during the Tokyo round. It requires national treatment and nondiscrimination for purchases by government entities, and establishes rather detailed rules to enhance the transparency of tendering procedures. The tradeoff for what is essentially a "free trade agreement" for procurement—a large market in any country—was that the disciplines of the agreement apply only to those governments that sign it, and then only for specific entities that are listed in the Annexes (schedules) for each of the signatory nations. The agreement was renegotiated in 1986 and during the Uruguay round. The post-Uruguay round GPA entered into force in January 1996.

The GPA prohibits preferences for domestic firms through the application of the national treatment and nondiscrimination rules. These principles apply to both trade (cross-border supply) *and* tenders by foreign firms that are locally established. Three types of bodies are covered by the GPA: central government entities, such as Ministries, sub-central government entities, and a catch-all of "all other entities" that are required to follow the GPA's rules (in practice mostly public utilities). The extent to which bodies belonging to each of these three groups are covered depends on the schedules that are negotiated between the signatories. The GPA applies to all contracts (calls for tender) by listed central government entities that exceed SDR 130,000 or approximately $182,000. Higher thresholds apply to procurement by sub-central entities (usually around SDR 200,000) and utilities (around SDR 400,000). The GPA's scope was enhanced in the Uruguay round not only by the expansion of entities covered, but also by the inclusion of services and construction contracts. Procurement of the latter is again covered only for listed entities, and then only for those services that are explicitly listed for each signatory.

The GPA contains detailed rules regarding the tendering procedures that are to be followed by covered entities. It reduces the scope for so-called single or limited tendering, where a firm is directly approached and invited to bid (or simply awarded the contract outright). Tendering is to be competitive, either being open to all firms, or open to all pre-qualified firms. If qualification is a pre-condition, the GPA establishes detailed rules regarding the procedures and modalities for allowing foreign firms to qualify and ensuring that this process does not work to shut out foreign competition. There are also detailed requirements concerning technical specifications used in invitations to bid, publication requirements, time limits, and the content of tender documentation to be provided to potential suppliers. Signatories must establish mechanisms allowing awards to be contested by bidders and to compensate them should it be found that a decision violates GPA rules and procedures. Thus, firms that believe that the agreement's rules are being circumvented in the case of a specific tender may challenge an ongoing procurement process before a *domestic* court or an independent review body that is subject to judicial review. In some sense this implies that the GPA has direct effect in signatories. A complainant firm that contests a procurement process may benefit from "rapid interim measures", which could consist of compensation or of suspension of bidding and tendering.

Although in principle no discrimination is allowed in favor of domestic firms by covered entities, developing countries may negotiate "mutually acceptable exclusions from the rules on national treatment with respect to certain entities, products, or services that are included in their lists of entities." Such negotiations may also be initiated *ex post,* after signing the agreement. However, the option is limited to *certain* entities, products or services. Many countries have concluded that the GPA is too far-reaching in its implications. Membership of the GPA is quite limited, with only 13 signatories (counting the EU as one). Indeed, not all OECD countries have signed it. There is therefore a large hole in the WTO, as public procurement constitutes a large source of demand for goods and services in most countries. The conditional-MFN approach based on reciprocal negotiation of entity lists has not proven successful in inducing large membership.

Two possibilities arise to improve the situation. The first is to pursue conditional tariffication which allows price preferences subject to a determination that certain necessary conditions have been met (these will have to be negotiated). The second is to allow for tariffication of procurement preferences more generally by developing countries (Hoekman and Mavroidis 1995). The first option is analogous to the pursuit of competition policy disciplines, and is therefore subject to the general arguments that can be raised against such efforts. As long as agreement can be reached regarding the economics of the issue, progress along this dimension may well be feasible. Involvement of competition-type bodies could be useful in the procurement area by establishing conditions under which negotiated criteria allowing for the use of price preferences (or local content/offset requirements) have been met. No economic criteria are currently defined under which a government may diverge from the ban on discrimination. General tariffication is the more straightforward approach, although not necessarily the optimal one from an economic perspective.

The potential gains from trade are clear on this issue. Developing countries offer potential markets for current signatories, whereas governments that are concerned with minimizing their budgetary outlays have a stake in adopting procurement practices that maximize national welfare. As in other areas, the key issue appears to be one of information: often it may not be clear to policymakers what procurement policy is the most beneficial. More research on this question could therefore be very useful in itself, as well as in terms of extending the reach of the GPA. As in the case of services, no attempts have been made to calculate tariff or producer subsidy equivalents implied by existing policies. Indeed, very little is known about the product composition of procurement, its absolute magnitude, the average size of contracts, and the opportunity costs of current practices. The first step must therefore be data collection.

Anti-dumping

GATT data reveal that some 2,000 anti-dumping cases were initiated after 1980 by OECD countries, with most of the growth occurring in more recent years. Without disciplining the use of this form of contingent protection, developing countries and economies in transition will find their access to markets diminished or uncertain, thus frustrating their drive to integrate themselves into the world economy. A key issue confronting policymakers in the coming years is to decide on how to undertake the required surgery. Affected trading partners will have to help. A passive strategy or one that is limited to pointing out the absurdities and hypocrisy of maintaining anti-dumping will not be effective. What is required is to deal with the rhetoric of 'unfairness' first. Advocates of anti-dumping policies argue that they are a justifiable attempt by importing country governments to offset the market access restrictions existing in an exporting firm's home country that underlie the ability of such firms to dump.[12] Such restrictions may consist of import barriers preventing arbitrage, but may also reflect the non-existence or non-enforcement of competition law by the exporting country. Anti-dumping may then be defended as a second-best instrument to offset such "government-made" competitive differences, the first-best solution being held to be the adoption of common competition policies. Whatever one thinks of the economics of this argument, it appears to be supported by regional experience, which suggests that there are at least three necessary conditions for the abolition of contingent protection: (1) free trade and freedom of investment; (2) disciplines on the ability of governments to assist firms and industries located in their territory; and (3) the existence and enforcement of competition (antitrust) legislation. All three elements can be regarded as forming an implicit market access guarantee, the objective being to safeguard the conditions of competition on regional markets.

Enhancing the contestability of services and procurement markets could do much to reduce rhetorical claims of "unfair trade", but cannot guarantee a significant fall in the incidence of antidumping harassment. Even economies such as Singapore and Hong Kong are subjected to anti-dumping by OECD countries. One possible remedy is to enhance the role of competition policy disciplines in the anti-dumping context by seeking multilateral agreement on a limited number of common standards. Political realities will require that the antidumping option be maintained in the immediate future. But it may be possible to make anti-dumping just one of a number of available remedies. For example, agreement could be sought that allegations of dumping are first investigated by the antitrust authorities of the exporter's home country. The objective of this investigation would be to determine whether the exporting firm or industry engages in anti-competitive practices, or benefits from government-created or government-supported entry barriers that have a significant impact on the contestability of its home market. The benchmark used in investigations would be the home country's competition laws. The importing country's competition authorities would be invited to participate in the investigation, and would be provided with all relevant data collected and used. If anti-competitive behavior is found to exist, a previously agreed remedy would be applied. Strict time limits would have to be agreed to ensure that allegations of unfair trade could be dealt with rapidly.

If the importing country government disagrees with the conclusion of the investigation by the exporter's competition office, it would be encouraged to invoke the WTO dispute settlement mechanism. More specifically, a so-called non-violation complaint could be brought. Under a non-violation complaint, the policy to which a country objects does *not* violate any

GATT disciplines, but is nonetheless alleged to worsen the conditions of competition (i.e. market access). Under this approach it would be left to multilateral mechanisms to determine the facts of the case. Although it would be encouraged to seek GATT arbitration, political realities dictate that the importing country retain the option of initiating anti-dumping investigations. But agreement should be sought that a necessary condition for this is that the investigation and data collected by the competition authorities have revealed the existence of significant barriers to entry in the exporter's home market. These barriers could be either purely private or be created or supported by government actions.[13] Given that a rationale offered by proponents for anti-dumping is the existence of non-contestable markets this should be made an explicit criterion. This would go some way towards defining unfairness as injury to competition (the antitrust standard), rather than injury to competitors (the anti-dumping standard), and ensuring that unfairness is demonstrated to exist, rather than merely alleged.

It is not clear that the foregoing satisfies the MTN reciprocity constraint. While potentially affected exporters may support a proposal along the lines suggested above, the import-competing lobbies that support anti-dumping most likely will not. The main group that should favor the use of more competition policy-based tests and criteria in the application of anti-dumping are consumers (both firms and households). As argued by Finger (1993), anti-dumping will ultimately have to be dealt with in the domestic arena. For this to occur a necessary condition is information. A very significant amount of work has been done on the effects of anti-dumping, but mostly in a partial equilibrium context. The existence of anti-dumping and the threat of its use can be regarded as raising the average expected tariff confronting exporters above the actual average applied rate (or the rate bound under the GATT). Efforts to estimate how high this margin is, and the effects of the concomitant uncertainty regarding the tariff that may exist in the future, could be helpful both in the domestic political arena and in the multilateral context. In turn, another way of exploiting the concept of tariffication in negotiations could be to seek to put upper bounds on anti-dumping duties. These bounds—which could be absolute or relative to the applied nominal rate—could then become the focus of reciprocal reductions.

Concluding Remarks

In the domestic setting governments and legislatures decided at some point in time that competition laws and enforcement offices were necessary to safeguard the interests of consumers. Their focus is limited to the behavior of private entities, and their substantive content varies significantly across countries. In the MTN setting, the question is how to deal with the anti-competitive effects of state behavior meaning actions that are generally *beyond* the purview of domestic competition laws and agencies. Although the pursuit of multilateral competition-policy disciplines per se through MTNs may be useful to help address some market access concerns (such as anti-dumping) it is not likely to prove very fruitful, given the differences in approaches to antitrust. Attempts to enhance market access and the contestability of markets should be informed by competition policy principles.

With the gradual reduction of average tariffs to rather low levels, it has become more difficult for MTNs to ensure that negotiated disciplines are directly competition-enhancing. This is well illustrated by the GATS, where negotiators were confronted with a policy universe that was difficult to identify, let alone quantify. As the level of tariffs has fallen towards zero, incentives were created to shift MTNs towards the negotiation of policy-specific rules, and to the adoption of market access commitments with explicit or implicit sectoral reciprocity objectives and constraints. Such commitments are potentially inconsistent with the aim of generating greater competition in that they are less or transparent, involving greater opportunities or need for management. The rising prominence of domestic regulatory regimes as market access barriers has also led to increasing pressure for harmonization of regulatory policies (Bhagwati 1994).

The use of price-based measures as focal points, as opposed to actual imposition of taxes, in areas such as services and procurement could help to ensure that MTNs will move the world towards a more competitive environment. Tariff-like focal points can be useful not only in harnessing the mercantilist bias of policymakers in international negotiations, but can also help offset the lack of information on the costs and benefits of status quo policies pertaining to areas such as services and procurement. Greater information and better data are crucial for momentum towards liberalization to be maintained. It is a truism that the main constraint affecting liberalization is the asymmetry in incentives confronting the gainers and losers from state-sanctioned entry barriers. But to some degree this reflects an asymmetry in information. On issues such as services and procurement too little is known regarding the costs of the status quo and the potential benefits of greater competition. In part this is because basic data are not collected on variables of economic interest. There is a clear role here for international organizations such as the WTO or the OECD to provide data and analysis of the costs and benefits of existing policies and possible alternatives. Quantifying the tariff-equivalent of discriminatory and nondiscriminatory entry barriers and their welfare costs may prove very fruitful in mobilizing interest groups that support liberalization and greater competition. But, as Bob Stern has been propounding for many years (see, e.g., Stern 1985, 1994) before analysis is possible, data are required. Compiling the requisite data sets to allow further use of "tariffication" in multilateral trade negotiations is not a trivial task, but is likely to be well worth pursuing.

NOTES

1. Many jurisdictions recognize that specific agreements between firms that may reduce competition could be welfare enhancing, and make allowance for such agreements. However, the burden of proof in such instances is usually upon the participants in such arrangements.

2. The distinction between trade policy and trade liberalization is often neglected. In OECD deliberations, for example, one often encounters the proposition that trade and competition policies have congruent objectives, i.e. efficient resource allocation (e.g., OECD 1994). While this may be the case for trade liberalization, the fact remains that trade policy officials have the task of designing and implementing barriers to trade. Only through recurring rounds of multilateral trade negotiations has it been possible to incrementally reduce tariffs, as policymakers generally have not been willing or able to engage in unilateral liberalization. And progress towards free trade has been slow, reflecting a strong desire to maintain a sufficiently powerful arsenal of instruments of contingent protection such as antidumping legislation.

3. See, e.g., Caves and Uekusa (1976) or Nakatani (1984).

4. This is not to deny that market access commitments cannot or will not be procompetitive, simply that: (1) greater competition will not necessarily follow; and (2) the level of competition in a market may not really be at issue.

5. The GATT's focus is on "like" or "directly competitive or substitutable" products. While implicitly the degree of substitutability between products is a major factor underlying the determination of what are "like" products, GATT case law has not developed clear definitions or criteria. In a 1987 panel report on Japanese taxes on imported alcoholic beverages, the panel used economic criteria (cross-elasticities of demand) explicitly for the first time (GATT 1994, 147). Subsequent panels have not followed this precedent, however.

6. See Fung (1991) and Dick (1993), who argue that differences in competition laws may not have an obvious impact on competition. Exemptions, for example, may alter the form of competition (e.g., induce a shift from price to non-price competition), which can be both pro-competitive and welfare enhancing.

7. For more on this topic, see Dutz (1993) and Hoekman and Mavroidis (1994) and the references cited therein.

8. As with VERs, a VIE may be detrimental to the country seeking it, insofar as the guaranteed access stimulates production by firms that are not competitive and draws resources away from more economically beneficial activities (Bhagwati 1988).

9. Space considerations prohibit a detailed discussion of the contents of the GPA or the GATS. See Hoekman and Mavroidis (1995) and Hoekman (1995).

10. This fluidity is also reflected in changes in enforcement practices over time. See Sapir et al. (1993).

11. Most GATS schedules embody greater limitations on market access than on national treatment. In the latter category one often finds the label "unbound" for sectors, rather than specific measures. This suggests that the status quo may be liberal (see Hoekman 1996).

12. What follows draws on Hoekman and Mavroidis (1994).

13. Both types of barriers may not be addressable through the application of the home country's competition law. For example, the law might exempt certain practices on the basis of economic efficiency. Government policies will usually be exempt altogether from the reach of antitrust.

REFERENCES

Baldwin, Robert. 1970. *Nontariff Distortions to International Trade.* Washington: Brookings.

Bhagwati, Jagdish. 1988. *Protectionism.* Cambridge: MIT Press.

Bhagwati, Jagdish. 1994. "Fair Trade, Reciprocity and Harmonization: The New Challenge to the Theory and Policy of Free Trade." In Alan Deardorff and Robert Stern, eds., *Analytical and Negotiating Issues in the Global Trading System.* Ann Arbor: University of Michigan Press.

Caves, Richard, and Uekusa, Masu. 1976. *Industrial Organization in Japan.* Washington D.C.: Brookings Institution.

Deardorff, Alan. 1994. "Market Access." In *The New World Trading System: Readings.* Paris: OECD.

Deardorff, Alan V., and Stern, Robert M. 1985. *Methods of Measurement of Non-Tariff Barriers.* Geneva: UNCTAD.

Deardorff, Alan V., and Stern, Robert M. Stern. 1986. *The Michigan Model of World Production and Trade.* Cambridge: MIT Press.

Deardorff, Alan, and Stern, Robert. 1987. "Current Issues in Trade Policy: An Overview." In Robert Stern, ed., *U.S. Trade Polices in a Changing World Economy.* Cambridge, MA.: MIT Press.

Deardorff, Alan, and Stern, Robert. 1990. *Computational Analysis of Global Trading Arrangements.* Ann Arbor: University of Michigan Press.

Dick, Andrew. 1993. "Japanese Antitrust: Reconciling Theory and Evidence." *Contemporary Policy Issues* 9:50–60.

Dutz, Mark. 1993. "Enforcement of Canadian 'Unfair' Trade Laws: The Case for Competition Policies as an Antidote for Protection." In J.M. Finger, ed., *Antidumping: How it Works and Who Gets Hurt.* Ann Arbor: University of Michigan Press.

Finger, J. Michael, ed. 1993. *Antidumping: How it Works and Who Gets Hurt.* Ann Arbor: University of Michigan Press.

Fung, K.C. 1991. "Characteristics of Japanese Industrial Groups and Their Potential Impact on U.S.-Japan Trade." In Robert Baldwin, ed., *Empirical Studies of Commercial Trade Policy.* Chicago: University of Chicago Press.

GATT. 1994. *Analytical Index.* Geneva: GATT.

Graham, Edward M., and Richardson, J. D. 1994. "Summary of the Institute for International Economics Project on International Competition Policies." In process.

Hoekman, Bernard. 1996. "Tentative First Steps: An Assessment of the Uruguay Round Agreement on Services." In Will Martin and Alan Winters, eds., *The Uruguay Round and the Developing Economies.* Cambridge: Cambridge University Press. Hoekman, Bernard, and Mavroidis, Petros C. 1994. "Antitrust-based Remedies and Dumping in International Trade." Cambridge: Cambridge University Press.

Hoekman, Bernard, and Mavroidis, Petros C. 1995. "The WTO's Agreement on Government Procurement: Expanding Disciplines, Declining Membership?" *Public Procurement Law Review* 4:63–79.

McAfee, R. Preston, and McMillan, John. 1989. "Government Procurement and International Trade." *Journal of International Economics* 26:291–308.

Nakatani, Iwao. 1984. "The Economic Role of Financial Corporate Grouping." In M. Aoki, ed., *The Economic Analysis of the Japanese Firm.* Amsterdam: North Holland.

OECD. 1994. *Trade and Competition Policy: Comparing Objectives and Methods.* Paris: OECD.

Sapir, André; Buigues, Pierre; and Jacquemin, Alexis. 1993. "European Competition Policy in Manufacturing and Services: A Two-speed Approach?" *Oxford Review of Economic Policy* 9:113–32.

Spriggs, John. 1991. "Towards an International Transparency Institution: Australian Style." *The World Economy* 14:165–80.

Stern, Robert M. 1985. "Global Dimensions and Determinants of International Trade and Investment in Services." In Robert M. Stern, ed., *Trade and Investment in Services: Canada/U.S. Perspectives.* Toronto: University of Toronto Press for the Ontario Economic Council.

Stern, Robert M. 1994. "Liberalization." In *The New World Trading System: Readings.* Paris: OECD.

Stern, Robert M.; Jackson, John H.; and Hoekman, Bernard. 1986. *Assessment of the GATT Codes of Conduct.* Research Seminar in International Economics Discussion Paper No. 174. Ann Arbor: University of Michigan.

CHAPTER 9

Do Trading Blocs Enhance the Case for Strategic Trade Policy?

Wilhelm Kohler

Recent years have witnessed significant efforts on the part of EU as well as EFTA countries to increase their degree of economic integration. Thus, the EU has completed its Internal Market Programme, called Europe 1992, and it has set out to achieve European Monetary Union (EMU) in the hotly debated Maastricht Treaty of 1991. In addition, EFTA countries have secured much of the gains from Europe 1992 by forming what is sometimes referred to as the European Economic Area, and some of them (Austria, Finland and Sweden) formally joined the EU in 1995. While there is a good deal of controversy among economists as to the pros and cons of EMU as envisaged in Maastricht, there is much less disagreement on the gains from Europe 1992. The accepted framework within which economists discuss the effects of Europe 1992 emphasizes three different channels for static efficiency gains: lower real trade costs, more competitive conduct due to lower market segmentation, and increased factor mobility. In addition, there are dynamic effects of integration, operating through capital formation and endogenous growth channels, but these have so far received very little attention in the literature on Europe 1992.[1]

But there are also misgivings. Some observers have expressed fears that countries entering a trading bloc will find themselves in a new environment which may prompt them to be more protectionist with respect to third countries than they would be otherwise, giving rise to the notion of "Fortress Europe." Such fears have additionally been fueled by the Maastricht Treaty bestowing upon the European Commission the right to pursue a common industrial policy vis a vis the rest of the world in Article 130. Indeed, even before the treaty was drafted, there was the general perception that Europe 1992 was also intended as an industrial policy initiative. However, misgivings have been arising also within the EU itself. Thus, the Commission has repeatedly expressed concern about the possibility that the gains from Europe 1992 might be jeopardized by EU countries gearing up their industrial policies, in particular as regards their subsidy programs, *as a result of Europe 1992.*[2]

What, precisely, are the channels through which Europe 1992 might lead EU countries to become more activist in their industrial policies? This paper singles out one of several possibly relevant incentives: the presence of international strategic distortions in oligopolistic markets, as emphasized in the modern trade policy literature. Suppose, then, that European countries try to target international strategic distortions in oligopolistic industries by means of appropriately specified production subsidies and taxes (instead of targeted export or import subsidies and taxes, which are largely ruled out by both multilateral and preferential arrangements). Suppose, moreover, that Europe 1992 does lower real trade costs for intra-European trade as is commonly assumed, while leaving real trade costs unchanged for external trade.[3] Once firms and consumers have reacted to this change, will national governments in Europe and elsewhere face an incentive to increase or lower their production interventions, if they act non-cooperatively? To what extent will the result differ if they behave cooperatively, say under the common industrial policy provision of Article 130 of the Maastricht treaty?

I shall pursue these questions under the assumption that market segmentation prevails both before and after the trading bloc is formed. This is not to deny the pro-competitive effect of a relaxation of market segmentation that many observers expect from Europe 1992. Indeed, we shall see below that lower trade costs do entail lower oligopolistic markups even if markets remain segmented. In this sense, the *degree* of market segmentation is reduced. There may, however, be additional channels for such pro-competitive effects which I do not address in this paper.[4] The aim here is to focus clearly on lower real trade costs, which are arguably the most direct effect of European integration.

Although I shall use the welfare terminology familiar from the normative literature, my aim here is not to advocate such strategically motivated policies. Much has been said about the limits to the strategic trade and industrial policy literature as a workable tool of policy prescription. Instead, my aim is a positive one. The fundamental premise of my analysis is that, for better or for worse, governments may feel the kind of incentives emphasized by the strategic trade policy literature. Indeed, strategic considerations of this type may to a large extent also underlie political-economy forces to which governments feel exposed. My concern here is to study how trade integration of the kind envisaged by Europe 1992 affects these incentives.

I proceed as follows. The next section puts the subsequent theoretical treatment into perspective by presenting some empirical evidence on industrial subsidies in the EU. The following section outlines a conjectural variations oligopoly model covering three countries, which is suitable for an integration scenario of the type in question. The industry equilibrium for the model is then derived and equilibrium policies are determined in the ensuing section. If looked at from a normative perspective, these policies are second-best in that they try to correct several strategic distortions plus a mixture of oligopoly and terms-of-trade distortions with the single instrument of a general production subsidy or tax. I then show that the strategic part of these policies can be interpreted as a weighted average of the various single-market policy prescriptions that are already familiar from the literature. As will become evident, the ultimate policy outcome crucially depends on how governments react to each others' policy changes. Hence, a succeeding section investigates whether production subsidies and taxes are strategic substitutes or complements in the non-cooperative game played by governments. I then move on to the central question of whether a reduction in real trade costs for intra-European trade increases or reduces the strategic distortions that European countries and a third country face. The last part of the analysis considers strategic interactions with third countries and briefly explores extensions to the case of non-constant marginal costs. I then close the paper with a few summary remarks and suggestions for further research.

Industrial Subsidies in the European Union

To put the theoretical analysis into perspective, this section offers some empirical evidence on industrial subsidies. Since the paper is primarily motivated by recent developments in the European Union, the evidence presented is restricted to the EU. The general results of the paper are applicable to other trading blocs as well.

Subsidization has traditionally been an integral part of national industrial policies in all European countries. From its inception in the late 1950s, the EC has recognized such subsidization practices as an element that could limit European integration. The initial EC treaty, therefore, took a restrictive stance on industrial subsidies: they were ruled out unless explicitly allowed by the treaty, or unless exemption was granted by EC authorities on the basis of the Treaty. This principle has survived in the Maastricht Treaty of 1991 (Article 92). But whenever there are exemptions, there is danger of excessive use. In addition, not all kinds of subsidies are sufficiently visible for such a principle to operate fully in all conceivable instances. Hence, the Treaty put the Commission in charge of extensive surveillance and control with respect to national subsidization practices. Whatever the success in terms of curtailing these practices, a welcome side effect has been that the Commission produces a sizable body of empirical evidence in an area where national governments are hesitant to go public.

The figures presented here are from a special study published by the Commission of the EC (1991), and from the third survey of state aids by the Commission of the EC (1992). An important caveat has to be mentioned before looking at the details, however. Subsidies do not leave paper trails that allow us to identify the underlying motivation or incentive. The figures presented cannot, therefore, be taken as evidence for *strategically motivated* subsidization. They are only intended to give a broad idea of the extent to which subsidization as such, whether granted on strategic grounds or otherwise, is going on in EU countries. Important structural features that relate, however tenuously, to the issues considered below are also presented. The subsidies reported are parts of national industrial policies, although they may also involve EU funds. A coherent EU industrial policy has only recently been envisaged by Article 130 of the Maastricht Treaty. Whether or not such a policy will in fact evolve, given the controversy surrounding it, remains to be seen.

The average annual amount of subsidies paid by all 12 EU countries between 1986 and 1988 was 82 billion ECU (in 1987 prices), which is 2.2 percent of EU GDP. This is a sizable amount which explains the continuing attention of the European Commission to subsidy payments. One would perhaps expect a few "classical recipients," such as agriculture, mining and transport, to loom large in the overall picture. It is therefore interesting to note that subsidies to manufacturing command by far the largest share of all subsidies recorded. The average annual figure for 1986–88 was 39.095 billion ECU (in 1989 prices) which is roughly 42 percent of all subsidies, as opposed to roughly 31 percent for transport, 15 percent for coal mining, and only 13 percent for agriculture.[5] Table 1 highlights international differences in manufacturing subsidies paid by EU countries in the two periods 1986–88 and 1988–90. We observe a moderate overall reduction that does not, however, uniformly show up for every country. Greece, Spain and Ireland exhibit significant reductions, while Portugal, Luxemburg and Denmark have increased their manufacturing subsidies expressed in percent of manufacturing value added. Moreover, looking at annual changes, manufacturing subsidies on the EU level have picked up again in both 1988 and 1990, after falling from 1986 to1987 and from 1988 to 1989. For this reason, the Commission is explicitly hesitant to identify a long-term downward trend in manufacturing subsidization (Commission of the EC 1992, 9–10). As to the purpose pursued, we observe an overall shift from sectoral targeting to general purpose and regional subsidies. But again, the aggregate figures mask a con-

TABLE 1. Subsidies to Manufacturing in EU Countries
Average Annual Figures, 1989 Prices

	Mio ECU		% (1)		ECU/empl.		Gen. (2)		Targ. (2)		Reg. (2)	
	86–88	88–90	86–88	88–90	86–88	88–90	86–88	88–90	86–88	88–90	86–88	88–90
BEL	1175	1211	4.3	4.1	1606	1655	67.7	75.9	11.9	3.5	20.4	20.6
DK	316	333	1.9	2.1	593	634	72.7	59.1	21.1	37.7	6.2	3.2
GER	7869	7865	2.7	2.5	994	984	34.3	28.6	7.1	10.8	58.6	60.7
GRC	2074	1072	24.3	14.6	2983	1502	41.2	80.7	19.9	4.5	39.0	14.8
SP	4491	2499	6.8	3.6	1749	936	12.5	27.7	85.3	67.1	2.2	5.2
FR	6479	6106	3.8	3.5	1437	1380	46.4	66.0	45.9	25.3	7.7	8.7
IRL	447	368	6.4	4.9	2114	1734	47.3	49.6	13.7	8.8	39.0	41.6
IT	10760	11027	6.2	6.0	2139	2175	31.9	29.8	16.7	14.8	51.4	55.4
LX	37	48	2.3	2.6	988	1270	44.1	39.0	0.0	0.3	55.9	60.7
NL	1101	1225	3.1	3.1	1215	1327	78.5	77.0	6.4	10.8	15.0	12.2
POR	245	616	2.2	5.3	302	758	64.7	17.1	31.2	77.6	4.1	5.3
UK	4101	3133	2.6	2.0	770	582	34.2	45.5	33.6	20.4	32.1	34.1
EU 12	39095	35503	4.0	3.5	1325	1203	37.3	42.0	27.0	20.3	35.7	37.7

Source: Commission of the EC (1991, 1992).

Notes: These figures do not include subsidies to coal mining and transport. 1990 figures for Germany do not include transfer programs to former East Germany. (1): Percent of manufacturing value added. (2): Percent of total manufacturing. Gen.: general purpose, i.e., granted to firms in all sectors on the basis of general criteria, such as R&D, small scale firms, exports, or investment. Targ.: targeted, i.e., selectively granted to firms in individual sectors. Reg.: regional, i.e., granted under the general exemption of Article 92 of the Maastricht treaty.

siderable amount of international variation, with Denmark, Germany, and Portugal exhibiting a reverse shift.

It is tempting to argue that it is only targeted subsidies that may potentially fall under the type of policy analyzed in subsequent sections, and these are a relatively small share of total manufacturing subsidies in most countries (the major exceptions being Spain and France). However, the Commission of the EC (1991, 39) explicitly mentions that, de facto, the so-called general purpose subsidies are quite frequently aimed at what is perceived as "strategic industries" in the respective countries (see also the OECD study mentioned below). And Franzmeyer (1991/92, 158) points out that the regional policy exemption of Article 92 has increasingly been drawn upon to justify quite selective policies towards individual industries. Obviously, the less diversified the industry of a given region the more will regional subsidies come close to industrial targeting. A rough sectoral breakdown of targeted subsidies is provided by table 2. Steel and shipbuilding have been singled out by the Commission report presumably because of the enormous pressure of capacity cuts and restructuring that these sectors have been exposed to and which was supposedly eased by the subsidies paid. While strategic aspects of trade or industrial policies have mostly been emphasized with respect to "sunrise" rather than "sunset" industries, there is nothing fundamental that would rule out the importance of such aspects also for "sunset" industries like steel or shipbuilding. In any case, in 1988–90 other sectors appear to be as important targets as are shipbuilding and steel taken together. In 1986–88 they received more than double the amount of subsidies targeted towards steel and shipbuilding. Unfortunately, there is no further breakdown of the data for other sectors, but there is reason to assume that the automobile industry is an important recipient in this category [see Commission of the EC (1991, 43)].

It is important to realize that the figures presented above are certainly not exhaustive. Although the Commission took pains to define subsidies in a reasonably broad way, there remains a serious problem of transparency. It must be assumed that there is a significant amount of subsidization which is sufficiently indirect and limited in transparency to escape even the most ambitious attempt at documentation. For instance, work by Abraham and Dewit (1992) reveals that insurance against non-payment of exports, as offered by many European governments, may involve selective implicit subsidies with a distinct flavor of targeting.

It would be interesting to compare industrial subsidization practices of EU countries with those of non-European countries. A recent study by the OECD (1992), which is structured along criteria similar to those used by the Commission of the EC (1991, 1992), does extend to non-European countries, but unlike the EU studies it is careful to avoid any direct international comparison of support levels. A few observations are nevertheless worth mentioning. The net cost to governments of reported programs amount to 3.3 percent of OECD manufacturing value added in 1986, which is slightly less than the EU average for 1986–88 reported in table 1 above. While the EU figure has dropped to 3.5 percent for 1988–1990, the OECD-wide figure was down to 1.8 percent in 1989. Of particular relevance to the issue raised by the present paper, however, the OECD notes that the overall reduction in the level of government support to industry was paralleled by a significant shift away from general purpose policies to more focused and selectively available support measures, "favoring for example certain technology areas or certain types of enterprises" (OECD 1992, 63).

The evidence available thus indicates that European as well as non-European governments pursue industrial policies by means of state aids to individual sectors. While it is impossible to trace in detail the sectoral targeting involved, one may nevertheless safely assume that a significant amount of targeting is involved. Industrial policies of this sort continue to be a prime concern to many policy observers and to the European Commission. The subsequent theoretical analysis tries to identify the impact of trading blocs on strategic incentives that governments may feel to pursue industrial policies. As is well-known, these incentives may also operate towards taxing rather than subsidizing firms in individual sectors, whereas

TABLE 2. Targeted Subsidies in EU Countries Average Annual Figures

	Steel			Shipbuilding			Other Sectors		
	Mio ECU	in %		Mio ECU	in %		Mio ECU	in %	
	88–90	88–90	86–88	88–90	88–90	86–88	88–90	88–90	86–88
BEL	0.000	0.0	0.0	16.452	1.4	2.9	26.263	2.2	8.9
DK	0.000	0.0	0.0	107.220	32.2	20.7	18.554	5.6	0.4
GER	39.140	0.5	0.8	228.310	2.9	2.2	579.903	7.4	4.1
GRC	1.953	0.2	0.0	34.231	3.2	0.0	12.489	1.2	19.9
SP	726.653	29.1	30.4	249.380	10.0	3.5	699.809	28.0	51.4
FR	16.240	0.3	0.3	262.490	4.3	8.4	1264.760	20.7	37.2
IRL	0.000	0.0	0.0	0.000	0.0	0.0	32.276	8.8	13.7
IT	677.850	6.1	3.7	396.370	3.6	2.3	556.152	5.0	10.6
LX	0.000	0.0	0.0	0.000	0.0	0.0	0.123	0.3	0.0
NL	0.000	0.0	0.0	88.391	7.2	2.8	44.096	3.6	3.6
POR	143.708	23.3	4.6	166.530	27.0	5.2	167.660	27.2	21.4
UK	2.660	0.1	0.6	234.200	7.5	12.7	402.407	12.8	20.4
EU 12	1608.204	4.5	4.0	1783.600	5.0	4.6	3804.492	10.7	18.3

Source: Commission of the EC (1991, 1992).

Notes: % = Percent of total manufacturing subsidies, as in column 1 of table 1.

the above evidence is restricted to subsidization practices. Theoretical reasons for the prevalence of subsidies rather than taxes will be given below.

Outline of the Model

To make the analysis tractable, I use a stylized model of the world economy. Thus, suppose the world consists of three countries, two European (labeled 1 and 2) and one non-European (labeled 3). I assume that these countries coincide with three segmented markets. Each of them has a given number, n^i, of identical firms producing a homogeneous good which they ship to all three countries. Though homogeneous within a given country of origin, products may be differentiated by country of origin. Demand is represented by the following type of revenue function for a typical firm of country 1 shipping to country j

$$R_j^1 = R_j^1(q_j^1, \overline{Q}_j^1, Q_j^2, Q_j^3), \qquad j = 1, 2, 3, \qquad (1)$$

where capital letters denote total sales by all firms of a given country to a given market, and $\overline{Q}_j^1 \equiv Q_j^1 - q_j^1$. By symmetry, $\overline{Q}_j^1 = n^i q_j^i$. For simplicity, I assume that all foreign firms' sales always enter a domestic firm's revenue function symmetrically:[6] $R_{j,2}^1 \equiv \partial R_j^1/\partial Q_j^2 = \partial R_j^1/\partial Q_j^3$. Moreover I use $R_{j,0}^1$ to denote $\partial R_j^1/\partial q_j^1$, and $R_{j,1}^1 \equiv \partial R_j^1/\partial \overline{Q}_j^1$. I shall subsequently refer to these derivatives as *direct* marginal revenues, as opposed to *perceived* and *true* marginal revenues, to be defined below. Part of the subsequent analysis is restricted to the case of linear inverse demand functions. In this case, the slopes of all *direct* marginal revenue schedules are constant, and $R_{j,1}^1$ and $R_{j,2}^1$ do not change as competitors vary their sales. These slopes will subsequently be denoted by $R_{j,10}^i \equiv \partial R_{j,1}^i/\partial q_j^i$, $R_{j,11}^i \equiv \partial R_{j,1}^i/\partial \overline{Q}_j^i$, and $R_{j,12}^i \equiv \partial R_{j,1}^i/\partial Q_j^{k \neq i}$, for $i, j = 1, 2, 3$ and $l = 0, 1, 2$. It is assumed that $R_{j,0}^i$ is decreasing in firm i's own sales as well as in all of its competitors' sales. This is guaranteed if domestic and foreign goods are substitutes, as long as inverse demand functions are not too convex. Moreover, I assume that "own effects" on revenues always dominate "cross effects": $R_{j,1}^1 < R_{j,2}^1$ and $R_{j,01}^1 < R_{j,02}^1$.[7]

I first take the simplest case of constant marginal cost of production, denoted by c^i, and I shall briefly explore the consequences of more complex cost structures, such as those stipulated by Krugman (1984), later in the paper.[8] In addition to cost of production, each firm faces a constant marginal cost of shipping to foreign markets. Let this marginal real trade cost be t_e for cross-border shipments within Europe, and t_n for shipments to and from Europe. Integration lowers t_e, but leaves t_n unchanged. I am not concerned with the detailed nature of these trade costs and why t_e is reduced in the process of European integration,[9] but it is important to note that, in line with the accepted framework mentioned in the introduction, forming a such a trading bloc is assumed to lower real trade costs rather than simply removing a price distortion.

I use the familiar Nash equilibrium concept to analyze non-cooperative behavior, and I model market conduct by means of conjectural variations. I define γ_1^i and γ_1^i to indicate the response of a representative domestic and foreign competitor, respectively, that a representative firm of country i believes will follow a unit increase of its own sales. Thus, firms of any one country entertain identical conjectures about their rivals' behavior, and these are identical for all markets, but differ as between domestic and foreign competitors. Subject to these conjectures, firms maximize profits. By assumption, positive profits do not induce entry. The number of firms in each country remains fixed.

Using conjectural variations in static games is open to criticism. In a sense it amounts to incorporating inherently dynamic notions, such as assumed *changes* in competitors' sales, without actually making the model truly dynamic.[10] However, a recent paper by Dockner (1992) establishes that static conjectural variations equilibria may under certain conditions be interpreted as steady state closed-loop equilibria of differential games. Dockner's analysis importantly complements the traditional justification for using conjectural variations, which simply points out its usefulness in allowing one to capture the idea of varying degrees of competition in a unified model [see Dixit (1986, 107–8)].[11] Exploiting symmetry, *perceived* marginal revenue of a representative country i firm may be written as[12]

$$\widetilde{MR}_j^i = R_{j,0}^i + (n^i - 1) R_{j,1}^i \gamma_1^i + N^i R_{j,2}^i \gamma_2^i, \tag{2}$$

where N^i is the total number of firms *outside* country i.

The policy variable is a general production subsidy or tax, denoted by s^i. As indicated in the introduction, a key feature of trading blocs is that trade policy measures are no longer available with respect to intra-bloc trade. Moreover, they are to a large extent subject to international obligations even for external trade.[13] The model captures this in a stylized way by assuming that there are no trade barriers other than real trade costs which are, in turn, treated as exogenous when governments decide upon their production subsidies and taxes. Hence, integration is similarly treated as an exogenous reduction in real trade costs, and our main question simply is how this affects the endogenous production subsidy or tax. From a broader perspective, one can argue that the decision to integrate and thereby reduce real trade costs and the choice of a particular production subsidy or tax should be treated on an equal footing, rather than taking one as being exogenous to the other. However, real trade costs are not determined directly by governments. Instead, they are the outcome of a potentially large number of national regulations with diverse objectives, which are almost impossible to deal with in a unified approach. Moreover, Europe 1992 is based on mutual recognition rather than a grand uniform design, grounded in the belief that the ensuing gains from lower trade costs and enhanced competition will more than outweigh the cost of losing regulatory power on imported goods. Bearing all this in mind, it is hard to envisage any more satisfactory treatment of the issue than simply postulating an exogenous reduction in real trade costs.[14]

In line with the bulk of the literature, I assume that the sequence of events is such that governments choose their policies prior to firms playing their non-cooperative game, and that in doing so they fully internalize the Nash equilibrium of the subgame on the firm level (subgame perfection). Policy makers are assumed to maximize welfare, which is measured as usual by industry profits plus consumer surplus minus the subsidy cost-plus tax receipts (see below).

Equilibrium at the Firm Level

Profits of representative firms of the three countries may be written as

$$(a) \quad \Pi^i = \sum_j R_j^i(.) - (c^i - s^i) \sum_j q_j^i - t^e q_k^i - t_n q_3^i, \quad j = 1, 2, 3; k \neq i = 1, 2,$$

$$(b) \quad \Pi^3 = \sum_j R_j^3(.) - (c^3 - s^3) \sum_j q_j^3 - t^n \sum_h q_h^3, \quad j = 1, 2, 3; h = 1, 2.$$

(3)

The non-cooperative equilibrium on the firm level is determined by the condition that *perceived* marginal profits are equal to zero for $i = 1, 2, 3$ and $j = 1, 2, 3$. This gives 9 equations which jointly determine sales by the three representative firms to the three markets. It should be noted that each firm's decision relating to a given market is independent of its decision on sales to other markets, as long as markets are not interrelated by joint economies or diseconomies or demand links [see Krugman (1984), and Bulow, Geanakoplos and Klemperer (1985)]. Sales to the European market 1 are, for instance, determined by the following first order conditions for representative firms of the three countries:

$$(a) \quad \widetilde{MR}_1^1 - c^1 + s^1 = 0.$$
$$(b) \quad \widetilde{MR}_1^2 - c^2 - t_e + s^2 = 0.$$
$$(c) \quad \widetilde{MR}_1^3 - c^3 - t_n - s^3 = 0.$$

(4)

where $\widetilde{MR}^i_j$ is perceived marginal revenue as defined above. Fulfillment of the second order conditions is discussed in the appendix. Sales to markets 2 and 3 are analogously determined. I assume that all firms serve all markets, giving rise to what Brander and Krugman (1983) have called "reciprocal dumping". This requires that without trade the oligopoly markups in all countries would exceed real trade costs. The comparative static properties of this equilibrium hinge upon the signs and magnitudes of the various partial derivatives of perceived marginal revenues. We can write the first order conditions in differentiated form as:

$$
\begin{bmatrix}
\left(\begin{array}{c} \widetilde{MR}^1_{1,0} \\ + (n^1-1)\,\widetilde{MR}^1_{1,1} \end{array} \right) & n^2\widetilde{MR}^1_{1,2} & n^3\widetilde{MR}^1_{1,2} \\[2em]
n^1\widetilde{MR}^2_{1,2} & \left(\begin{array}{c} \widetilde{MR}^2_{1,0} \\ + (n^2-1)\,\widetilde{MR}^2_{1,1} \end{array} \right) & n^3\widetilde{MR}^2_{1,2} \\[2em]
n^1\widetilde{MR}^3_{1,2} & n^2\widetilde{MR}^3_{1,2} & \left(\begin{array}{c} \widetilde{MR}^3_{1,0} \\ + (n^3-1)\,\widetilde{MR}^3_{1,1} \end{array} \right)
\end{bmatrix}
\begin{bmatrix} dq^1_1 \\ dq^2_1 \\ dq^3_1 \end{bmatrix}
$$

$$
= \begin{bmatrix} dc^1 - ds^1 \\ dc^2 + dt_e - ds^2 \\ dc^3 + dt_n - ds^3 \end{bmatrix}, \tag{5}
$$

where we have exploited the assumption of complete symmetry within countries, and the assumption that all foreign sales (from whatever country) enter the revenue function of any domestic firm symmetrically (symmetric heterogeneity). In the above equations, subscript indices must be interpreted as with marginal revenues above, i.e., $\widetilde{MR}^i_{1,0} \equiv \partial\widetilde{MR}^i_1/\partial q^i_1$, $\widetilde{MR}^i_{1,1} \equiv \partial\widetilde{MR}^i_1/\partial \bar{Q}^i_1$, and $\widetilde{MR}^i_{1,2} \equiv \partial\widetilde{MR}^i_1/\partial Q^{k\neq i}_1$. Some of the results below are more readily understood in terms of aggregate changes. The above system may thus alternatively be expressed as

$$
\begin{bmatrix} dQ^1_1 \\ dQ^2_1 \\ dQ^3_1 \end{bmatrix} = [\mathbf{A}]^{-1} \begin{bmatrix} n^1(dc^1 - ds^1) \\ n^2(dc^2 + dt_e - ds^2) \\ n^3(dc^3 + dt_n - ds^3) \end{bmatrix}, \tag{6}
$$

where

$$
\mathbf{A} \equiv \begin{bmatrix}
\left(\begin{array}{c} \widetilde{MR}^1_{1,0} \\ + (n^1-1)\, MR^1_{1,1} \end{array} \right) & n^1 \widetilde{MR}^1_{1,2} & n^1 \widetilde{MR}^1_{1,2} \\[2em]
n^2 \widetilde{MR}^2_{1,2} & \left(\begin{array}{c} \widetilde{MR}^2_{1,0} \\ + (n^2-1)\, MR^2_{1,1} \end{array} \right) & n^2 \widetilde{MR}^2_{1,2} \\[2em]
n^3 \widetilde{MR}^3_{1,2} & n^3 \widetilde{MR}^3_{1,2} & \left(\begin{array}{c} \widetilde{MR}^3_{1,0} \\ + (n^3-1)\, \widetilde{MR}^3_{1,1} \end{array} \right)
\end{bmatrix}
$$

Due to the assumption of identical firms within any given country, we can draw upon Dixit (1986) to investigate stability of this equilibrium. Stability is not guaranteed for arbitrary firm numbers and conjectural variations parameters. The same holds true for second order conditions. However, for obvious reasons conjectural variations should not be seen as independent on the number of firms. A more detailed discussion in the appendix shows that a reasonable condition can be imposed on the magnitudes of these parameters that guarantees fulfillment of the second order condition and makes stability "very likely".

Given stability, the slopes of the reaction functions depend on the signs of off-diagonal elements of the above matrices. It must be emphasized that, in general, substitutability in demand does not imply negative off-diagonal elements. This has to do with the distinction between *substitutability in demand* and the concept of *strategic substitutes*. The former depends on changes in profits as rivals change their sales, whereas the latter relates to changes in *perceived marginal* profits. However, I do assume that off-diagonal elements are negative, giving rise to downward sloping reaction functions.[15]

Exploiting symmetry and using a notation similar to the one introduced above, the following expression may be derived for the slope of the reaction function of a typical country k firm with respect to sales of a typical country i firm:[16]

$$
\rho^{k,i}_j \equiv \frac{\partial q^k_k}{\partial q^i_j} = - \frac{n^i \widetilde{MR}^k_{j,2}}{\widetilde{MR}^k_{j,0} + (n^k-1)\, \widetilde{MR}^k_{j,1}} < 0. \tag{7}
$$

Diagonal dominance, as required for stability, implies The aggregate reaction functions have a slope of

$$\Phi_j^{k,i} \equiv \frac{\partial Q_j^k}{\partial Q_j^i} = \frac{n^k}{n^i} \rho_j^{k,i} < 0. \tag{8}$$

It should be noted that the slopes of these reaction functions depend on the number of firms, directly and indirectly through the slopes of the marginal revenue functions. From the above assumptions we have $\Phi_j^{2,1} = \Phi_j^{3,1}$, and analogously for countries 2 and 3.

We finally note that the matrix $\mathbf{A}$ in equation (6) above has two useful properties. First, its off-diagonal elements are identical within any row. And secondly, stability requires that they are individually negative and smaller in absolute value than the diagonal element of the same row. This, in turn, implies $\Phi_j^{2,1} > -1$ plus the following properties of the inverse $[\mathbf{A}]^{-1}$: (a) It has negative diagonal elements and positive off-diagonal elements, and (b) its column sums are less than zero. As a result of any country increasing its subsidy, its own firms increase sales to all markets at the expense of other countries' firms, and *total* sales to any given market increase [see Dixit (1986, 120)]. Analogously, if real trade costs fall for intra-European trade, *total* sales to all European markets increase. For homogeneous products, it follows immediately that prices fall in these markets. If imports are imperfect substitutes, then import prices fall by the assumption that "own effects" dominate. But without any further assumption it is unclear how home prices move, and we may note the possibility that they increase. The opposite holds true if the home government increases its subsidy.

Government Policy

As motivated above, I assume that governments only have one instrument, viz. a general production subsidy or tax, and that it maximizes the usual industry-specific welfare measure consisting of industry profits plus consumer surplus less subsidy cost (plus tax revenue). Inverse demand functions of the kind assumed above imply a direct utility function of the quasi-linear form $u_1[z_i(z_i^1, z_i^2, z_i^3)] + m_1$, where z_i^j is consumption by country i residents of commodities supplied by country j's firms, $z_i(\cdot)$ is a quasi-concave and linearly homogeneous subutility index, $u_i(\cdot)$ is quasi-concave, and m_i is consumption of some numéraire good. For homogeneous goods, z_i simply is consumption of country i. If consumers maximize utility, then all income effects exclusively affect numéraire good consumption, and the differential of our welfare measure, which the present government cares about, may be written as

$$dW^i = -z_i dp_i + n^i \left[d\Pi^i - d(s^i \sum_j q_j^i) \right],$$ (9)

where p_i denotes the unit expenditure function associated with the subutility index $z_i(\cdot)$.[17] The terms ρ_i/ρ_i are determined by individual relative price changes according to initial budget shares. For the case of homogeneous goods, dp_i is simply the price change.[18]

Profit changes for a European firm i can be expressed as

$$d\Pi^i = \sum_j MR_j^i dq_j^i - c^1 \sum_j dq_j^i - t_e dq_k^i - t_n dq_3^i + \sum_j (s^i dq_j^i + ds^i q_j^i),$$ (10)

where $k \neq i = 1, 2, j = 1, 2, 3$, and MR_j^i denotes *true marginal revenue* to firm i from sales to market j. I shall return to this true marginal revenue in a minute. The optimal policy may now be found by incorporating firm behavior into the above differentials. In doing so, I follow Helpman and Krugman (1989) who have emphasized that strategic trade policy should be viewed as a special case of the traditional principle of targeting distortions. Pivotal to this view is the difference between *true* and *perceived* marginal revenue which I shall call the *strategic distortion*.[19] I shall, accordingly, first formulate the optimal policy using this difference and subsequently point out the essential elements determining its algebraic value. If we write

$$v_j^i \equiv MR_j^i - \widetilde{MR}_j^i,$$ (11)

and if we use the above first order conditions for profit maximization, then the welfare differential obtains as

$$dW^i = -z_i dp_i + n^i \left[\sum_j v_j^i dq_j^i - s^i \sum_j dq_j^i \right],$$ (12)

where the dq_j^is must be interpreted as part of the comparative static solution of system (5) above. Thus, they represent changes in the Nash equilibrium of the subgame on the firm level. This reflects the assumption of subgame perfection. If we restrict ourselves to changes in the subsidy or tax s^i, we may write

$$\frac{dW^i}{ds^i} = z_i \frac{dp_i}{ds^i} + n^i \left[\sum_j v_j^i \frac{dq_j^i}{ds^i} - s^i \sum_j \frac{dq_j^i}{ds^i} \right],$$ (13)

where we have assumed constant levels of foreign subsidies and taxes. Governments are thus treated as non-cooperative Cournot players. Setting this derivative equal to zero, we obtain the condition of an optimal subsidy or tax:

$$s^{i*} = \sum_j \alpha_j^i v_j^i - z_i \frac{dp_i}{ds^i} / \sum_j \frac{dQ_j^i}{ds^i}, \tag{14}$$

where $\alpha_j^i \equiv (dq_j^i/ds^i)/\Sigma_j(dq_j^i/ds^i) > 0$ (for all j). The sum $\Sigma_j \alpha_j^i = 1$, may be thought of as weights for the different markets. We may state the following:

PROPOSITION 1: *If domestic firms sell to several segmented oligopolistic markets and if the government wants to correct the different strategic distortions involved with a single production subsidy or tax, then it must do so by looking at the weighted average of strategic distortions, with the relative comparative static quantity effects of its subsidy serving as weights.*

If there is home consumption of the commodities involved, due concern must also be given to consumer surplus effects of the subsidy or tax, and this is represented by the second term of (14). This has already been emphasized in the literature, among others by Brander and Spencer (1985), and Krishna and Thursby (1991). In the general case of heterogeneous products, the term dp_i/ds^i involves a mixture of an oligopoly distortion and a terms of trade effect. The term is the change in the unit expenditure function for z_i and is composed of a change in the import price, which may be called a terms of trade effect, and a change in the price of the domestic good, according to initial budget shares. We have already noted above that the cross-price effects of a subsidy are ambiguous. Hence, a positive subsidy may involve an unfavorable terms of trade effect because foreign firms supply less imports, which tends to raise their price. At the same time, however, the domestic oligopoly distortion is reduced since domestic firms increase their sales, thus lowering the markup between marginal cost and price. With a sufficient share of domestic goods in the consumption aggregate z_i, the net effect [i.e., the second term in equation (14)], is positive. For easier wording, I shall simply call $-z_i dp_i/ds^i$ the oligopoly distortion in what follows.

The policy determined in this way is inevitably second best because the government tries to correct several distortions with but a single instrument. In a sense, the situation is just the opposite of what critics of using trade policy to correct distortions have always pointed out. The usual argument is that most distortions are domestic, and dealing with them via trade policy necessarily introduces what Corden has called a by-product distortion.[20] By way of contrast, in the present context we have genuine trade distortions alongside the oligopoly distortion, and we assume that only a domestic policy is available. Efficient targeting would require the use of a differentiated export subsidy to target the different strategic distortions on the export side, and a general production subsidy or tax plus a domestic consumption subsidy or tax (jointly determined) to target the strategic distortion and the oligopoly distortion on the domestic market.[21] Traditionally, tariffs (or import subsidies) have been advocated as the appropriate policy for the case of imperfectly competitive import supply (see Dixit 1984, Brander and Spencer 1984, Helpman and Krugman 1989, and Collie 1991). But a tariff is equivalent to a consumption tax plus a production subsidy of equal rates. Hence, there is no fundamental difference between the two views, and efficient targeting in our model setup could equally well be pursued by means of export subsidies and taxes plus a production subsidy or tax and a tariff, as in Dixit (1984) and Collie (1991), or by means of export subsidies and taxes plus a production subsidy or tax and a consumption subsidy or tax, as in Krishna and Thursby (1991).[22] I deliberately abstain from identifying the first best policy in any more detail on the grounds that governments are typically constrained in the availability of instruments. However, a certain degree of targeting might nevertheless sometimes be possible. In particular, as I have already pointed out above, the case of differentiated export subsidies should not be dismissed too quickly. It is easy to see what this case would imply for the optimal policy. Export subsidies would be determined by individual strategic distortions, v_j^i, while a subsidy or tax on domestic firms' home sales might be used to trade off the domestic strategic distortion against the oligopoly distortion. Since the subsequent analysis will primarily focus on changes in the strategic distortions, the results can easily be interpreted for whatever the reader believes is the more relevant case.

Sources of Strategic Distortions

What determines the marginal revenue distortions v_j^i? Exploiting the symmetry assumption, *true* marginal revenue may be expressed as

$$MR_j^i = R_{j,0}^i + (n^i - 1) R_{j,1}^i + R_{j,2}^i \sum_{k \neq i} n^k \rho_j^{k,i}. \tag{15}$$

From this, and the above expression (2) for we obtain

$$v_j^i = (n^i - 1) R_{j,1}^i (1 - \gamma_1^i) + R_{j,2}^i \sum_{k \neq i} n^k (\rho_j^{k,i} - \gamma_2^i), \quad \text{or}$$

$$= (n^i - 1) R_{j,1}^i (1 - \gamma_1^i) + R_{j,2}^i 2n^i \sum_{k \neq i} (\Phi^{k,i} - \Gamma^{k,i}),$$

(16)

where $\Gamma^{k,i} \equiv (n^k/n^i)\gamma_2^i$. This equation incorporates in a general way the two sources of strategic distortions that have been identified in the literature. The first term represents an *externality* that domestic firms confer upon each other if they fail to cooperate. A symmetric cartel would be equivalent to domestic firms setting conjectural variation equal to unity for each other: $\gamma_1^i = 1$, and the first term vanishes. In the non-cooperative situation, $\gamma_1^k < 1$, and the first term becomes negative, calling for an export tax. This is the well known rationale for taxing exports if export demand is less than perfectly elastic (see Dixit 1984, Eaton and Grossman 1986, and Helpman and Krugman 1989, chapter 5). Of course, the problem trivially disappears if there is but one domestic firm. The second term represents the equally well-known strategic concern of trade policy. If the conjectural variation γ_2^i is algebraically greater than the slope of a reaction function then this constitutes a case for subsidizing production, and vice versa. The optimal policy under strategic distortions in oligopolistic markets thus crucially depends on market conduct, as is now well known due to Eaton and Grossman (1986).

We may add a few more words on the magnitude of conjectural variations. As indicated above, new results in oligopoly theory justify viewing conjectural variations as capturing truly dynamic competition (see Dockner 1992).[23] More precisely, static equilibria like the one above may be interpreted as steady state, closed-loop equilibria of a dynamic game. Thus, the conjectural variations approach does make dynamic sense. However, this does not hold for arbitrary conjectural variations, for these are endogenous in a dynamic game. Dockner provides a detailed characterization of a special case with linear demand that is quite illuminating for the present purpose (see Dockner 1992, 386–393). In addition to quadratic adjustment costs, which are assumed to be symmetric across firms, Dockner assumes production costs that are asymmetric across firms with respect to a linear term, but symmetric with respect to the quadratic term (which is zero in our case). In the present context, the asymmetry in the linear term can be identified with real trade costs, which are different for bloc members and outside countries. Dockner derives an expression for the conjectural variations parameter, which turns out to be (1) constant and symmetric (despite the asymmetry in the linear cost term), and (2) negative but greater in algebraic value than consistent conjectural variations in the sense of Eaton and Grossman (1986). This has striking implications for strategic trade policy. If firms play differential games with Markov strategies, then the long run equilibrium is more competitive than that of a static Cournot game, but under the Dockner conditions it will not be competitive enough for strategic distortions as defined above to be negative. In other words, if one justifies the use of conjectural variations in a static oligopoly model along the lines suggested by Dockner, this implies that the strategic distortions that may be targeted by policy makers are positive. This is in line with the fact that industrial policies in practice are largely restricted to subsidization rather than taxation (see section 2 above). Tanaka (1994) provides an explicit treatment of strategic trade policy for a dynamic duopoly game. As one expects from the above, the optimal subsidy is positive but lower than in the static Cournot game. A further important consequence of Dockner's result is that we may indeed treat conjectural variations parameters as constants when exploring the strategic implications of reductions in real trade costs, as long as such trade costs appear in linear fashion.

There is nothing fundamental suggesting that firms play identical games in different segmented markets. It would thus appear that there is a possibility of strategic distortions in several markets offsetting each other, conceivably leading to a near-zero optimal subsidy despite the presence of strategic distortions. Moreover, a different number of firms might also be active in different markets, whereby the rationale for taxing exports would receive different weights in different markets.

The remainder of the paper carries out various forms of comparative static analysis of the optimal subsidy or tax. In the general case, this is rather complex because in addition to changes in the strategic distortions, v_j^i, one would also have to look at changes in their weights, α_j^i. The situation becomes much more tractable if we restrict ourselves to linear inverse demand functions. If demands are linear, then the terms $R_{j,kh}^i$ are zero for all $k \neq 0$ and $h \neq 0$ (see appendix). Hence, we have constant slopes of perceived as well as true marginal revenues, and thus constant comparative static coefficients for the subgame on the firm level. Optimal subsidies are thus driven by changes in the strategic distortions, v_j^i, and aggregate consumption, z_i, across equilibria. Hence, the following analysis will always first trace out the adjustment of firms and consumers to some exogenous change under the assumption of an unchanged domestic subsidy. The resulting changes in strategic distortions and the oligopoly distortion then tell us whether the domestic government finds an incentive to increase or lower its subsidy or tax.

Government Reaction Functions

Suppose country 1 is the home country, and suppose that country 2 increases its subsidy (lowers its tax). Firm reactions can best be thought of as taking place in two steps. We identify as the *first step* the reactions (to an increase in s^2) of countries 2 and 3, with notionally unchanged sales by our own firms. This displaces both the perceived and the true marginal revenue schedules for domestic firms. We identify these shifts and then focus on how domestic firms react to them, along with ensuing further reactions of foreign firms, as the *second step* of the overall adjustment. It should be noticed already at this stage that the following argument carries over to the case where a competing country enjoys lower trade costs for a given market. We shall return to this in sections 7 and 8 below.

In the first step, country 2 firms increase their sales, while country 3 firms cut their sales to all markets. Under the stability conditions discussed in the appendix, the former effect dominates so that aggregate foreign firms' sales increase, say by $dQ_j^{23} > 0$, in market j. The resulting shift in the marginal revenue schedules for domestic firms pertaining to market j is simply $d(\widetilde{MR}_j^1) = d(\widetilde{MR}_j^1) = R_{j,02}^1 dQ_j^{23} < 0$. All other derivatives of direct marginal revenues vanish due to assumed linearity of demand. The most important thing to note is that the first step does not entail any change in the strategic distortions v_j^1.

In the second step, domestic firms cut their sales so as to equate perceived marginal revenues to unchanged marginal costs, as required by the first order conditions. We denote this adjustment by $d(q_j^1)^0 < 0$. Noting that the first step did not affect strategic distortions, we may characterize the second step as

$$dv_j^1 = (MR_{j,0}^1 - \widetilde{MR}_{j,0}^1) \, d(q_j^1)^0 + (n^1 - 1)(\widetilde{MR}_{j,1}^1 - _{j,1}^1) \, d(q_j^1)^0$$
$$+ (MR_{j,2}^1 - \widetilde{MR}_{j,2}^1) \sum_{k=2}^{3} n^k d(q_j^k)^0, \tag{17}$$

where $d(q_j^k)^0 = \rho_j^{k,1} d(q_j^1)^0$, and where we have again exploited the symmetry assumption. With linear demand, we have $\widetilde{MR}_{j,1}^1 = \widetilde{MR}_{j,1}^1$ and $\widetilde{MR}_{j,2}^1 = \widetilde{MR}_{j,2}^1$, hence the strategic distortion is ultimately driven by the first term in the above equation. It can easily be shown that $MR_{j,0}^1 - \widetilde{MR}_{j,0}^1$ is positive if and only if[24]

$$(n^1 - 1) R_{j,10}^1 (1 - \gamma_1^1) + R_{j,20}^1 \sum_{k=2}^{3} n^k (\rho_j^{k,1} - \gamma_2^1) > 0. \tag{18}$$

Comparing this to the above expression for the strategic distortion, and noting that due to the assumed linearity of demand $R^1_{j,1} = q^1_j D^1_{j,1}$ and $R^1_{j,10} = D^1_{j,1}$ (and analogously for $R^1_{j,2}$ and $R^1_{j,20}$), we realize that this condition reduces to $v^i_j > 0$ initially, since $q^1_j > 0$. This establishes the following:

PROPOSITION 2: *For linear demand functions, the strategic interactions between individual governments may be described as follows. If we have positive strategic distortions throughout and if there is no oligopoly distortion (every country has a positive subsidy), then a small increase in any one country's subsidy causes other countries to lower their subsidies. If we have negative strategic distortions throughout (every country has a negative subsidy, or a tax), then a small increase in any one country's tax causes other countries to increase their taxes as well. In this sense it can be said that subsidies are strategic substitutes, whereas taxes are strategic complements.*[25]

The proposition seems to rest uneasily upon the assumption of constant marginal costs. It is, however, relatively easy to see how non-constant marginal costs would affect the result.[26] If marginal costs are increasing, then any cut in domestic firms' output (due to an increase in the foreign subsidy, say) lowers their marginal cost and their reaction is thus more moderate. In turn, this implies that the strategic substitution effect in the case of positive distortions is dampened. The opposite holds true for decreasing marginal costs. By complete analogy, we may note that increasing (decreasing) marginal costs will similarly dampen (strengthen) strategic complementarity in the case of negative strategic distortions. Whatever type of distortion is prevalent, increasing (decreasing) marginal costs always make domestic firms less (more) sensitive towards foreign policy measures, and this translates into a smaller (larger) change in the strategic distortion. In all cases, however, the above proposition continues to hold in qualitative terms. Finally, if the oligopoly distortion is considered as well, any comparative static increase in z_1, such as that brought about by an increase in a foreign subsidy, would weaken the case for lowering the domestic subsidy, possibly even overturning the substitutability relationship of proposition 2. Conversely, if such an increase is brought about by foreign countries lowering their tax, it effectively strengthens the case for lowering the domestic tax, and thereby also strengthens the complementarity relationship of proposition 2.

Optimal Subsidy/Tax with Lower Real Trade Costs

As argued in the introduction, an important aspect of Europe 1992 is that real trade costs within Europe are reduced. I shall now explore how this affects optimal policies of the three countries under the assumption that market segmentation is maintained. This is a conservative scenario in that it disregards any direct effect that integration might have on the degree of market segmentation. One way of modeling a decrease in market segmentation would be to assume that integration changes conjectural variations in such a way that price gaps between national markets are narrowed, as in Venables (1990). However, it is somewhat difficult to imagine exactly why firms should change their conjectures as a result of integration.[27] Arguably, the most direct and least questionable effect of integration is a reduction in trade costs. By assuming post-integration market segmentation, we simply postulate that trade costs (including transport costs) remain high enough, and cross country price gaps low enough, after integration that they preclude arbitrage activities in the Nash equilibrium.[28]

As a result of a reduction in t_e, country 1 firms increase their sales to market 2, at the expense not only of country 2 firms, but also of non-European firms from country 3. At the same time, and for the same reason, country 2 firms increase their sales in market 1 at the expense of country 1's domestic sales and sales by non-European firms. Under constant marginal costs and absent any demand links, market 3 is not affected in any direct way. There are, however, indirect effects as we shall see below. How do these comparative static effects change strategic distortions? It is obvious that with respect to domestic markets each European country is affected in exactly the same way as it would be by the European partner country increasing its subsidy, or lowering its tax. We can therefore apply reasoning similar to that underlying proposition 2 to arrive at the following:

PROPOSITION 3: *A reduction in real trade costs for intra-European trade lowers (increases) strategic distortions in respective home markets of bloc countries, if these were positive (negative) prior to integration.*

As regards intra-bloc export markets, firms will find the first order condition violated once they perceive lower real trade costs. Perceived marginal revenue is above marginal costs and this causes them to increase intra-union exports. In the process of doing so, they change both perceived and true marginal revenue and, thus, the strategic distortion in a way that can be described by equation (17) above, if we set $j = 2$ (i.e., $d(q_j^1)^0 = d(q_2^1)^0 > 0$). A completely analogous argument applies for country 2, and we obtain:

PROPOSITION 4: *A reduction in real trade costs for intra-European trade increases (lowers) strategic distortions in intra-union export markets, if these were positive (negative) prior to integration.*

How propositions 3 and 4 translate into a change in policy depends on the weights of the different markets (i.e., on the 's), as well as on how integration affects the oligopoly distortion. If goods are homogeneous, prices p_i are lower and domestic consumption z_i is higher in both European markets after integration. If foreign goods are imperfect substitutes there is a potential for home price increases as domestic firms cut their sales. However, to keep the analysis more in line with the literature, which largely assumes homogeneous products, I assume a sufficiently high budget share of foreign goods for the price index p_i to fall upon integration even in this case. This seems warranted in view of the high degree of mutual market penetration observed in European countries. The overall situation is then summarized by table 3.[29]

What is the intuition behind the change in strategic distortions? If the government has initially subsidized production, it is because its firms were selling less than would have been socially optimal. We might expect that a reduction in trade costs would do part of this job so that the subsidy can be reduced. This is not true here because trade costs are *real* costs and if they fall the optimal level of exports also increases. Firms have initially failed to achieve the optimal level of exports, and they fail even more so now that the optimal level of exports has risen.[30] In contrast, the optimal level of domestic sales from a strategic point of view is now lower since partner country firms have gained a *real* advantage by way of lower trade costs. Firms do not fully accommodate the required change when sliding along their reaction functions and this, in turn, weakens the need for a credible commitment to a higher level of domestic sales. On the other hand, if the government has initially chosen to tax domestic production, it is because domestic firms were, on average, selling too much. We might expect this to be partially remedied by the fact that the optimal level of exports is now increased, so that the tax can be reduced. Again, this is false because the fall in trade costs has also changed the firms' environment, causing them to export more. In a sense, they overreact, and this calls for an increase in the tax. On the domestic market, they overreact as well, cutting sales by more than is required, so that the tax should be reduced.

TABLE 3.   Falling Trade Costs and Associated Changes in Optimal Subsidies

	Strategic distortions		Oligopoly distortion
	in export markets	in domestic markets	
positive strategic distortions initially	rising $\Rightarrow$ higher subsidy	falling $\Rightarrow$ lower subsidy	calls for higher subsidy
negative strategic distortions initially	falling $\Rightarrow$ higher tax	rising $\Rightarrow$ lower tax	calls for lower tax

According to the summary information given by table 3, one cannot unambiguously say whether integration reinforces or weakens the case for strategic trade policy. However, if all markets are completely symmetric, then we know from the comparative statics on the firm level that $dq_2^1 > |dq_1^1|$ and $dq_1^2 > |dq_2^2|$, in which case the export side dominates the strategic part of the policy change for both countries.[31] This is clearly aggravated if the home market is one of many intra-bloc markets, instead of only two as in this model. Hence, export markets are very likely to dominate the strategic concern of the policy. The oligopoly distortion unambiguously calls for a higher subsidy or lower tax, and this reinforces the effect of dominant export markets if strategic distortions are positive. For negative distortions, however, the strategic concern on intra-bloc export markets and the oligopoly distortion pull in opposite directions. But it is worth pointing out once more that the case of negative distortions is called into question by recent theoretical results on dynamic oligopolistic competition (see above). Moreover, political-economy arguments would suggest that governments attach a relatively low weight to the oligopoly distortion anyway, so that we may conclude an overall presumption that the formation of trading blocs increases the strategic incentives faced by national governments to subsidize domestic firms. Finally, policy results would become more clear-cut, of course, if governments were to have at their disposal a sufficient number of independent instruments to pursue efficient targeting.

Strategic Interactions with the Third Country

All the results stated so far hold for notionally unchanged strategic policies of the respective foreign governments. We can now complete the analysis by considering *strategic interactions among governments.* This is quite easily accomplished on the basis of the above propositions, if we are willing to disregard the oligopoly distortion. First, country 3 is to some extent driven out of European markets, and it therefore faces an incentive to lower its tax or subsidy in place according to the type of distortions it is facing in European markets. This follows from reasoning similar to that underlying proposition 3. Its reaction function (showing how its optimal subsidy s^3 depends on s^1 and s^2) shifts even though it does not experience any change in trade costs. Suppose we have positive distortions throughout to begin with, so that country 3's reaction function shifts inward. We already know that in this case reaction functions of European governments shift outwards as a result of forming a trading bloc. It is then clear that strategic interactions reinforce the type of presumption that we have pointed out above. The situation is depicted in figure 1, which assumes that European

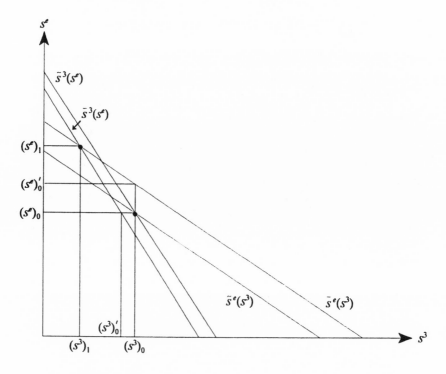

Fig. 1. Strategic interactions among governments in the case of positive distortions

countries are completely symmetric.[32] The term s^e denotes the common subsidy that the two European countries choose and the curve labeled $\tilde{s}^e(s^3)$ depicts the pre-integration Nash equilibrium subsidy of European countries for alternative values of the non-European subsidy s^3.[33] Similarly, $\tilde{s}^3(s^e)$ depicts how country 3 chooses its subsidy depending on the common subsidy of European countries. Pre-integration equilibrium subsidies are given by the pair $\{(s^3)_0, (s^e)_0\}$. As the fall of intra-European trade costs and the ensuing mutual market penetration within the union increases strategic distortions, the European Nash equilibrium schedule shifts from $\tilde{s}^e(s^3)$ to $\bar{s}^e(s^3)$, leading to a common European subsidy of $(s^e)'_0$, if country 3 were to maintain its original subsidy $(s^3)_0$. Note that the move from $(s^e)_0$ to $(s^e)'_0$ involves strategic interactions among European governments. It is a move from one Nash equilibrium to another of a *non-cooperative* game played by European governments under a notionally constant non-European subsidy. But country 3 finds a change in distortions along the lines of proposition 3 above, and this will shift its reaction function from $s^3(s^e)$ to $s^{-3}(s^e)$. The new equilibrium situation, then, is $\{(s^3)_1, (s^e)_1\}$. Strategic interactions among governments thus magnify the effect of integration on the European subsidy.

Interrelated Markets

To be able to treat all markets separately, we have so far assumed constant marginal costs. Krugman (1984) has shown various ways in which marginal cost may decrease as total sales increase, and how protecting domestic firms in any one market then favorably affects its position on all other markets. Referring to this type of interrelationship, he states in Krugman (1989, 362) that "European integration itself is a kind of strategic trade policy". What he has in mind is that a shift in the reaction function of a given firm relating to any one market, such as the European export market in the case of falling trade costs, will subsequently also shift all other reaction functions of this firm. But European firms don't just gain shares in their respective intra-union export markets, they also lose market shares at home. And if home market effects dominate they would be adversely affected on the cost side. However, it was already pointed out above that it is export market effects that are likely to be dominant, so that the loss in home sales is smaller than the gain in foreign sales. In this case the Krugman effect obtains. Applying the logic of the two previous subsections, we see that the resultant fall in marginal cost of production reinforces the above mentioned presumption towards increased subsidization in European countries, and lower subsidies in non-European countries. We may, however, add that if cost functions are convex, then market interrelationships work in the opposite direction [see Bulow, Geanakoplos and Klemperer (1985)].

Conclusion

The above analysis has shown that the formation of a trading bloc of the type envisaged by Europe 1992 systematically changes international strategic distortions in oligopolistic markets. If governments target these distortions, it is to be expected that integration has spillover effects on such strategically motivated policies. Moreover, given that trade policy measures are to a large extent subject to international obligations, the spillover effect might show up in industrial policies, such as production subsidies and taxes, more than in trade policy proper. This, however, typically makes the policy second best and, in general, negates a clear conclusion as to where optimal policy moves upon integration, even though individual distortions change in a predictable way. One can nevertheless conclude that there is a presumption that integration increases the strategic incentives faced by European governments to subsidize domestic firms. This is aggravated by the strategic interactions between European and non-European countries that arise if countries behave non-cooperatively. The concern expressed by the European Commission and policy observers about increased subsidization as a result of Europe 1992 thus appears to be justified, if looked at from a strategic industrial or trade policy perspective.

An obvious suggestion for further research is to address cross-country welfare effects of such policy changes and, ultimately, to allow for cooperation between union governments. It has long been emphasized that non-cooperative policy games of the sort analyzed above carry a potential for welfare-improving cooperation. In particular, it has frequently been pointed out that if countries find it individually optimal to subsidize their exports, they do so to a more than jointly optimal extent in a Nash subsidy equilibrium. Policy changes such as the ones portrayed above may thus be to the mutual disadvantage of union countries. This, in turn, begs the question of whether or not the formation of a trading bloc might also enhance the means of coordination and enforcement, perhaps even to the extent of allowing member countries to achieve cooperative instead of non-cooperative equilibria vis-à-vis non-member countries. This is particularly relevant for the case of European integration where harmonization of policies, according to the Maastricht treaty including industrial policy, is an important part of the agenda. An obvious consequence of such a scenario would be that, whereas in the present paper each European government was concerned about shifting profits from foreign European firms, under cooperation they would continue to do so jointly only from non-European firms. This implies a shift from a profit-snatching concern to an externality concern, giving more weight to the case for taxation than would be the case in a non-cooperative environment. A similar effect obtains if integration mutually increases foreign ownership of domestic firms through increased foreign investment [see Welzel (1994)].

Whether or not the formation of trading blocs will enhance the case for strategically motivated policies thus crucially depends on whether such trading blocs are also equipped with ways and means to foster international cooperation on the government level, or whether governments continue to behave non-cooperatively. The above results appear to suggest that if integration only affects the trading environment, its spillover effects on industrial policies are likely to aggravate the unfavorable consequences of non-cooperative government behavior. In their survey of theoretical issues in trade policy, Deardorff and Stern (1987, 54) have pointed out that

" . . . the question of how policymakers should act in a world of exploitative trade intervention may well be one of the great unresolved questions in the trade policy field today." The results of this paper suggest, somewhat paradoxically, that trade integration of the type accomplished by Europe 1992 may well make this question even more pressing. As a consequence, one is tempted to advise policymakers to extend their integration efforts to harmonization of trade and industrial policies, in addition to simply removing trade barriers. The common industrial policy envisaged by the Maastricht Treaty, which is so heavily questioned by advocates of a "laissez faire" policy, may at least be better than a world where governments resort to activist industrial policies in a non-cooperative way. However, two important qualifications need to be added in this regard. First, harmonization of policies should not be taken necessarily to imply cooperative outcomes. As highlighted in two recent contributions by Gatsios and Karp (1991, 1992), cooperative outcomes may not be optimal, and possibly even worse than non-cooperative outcomes, if strategic interactions with third countries are duly taken into account. And secondly, formal or informal measures that increase the likelihood of retaliation may be a somewhat less demanding and, therefore, attractive alternative to formal cooperation.

Appendix

This appendix first derives the slopes of the various *direct* marginal revenues, and it discusses the second order condition and stability of the oligopoly equilibrium focused on in the paper.

Slopes of Marginal Revenues

If we write $D^1_j(Q^1_j, Q^2_j, Q^3_j)$ for the inverse demand function for country 1 products in market j, $D^1_{j,i}$ for its derivative with respect to argument i, and $D^1_{j,ik}$ for the second order derivative with respect to argument k, then we have (omitting the arguments for ease of notation):

$$
\begin{aligned}
(a) \quad & R^1_{j,0} = D^1_j + q^1_j D^1_{j,1}, \\
(b) \quad & R^1_{j,1} = q^1_j D^1_{j,1}, \\
(c) \quad & R^1_{j,2} = q^1_j D^1_{j,2} = q^1_j D_{j,3}^1.
\end{aligned}
\tag{19}
$$

(a) $R_{j,00}^1 = 2D_{j,1}^1 + q_j^1 D_{j,11}1,$

(b) $R_{j,01}^1 = D_{j,1}^1 + q_j^1 D_{j,11}^1,$ (20)

(c) $R_{j,02}^1 = D_{j,2}^1 + q_j^1 D_{j,12}^1.$

(a) $R_{j,10}^1 = D_j^1 + q_j^1 D_{j,11}^1 = R_{j,01}^1,$

(b) $R_{j,11}^1 = q_j^1 D_{j,11}^1,$ (21)

(c) $R_{j,12}^1 = q_j^1 D_{j,12}^1.$

And finally

(a) $R_{j,20}^1 = D_{j,2}^1 + q_j^1 D_{j,21}^1 = R_{j,02}^1,$

(b) $R_{j,21}^1 = q_j^1 D_{j,21}^1 = R_{j,12}^1,$ (22)

(c) $R_{j,22}^1 = q_j^1 D_{j,22}^1.$

Analogous expressions hold for representative firms of countries 2 and 3. Equating symmetric second order derivatives of the demand function implies that they are continuous (Young's theorem). If market demand is linear, then all second order derivatives of D_j^i vanish, the slopes of all *direct* marginal revenue schedules are constant, and marginal revenue with respect to competitors' sales, $R_{j,1}^1$ and $R_{j,2}^1$ does not change with changes in competitors' sales. Assuming substitutability in demand, we have $D_{j,2}^1 = D_{j,3}^1 < 0$. In addition, the paper assumes that $D_{j,1}^1 < D_{j,2}^1$, as well as $R_{j,01}^1 < 0$, which implies $R_{j,00}^1 < R_{j,01}^1$, and $R_{j,1}^1 < R_{j,2}^1$. Firms of countries 2 and 3 are treated by complete analogy.

Second Order Condition and Stability

The crucial thing to note is that these assumptions do not uniquely determine the derivatives of *perceived* marginal revenues, which appear in the second order condition and determine stability in the sense of Dixit (1986). Following Eaton and Grossman (1986, appendix), the slopes of perceived marginal revenues can be written as:

(a) $\widetilde{MR}_{j,0}^i = R_{j,00}^i + (n^i - 1)\gamma_1^i R_{j,10}^i + N^i \gamma_2^i R_{j,20}^i,$

(b) $\widetilde{MR}_{j,1}^i = R_{j,01}^i + (n^i - 1)\gamma_1^i R_{j,11}^i + N^i \gamma_2^i R_{j,21}^i,$ (23)

(c) $\widetilde{MR}_{j,2}^i = R_{j,02}^i + (n^i - 1)\gamma_1^i R_{j,12}^i + N^i \gamma_2^i R_{j,22}^i.$

The problem we face here is that the second order condition for profit maximization, as well as stability, crucially depend on the number of firms and the conjectural variations parameters. It can, however, be demonstrated that for linear inverse demand functions a reasonable condition on the relationship between the number of firms and conjectural variations guarantees the second order condition and makes stability "very likely".

Conjectural variations parameters capture the degree of competition or collusion that prevails in the market. For instance, for homogeneous products perfect collusion under symmetry implies conjectural variations equal to unity. Cournot behavior implies zero conjectural variations, whereas if market conduct is still more competitive conjectural variations become negative. A reasonable lower limit seems to be given by the case where each competitor conjectures rivals' responses that would, in their entirety, just leave *her own* price unchanged. This is not quite the same as Bertrand conduct where competitors are assumed to react in such a way as to keep *their* prices unchanged. Only for homogeneous products does this distinction disappear. In any case, this limit amounts to perfectly competitive behavior, with each firm taking the price as given. Ruling out such perfectly competitive conduct for our oligopolistic industry, conjectural variations must satisfy the following condition:[34]

$$\left[1 + (n^i - 1) \, \gamma_1^i \right] D_{j,1}^i + N^i \gamma_2^i D_{j,2}^i < 0, \tag{24}$$

where $D_{j,1}^i$ and $D_{j,2}^i$ denote the derivatives of country j's inverse demand function for the country i good with respect to country i's own sales to j, and foreign firms' sales to j. Thus, any country i firm conjectures that if it increases sales to market j, its competitors do not react in such a way that they would prevent this firm's price in that market from falling. Conversely, if it cuts sales, then competitors' reactions would not prevent its price from increasing. Now consider the second order condition for profit maximization:

$$\widetilde{MR}_{1,0}^i + (n^i - 1) \, \gamma_1^i \widetilde{MR}_{1,1}^i + N^i \gamma_2^i \widetilde{MR}_{1,2}^i < 0, \tag{25}$$

For linear demand, this reduces to

$$2D_{j,1}^i \left[1 + (n^i - 1) \, \gamma_1^i \right] + 2N^i \gamma_2^i D_{j,2}^i < 0. \tag{26}$$

It is immediately clear that the above restriction on market conduct guarantees that this condition is satisfied.

I now investigate stability of the industry equilibrium described in the text along the lines suggested by Dixit (1986). Equation (6) captures the comparative statics of the aggregate equilibrium. Dixit stipulates an adjustment process according to which firms expand their sales to a given market if they perceive positive marginal profits from doing so, with the precise reactions being governed by arbitrary adjustment speed parameters. This gives rise to a system of differential equations which may be linearized around the equilibrium described by the first order conditions. In our case, stability requirements pertain to the matrix $\mathbf{A}$ appearing in equation (6). In particular, Dixit shows that a necessary condition is that all diagonal elements of $\mathbf{A}$ be negative, and that stability is guaranteed if this matrix has a dominant diagonal in the sense that $|a_{ii}| > \Sigma_{j \neq i} |a_{i,j}|$.

We first look at the diagonal elements of $\mathbf{A}$, which are required to be negative:

$$\widetilde{MR}^i_{j,0} + (n^i - 1)\, \widetilde{MR}^{\,i}_{j,1} < 0. \tag{27}$$

For linear demand this reduces to

$$2D^i_{j,1} + (n^i - 1)\,(1 + \gamma^i_1)\, D^i_{j,1} + N^i \gamma^i_2 D^i_{j,2}$$
$$= \left[1 + (n^i - 1)\,\gamma^i_1 \right] D^i_{j,1} + N^i \gamma^i_2 D^i_{j,2} + n^i D^i_{j,1} < 0. \tag{28}$$

As it follows immediately that the above restriction guarantees negativity as required. The sufficient condition of diagonal dominance requires that within any row the diagonal element is larger in absolute value than the sum of all off-diagonal elements. Under our assumptions all elements are negative, hence diagonal dominance requires, again assuming linear demand, that

$$(a) \quad \widetilde{MR}^{\,i}_{j,0} + (n^i - 1)\, \widetilde{MR}^{\,i}_{j,1} - 2n^i \widetilde{MR}^{\,i}_{j,2} < 0,$$
$$(b) \quad \left[1 + (n^i - 1)\,\gamma^i_1 \right] D^i_{j,1} + N^i \gamma^i_2 D^i_{j,2} + n^i D^i_{j,1} - 2n^i D^i_{j,2} < 0. \tag{29}$$

Given the above restriction on conjectural variations, a sufficient, but not necessary, condition for diagonal dominance is

$$\frac{1}{2} \geq \frac{D^i_{j,2}}{D^i_{j,1}}. \tag{30}$$

That is, stability is guaranteed if the absolute value of the cross price coefficient in the inverse demand functions is less than or equal to half the absolute direct price coefficient. It should be noted, however, that this restriction is not necessary for stability. Specifically, the smaller is the left-hand side of equation (24), the closer the two coefficients may be.

NOTES

1. Thus, in a recent survey, Harry Flam (1992, 6) states that " . . . the '1992' effort has clearly been spurred in part by an ambition to promote European indus-try and make it more competitive in the world market." For a similar statement, see Stegemann (1989, 79): " . . . proponents of a common industrial policy for the European Community have insisted on treating internal-market policies and exter-nal-trade policies as integral parts of a unified strategy aimed at helping European advanced-technology sectors to become competitive with their American and Japanese rivals".

2. See, for instance, Commission of the EC (1991, 15), and Franzmeyer (1992/1993, 151).

3. Estimates of European trade cost reductions due to Europe 1992 vary from 1 to 3 percent. See the discussion in Baldwin (1993, 132).

4. Harrison, Rutherford, and Tarr (1994) argue, for instance, that Europe 1992 also increases the elasticity of substitution between products of different European origins, ultimately increasing perceived price elasticities of demand and thus reduc-ing markups.

5. It still holds true, however, that agriculture receives by far the highest level of support if expressed relative to value added.

6 This assumption is for tractability, and it is called symmetric heterogeneity in Dixit (1986, 119). In the present setup, it implies that country 1 consumers view country 2 and country 3 products as perfect substitutes, while country 2 consumers view country 1 and country 3 products as perfect substitutes, and similarly for country 3 consumers. Consumers thus have different preferences across countries.

7. See the appendix for details.

8. A possible interpretation of constant marginal costs, from a general equilib-rium perspective, is a case in which all goods are produced subject to constant returns to scale and with identical factor bundles, and where the economy is diversified in production.

9. For a detailed account of the type of barriers targeted by Europe 1992, and why this involves a reduction in real trade costs, see Flam (1992).

10. For a detailed formulation of this criticism, see Helpman and Krugman (1989, 160).

11. I am grateful to Gerard Gaudet for pointing this out to me.

12. I follow the notation used by Dixit (1987).

13. Tariffs have long been eliminated within the EC. Moreover, the GATT pro-hibits tariff increases irrespective of any trading bloc, except for anti-dumping, countervailing duty and safeguard measures, and it prohibits export subsidies. Whether or not countries abide, however, is a different issue. See, for instance, Abraham and Dewit (1992).

14. Further, treating governments as single decision units would do violence to the diversity existing even within administrations as to the objectives pursued and the information and instruments available.

15. Dixit (1986, 118–119) refers to this as the "generalized Hahn condition". It is generalized because it relates to *perceived* marginal revenue, whereas the original Hahn condition would require that $R_{j,0}^k$ be decreasing in other firms' outputs [see also Dixit (1986, 110)]. However, in the linear case or with Cournot conduct the distinction disappears.

16. Talking about reaction functions in this regard is a bit misleading. We are not analyzing reactions of individual domestic firms with respect to its competitors. Instead, we are analyzing how Nash equilibrium sales of symmetric domestic firms vary as foreign firms change their sales. A somewhat more appropriate term to describe this would be a movement along a "collective reaction function".

17. Generally, subscript indices refer to countries where goods are sold and consumed, whereas superscript indices refer to countries where firms are located.

18. I should like to emphasize that a "benevolent dictator" view is not the only, or indeed the most sensible, interpretation of such government behavior. A "benevolent dictator" would have to take into account the general equilibrium repercussions pointed out by Dixit and Grossman (1986), whereas our government cares only about profits in the industry under question. Arguably, the most obvious reason for this is that the industry is for some reason powerful politically. The only additional considerations on the part of the government are the subsidy cost or tax revenue and the distortionary effect of its policy on consumers. Even though the present model does not attempt to explain why it is that our industry succeeds in lobbying, one can nevertheless argue that because the government cares about profits in a specific industry, with an added concern for the distortionary and budgetary consequences of its policy, it is more of a political-economy type government than a "benevolent dictator". Indeed, the model could quite easily accommodate additional political economy arguments by adding a scaling factor to the first term in the differentiated objective function above, thus capturing the frequently made point that consumer interests are less powerful politically than producer interests.

19. Among the first to point out the rationale for strategic trade policy as an attempt to correct a distortion were Deardorff and Stern (1987).

20. See Deardorff and Stern (1987, 38–42) for a lucid exposition of this line of argument.

21. The general production subsidy or tax would also affect export markets and thus importantly influence the export subsidies and taxes needed to offset the strategic export distortions. Alternatively, one might also envisage a subsidy or tax for home firms' domestic sales, as for instance in Dixit (1984).

22. Collie (1991) has the domestic country retaliating a foreign export subsidy by means of a production subsidy plus a tariff. In a sense, we could also talk about retaliation in our case, except for the fact that we have but a single instrument which must also capture rent shifting aspects on export markets. In addition, we do not assume Stackelberg leadership on the part of the exporting country, but,

instead, complete symmetry between governments. As Collie has shown, if the exporting country anticipates retaliation in the sense of Stackelberg leadership, then the rent shifting argument for export subsidies would to a considerable extent disappear in the Cournot case.

23. It should be mentioned that Dockner's analysis is restricted to the duopoly case. The following argument assumes that the general thrust of the analysis generalizes to the present multi-firm oligopoly.

24. Linear demand also implies that $\rho_j^{k,i}$ $(k \neq i)$ is constant.

25. Gatsios and Karp (1992) indicate a similar proposition relating to two subgroups of an arbitrary number of countries, instead of singling out the reaction of individual countries to any foreign country's policy.

26. Non-constant marginal costs will be taken up again below.

27. We have already noted above that the results produced by Dockner (1992) provide strong theoretical support for constant conjectural variations, even if firms are facing a change in their costs, as long as the change occurs in the linear terms of their cost functions. We have assumed from the outset that trade costs appear in linear fashion.

28. On the extent of market segmentation after Europe 1992, see Flam (1992).

29. It should be emphasized that the distortions do not change parametrically. In particular, one cannot just plug in the new values of various distortions and then calculate the new optimal subsidy from the above equation (15). We have only identified the direction in which various strategic distortions pull the subsidy. If the subsidy is changed, this then feeds back into the distortions.

30. There is a close similarity between this result and de Meza (1986), as well as Neary's (1994) finding that in the case of cost asymmetries governments should more heavily subsidize low cost producers, instead of "helping losers." In addition to the linear case, Neary also considers non-linear demand. In doing so, he focuses on how *relative* subsidies of two countries are related to cost advantages. It turns out that this relationship is positive for non-concave inverse demand functions. It is not clear to me, however, how this approach might be carried over to the present context which is more general in terms of dimensionality as well as market conduct. Hence, we stay with the linear case.

31. The above inequalities follow from the fact that lower trade costs increase *total* sales to all European markets.

32. An analogous figure could be produced for negative distortions, but that case is less interesting for reasons pointed out above.

33. Gatsios and Karp (1992) offer a similar graphical exposition, but there the union countries lower their common subsidy due to cooperation, whereas here they increase it without entering cooperation. For this reason the welfare result of Gatsios and Karp does not apply for the present case. Notice also that unlike Collie (1991) we have not allowed the third country to use tariffs in addition to a production subsidy for retaliation, and European Governments do not act as Stackelberg leaders vis-à-vis the third country.

34. Under competitive conduct, perceived profits are no longer concave and sales cannot be determined via profit maximization.

REFERENCES

Abraham, Filip, and Dewit, Gerda. 1992. *Strategic Export Insurance Subsidies and Compliance with the GATT Subsidy Code.* University of Michigan, Research Forum on International Economics, Discussion Paper No. 319.

Baldwin, Richard. 1993.""On the Measurement of Dynamic Effects of Integration." *Empirica* 20:129–145.

Brander, James A. and Krugman, Paul R. 1983. "Reciprocal Dumping in International Trade." *Journal of International Economics* 15:313–321.

Brander, James A. and Spencer, Barbara J. 1984. "Tariff Protection and Imperfect Competition." In H. Kierzkowsky, ed., *Monopolistic Competition and International Trade.* Oxford: Oxford University Press. Reprinted in Gene M. Grossman, ed., *Imperfect Competition and International Trade.* Cambridge: MIT Press, 1992, 107–119.

Brander, James A. and Spencer, Barbara J. 1985. "Export Subsidies and International Market Share Rivalry." *Journal of International Economics* 18:83–100.

Bulow, Jeremy I.; Geanakoplos, John D.; and Klemperer, Paul D. 1985. "Multimarket Oligopoly: Strategic Substitutes and Complements." *Journal of Political Economy* 93:488–511.

Collie, David. 1991. "Export Subsidies and Countervailing Tariffs." *Journal of International Economics* 31:309–324.

Commission of the EC. 1991. "Fair Competition in the Internal Market: Community State Aid Policy." *European Economy* No. 48, 7–123.

Commission of the EC. 1992. "Third Survey on State Aids." Brussels - Luxemburg.

Deardorff, Alan, and Stern, Robert M. 1987. "Current Issues in Trade Policy: An Overview." In Robert M. Stern, ed., *U.S. Trade Policies in a Changing World Economy.* Cambridge: MIT Press, 15–68.

De Meza, David. 1986. "Export Subsidies and High Productivity: Cause or Effect." *Canadian Journal of Economics* 19:347–350.

Dixit, Avinash. 1984. "International Trade Policy for Oligopolistic Industries." *Economic Journal* 94:1–16.

Dixit, Avinash. 1986. "Comparative Statics for Oligopoly." *International Economic Review* 27:107–122.

Dixit, Avinash. 1987. "Strategic Aspects of Trade Policy." In Truman F. Bewley, ed., *Advances in Economic Theory: Fifth World Congress.* Cambridge: Cambridge University Press, 329–362.

Dixit, Avinash, and Grossman, Gene M. 1986. "Targeted Export Promotion with Several Oligopolistic Industries." *Journal of International Economics* 21:233–250.

Dockner, Engelbert. 1992. "A Dynamic Theory of Conjectural Variations." *The Journal of Industrial Economics* 40:377–395.

Eaton, Jonathan and Grossman, Gene M. 1986. "Optimal Trade and Industrial Policy under Oligopoly." *Quarterly Journal of Economics* 101:383–406.

Flam, Harry. 1992. "Product Markets and 1992: Full Integration, Large Gains?" *Journal of Economic Perspectives* 6:7–30.

Franzmeyer, Fritz. 1991/92. "Wettbewerbs- und Industriepolitik." *Jahrbuch der Europäischen Integration* 1991/1992, 157–164.

Franzmeyer, Fritz. 1992/93. "Wettbewerbs- und Industriepolitik." *Jahrbuch der Europäischen Integration* 1992/1993, 151–158.

Gatsios, Konstantine, and Karp, Larry. 1991. "Delegation Games in Customs Unions." *Review of Economic Studies* 58:391–397.

Gatsios, Konstantine, and Karp, Larry. 1992. "The Welfare Effects of Imperfect Harmonisation of Trade and Industrial Policy." *Economic Journal* 102:107–116.

Harrison, Glenn; Rutherford, Thomas; and Tarr, David. 1994. *Product Standards, Imperfect Competition, and Completion of the Market in the European Union.* Policy Research Working Paper No. 1293, Washington D.C.: The World Bank.

Helpman, Elhanan, and Krugman, Paul R. 1989. *Trade Policy and Market Structure.* Cambridge/Mass: MIT Press.

Krishna, Kala, and Thursby, Marie. 1991. "Optimal Policies With Strategic Distortions." *Journal of International Economics* 31:291–308.

Krugman, Paul R. 1984. "Import Protection as Export Promotion: International Competition in the Presence of Oligopoly and Economies of Scale." In Henryk Kierzkowski, ed., *Monopolistic Competition and International Trade.* Oxford: Oxford University Press, 180–193.

Krugman, Paul R. 1989. "Economic Integration in Europe: Some Conceptual Issues." In Alexis Jacquemin, and Andre Sapir, eds., *The European Internal Market: Trade and Competition.* Oxford: Oxford University Press, 357–380.

Neary, J. Peter. 1994. "Cost Asymmetries in International Subsidy Games: Should Governments Help Winners or Losers?" *Journal of International Economics* 37:197–218.

OECD. 1992. *Industrial Support Policies in the OECD Countries 1986–1989.* Paris: OCDE/GD(92)126.

Smith, Alasdair, and Venables, Anthony J. 1988. "Completing the Internal Market in the European Community: Some Industry Simulations." *European Economic Review* 32:1501–1525.

Stegemann, Klaus. 1989. "Policy Rivalry among Industrial States: What can we Learn from Models of Strategic Trade Policy?" *International Organization* 43:73–100.

Tanaka, Yasihito. 1994. "Export Subsidies under Dynamic Duopoly." *European Economic Review* 38:1139–1151.

Venables, Anthony J. 1990. "The Economic Integration of Oligopolistic Markets."

Welzel, Peter. 1994. *Strategic Trade Policy with Internationally Owned Firms.* Institut für Volkswirtschaftslehre der Universität Augsburg, Volkswirtschaftliche Diskussionsreihe, Beitrag Nr. 110, Augsburg, forthcoming in *Bulletin of Economic Research.*

Part Three:
International
Financial Analysis

CHAPTER 10

International Comparisons of the Levels of Unit Labor Costs in Manufacturing

Peter M. Hooper and Elizabeth Vrankovich

Wide swings in nominal exchange rates among the currencies of industrial countries over the past two decades have produced substantial shifts in the relative costs of production in manufacturing across these countries. While movements over time in relative costs are monitored fairly intensively by various national and international statistical agencies, less is known about the comparative absolute levels of these costs at any given point in time. This paper presents estimates of unit labor cost levels for the Group of Seven (G-7) major industrial countries.

Measurement of the comparative levels of labor costs is of interest for a variety of possible reasons. First, they provide a summary statement of a key element in a country's international cost competitiveness. Researchers ranging from Stern (1962) to Golub (1994) have found that differences in unit labor cost levels influence the relative export performance, across industries, of major industrial countries. Second, to the extent that prices of tradable goods across countries converge over time, significant differences in the levels of production costs provide some indication of the possible path of exchange rates and domestic cost levels in the longer term. In support of this view, various studies, including Frankel (1986), Edison (1987), Boucher Breuer (1994), Froot and Rogoff (1995), and Wei and Parsley (1995), have found considerable evidence that real exchange rates revert to their historical means over long periods of time. Third, cost differentials may also have implications for the location of production facilities and the flow of direct investment as firms seek to minimize their costs of production globally.

Over the years, a variety of researchers have striven to measure the comparative levels of unit labor costs in manufacturing among the major industrial countries. Data on comparative levels of the numerator of unit labor costs are readily available across countries since compensation rates can be translated from local currencies to common currency units using nominal exchange rates. The challenge in this line of research is translating the denominator of unit labor costs (productivity or output levels) across countries into common currency units. To do so, one needs measures of relative national price levels specific to manufacturing, which can differ widely from nominal exchange rates. Two approaches have been pursued in the computation of such relative price levels or output price ratios. One approach has been to employ unit values ratios (UVRs) constructed from detailed census of manufactures data. The second approach has been to employ expenditure purchasing power parities (EPPPs) produced by the UN International Comparison Project (and more recently by Eurostat and the OECD). As the Bureau of Labor Statistics and others have noted, both approaches have their drawbacks. The present paper focuses primarily on the second (or EPPP) approach and attempts to correct for the more important conceptual and empirical problems underlying that approach. We also compare our results with recent estimates that are based exclusively on the first (or UVR) approach.

We begin the next section by describing and comparing the methodology underlying the two approaches and outlining our adjustments to correct for deficiencies in the EPPP approach. These adjustments pertain to correcting the EPPPs for factors that cause them to deviate from relative output prices (i.e., cross-country differences in distribution margins, indirect tax rates and the influences of import and export prices).

In the subsequent section we compute output prices ratios for the United States vis-a-vis each of the other G-7 countries (Japan, Germany, France, Italy, the United Kingdom, and Canada) for total manufacturing and for each of five major subsectors of manufacturing, starting with expenditure purchasing power parities for 1990. The EPPPs indicate that in recent years, final expenditure prices for goods have been significantly higher in Europe and Japan than in the United States. Conventional wisdom holds that these price differences have reflected, to a significant degree, higher indirect taxes and less efficient distribution systems in these countries than in the United States. We find that after adjusting expenditure prices for these and other factors, our estimates of output price levels in Japan and Europe show an even greater premium over the U.S. price level than is the case for expenditure prices. Contrary to the conventional wisdom, recent research has shown distribution margins to be higher in the United States than in other major industrial countries on average. We find that differences in net indirect tax rates and other factors that affect the spread between expenditure prices and output prices also appear to be larger on balance in the United States than in other major industrial countries on average.

We next present and analyze data on the comparative levels of labor productivity, compensation, and unit labor costs across countries and industries and compare our results with those reported in other recent studies. Using the output price ratios derived earlier, we compute productivity level estimates that show that in 1990 U.S. productivity in total manufacturing was significantly higher than that in other G-7 countries. Since U.S. compensation rates were about in line with average rates abroad at that time, U.S. unit labor costs were significantly below those in other G-7 industrial countries on average. When extrapolated to 1995 using indexes of domestic unit labor costs and nominal exchange rates, we find that U.S. manufacturing unit labor costs were 45 to 50 percent below those in Germany and Japan. Differences with other G-7 countries were a good deal smaller.

Our results show the relative level of U.S. productivity to be somewhat higher and the relative level of U.S. unit labor costs to be somewhat lower than estimates based on the UVR approach. However, estimates based on both approaches find the level of manufacturing unit labor costs in the United States currently to be well below those in Japan and Germany. Our analysis of differences in productivity, compensation and unit labor costs among different subsectors of manufacturing suggests that within Japan productivity is relatively low and unit labor costs correspondingly high in the food and textiles subsectors, and vice versa in the machinery, basic metals and chemicals industries. In Europe and the United States, textiles and apparel stand out as a low-productivity, high-unit labor cost subsector, but food and beverages are just the opposite. Our conclusions are presented in the final section.

International Comparisons of Labor Cost Levels: Methodology

The simplest basis for comparing the levels of labor costs across countries is the rate of nominal compensation (C) per worker or per hour worked (H). Because differences in compensation rates across countries tend to reflect differences in labor productivity, however, the preferred basis for cross-country comparison of labor costs is unit labor costs (ULC), defined as total labor compensation per hour, divided by productivity or real output (O) per hour, which simplifies to compensation divided by output: $ULC = (C/H)/(O/H) = C/O$.

Conversion to Common Currency Units

The key methodological issue underlying intercountry comparisons of labor costs is how to translate the unit labor costs calculated for individual countries into comparable or common-currency units. Nominal compensation in different countries can readily be translated into a common currency using nominal market exchange rates.[1] The translation of real outputs measured in national currencies into common currency units presents more of a challenge. In principle, country j's output for industry i (O_{ij}), for example, should be translated into U.S. dollars ($O_{ij}^\$$) using the ratio of j's average local-currency price level for the output of industry i. (P_{ij}) to the average U.S. (dollar) price level for that industry (P_{iUS}):

$$O_{ij}^\$ \;=\; \frac{O_{ij}}{P_{ij}\ /P_{iUS}} \tag{1}$$

Nominal exchange rates have been used as proxies for the output price ratio (P_{ij}/P_{iUS}, henceforth "OPR") but they are particularly ill suited for this purpose. Exchange rates between the United States and most other major industrial countries, for example, tend to be much more volatile that output price ratios, and at any given point in time they can differ widely from those price ratios.[2]

Two approaches have been used to estimate OPRs for manufacturing more directly: the unit value ratio or UVR approach, and the expenditure purchasing power parity or EPPP approach. We outline each in turn.

The UVR Approach

The UVR approach involves estimating local-currency output price levels (in the countries whose output levels are being compared) with unit values. Unit values are computed by dividing the value of manufacturing output at the industry or sub-industry level by measures of the quantities of those outputs (tons of steel, pairs of shoes, and so on), typically with data taken from the census of manufactures. This approach has been used by a variety of researchers. Paige and Bombach (1959) computed UVRs to compare productivity levels in the U.K. and U.S. manufacturing sectors in the 1950s. Smith, Hitchins and Davies (1982) updated Paige and Bombach's estimates and extended them to include a U.K.-German comparison in the 1970s. O'Mahony (1992) has made a U.K.- German comparison using this methodology with more recent (1987) data.[3]

The most prominent work in this area over the past decade has been pursued by the International Comparison of Output and Productivity (ICOP) project of the University of Groningen (Netherlands). Maddison and van Ark (1994) and van Ark (1993) provide overviews of the project. Pilat and van Ark (1993, 1994) report UVR-based price level and productivity comparisons between the United States and both Japan and Germany for 1987 and 1990. Van Ark (1992) reports U.S.-U.K. comparisons for 1987, and van Ark and Kouwenhoven (1994) do the same for U.S.-French comparisons. Much of this work is summarized in Van Ark (1995).

One drawback to the UVR approach is the difficulty involved in matching units or measures of output quantity across countries due to differences in product definitions, product qualities, product mixes at the individual industry level, and units of quantity measurement. UVRs that have been computed in the ICOP project for the United States vis-a-vis four other major industrial countries (Japan, Germany, France, and the United Kingdom) are based on products accounting for less than one-fourth of the value of total manufacturing output (ranging from 15 percent for U.S.-French comparisons to 24 percent for U.S.-German. comparisons). Moreover, the coverage tends to be more complete in the more homogeneous and less technologically sophisticated product categories, such as food and textiles, and less complete in the more sophisticated categories, such as machinery and equipment.

Another drawback to the UVR approach is that unit values have generally proven to be inferior indicators of actual price movements. As noted by Lichtenberg and Griliches (1989), survey-based producer price indexes tend to be more reliable measures of U.S. output prices than unit values based on the census of manufactures. The methodology underlying the construction of expenditure purchasing power parities (discussed below) is closer to the construction of price indexes than the methodology underlying unit values.

The EPPP Approach

The second approach to estimating output price ratios has been to employ expenditure purchasing power parities (EPPPs) as proxies. The EPPPs are those for total GDP and disaggregated expenditure components that have been compiled during the past four decades by the U.N. International Comparison Project and more recently Eurostat and the OECD. Some researchers, for example Dollar and Wolff (1988, 1993) and Golub (1994), have simply used the aggregate EPPPs for total GDP as proxies for manufacturing OPRs.[4] Others have attempted to refine these proxies by computing weighted averages of disaggregated EPPPs specific to manufactured goods categories. Prais (1981) used this technique to compare manufacturing output in the United States, Germany and the United Kingdom in the 1970s. Roy (1982) and Roy (1987) did much the same for a wider set of countries in 1975 and 1980, as did Hooper and Larin (1989) for the ten major industrial countries and Turner and Van't dack (1993) for a smaller set of countries during the 1980s.

As has been noted, perhaps most prominently by the Bureau of Labor

Statistics (see, for example, Neef et al., 1993), the use of EPPPs as proxies for manufacturing output price ratios has several potentially significant drawbacks. First, expenditure (or purchaser) prices reflect cross-country differences in wholesale and retail distribution margins and transportation costs, while output (or producer) prices do not. Second, expenditure prices include indirect taxes and subsidies (which can vary across countries), while output prices do not. Third, expenditures include imports (which do not affect output prices directly), while they exclude exports, which are reflected directly in output prices. To the extent that import and export prices differ from the prices of domestic output that is sold domestically and trade in the sector in question is imbalanced, expenditure prices will differ from domestic output prices. Finally, EPPPs pertain to final expenditures and do not lend themselves to the comparison of price levels for sectors that produce intermediate rather than final products.

Initial attempts have been made to deal with some of these problems. Specifically, Jorgenson and Kuroda (1992) used EPPPs for the mid-1980s to compare U.S.-Japanese manufacturing outputs and adjusted the EPPPs for trade and transportation margins and indirect taxes. Some work has begun at the OECD to adjust EPPPs for indirect taxes and the influences of import and export prices for a wider set of countries.

This paper continues in the spirit of the EPPP approach and strives to deal with some of its major shortcomings by making adjustments to the EPPPs for indirect taxes and subsidies, distribution margins, and the influence of import and export prices. In doing so, it extends the scope of earlier published estimates using this approach to a broader set of countries and by making use of data on EPPPs that have recently been made available by the World Bank at a more detailed level of disaggregation than was the case previously.[5] An initial attempt also is made to fill in some of the gaps in this approach with respect to intermediate goods prices by using UVR-based estimates for the basic metals industry.

Computation of EPPPs

The starting point for this approach is the ICOP EPPPs for 101 final expenditure categories for each of six major industrial countries (Canada, France, Germany, Italy, Japan, and the United Kingdom) vis-a-vis the United States. The EPPPs for the 101 "basic heading" categories (e.g., bread, beef, poultry), in turn, reflect averages of EPPPs for up to 500 (or roughly 5 per category) individual products or "items". The basic-heading EPPPs are aggregated into five manufacturing subsectors.[6] The weights used in this first level of aggregation are the shares of expenditures on the basic heading categories (k) in the total expenditures across all seven countries (j) on the manufacturing subsector (i). This weighted average is written:

$$EPPP_{ij} \;=\; \sum_{k=1}^{n} \frac{\displaystyle\sum_{j=1}^{7} E_{ijk}}{\displaystyle\sum_{j=1}^{7}\sum_{k=1}^{n} E_{ijk}\;\; EPPP_{ijk}} \tag{2}$$

where E_{ijk} = the value of expenditures in dollars (translated from local currencies using the EPPPs) in country j on the basic heading category k in subsector i.

Adjustments

The first adjustment to the EPPPs is for cross-country differences in distribution margins. The distribution margin is defined as the ratio of the retail distributor's selling price to the factory gate price. Where $EPPP_{ij}$ is defined as the ratio of expenditure prices (PE) in country j relative to those in the United States:

$$EPPP_{ij} \;=\; \frac{PE_{ij}}{PE_{iUS}}, \tag{3}$$

the EPPP adjusted for distribution margins can be defined as:

$$EPPP_{ij}^{m} \;=\; \frac{PE_{ij}/(1\;+\;\delta_{ij})}{PE_{iUS}/(1\;+\;\delta_{iUS})} \;=\; \frac{1\;+\;\delta_{iUS}}{1\;+\;\delta_{ij}}\;EPPP_{ij} \tag{4}$$

where δ_{ij} = the combined wholesale and retail distribution markup over producer prices for subsector i in country j. To the extent that distribution margins in other countries exceed those in the United States, their EPPPs adjusted to exclude those margins will be less than the unadjusted EPPPs.

Second, a similar adjustment to the $EPPP_{ij}$s is made for the influence of net indirect taxes and subsidies:

$$EPPP_{ij}^{*} \;=\; \frac{1+\;t_{iUS}}{1+\;t_{ij}}\;EPPP_{ij}^{m} \tag{5}$$

where t_{ij} = indirect tax rate net of subsidies on goods from subsector i in country j. As with the distribution margins, the adjustment for taxes and subsidies is made both for country j and for the United States.[7] To the extent that indirect taxes net of subsidies are greater in other countries than in the United States, the PPP in terms of expenditure prices will be greater than that in terms of output prices (or in terms of expenditure prices net of taxes and subsidies).

Third, a crude adjustment is made to the EPPP*s for the net influence of import and export prices on the difference between expenditure and output prices. This adjustment begins with the definition of the domestic expenditure price index (net of indirect taxes and subsidies and distribution margins) as a weighted sum of the price of imports (PM) and the price of domestic output that is sold domestically (PD):

$$PE^* \ = \ \frac{M}{E^*} \ PM \ + \ \frac{E^* - M}{E^*} \ PD \tag{6}$$

where M = imports and E^* = domestic expenditure net of indirect taxes and subsidies and distribution margins. Solving for PD yields:

$$PD \ = \ \frac{E^*}{E^* - M} \ PE^* \ - \ \frac{M}{E^* - M} \ PM \tag{7}$$

The price of total domestic output (P) is defined as a weighted sum of the price of exported goods (PX) and PD:

$$P \ = \ \frac{X}{O} \ PX \ + \ \frac{O - X}{O} \ PD \tag{8}$$

where X = exports and O = total domestic output. To solve for P in terms of PE*, note that expenditures are equal to output plus imports minus exports:

$$E^* \ = \ O + M - X \tag{9}$$

Next, assume that for each category of goods, both imports and exports are priced at the average world price level (PW) where all prices are measured in a common currency (i.e., dollars):

$$PM = PX = PW \tag{10}$$

Substituting equations (7), (9), and (10) into equation (8) and rearranging terms yields:

$$P = PE^* + \frac{X - M}{O}(PW - PE^*) \tag{11}$$

Equation (11) indicates that the domestic output price will exceed the domestic expenditure price if the world price exceeds the domestic expenditure price and the country is running a trade surplus in the category of goods in question. In this case, the price of exports and imports will be above the price of domestic output sold domestically, and with exports being greater than imports, they will have a greater positive effect on the output price than imports will have on the expenditure price.

The "world" price level (in dollars) is defined as the output-weighted average of each country's expenditure price level in dollars (net of indirect taxes and subsidies) for the manufacturing subsector in question:

$$PW_i^\$ = \sum_{j=1}^{7} \frac{O_{ij}/EPPP_{ij}^*}{\sum_{j=1}^{7} O_{ij}/EPPP_{ij}^*} \quad PE_{ij}^\$ \tag{12}$$

where each country's output in dollars is defined, at this stage, as output in local currency (O) divided by the EPPP adjusted for distribution margins and indirect taxes (EPPP*). With the EPPP*s normalized to a U.S. price level (PE*$_{US}$) of 1.0, the other countries' expenditure price levels in dollars are derived as their EPPP*s divided by their nominal dollar exchange rates:

$$PE_{ij}^\$ = \frac{EPPP_{ij}^*}{ER_j} \tag{13}$$

The output price ratio (OPR) for each country j is now computed as the ratio of j's output price to the U.S. output price (or the ratio of PE*s adjusted for import and export price effects):

$$OPR_{ij} = \frac{P_{ij}}{P_{iUS}} = \frac{PE_{ij}^* + \frac{(X_{ij} - M_{ij})}{O_{ij}}(PW_i - PE_{ij}^*)}{PE_{iUS}^* + \frac{(X_{iUS} - M_{iUS})}{O_{iUS}}(PW_i - PE_{iUS}^*)} \qquad (14)$$

Recall from the discussion of equation (11) that if country j is running a trade surplus in commodity category i, and the world price exceeds its domestic price, its output price will exceed its expenditure price. In this case, country j's OPR will exceed its EPPP* so long as the U.S. output price exceeds the U.S. expenditure price by a proportionately smaller amount than is the case for country j.

The adjustment for import and export prices is based on several heroic assumptions. First, it assumes that each country is a price-taker in the world market. That is, each country prices its exports at the world market price and pays for its imports at the world market price. Several of the countries considered (most notably the United States) are large enough to have some degree of control over the prices of their imports and exports. Second, it abstracts from tariffs and non-tariff barriers, which may cause the domestic price of imported goods to differ from the world price level. Third, it uses the average price level for the G-7 countries as a proxy for the "world" price level. Trade among these seven countries actually accounts for only about half of their total international trade, and the actual "true" price level could differ significantly from the one constructed here. For these reasons, the empirical section that follows considers the sensitivity of these estimates to plausible alternative assumptions about the behavior of import and export prices.

One final conceptual problem with the EPPP methodology is that after the adjustments outlined above have been made, the resulting output price ratio pertains to the gross output of the sector in question, not to value added. This is a potentially important consideration because value added data are much more readily available on a consistent basis across countries than gross output data. To the extent that the relative cost of a sector's inputs (between two countries) differs from the relative price of the sector's outputs, application of the OPR defined above to the value added for that sector will yield a biased translation of that value added into common currency units.[8] The potential bias is greater the greater the share of inputs in gross output (i.e., especially at the subsectoral level). Conversely, the problem is presumably less serious the more highly aggregated the level of analysis (e.g., total manufacturing). Nevertheless, in principle at least, before they are applied to value added data, the OPRs should first be adjusted for differences in input price ratios, or "double deflated." This is a nontrivial task that is left for future research.

Empirical Estimation of the OPRs

The EPPPs

The derivation of OPRs for total manufacturing and by major manufacturing sector begins with the averaging of ICP expenditure PPPs (EPPPs). The EPPPs used are the 1990 "EKS" PPPs published in summary form in OECD (1992) and available in greater detail in World Bank (1993).[9] The goods categories selected for each manufacturing subsector are shown in table 1. The food, beverages and tobacco products subsector includes over 40 basic heading entries, the machinery and equipment subsector over 30 entries and the other three subsectors 8 to 10 entries each. There are no entries for basic metals, which are primarily intermediate goods. Table 1 also shows the EPPPs for each of the basic heading entries across countries (the $EPPP_{ijk}$s). The two right-hand columns of the table show total G-7 expenditures (in dollars) on these goods categories and each category's share in the total expenditures for the particular manufacturing sector. These expenditure shares are the weights used to compute the $EPPP_{ij}$s defined in equation (3). The computed values of the $EPPP_{ij}$s are shown at the bottom of each manufacturing sector group in the table.

The level of disaggregation used here captures some but by no means all of the dispersion of PPP levels across commodity categories. In the case of Japan, for example (the first column of numbers in the table), $EPPP_{ij}$s range from a high of 281 yen per dollar for food, beverages and tobacco, to a low of 190 yen per dollar for machinery and equipment (169 excluding office machinery). The individual $EPPP_{ijk}$s within these sectors range even more widely. For example, in the food sector, beef and veal show a high of 549 yen per dollar, while seafood ranges as low as 133 yen per dollar. And, in the machinery and equipment sector, some household appliances range as high as 300 to 400 yen per dollar, while the EPPPs for transportation equipment are generally in the 100 to 150 range.

The EPPPs for office machinery (which include computers) look suspect and could reflect artificial differences in price measurement practices across countries. The 1985 EPPPs for the same category were only about one tenth as large. It would appear that the 1990 EPPPs were derived by extrapolating in the 1985 EPPPs with relative deflators for office machinery. The United States measures movements in computer prices over time with a hedonic index that shows a strong downward trend. Most other

TABLE 1.   1990 ICP Expenditures PPPs, Expenditures and Expenditure Shares

Expenditure Category	Expenditure PPPs (units of own currency per $)						G-7 Expenditures	
	Jap	Ger	Fra	Ita	UK	Can	B $	% share
Food, Beverages, and Tobacco								
Rice	349	2.44	6.11	1582	0.85	1.27	13.3	1.2
Flour, other cereals	290	1.59	7.27	1658	0.52	1.53	5.0	0.4
Bread	246	1.64	6.07	958	0.39	1.15	55.4	4.9
Bakery products, biscuits, cakes	226	2.09	7.06	1853	0.52	1.61	38.0	3.3
Noodles, Macaroni, Spaghetti	328	1.87	5.62	1469	0.52	1.28	12.0	1.1
Cereal Preparations	260	1.70	6.11	2111	0.56	1.32	32.1	2.8
Beef and Veal	549	2.48	7.73	1638	0.68	1.53	64.0	5.6
Pork	262	1.65	6.02	1442	0.52	1.13	24.1	2.1
Lamb, goat, and mutton	296	2.56	8.00	1530	0.53	1.02	8.7	0.8
Poultry	347	3.15	12.13	2538	0.96	1.90	20.7	1.8
Dried or processed meat, etc.	365	2.94	13.39	2484	0.67	1.58	72.0	6.3
Fish fresh, frozen	223	2.03	6.94	2013	0.57	1.20	29.8	2.6
Processed fish/seafood, canned	238	1.71	6.87	1607	0.47	1.29	13.0	1.1
Smoked or preserved fish/seafood	230	2.05	7.23	1891	0.68	1.25	11.0	1.0
Other seafood	133	3.44	11.25	3413	0.70	1.37	10.1	0.9
Milk fresh	315	1.61	6.88	2027	0.71	1.64	44.9	4.0
Milk preserved	237	1.85	6.08	3250	0.48	1.33	6.3	0.6
Other milk products	289	1.36	6.78	2027	0.77	1.88	13.5	1.2
Cheese	246	1.98	6.44	1332	0.54	1.44	34.6	3.0
Egg and egg products	239	2.41	13.09	2536	1.20	1.55	10.7	0.9
Butter	353	1.72	7.39	2052	0.61	1.34	6.6	0.6
Margarine, edible oils, and lard	383	1.78	6.44	1484	0.46	1.22	13.2	1.2
Fresh fruits	254	2.48	7.42	970	0.60	1.09	49.1	4.3
Dried, frozen, preserved juices	194	1.31	6.69	1272	0.43	1.21	33.4	2.9
Fresh vegetables	204	1.80	6.48	1080	0.76	1.02	48.1	4.2
Dried, froz., preserved vegetables	395	2.37	9.04	2366	0.83	1.45	26.0	2.3
Tubers, including potatoes	249	1.74	6.26	1240	0.57	1.40	17.6	1.5
Coffee	249	2.51	3.60	1755	0.75	1.46	26.6	2.3
Tea	429	4.04	10.27	2926	0.55	0.85	6.0	0.5
Cocoa	409	2.34	10.10	1149	0.76	1.67	3.2	0.3
Sugar	240	1.70	5.73	1125	0.54	1.01	8.9	0.8
Jam, syrup, honey, etc.	243	2.09	5.06	2024	0.56	0.99	6.4	0.6
Chocolate, ice cream, etc.	308	2.05	7.40	2506	0.62	1.48	68.4	6.0
Condiments, spices, salt, etc.	245	2.74	9.83	2091	0.87	2.28	21.5	1.9
Mineral water	230	0.92	2.41	429	0.27	1.56	12.8	1.1
Soft drinks	309	2.18	7.15	2020	0.75	1.86	36.6	3.2
Liquors and spirits	274	2.08	7.30	1228	0.98	1.90	26.4	2.3
Wine, cider	204	0.89	2.83	357	0.52	1.19	44.6	3.9
Beer	315	1.09	5.14	1291	0.68	1.92	49.4	4.3
Other alcoholic beverages	347	2.56	10.44	2137	1.15	2.66	10.4	0.9
Cigarettes	132	2.52	5.75	1389	0.93	2.36	96.5	8.5
Other tobacco products and stimulants	497	2.72	7.18	1625	1.05	2.72	6.4	0.6
Total food, beverages, and tobacco	281	2.07	6.97	1666	0.67	1.54	1137.2	100.0

TABLE 1.— *Continued*

| Expenditure Category | Expenditure PPPs (units of own currency per $) | | | | | | G-7 Expenditures | |
	Jap	Ger	Fra	Ita	UK	Can	B $	% share
Textile, apparel, and leather products								
Men's clothing	210	2.70	10.16	2116	0.64	1.51	131.1	25.0
Women's clothing	226	2.62	9.85	2000	0.64	1.49	150.2	28.7
Children's clothing	405	4.35	18.53	3599	1.06	1.49	54.4	10.4
Clothing accessories	229	3.70	14.55	2808	1.05	1.35	33.4	6.4
Clothing, rental and repair	140	2.14	9.61	1833	0.97	1.21	10.6	2.0
Footwear, men's	173	2.33	9.65	1774	0.54	1.56	21.4	4.1
Footwear, women's	232	3.09	11.56	2300	0.81	2.24	26.0	5.0
Footwear, children's, infants'	98	2.47	8.94	1807	0.51	1.21	21.1	4.0
Household textiles, etc.	82	1.53	7.15	1047	0.44	1.48	53.4	10.2
Floor coverings	222	1.52	6.27	1705	0.48	1.53	22.5	4.3
Total textile, apparel, and leather products	217	2.73	10.73	2131	0.69	1.51	524.1	100.0
Chemical, petroleum, rubber, and plastic products								
Gas	481	3.46	13.49	2715	1.15	1.23	45.2	5.1
Liquid heating fuels	210	1.80	7.39	1965	0.73	1.08	46.3	5.2
Automotive fuel and lubricant	394	4.51	16.04	4279	1.51	1.88	154.2	17.4
Other fuels	1062	4.91	20.61	3467	1.50	1.88	3.6	0.4
Tires, tubes, accessories	217	1.68	7.63	1744	0.88	1.46	71.7	8.1
Cleaning maintenance supplies	205	2.68	7.61	1714	0.72	1.43	35.5	4.0
Drugs and medical preparations	78	1.60	2.87	713	0.35	1.10	419.4	47.4
Medical supplies	153	2.19	4.75	777	0.49	1.26	34.8	3.9
Toilet articles (all kinds)	315	2.58	9.97	2036	0.89	1.66	74.7	8.4
Total chemical, petroleum, rubber, and plastic products	204	2.38	7.26	1751	0.73	1.34	885.4	100.0
Machinery, equipment, and fabricated metal products								
Cutlery and flatware	420	3.13	7.87	1944	0.90	1.94	2.8	0.2
Domestic utensils without motor	228	1.93	7.13	1331	0.75	1.55	21.0	1.3
Refrigerators, freezers, etc.	314	2.19	10.31	1502	0.71	1.77	10.6	0.7
Washing and cleaning appliances	121	1.46	5.78	1087	0.38	1.49	24.1	1.5
Cooking and other food warming appliances	217	2.27	9.81	2003	0.92	1.49	15.0	0.9
Sewing machines, fans, toasters	332	3.06	12.26	2743	0.95	1.41	10.4	0.7
Room climate control equipment	403	1.35	5.64	1146	0.39	1.22	11.4	0.7
Garden appliances	287	2.77	10.51	3308	1.68	1.97	1.7	0.1
Light-bulb, cable, switches, etc.	128	2.16	7.71	1180	0.97	1.07	11.6	0.7
Therapeutic appliances and equip	183	1.73	5.74	1692	0.57	1.01	66.0	4.1
Radios, televisions, phonographs	144	2.63	10.11	2149	0.68	1.69	60.6	3.8
Musical instruments, boats, etc.	179	1.76	7.58	1321	0.40	1.03	22.6	1.4
Camera, VCR, and other optical equipment	164	2.12	8.97	1670	0.63	1.51	51.2	3.2
Engines, turbines	222	2.47	9.73	1913	0.78	1.79	19.2	1.2
Agricultural machinery	179	1.61	5.98	1247	0.66	0.97	54.1	3.4
Office machinery and equipment	993	10.49	43.79	10211	3.89	6.80	40.6	2.6

(*continued*)

TABLE 1.— Continued

Expenditure Category	Expenditure PPPs (units of own currency per $)						G-7 Expenditures	
	Jap	Ger	Fra	Ita	UK	Can	B $	% share
Metal and woodworking mach.	304	3.00	10.26	2489	1.05	1.60	80.5	5.1
Tool, finished metal	206	3.31	9.63	2297	0.57	1.15	33.6	2.1
Construction, mining, oil field	139	1.95	6.89	1758	0.62	1.10	80.9	5.1
Textile/leather working mach.	127	2.40	11.90	2094	0.87	1.17	11.0	0.7
Other machinery equipment	206	2.13	6.06	1403	0.67	1.46	86.4	5.4
Precision, optical instruments	189	1.59	6.36	1602	0.68	0.84	61.3	3.9
Electrical equip., including lights	222	2.95	10.62	2311	1.00	1.24	71.9	4.5
Other electrical equipment	60	1.01	5.30	1182	0.44	0.66	46.4	2.9
Telecom. and measuring instr.	115	2.48	7.18	1468	0.52	1.22	113.5	7.1
Passenger cars (consumption)	145	1.95	7.17	1548	0.77	1.41	330.6	20.8
Other personal transport	150	1.96	7.02	1587	0.65	0.86	20.6	1.3
Motor vehicles, engines	157	2.87	10.31	2263	1.00	1.53	178.2	11.2
Railway vehicles	99	1.68	5.64	1855	0.84	1.73	12.6	0.8
Aircraft	104	1.94	6.94	1812	0.95	1.54	18.0	1.1
Ship, boats	104	1.94	6.94	1812	0.95	1.54	17.3	1.1
Other transport equipment	104	2.03	7.55	1718	0.99	1.44	4.7	0.3
Total machinery, equipment, and fabricated metal products	190	2.42	8.84	1972	0.83	1.47	1590.3	100.0
Total machinery, etc. excl. office machinery	169	2.21	7.92	1756	0.75	1.33	1549.7	
Other manufactured products								
Furniture, fixtures	243	1.91	7.05	1500	0.59	1.40	116.2	26.8
Books, newspapers, magazines	227	2.47	5.93	1814	0.61	1.56	80.4	18.5
Stationery: noneducational	377	3.14	10.67	2267	0.78	1.84	18.3	4.2
Glassware and tableware	50	0.55	1.48	251	0.15	0.46		0.0
Jewelry, watches, etc.	237	2.94	11.22	1720	0.91	1.76	60.6	14.0
Other personal care goods	169	2.11	6.25	1870	0.74	1.42	38.3	8.8
Other nondurable household products	217	2.31	9.99	2986	0.57	1.67	52.6	12.1
Semi and nondurable recreation goods	182	2.04	7.34	1729	0.51	1.79	68.0	15.7
Total other manufactured products	225	2.30	7.91	1870	0.64	1.59	434.2	100.0

countries do not use this methodology, and their computer price indexes tend to show increases or only moderate declines over time. This difference in price measurement practices could introduce a significant bias into the estimation of the OPRs for machinery and total manufacturing.[10] As indicated in the table (at the bottom of the machinery subsector), when office machinery is excluded from that subtotal, the EPPP is lowered by about 10 percent for each country. Given the weight of machinery in total manufacturing, this exclusion lowers the OPR for total manufacturing by about

5 percent in most of the countries. In light of this potential bias, office machinery (which accounted for 2.5 percent of total G-7 expenditures on machinery and equipment in 1990) was excluded from the EPPP calculations.

The EPPP$_{ij}$s are presented again in table 2, which shows the derivation of OPRs from the EPPPs. This derivation can be seen more clearly when the EPPPs are translated to expenditure price (PE) levels by dividing through by the 1990 nominal exchange rates. The corresponding price levels, indexed to a U.S. PE of 1.0, are shown in table 3. The foreign PEs in 1990 were uniformly higher than the U.S. PEs. While it is difficult to generalize, this difference tended to be maximized in the textile and apparel sector for most countries and in the food sector for Japan, where expenditure prices were nearly double the U.S. level.

Averaging across sectors, Italy shows the largest expenditure price premium over the U.S. price level for total manufacturing (at more than 50 percent), while Canada and the United Kingdom show the smallest.[11] The weights used to compute the averages for total manufacturing are the sector shares in total G-7 output, shown in the bottom panel of table 4.[12] Machinery and equipment has the largest output weight, at about 45 percent, while the textiles and apparel sector has the smallest, at 4 percent. This is generally true across countries, as indicated in the upper panel of the table, although textiles and apparel figure much more importantly in Italian output than in that of other countries. The table also shows, for comparison, the shares of the manufacturing sectors in total G-7 expenditures in 1990. The shares of food, textiles, and petroleum (where the G-7 countries are net importers on average) are larger in expenditures than in output, while the opposite is true for machinery and other manufactured products (where these countries are net exporters on average).

Adjustments

The first adjustment to the expenditure prices is to remove wholesale and retail distribution margins. Estimates of these margins for total manufacturing were obtained from a series of recent papers written as part of an OECD project to analyze the distribution systems of the major industrial countries.[13] These margins, which include the total value added (the cost of labor, other inputs and profit margins) of the distribution sectors, excluding transportation costs and indirect taxes, are shown in table 5.[14] One surprising result from these studies is that total wholesale plus retail margins in the United States, which is typically thought to be have a relatively efficient distribution system, were found to be at the high end of the range for these countries (roughly 40 to 60 percent in 1987), while margins

TABLE 2. 1990 Purchasing Power Parities (Units of Local Currency per Dollar)

	Japan	Germany	France	Italy	UK	Canada
Food Beverages and Tobacco						
OPR	285	1.96	7.67	1788	0.73	1.67
UVR	203	1.88	6.91		0.74	
OPR/UVR	1.41	1.04	1.11		0.98	
Textile, Apparel, and Leather Products						
OPR	335	4.71	15.94	2736	0.99	1.89
UVR	186	2.71	8.05		0.77	
OPR/UVR	1.80	1.73	1.98		1.28	
Chemical, Petroleum, Rubber, and Plastic Products						
OPR	208	2.25	6.18	2246	0.75	1.40
UVR	160	2.12	6.22		0.54	
OPR/UVR	1.30	1.06	0.99		1.38	
Basic Metals						
UVR	166	2.02	6.99		0.66	
Machinery, Equipment, and Fabricated Metal Products						
OPR	186	2.25	8.16	1918	0.86	1.28
UVR	123	2.14	7.41		0.73	
OPR/UVR	1.52	1.05	1.10		1.18	
Other Manufactured Products						
OPR	256	2.52	8.20	2016	0.72	1.60
UVR	200	2.22	6.99		0.90	
OPR/UVR	1.28	1.13	1.17		0.80	
Total Manufacturing						
OPR	218	2.36	8.07	2005	0.79	1.43
UVR	157	2.14	7.10		0.74	
UVR*	155	2.14	7.03		0.74	
OPR/UVR	1.39	1.10	1.14		1.08	
EPPP	198	2.25	7.78	1794	0.71	1.41
GDP PPP	223	2.49	7.31	1310	0.57	1.23
ER	145	1.61	5.46	1195	0.56	1.17

EPPP = Expenditure PPP
EPPPm = Expenditure PPP adjusted for wholesale and retail distribution margins
EPPP* = EPPPm adjusted for net taxes and subsidies
OPR = Output price ratio (EPPP* adjusted for import and export prices)
UVR = Van Ark-Pilat Unit Value Ratio
ER = Nominal exchange rate

TABLE 3. 1990 Dollar Price Levels (US Expenditure Price Level = 1.0)

	US	Japan	Germany	France	Italy	UK	Canada	G-7 Dollar Price Level
Food Beverages and Tobacco								
PE	1.00	1.94	1.28	1.28	1.39	1.20	1.32	
PEm	0.63	1.37	0.85	0.80	0.93	0.82	0.83	
PE*	0.56	1.04	0.69	0.81	0.81	0.73	0.81	0.72
P	0.56	1.11	0.69	0.79	0.84	0.73	0.81	
Textile, Apparel, and Leather Products								
PE	1.00	1.50	1.69	1.98	1.78	1.23	1.29	
PEm	0.63	1.06	1.12	1.24	1.19	0.84	0.81	
PE*	0.62	0.97	1.10	1.20	1.18	0.82	0.80	0.86
P	0.45	1.05	1.32	1.33	1.03	0.80	0.73	
Chemical, Petroleum, Rubber, and Plastic Products								
PE	1.00	1.41	1.48	1.34	1.46	1.30	1.15	
PEm	0.63	0.99	0.98	0.84	0.97	0.89	0.72	
PE*	0.57	0.81	0.81	0.65	0.97	0.76	0.68	0.69
P	0.57	0.81	0.79	0.64	1.06	0.75	0.68	
Basic Metal Industries								
UVR/E	1.00	1.15	1.25	1.29		1.18		
Machinery, Equipment, and Fabricated Metal Products								
PE	1.00	1.17	1.37	1.46	1.47	1.33	1.14	
PEm	0.63	0.83	0.91	0.91	0.98	0.91	0.72	
PE*	0.61	0.78	0.90	0.90	0.99	0.91	0.70	0.76
P	0.60	0.77	0.84	0.90	0.96	0.92	0.66	
Other Manufactured Products								
PE	1.00	1.56	1.42	1.46	1.56	1.15	1.36	
PEm	0.63	1.10	0.95	0.91	1.04	0.78	0.86	
PE*	0.61	1.04	0.92	0.88	1.04	0.77	0.83	0.81
P	0.59	1.05	0.92	0.90	1.00	0.76	0.82	
Total Manufacturing								
PE	1.00	1.32	1.38	1.42	1.52	1.25	1.22	
PEm	0.64	0.97	0.95	0.92	1.04	0.87	0.80	
PE*	0.62	0.89	0.90	0.87	1.03	0.83	0.77	
P	0.60	0.89	0.87	0.88	1.01	0.83	0.75	
ER	1.00	145	1.61	5.43	1195	0.56	1.17	

PE = Expenditure price level
PEm = Expenditure price level adjusted for wholesale and retail distribution margins
PE* = PEm adjusted for net taxes and subsidies
OPR = Output price (PE* adjusted for import and export prices)
UVR = Van Ark-Pilat Unit Value Ratio
ER = Nominal exchange rate
G-7 dollar price level is a weighted average based on outputs translated to dollars with tax-adjusted expenditure PPPs.

in Germany, the United Kingdom, and especially Japan were found to be lower.[15] These results are corroborated by a separate study by Ito and Maruyama (1991), whose results are also reported in the table, and an independent study by Nishimura (1993).[16]

The OECD project did not provide details on distribution margins at the manufacturing subsector level consistently across countries. Adjustments for these margins at the subsector level is therefore based on the average margins for total manufacturing, which undoubtedly entails some bias at the subsector level. Based on U.S. input-output data (U.S. Department of Commerce, 1994), total distribution margins tend to be substantially higher than average in the area of consumer expenditures (as high as 75 to 100 percent on food, apparel and footwear, and many consumer durables, for example) and noticeably lower than average for producer durables. To the extent that these differences across subsectors are similar across countries, however, this particular source of bias in comparisons at the subsector level is mitigated. As noted above, the estimates may also be

TABLE 4.   1990 Output in Billions of Dollars Translated at PPP, factor cost

	US	Japan	Germany	France	Italy	UK	Canada
Food, Beverages, and Tobacco	85.7	31.9	30.4	23.3	17.0	31.0	9.2
Textiles, Apparel, and Leather Products	48.4	6.4	5.8	5.2	17.1	6.2	3.1
Chemical, Petroleum, Rubber, and Plastic Products	149.1	54.8	46.8	29.9	17.0	21.0	10.2
Basic Metals	35.1	58.0	27.0	10.6	6.5	6.2	5.0
Machinery, Equipment, and Fabricated Metal Products	379.4	285.5	156.8	67.2	55.8	53.3	27.1
Other Manufactured Products	202.3	105.5	35.8	27.8	29.3	30.7	18.6
Total Manufacturing	900.1	541.0	302.6	163.9	142.7	148.4	73.1

1990 G-7 Output and Expenditures

	Output ($b)	% Share	Expenditure ($b)	% Share
Food, Beverages, and Tobacco	228	10.1	1137	25.1
Textiles, Apparel, and Leather Products	92	4.1	524	11.6
Chemical, Petroleum, Rubber, and Plastic Products	328	14.4	885	19.5
Basic Metals	148	6.5		0.0
Machinery, Equipment, and Fabricated Metal Products	1025	45.1	1550	34.2
Other Manufactured Products	450	19.8	434	9.6
Total Manufacturing	2272	100.0	4531	100.0

Source: OECD ISDB and National Accounts, ICP PPPs and expenditures and authors' calculations.

Note: Output at market price for France, Germany, Japan, and the United States were adjusted to factor cost using OECD data on net taxes and subsidies.

biased by the absence of adjustment for differences in domestic transportation margins, although the bias in this case is likely to be small because transportation margins tend to be small.

The effects of adjusting for distribution margins are shown by comparing the top two lines in each subsector panel of both table 2 (compare the unadjusted EPPPs and the adjusted EPPPms) and table 3 (compare the PEs and the PEms). When adjusted for distribution margins, the price levels in Japan, Germany, and the United Kingdom relative to the United States (i.e., the EPPPms) are higher than on an unadjusted basis. In the Japanese case they are nearly 13 percent higher.

The next adjustment is for indirect taxes and subsidies. Net indirect tax rates are computed as the difference between taxes paid and subsidies received in each subsector divided by subsector value added, using data obtained from the OECD International Sectoral Database (1993) and OECD Annual National Accounts (1994).[17] This approach is based on tax collections imputed to value added in the manufacturing sector, and implicitly assumes that the same tax rates apply to value added in the distribution of these goods at the wholesale and retail sector level.[18]

The net indirect tax rates for the manufacturing subsectors are shown in table 6. The OECD reports relatively large net indirect taxes for Japan, especially in the food sector (32 percent), and relatively low net rates for

TABLE 5.   Manufacturing Wholesale and Retail Distribution Margins (percent of sales)

	US	Japan	Germany	France	Italy	UK	Canada
Wholesale	20.1	11.2	16.8	23.1	22.4	13.4	20.1
Retail	32.3	27.1	29.0	29.7	22.9	28.8	32.3
Total	58.9	41.3	50.7	59.7	50.4	46.1	58.9

Margins reported by Ito and Maruyama (1993) for year shown

	US	Japan	Germany	France	Italy	UK	Canada
	1986	1986	1985	1985		1984	
Wholesale	19.4	11.2	12.6	21.8		13.4	
Retail	31	27.1	34.2	29.6		27.6	
Total	56.4	41.3	51.1	57.9		44.7	

Sources:
France: Messerlin (1993) pp. 32–33 (data for 1987).
Germany: Lachner et. al. (1993) pp. 80, 129 (data for 1987).
Italy: Pellegrini and Cardini (1993) p. 34 (data for 1988).
Japan: Maruyama (1993) p. 60 (data for 1986).
UK: Dawson (1993) pp. 69–70 (data for 1984 and 1988).
US: Betancourt (1993) pp. 26, 30 (data are for 1987).
Canadian margins are assumed to equal US margins.

Italy (where sizable subsidies largely offset slightly more sizable tax collections). U.S. rates are about average. Across subsectors, net indirect tax rates tend to be highest for food and for chemicals (including petroleum products). Notable exceptions to this rule are France, where net indirect taxes on food are about zero, and Italy, where net indirect taxes on chemicals and petroleum are about zero.

The effects of adjusting for taxes can be seen in table 2 by comparing the EPPPms (unadjusted) with the EPPP*s (adjusted), and in table 3 by comparing the PEms with the PE*s. This adjustment tends to reduce the relative price levels slightly in Japan, Germany and France (where net indirect tax rates are somewhat above U.S. rates on average). The downward adjustments are most pronounced for food and chemicals in Japan and Germany. The relative price levels in the other countries are raised slightly overall.

The final adjustment is for the prices of imports and exports as defined in equation (11). The requisite inputs are trade balances expressed as a percent of value added (which are reported in table 7) and an estimate of the "world price level", as defined in equation (12) above and reported in the far right-hand column of table 3. Recall that this adjustment will be greatest in cases where both a country's trade imbalance is large and the deviation of its domestic price level from the world price level is large. The largest trade imbalances tend to occur in the textile and apparel sector, with most countries showing substantial deficits and Italy showing a large surplus. Also, Germany and Japan show substantial surpluses and Canada a substantial deficit in machinery and equipment. In most cases, subsector imbalances tend to be offsetting within countries and the imbalances for total manufacturing are generally a good deal smaller. As indi-

TABLE 6.   Indirect Taxes Net of Subsidies (percent of value added)

	US	Japan	Germany	France	Italy	UK	Canada
Food, Beverages, and Tobacco	13.24	32.23	23.74	-0.39	13.90	12.42	2.57
Textile, Apparel, and Leather Products	1.57	9.25	2.14	3.08	0.33	1.85	2.34
Chemical, Petroleum, Rubber, and Plastic Products	10.73	23.04	20.56	29.79	0.51	16.95	6.54
Basic Metal Industries	4.85	5.67	-0.48	3.87	-5.15	-0.59	4.66
Machinery, Equipment, and Fabricated Metal Products	2.55	5.94	1.40	1.76	-1.18	0.66	2.95
Other Manufactured Products	2.38	6.18	2.59	3.25	-0.14	1.90	4.05
Total Manufacture	5.05	11.04	7.40	7.42	1.02	5.28	3.77

Source: Computed form OECD ISDB.
(UK indirect taxes assumed to equal average of France + Germany + Italy.)

cated by comparisons of the G-7 and single-country values of the PE*s in table 3, deviations from the world price level (at 1990 exchange rates) tend to be highest for textiles. Among countries, PE*s in Italy are at the high end of the range and those in the United States at the low end.

The effect of the adjustment for international trade prices can be seen by comparing the EPPP*s and the OPRs in table 2, as well as the PE*s and Ps in table 3. The largest adjustments occur in the textile and apparel sector. For example, Japan, Germany, and France have PE*s above the world price level, and since those countries run large trade deficits in textiles and apparel, their output prices are adjusted upward relative to their PE*s. The net result is an increase in the OPR relative to the EPPP* in table 2. The United States, too, runs a trade deficit in that sector, but with the U.S. expenditure price adjusted for taxes and margins (PE*) below the world price level, the U.S. output price (P) is adjusted down relative to PE*.[19] In Italy's case, however, despite a high PE* relative to the world price level, P and OPR are adjusted downward because Italy runs a large surplus in textiles and apparel. In the more important machinery and equipment subsector and for overall manufacturing, the adjustments for import and export prices generally are fairly small, either because of small trade imbalances or because of small deviations from the world price level.

Because of the strong assumptions underlying the adjustments for import and export prices, it is prudent to consider how the results would be affected if: (a) import and export prices fell midway between the world price level and the domestic price level, and (b) import prices were at the world price level and export prices at the domestic price level. In the former case, to a rough approximation, the adjustment is cut in half and has little net effect, except in the textile and apparel sector. In the latter case,

TABLE 7.   Trade Balance in 1990 (percent of value added)

	US	Japan	Germany	France	Italy	UK	Canada
Food, Beverages, and Tobacco	3.9	-22.1	-12.1	15.4	-29.8	-16.5	4.0
Textile, Apparel, and Leather Products	-68.7	-68.6	-93.6	-36.9	46.6	-72.4	-96.4
Chemical, Petroleum, Rubber, and Plastic Products	-2.0	-3.4	19.4	-1.9	-33.7	8.9	-10.1
Basic Metal Industries	-27.7	-0.5	1.9	-7.9	-41.2	-17.5	64.9
Machinery, Equipment, and Fabricated Metal Products	-9.1	44.9	43.5	-2.7	11.0	-10.4	-57.5
Other Manufactured Products	-11.6	-5.1	-2.6	-15.4	17.7	-30.1	50.2
Total Manufacture	-11.1	15.4	19.6	-4.8	6.1	-16.3	-7.1

Source: OECD ISDB.

the result is to produce an even greater upward adjustment in the output prices of all the other G-7 countries relative to the United States.

The Combined Adjustments

The net effect of the three adjustments to expenditure prices yields estimates of output prices that show, if anything, a *greater* premium of foreign prices over U.S. price levels at the output level than at the expenditure level. As indicated at the bottom of table 3, the PEs for total manufacturing in the foreign G-7 countries range between 22 and 52 percent above the U.S. level in 1990. And, as indicated in the bottom panel of table 8 (which shows the same data indexed to a U.S. output price level of 1.0), foreign output prices range between 26 and 68 percent above the U.S. level. Table 2 shows that the largest positive differences between OPRs and EPPPs are in the textile and apparel subsector. The only cases where the OPRs fall below the EPPPs are for food in Germany and chemicals and petroleum in Germany and France (in all three cases, high indirect tax rates account for most of the net downward adjustment).

Comparison of Alternative Measures of Relative Price Levels

Table 2 also shows the ICOP unit value ratios (UVRs).[20] A summary comparison of the OPRs and the UVRs is presented in table 9, which shows the two measures and ratios of the OPRs to the UVRs. In most cases the UVR's fall noticeably below the OPRs—by as much as 40 percent for total manufacturing in the case of Japan, and by between 10 and 15 percent for Germany, France, and the United Kingdom.[21]

Two sets of UVRs are shown for total manufacturing. The first, labeled UVR, are arithmetic weighted averages for which the weights are the output shares for the G-7 countries combined shown in the bottom panel of table 4. The second, labeled UVR*, are weighted averages reported in recent ICOP studies, which use Fisher indexes (geometric averages with output weights specific to the two countries being compared). The two weighting schemes make very little difference at this level of aggregation, except possibly in the case of France.

Table 9 also shows the 1990 EKS PPPs for total GDP, which have been used by various researchers as proxies for relative manufacturing price levels. In the case of Germany and Japan the PPPs are tolerably close to the OPRs (roughly within 5 percent). For the other countries, however, the PPPs understate the OPRs by amounts ranging from 10 percent for France to 35 percent for Italy.

TABLE 8.   1990 Dollar Price Levels (US Expenditure Price Level = 1.0)

	US	Japan	Germany	France	Italy	UK	Canada	G-7 Dollar
Food Beverages and Tobacco								
PE	1.78	3.45	2.28	2.28	2.48	2.13	2.35	
PEm	1.12	2.44	1.52	1.43	1.65	1.46	1.48	
PE*	0.99	1.84	1.23	1.44	1.45	1.30	1.44	1.28
P	1.00	1.97	1.22	1.41	1.50	1.30	1.44	
Textile, Apparel, and Leather Products								
PE	2.21	3.32	3.74	4.38	3.95	2.72	2.87	
PEm	1.39	2.35	2.49	2.74	2.63	1.86	1.80	
PE*	1.37	2.15	2.43	2.66	2.62	1.83	1.76	1.91
P	1.00	2.32	2.92	2.93	2.29	1.76	1.62	
Chemical, Petroleum, Rubber, and Plastic Product								
PE	1.77	2.48	2.61	2.36	2.59	2.29	2.03	
PEm	1.11	1.76	1.73	1.48	1.72	1.57	1.28	
PE*	1.00	1.43	1.44	1.14	1.71	1.34	1.20	1.21
P	1.00	1.44	1.39	1.14	1.88	1.33	1.20	
Basic Metal Industries								
UVR/E	0.57	0.81	0.79	0.64		0.75		
Machinery, Equipment, and Fabricated Metal Products								
PE	1.67	1.95	2.29	2.43	2.45	2.22	1.90	
PEm	1.05	1.38	1.52	1.52	1.63	1.52	1.19	
PE*	1.02	1.30	1.50	1.50	1.65	1.51	1.16	1.27
P	1.00	1.29	1.40	1.50	1.60	1.53	1.10	
Other Manufactured Products								
PE	1.69	2.63	2.40	2.46	2.64	1.93	2.30	
PEm	1.06	1.86	1.60	1.54	1.75	1.32	1.45	
PE*	1.04	1.75	1.56	1.49	1.76	1.30	1.39	1.36
P	1.00	1.77	1.56	1.51	1.69	1.28	1.38	
Total Manufacturing								
PE	1.68	2.20	2.31	2.37	2.55	2.09	2.05	
PEm	1.08	1.62	1.60	1.54	1.74	1.46	1.34	
PE*	1.03	1.49	1.51	1.46	1.72	1.39	1.29	
P	1.00	₁ 1.50	1.46	1.47	1.68	1.39	1.26	
ER	1.00	144.79	1.61	5.43	1195.35	0.56	1.17	

PE = Expenditure price level

PEm = Expenditure price level adjusted for wholesale and retail distribution margins

PE* = PEm adjusted for net taxes and subsidies

OPR = Output price (PE* adjusted for import and export prices)

UVR = Van Ark-Pilat Unit Value Ratio

ER = Nominal exchange rate

   G-7 dollar price level is a weighted average based on outputs translated to dollars with tax-adjusted expenditure PPPs.

TABLE 9. Comparison of 1990 Output PPPs with Van Ark-Pilat Unit Value Ratios

	Japan	Germany	France	Italy	UK	Canada
Food Beverages and Tobacco						
OPR	285	1.96	7.67	1788	0.73	1.67
UVR	203	1.88	6.91		0.74	
OPR/UVR	1.41	1.04	1.11		0.98	
Textile, Apparel, and Leather Products						
OPR	335	4.71	15.94	2736	0.99	1.89
UVR	186	2.71	8.05		0.77	
OPR/UVR	1.80	1.73	1.98		1.28	
Chemical, Petroleum, Rubber, and Plastic Products						
OPR	208	2.25	6.18	2246	0.75	1.40
UVR	160	2.12	6.22		0.54	
OPR/UVR	1.30	1.06	0.99		1.38	
Basic Metals						
UVR	166	2.02	6.99		0.66	
Machinery, Equipment, and Fabricated Metal Products						
OPR	186	2.25	8.16	1918	0.86	1.28
UVR	123	2.14	7.41		0.73	
OPR/UVR	1.52	1.05	1.10		1.18	
Other Manufactured Products						
OPR	256	2.52	8.20	2016	0.72	1.60
UVR	200	2.22	6.99		0.90	
OPR/UVR	1.28	1.13	1.17		0.80	
Total Manufacturing						
OPR	218	2.36	8.07	2005	0.79	1.43
UVR	157	2.14	7.10		0.74	
UVR*	155	2.14	7.03		0.74	
OPR/UVR	1.39	1.10	1.14		1.08	
EPPP	198	2.25	7.78	1794	0.71	1.41
GDP PPP	223	2.49	7.31	1310	0.57	1.23
ER	145	1.61	5.46	1195	0.56	1.17

OPR = Output price ratio

UVR = ICOP unit value ratio

UVR* = Aggregate UVR as computed by ICOP

EPPP = Expenditure PPP

GDP PPP = ICOP PPP for total GDP (EKS method)

ER = Nominal exchange rate

These comparisons, along with the large cross-country differences in absolute price levels for 1990 shown in tables 3 and 8, may lead one to wonder about the "plausibility" of these results. Our ability to capture the prices of many intermediate goods only indirectly through their contribution to final product prices is a potentially important source of error. The difference between the OPR and UVR estimates is greatest for textiles and apparel, an area where intermediate goods (which the UVR approach most likely captures better) figure importantly. At the same time, the OPR estimates are also generally significantly above the UVR estimates in the finished goods areas, where their coverage may well be superior. Moreover, several of the choices that have been made in constructing the adjustments—including the treatment of import and export prices and the extrapolation of UVRs to 1990 with value added deflators—probably have had the net effect of understating the difference between the UVR estimates and the OPR estimates.

Labor Costs: Data and Analysis

In this section we present and analyze the comparative levels of unit labor costs and their components, output per hour and compensation per hour, in each of the G-7 countries for total manufacturing and each of the six subsectors described in the preceding section. The analysis includes comparison of our results with those of other studies.

Productivity

The output price ratios (OPRs) derived in the preceding section were used to translate output per hour for 1990 in each of the non-U.S. G-7 countries from local currency into dollars. The output data for total manufacturing and for the subsectors are value added data from standardized national accounts as reported in the OECD International Sectoral Database (ISDB) and the OECD Annual National Accounts (1994). These sources contain sectoral data on nominal and real value added, compensation, employment, imports, exports, and net indirect taxes for many of the OECD countries.[22] (The OECD National Accounts contain the most recent observations of the historical series we took from the ISDB.) We also substituted the recently revised U.S. gross product originating (GPO) data for the value added data found in the ISDB.[23] The revised GPO data were only available for the 1977–91 period. We extended the data for total U.S. manufacturing back to 1970 using the growth rates in the previous (unrevised) data series.[24] For the United States, Japan, Germany and France, the value added in the national accounts is measured on a market-price basis rather than the preferred factor-cost basis. We used the net indirect tax data in the ISDB (updated where necessary) to convert market prices to factor costs.

Data on hours worked across countries and manufacturing subsectors were computed from subsectoral data on total employment from the ISDB (and the OECD National Accounts) and data on total hours worked in manufacturing provided by the BLS Office of Productivity and Technology. To estimate hours worked at the subsector level we multiplied hours worked in total manufacturing by the each subsector's share in total employment in manufacturing.[25]

Our results for productivity, measured in terms of 1990 dollars per hour indexed to a U.S. level of 100, are shown in the top panel of table 10. The bottom two panels show observations for 1985 and 1980, which were extrapolated back using growth rates in real output per hour measured in constant local currency units.[26] Movements in comparative productivity levels over time are shown more clearly in chart 1, which compares our measure of the U.S. level with those of each of the other G-7 countries. The reader should be cautioned that because of differences in the treatment of computer prices across countries, comparisons of relative productivity levels going back in time become less accurate the further one gets from the base period (1990). The computer price effect could bias downward our estimates of the levels of European and Japanese productivity in total manufacturing (and especially in the machinery and equipment subsector) in 1985 by as much as several percentage points.[27]

These data indicate that while there has been some convergence of productivity levels over time, the United States still had the highest level of total manufacturing productivity among the G-7 countries in 1990. Also in that year, France's productivity level had risen to second highest, ahead of Germany's, while the United Kingdom and Japan remained at the low end among the G-7. These results for total manufacturing mask a wide dispersion of relative productivity levels among manufacturing subsectors across countries. The United States had the most productive textile and apparel, machinery and equipment, and "other manufactures" subsectors, and it was near the top in food. But both Japan and France were clearly ahead in chemicals and basic metals.[28] Japan's overall productivity level is held back by very low productivity in the food subsector (consistent with the findings of McKinsey & Company 1993) and the textile subsector. As a note of caution, the usefulness of such comparisons at the subsector level is limited by both the imprecision of the EPPP adjustments at the subsector level and the fact that bias introduced by absence of double deflation is magnified at the subsector level.

Table 11 presents a comparison of the EPPP-based productivity estimates reported in table 11 for 1990 with recent ICOP UVR-based estimates reported in van Ark (1995). This comparison indicates that despite the very different analytical approaches and data sources employed, the two sets of estimates arrive at qualitatively quite similar estimates for total manufacturing productivity levels. Both show the same ranking of productivity levels, with the United States the highest, followed by France, Germany, Japan, and the United Kingdom in that order. The level estimates for both Germany and France are quantitatively quite similar between the two approaches; for Japan and the United Kingdom, the differences between the two sets of estimates are more noticeable, but still not large. In fact the comparative difference in the case of Japan is a good deal smaller than would be suggested by the difference between the OPR and

TABLE 10. Productivity (Indexed to US level = 100)

	US	Japan	Germany	France	Italy	UK	Canada
Total Manufacturing, 1990	100	67	83	94	72	60	83
Food, Beverages, and Tobacco	100	35	84	93	98	102	72
Textiles, Apparel, and Footwear	100	28	55	57	75	48	72
Chemical, Petroleum, and Products	100	128	70	126	50	51	71
Basic Metals	100	145	91	96	81	54	78
Machinery, Equipment, and Fabricated Metal	100	78	88	87	74	46	97
Other Manufactured Products	100	54	81	97	81	70	76
Total Manufacturing, 1985	100	59	87	85	73	57	95
Food, Beverages, and Tobacco	100	35	83	87	89	93	76
Textiles, Apparel, and Footwear	100	38	55	60	84	54	84
Chemical, Petroleum, and Products	100	134	83	91	54	51	87
Basic Metals	100	121	85	66	78	43	86
Machinery, Equipment, and Fabricated Metal	100	65	96	87	76	49	110
Other Manufactured Products	100	47	76	95	80	65	88
Total Manufacturing, 1980	100	56	85	81	65	50	91
Food, Beverages, and Tobacco	100	44	85	86	83	86	79
Textiles, Apparel, and Footwear	100	51	53	56	81	48	82
Chemical, Petroleum, and Products	100	98	86	85	52	46	88
Basic Metals	100	143	69	59	57	22	67
Machinery, Equipment, and Fabricated Metal	100	55	96	85	68	43	100
Other Manufactured Products	100	43	85	91	86	68	92

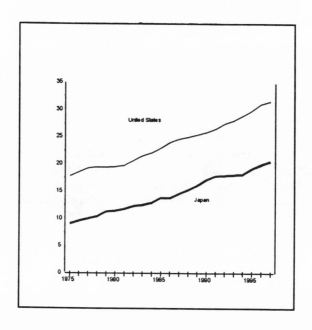

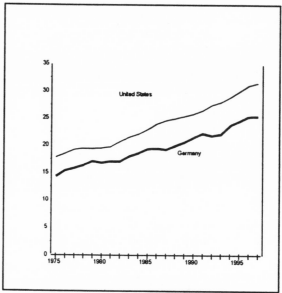

Chart 1. Manufacturing Productivity Levels (Real output per hour measured in 1990 U.S. dollars; Non-U.S. data translated to dollars using 1990 OPRs)

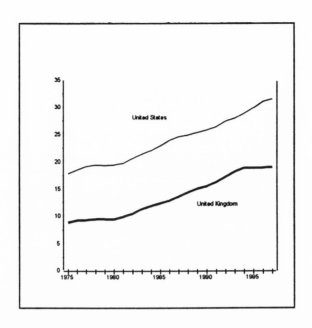

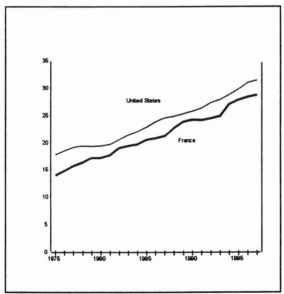

Chart 1. Manufacturing Productivity Levels (*continued*)

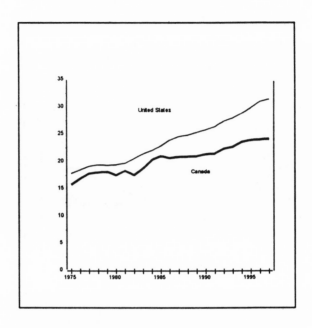

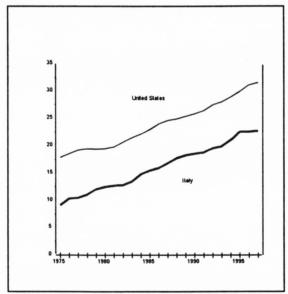

Chart 1. Manufacturing Productivity Levels (*continued*)

UVRs for total manufacturing reported in table 9. Apparently the difference in output price ratio estimates is partly offset by other differences in the output and labor input data underlying the two sets of productivity estimates.[29]

Across individual manufacturing subsectors much larger differences emerge. Some of the larger differences can be attributed to differences in definitions. For example, the EPPP estimate includes fabricated metal products with the machinery and equipment subsector, whereas the UVR estimates include those products with the basic metals subsector. The comparative estimates for those two subsectors suggest that labor productivity in Japan's fabricated metal products industry is quite low, since estimates for those subsectors are substantially lower when that industry is included than when it is not included. There are also some areas of striking agreement among the two sets of estimates. In particular, both the EPPP- and UVR-based estimates indicate that productivity in the Japanese food processing subsector is far below that in other countries.

TABLE 11. Comparison of EPPP and UVR Based Manufacturing Productivity Estimates for 1990 (Indexed to US level = 100)

		US	Japan	Germany	France	UK
Total Manufacturing, 1990	EPPP	100	67	83	94	60
	UVR	100	78	86	91	66
Food, Beverages, and Tobacco	EPPP	100	35	84	93	102
	UVR	100	37	76	79	54
Textiles, Apparel, and Footwear	EPPP	100	28	55	57	48
	UVR	100	48	88	89	65
Chemical, Petroleum, and Products	EPPP	100	128	70	126	51
	UVR	100	84	77	84	86
Basic Metals	EPPP	100	145	91	96	54
	UVR	100	96	99	93	80
Machinery, Equipment, and Fabricated Metal	EPPP	100	78	88	87	46
	UVR	100	114	88	98	66
Other Manufactured Products	EPPP	100	54	81	97	70
	UVR	100	55	79	90	60

Note:
EPPP = estimates from current study
UVR = estimates from the ICOP (reported in Van Ark (1995); the UVR estimates include fabricated metal products with basic metals instead of machinery and equipment.

Compensation

How productivity translates into unit labor cost levels depends on the level of labor compensation. Our comparison of compensation levels across countries is based on total wage and nonwage compensation, including health and retirement benefits, leave (including vacations and holidays), and employer expenditures for other legally required programs. These compensation data were also taken from OECD national accounts data and are defined on a consistent basis with the value added data.

Table 12 shows compensation per hour for the G-7 countries translated to U.S. dollars at current nominal exchange rates. Movements over time in comparative compensation rates for total manufacturing may be seen more clearly in chart 2, which shows each country's compensation per hour in dollars and in local currency, along with the U.S. level in dollars. These data indicate that exchange rate movements have had a dominant influence on the relative levels of compensation. Whereas U.S. compensation per hour was substantially above that in the other countries in all subsectors during 1985, by 1990 it had fallen below those in Germany and France in most cases as a result of the sharp depreciation of the dollar from its peak level in early 1985. As indicated in chart 2, this trend continued into the 1990s, and by 1995, compensation per hour for total manufacturing (measured in current dollars) in Germany, France, and Japan was substantially above the U.S. level.

The dispersion of compensation rates across sectors is somewhat wider in Japan and the United States than in the continental European countries (see table 12). The narrower dispersion in Europe no doubt reflects the greater significance of mandated government programs and employment protection legislation in those countries. In 1990, the ratio of nonwage or "additional" compensation (much of which is government mandated in Europe) to hourly earnings received by manufacturing production workers was more than 75 percent in Italy, France, and Germany, compared with only 18 percent in Japan. The United States and the United Kingdom were in the middle, at 38 percent and 34 percent respectively. Moreover, in the continental European countries, union contracts by law are extended to non-union workers. Gittleman and Wolff (1993) have found that the degree of cross-sector wage dispersion within countries is negatively correlated with the degree of unionization within countries. As indicated in the bottom two panels of table 13, our estimates of compensation rates in Japan and Germany (relative to the U.S. levels) are fairly similar to those calculated by the ICOP project.

Our estimates of unit labor costs are shown in table 13 and chart 3. The combination of a relatively high level of productivity and moderate level of compensation resulted in the United States having the lowest level of unit labor costs for total manufacturing among the G-7 countries in 1990. The strong influence of movements in nominal exchange rates on relative unit labor cost levels can be seen in the shift between 1985 and 1990. In 1985, when the dollar was at a peak level, U.S. unit labor costs for total manufacturing were uniformly higher than those in the other G-7 countries. Over much of the period shown in chart 3, foreign unit labor costs tended to fluctuate around the U.S. level; during the 1970s and 1980s, these pictures seem fully consistent with findings of mean reversion towards purchasing power parity.

When the estimates are extrapolated to the mid-1990s, however, differences vis-a-vis Japan and Germany appear to be outside the range of differences recorded during the 1970s and 1980s. At average nominal exchange rates prevailing during 1995, U.S. unit labor costs were as much

TABLE 12.   Compensation per Hours (Dollars per Hour)

	US	Japan	Germany	France	Italy	UK	Canada
Total Manufacturing, 1990	18	15	23	21	17	15	17
Food, Beverages, and Tobacco	16	12	17	21	18	14	16
Textiles, Apparel, and Footwear	10	8	16	16	12	9	12
Chemical, Petroleum, and Products	21	25	27	24	21	16	18
Basic Metals	21	19	23	18	20	12	19
Machinery, Equipment, and l Fabricated Meta	20	15	24	22	19	13	19
Other Manufactured Products	16	13	20	21	17	15	17
Total Manufacturing, 1985	15	7	10	10	8	7	12
Food, Beverages, and Tobacco	14	6	7	10	8	7	11
Textiles, Apparel, and Footwear	9	4	7	8	6	5	8
Chemical, Petroleum, and Products	17	12	12	12	10	7	12
Basic Metals	18	9	10	10	10	6	15
Machinery, Equipment, and Fabricated Metal	17	8	11	11	9	7	13
Other Manufactured Products	13	6	9	10	8	8	12
Total Manufacturing, 1980	11	6	12	12	8	8	9
Food, Beverages, and Tobacco	11	5	10	13	8	8	9
Textiles, Apparel, and Footwear	7	4	8	9	6	6	6
Chemical, Petroleum, and Products	13	9	15	14	10	9	10
Basic Metals	15	9	13	12	10	7	12
Machinery, Equipment, and Fabricated Metal	12	6	13	13	9	9	10
Other Manufactured Products	10	6	11	12	8	9	9

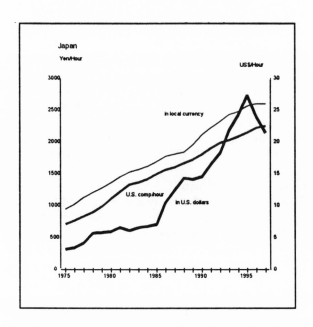

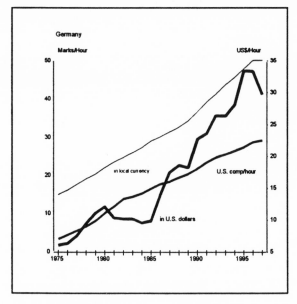

Chart 2. Compensation per Hour of Manufacturing Employees

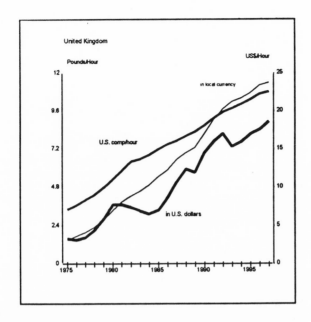

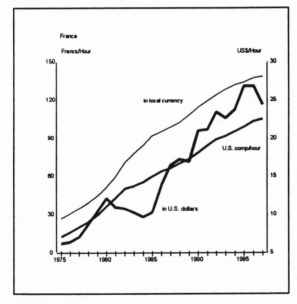

Chart 2. Compensation per Hour of Manufacturing Employees
(*continued*)

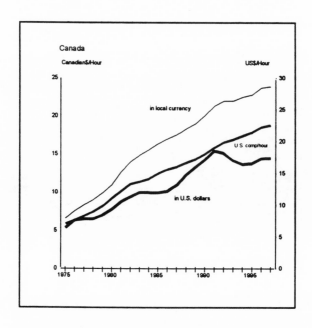

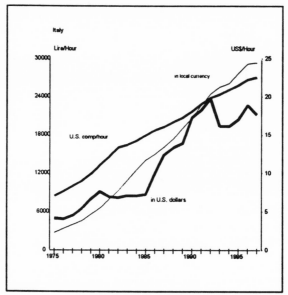

Chart 2. Compensation per Hour of Manufacturing Employees
(*continued*)

as 45 to 50 percent below those in Germany and Japan (see also table 14).[30] The widening of the gap between U.S. unit labor costs on the one hand and German and Japanese labor costs on the other hand between 1990 and 1995 can be attributed almost completely to movements in nominal exchange rates.[31] Unit labor costs in France and the United Kingdom were estimated to be noticeably above the U.S. level in 1995, although the gap was a good deal less than in the case of Japan and Germany. Unit labor costs in Italy and Canada were roughly in line with the U.S. level.

These outcomes for total manufacturing do not hold for all subsectors, although the subsectoral comparisons are somewhat more tentative. In 1990, productivity levels in Japan and France in the chemicals and basic metals subsectors appeared to be high enough relative to the U.S. levels to

TABLE 13. Unit Labor Cost Levels (Dollars per unit of Output)

	US	Japan	Germany	France	Italy	UK	Canada
Total Manufacturing, 1990	70	85	106	86	93	93	80
Food, Beverages, and Tobacco	53	116	65	73	59	46	73
Textiles, Apparel, and Footwear	76	200	207	199	120	142	118
Chemical, Petroleum, and Products	55	51	99	49	108	81	64
Basic Metals	77	46	90	67	90	82	97
Machinery, Equipment, and Fabricated Metal	79	76	109	97	99	113	76
Other Manufactured Products	68	107	106	93	88	91	95
Total Manufacturing, 1985	66	53	50	54	50	56	56
Food, Beverages, and Tobacco	46	57	31	40	32	25	50
Textiles, Apparel, and Footwear	74	94	105	108	65	78	80
Chemical, Petroleum, and Products	55	28	46	41	58	45	45
Basic Metals	69	29	45	56	48	53	67
Machinery, Equipment, and Fabricated Metal	79	54	52	60	54	71	55
Other Manufactured Products	61	62	52	50	45	54	62
Total Manufacturing, 1980	57	54	73	77	63	84	52
Food, Beverages, and Tobacco	40	42	43	57	37	34	43
Textiles, Apparel, and Footwear	66	82	156	154	75	117	77
Chemical, Petroleum, and Products	50	36	66	65	74	73	43
Basic Metals	55	22	69	75	63	115	68
Machinery, Equipment, and Fabricated Metal	67	62	74	84	69	109	55
Other Manufactured Products	54	69	71	71	48	70	54

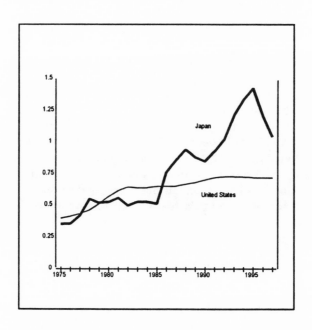

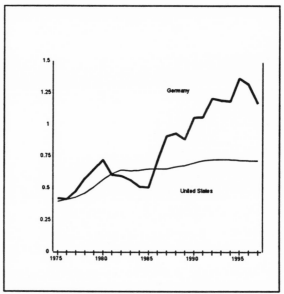

Chart 3. Manufacturing Unit Labor Costs (Dollars per unit of output; Output units measured in 1990 U.S. dollars)

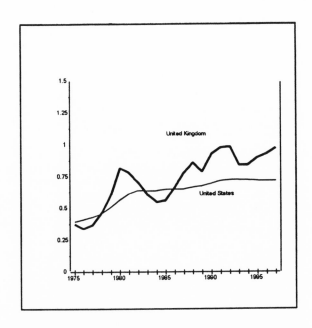

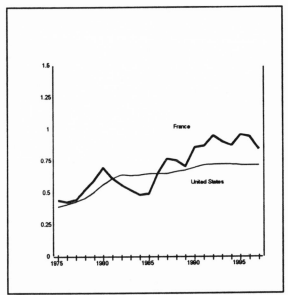

Chart 3. Manufacturing Unit Labor Costs (*continued*)

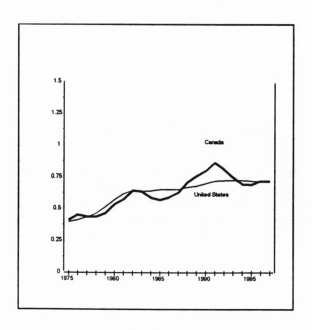

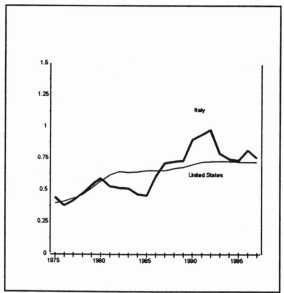

Chart 3. Manufacturing Unit Labor Costs (*continued*)

place their unit labor cost below the U.S. level. The same was true for machinery and equipment in Japan and Canada. At the other end of the spectrum, very low levels of productivity in the Japanese food and textile subsectors resulted in unit labor costs more than double the U.S. levels. The levels of unit labor costs in the European textiles and apparel and wood, paper, and nonmetallic mineral products subsectors also were extremely high, reflecting the combination of relatively high compensation rates (partly due to government mandated programs) and low productivity. In Europe and the United States, unlike Japan, food and beverages appears to be a relatively high-productivity, low-unit labor cost subsector. In Germany and Japan, the results for total manufacturing reflect those for the machinery and equipment subsector, which accounts for more than half of manufacturing output in those countries. This is a substantially greater share than in the other major industrial countries. Notwithstanding the strong international trade performance that both Germany and Japan have had in machinery, German unit labor costs in that subsector were as much as 40 percent above the U.S. level in 1990 by our estimates. By 1995, both German and Japanese unit labor costs would have been substantially above the U.S. level.

Table 14 compares our estimates of unit labor costs for total manufacturing (relative to a U.S. level of 100) with the ICOP or van Ark-Pilat estimates (reported by van Ark 1995), as well as with those reported in studies by Hooper and Larin (1989) and Turner and Van't dack (1993), both of which employed unadjusted weighted averages of EPPPs on goods, and by Golub (1994), which used the PPP for total GDP. Our estimates for 1990 tend to be somewhat higher than the others in the case of Japan and Germany, but below the estimates reported by Van't dack for the other countries. For Japan, the van Ark-Pilat estimate is somewhat below the other studies, and for Germany, the Golub estimate is noticeably below the others. In the earlier years, the Hooper-Larin result appears to be an outlier on the high side for Germany.

The table also shows our own estimates and the van Ark-Pilat estimates extrapolated to 1995. The results are qualitatively similar. The most notable quantitative difference is with respect to Japan: our estimates suggest that Japanese unit labor costs were more than 90 percent above the U.S. level at exchange rates prevailing in 1995, whereas the van Ark-Pilat estimates suggest the difference was closer to 60 percent. In the other cases, the two sets of estimates seem remarkably close in view of the differences in methodology and data employed.

Conclusion

Attempts to make international comparisons of levels of unit labor costs have had to contend with significant deficiencies in the data, particularly with respect to the derivation of output price ratios needed to compare labor productivity across countries. Unit value ratios are imperfect measures of relative manufacturing output prices, partly because they suffer from incomplete coverage of finished goods and especially more sophisticated products. Expenditure purchasing power parities are imperfect as well. They suffer from inadequate coverage of intermediate goods and from a variety of factors that cause PPPs to differ conceptually from output price ratios, including distribution margins, net indirect taxes, and import and export prices. Our empirical analysis has focused largely on these latter deficiencies in the EPPP approach. We find that for total man-

TABLE 14.   Alternative Estimates of Unit Labor Cost Levels for Total Manufacturing (Indexed to US level = 100)

	US	Japan	Germany	France	Italy	UK
1990						
Hooper-Vrankovich	100	121	152	124	133	115
Van Ark-Pilat*	100	100	142	112		137
Turner-Van't dack	100	110	154	144	134	145
Golub**	100	119	119			
1985						
Hooper-Vrankovich	100	79	76	82	76	85
Van Ark-Pilat*	100	66	70	78		88
Hooper-Larin	100	69	93	76	59	95
Golub	100	73	73			
1980						
Hooper-Vrankovich	100	95	128	136	110	147
Van Ark-Pilat*	100	79	112	123		146
Hooper-Larin	100	86	154	116	90	163
Golub	100	85	113			
1995* **						
Hooper-Vrankovich	100	198	179	130	100	138
Van Ark-Pilat*	100	159	174	124		114
Nominal Exchange Rate 1995 (local currency per US dollar)	1.00	94.00	1.43	4.99	1629.00	0.63

    * Van Ark (1995)
    ** Data are for 1989
    *** Estimates are extrapolated from 1990 levels using IMF manufacturing unit labor cost data for 1995:Q1-Q3 and nominal exchange rates are for the year 1995.

ufacturing at least, the deficiencies are less severe than might have been expected. Distribution margins do make a difference, but in most cases it is not large. Moreover, contrary to widely held perceptions, recent studies have suggested that distribution margins are actually wider in the United States than in other G-7 countries, so that U.S. output prices are even lower relative to those abroad than the EPPPs suggest. The effects of differences in net indirect tax rates appear to be still less important. Our adjustment for the influence of import and export prices had little effect on the outcome, although the adjustment was crude and incomplete at best. We also have taken initial steps to improve the coverage of intermediate goods prices by employing UVR-based estimates for the basic metals subsector.

Our results indicate that in 1990, among the G-7 countries, the United States had the lowest level of output prices, the highest level of labor productivity, and the lowest level of unit labor costs for total manufacturing. Extrapolated to 1995, our estimates suggest that U.S. unit labor costs in manufacturing were as much as 45 to 50 percent below those in Germany and Japan, although differences in the machinery and transportation equipment subsector were somewhat smaller and differences with other major industrial countries for total manufacturing were considerably smaller.

Our estimates differ somewhat from those of other studies. In particular, compared with the results of the ICOP project (based wholly on UVRs), we show a greater difference between U.S. and foreign unit labor costs, especially vis-a-vis Japan. Nevertheless, both approaches agree that at average nominal exchange rates prevailing during 1995, U.S. manufacturing unit labor costs were well below those in Japan and Germany. Moreover, in view of the differences in techniques and data employed by these two approaches, the results are in many cases remarkably similar.

We also considered relative price and productivity levels for various subsectors of manufacturing, though the data and our adjustments in this case are a good deal less precise than for total manufacturing. These disaggregated data suggest that the relatively high level of unit labor costs in the other (non-U.S.) G-7 countries reflects extremely low levels of productivity in the Japanese food and textile subsectors, and relatively high rates of labor compensation in Europe in subsectors where productivity is relatively low.

While our findings may answer some questions, they raise others, both substantive and methodological. Perhaps the key substantive finding is the large gap that prevailed during the first half of the 1990s between U.S. manufacturing unit labor costs on the one hand and German and especially Japanese unit labor costs on the other. Given the tendency for purchasing power parity to be mean-reverting, how would such unit labor cost gaps be likely to close over time—through adjustment of nominal exchange rates or adjustment of domestic prices, wages, or productivity? To what extent have downward pressures on wages and prices in Japan during the mid-1990s reflected such longer-term trend effects? How are these cost differentials reconciled with the persistence of large external deficits in the United States and large external surpluses in Japan, and does the existence of such cost differentials indicate the potential for adjustment of these external imbalances in the longer term?

The more central focus of this paper has been on methodological issues. We have made some advancements in the EPPP approach to measuring unit labor cost levels, but we also leave ample room for further work in this area. More could be done to refine estimates of distribution margins, especially at the level of manufacturing subsectors. Our adjustment for trade prices is at best only a crude first attempt. Finally, significant further improvements in the estimation of comparative unit labor cost levels might be made by taking greater advantage of complementary strengths of the EPPP and UVR approaches. The former approach provides better coverage of finished goods and the latter better coverage of intermediate goods. We have taken only a preliminary step in this direction, and there is scope for a more comprehensive effort to combine the two approaches.

NOTES

1. The use of nominal exchange rates to translate compensation levels into a common currency is appropriate from a "cost" perspective, such as the perspective of a firm or investors comparing current levels of labor costs across countries. From a welfare perspective (i.e., when comparing the command of labor compensation over expenditure on goods and services), it may be more appropriate to translate compensation at expenditure PPPs (defined below). The focus of the current paper is on the cost side.

2. The tendency for nominal exchange rates to diverge widely from movements over time in the ratios of domestic price levels (whether for nontradables or tradables) has been well established empirically. See, for example, Turner and Van't dack (1993).

3. O'Mahony also uses the EPPP approach (described further below) for some sectors where UVRs could not be obtained.

4. The OECD also uses this procedure in its International Sectoral Database to translate manufacturing outputs at the industry level across countries into common currency units.

5. The International Economics Department of the World Bank has constructed

spreadsheets containing detailed data from the U.N. International Comparison Program for 1975, 1980, 1985, and 1990. These spreadsheets are available on the World Bank's "STARS" diskettes and are described in World Bank (1993).

6. The subsectors include: (1) food, beverage, and tobacco products, (2) textiles, apparel, and footwear, (3) chemicals, petroleum refining, and rubber and plastic products, (4) machinery, equipment, and fabricated metal products, and (5) other manufactures, which include, among other products, paper and printing, wood and furniture products, and non-metallic mineral products.

7. If the indirect taxes are retail sales taxes, in principle, the tax adjustment would precede the adjustment for distribution margins as one works back from expenditure prices to factory gate prices. In many cases, however, indirect taxes are collected at other levels of production and distribution, as with value added taxes in Europe. In any event, it makes no difference algebraically whether the tax adjustment is made before or after the adjustment for distribution margins.

8. As noted by van Ark (1993), the UVR methodology suffers to a considerable extent from the same difficulty.

9. The EKS (Elteto-Koves-Szulc) method pertains to the way in which individual commodity PPPs are aggregated up to PPPs for total GDP. The EKS method gives roughly equal weight to the pattern of expenditures in all the countries being compared (in this case the OECD countries). Its main attraction is that it allows for consistent cross-country or third-country comparisons of relative price levels. Its main weakness is that it does not allow for arithmetic adding-up of individual expenditure components to total GDP in any given country. The primary competing method of aggregation is the Geary-Khamis (GK) method, which employs expenditure weights that are specific to any two countries that are being compared. This method does allow for adding-up of components, but it effectively gives greater weight to larger countries and entails less consistency in third-country comparisons. That is, the PPPs between countries A and B and between countries A and C may not yield a consistent comparison for countries B and C if country A's expenditure pattern differs significantly from those of the other two. The present analysis begins with PPPs at a relatively low level of aggregation and aggregates them with a methodology that lies somewhere between the GK and EKS methodologies. The method of aggregation in the present paper entails using average expenditure (and output) weights for the group of seven countries combined, which tends to increase the multilateral comparability of the results at the cost of somewhat reduced bilateral comparability. As will be shown, however, the different aggregation methods do not make a significant difference to the results. See Kravis et al. (1975) for a detailed description and discussion of the pros and cons of the alternative PPP aggregation methods. They also describe the "Walsh" method, which is essentially the one used here.

10. The problems that computer prices pose to international comparisons of output and productivity are discussed in greater detail in the next section and by Wyckoff (1993).

11. EPPPs were not available for basic metal industries; to compute weighted averages for total manufacturing the ICOP UVRs for basic metals as substitutes

was used wherever they were available. When UVRs were not available (as in the case of Italy and Canada), the EPPPs for machinery were used.

12. The outputs in table 4 are value added data from the OECD National Accounts, translated to dollars using the output price ratios computed in this paper.

13. The sources are listed in table 5.

14. In principle, this margin (as defined in equation 4) should include transportation costs, but this exclusion probably does not affect the results greatly. U.S. input-output data indicate that transportation costs typically amount to only about 2 to 3 percent of final sales—far less than wholesale and retail margins. (See U.S. Department of Commerce 1994.) Also, as noted below, Nishimura (1993) has found that U.S. and Japanese transportation margins are similar in magnitude.

15. The margins were shown to be relatively stable over time, which suggests that application of data on margins for 1987 (the latest year available) to the calculation of OPRs in 1990 probably is not a significant source of error. Retail margins were not reported for Italy or Canada. U.S. margins were used for Canada and an average of the French and German margins for Italy.

16. Nishimura corrects for several statistical shortcomings in the OECD project's (Maruyama's) estimates for Japanese distribution margins. He also compares transportation margins across U.S. and Japanese industries using input-output data and finds these margins to be both small (between 1 and 3 percent of final sales) and similar between the two countries.

17. In several cases where data were not available for 1990, data for 1989 (or if necessary, 1988) were used instead. Over the preceding ten years, net tax rates generally varied by less than 1 percentage point in each of these countries.

18. Based on OECD National Accounts data, the rates of net indirect taxes on value added in the wholesale and retail trade sectors overall are generally within several percentage points of those for total manufacturing in most countries. The tax rate for U.S. distribution sectors is slightly higher than for manufacturing, and that in most other countries is somewhat lower than that for manufacturing. Thus, differences are in a direction that would tend to increase the margin by which the adjusted U.S. price level falls below that in Japan and Europe.

19. This result for the United States is somewhat counterintuitive. Why should a country whose output price is below the "world" price be running a large deficit in that sector? Part of the problem is that the measure of the world price level is limited to an average for G-7 countries. In the case of textiles and apparel in particular, this limitation probably overstates the level that would be derived if the production and prices of developing countries were taken into account. Nevertheless, a more accurate (i.e., lower) measure of world prices for purposes of this adjustment would not greatly affect the comparison of price levels, at least among the G-7 countries that run trade deficits in this sector. This is because the greater upward adjustment of German and Japanese output prices, for example, would be largely offset by a smaller downward adjustment of U.S. output prices.

20. In the case of Japan and Germany UVRs were available for 1990; for the United Kingdom, UVRs for 1987 were extrapolated using relative value added

deflators obtained from OECD national accounts data. Van Ark and Pilat used the same methodology to extrapolate their 1987 UVRs for Germany and Japan to 1990.

21. Indeed, because of the way the UVRs were extrapolated from 1987 to 1990 (with unit-value deflators), the numbers shown here may actually understate the difference between the OPRs and the UVRs. That is, because of differences in the measurement of computer prices in the United States (where they are falling rapidly) and the other countries (where they are relatively stable), the UVRs reported here are probably biased *upward* by between 5 and 10 percent for total manufacturing and between 15 and 20 percent for machinery and equipment.

22. See OECD (1988 and 1993) for a full description of the ISDB.

23. Due to criticism of its methodology for calculating real output for industry, the Bureau of Economic Analysis (BEA) suspended publication of its data in 1989 and began an efforts to address some of the complaints. Lawrence (1991) provides a discussion of many of the criticisms of the data. See Parker (1993) for a full description of the improvements BEA made to the gross product originating data.

24. To the extent that the other countries have not undertaken similar steps to improve their estimates of real output, additional biases to the comparability of results across countries could have been introduced by using the updated U.S. data.

25. Data on hours at the subsector level are available from national accounts for the United States and Canada. In both countries, hours per employee appear to be relatively stable across subsectors. Nevertheless, hours are preferable over employment in cross-country comparisons of productivity, because of significant cross-country differences in hours per employee in total manufacturing (with the Japanese ratio far exceeding the German ratio for example). Any mismeasurement of hours at the subsector level does not affect our estimation of unit labor costs below, since hours cancel out of the numerator and the denominator of unit labor costs.

26. These extrapolations and the data underlying charts 1–3 below, which show movements over time in unit labor costs and their components, are based on indexes constructed by the BLS and the IMF.

27. Wyckoff (1993) examines how the methods used by various countries to calculate computer price deflators affects comparisons of labor productivity. He finds that the use of hedonic versus matched-model methods can lead to substantial differences in estimates of productivity growth, with the difference increasing at each level of disaggregation. Substituting the U.S. hedonic computer price index for Germany's non-hedonic index, for example, raised the annual growth rate of Germany's overall manufacturing real output and labor productivity by 20 percent. The same substitution raised the rate of growth of output and productivity in nonelectrical machinery in Germany and several other countries by a factor of two or three. Of the G-7 countries, only the United States and Canada use hedonic price indexes for computers. This factor would not have caused a further bias in our comparisons prior to 1985, since the United States did not adopt the hedonic index for computers until 1987.

28. The Japanese data for the chemical subsector are not fully comparable with the other countries because the Japanese national accounts do not include plastics and rubber products in the chemicals subsector. The Japanese textile subsector also differed from those of other countries in that apparel is included not there but with "other manufactures" instead.

29. The ICOP UVR-based productivity estimates are based on output and labor input data taken from the census of manufactures, whereas the EPPP-based estimates are computed using data from national income and product accounts and the BLS.

30. The extrapolations were based in part on BLS and IMF manufacturing unit-labor cost indexes and their components.

31. Between 1990 and early 1995, U.S. unit labor costs rose faster than those in Japan (measured in local currencies), and about the same as those in Germany.

REFERENCES

Betancourt, Roger R. 1993. "An Analysis of the U.S. Distribution System." OECD Working Papers, no. 135, Paris.

Boucher Breuer, Janice. 1994. "An Assessment of the Evidence on Purchasing Power Parity." In John Williamson, ed., *Estimating Equilibrium Exchange Rates.* Washington: Institute for International Economics, pp. 245–277.

Davis, Steven J. 1992. "Cross-Country Patterns of Change in Relative Wages." National Bureau of Economic Research, Inc., Working Paper, no. 4085, June.

Dawson, John A. 1993. 'The Distribution Sector in the United Kingdom." OECD Working Papers, no. 140, Paris.

Dollar, David, and Wolff, Edward N. 1988. "Convergence of Industry Labor Productivity Among Advanced Economies, 1963–1982." *The Review of Economics and Statistics* 4:549–558.

Edison, Hali. 1987. "Purchasing Power Parity in the Long Run: A Test of the Dollar/Pound Exchange Rate (1890–78)." *Journal of Money, Credit, and Banking* 19:376–87.

Frankel, Jeffrey. 1986. "International Capital Mobility and Crowding-out in the U.S. Economy: Imperfect Integration of Financial Markets or of Goods Markets?" In Ruth Hafer, ed., *How Open is the U.S. Economy.* Lexington, Mass: Lexington, pp. 33–74.

Froot, Kenneth, and Rogoff, Kenneth. 1995. "Perspectives on PPP and Long-Run Real Exchange Rates." In Gene M. Grossman and Kenneth Rogoff, eds., *Handbook of International Economics.*

Gault, Nigel. 1985. "The Competitiveness of U.S. Manufacturing Industry: International Comparisons of Labor, Energy, and Capital Costs." Data Resources, Inc.

Gittleman, Maury, and Wolff, Edward N. 1993. "International Comparisons of Inter-Industry Wage Differentials." *Journal of the International Association for Research in Income and Wealth* 39:295–312.

Golub, Stephen S. 1994. "Comparative Advantage, Exchange Rates, and G-7 Sectoral Trade Balances." IMF Working Paper 94/5.

Hooper, Peter, and Larin, Kathryn A. 1989. "International Comparisons of Labor Costs in Manufacturing." *Review of Income and Wealth* 35:161–175.

Ito, Takatoshi, and Maruyama, Masayoshi. 1991. "Is the Japanese Distribution System Really Inefficient." In Paul Krugman, ed., *Trade with Japan.* The University of Chicago Press, pp. 149–173.

Jorgenson, Dale W., and Kuroda, Masahiro. 1992. "Productivity and International Competitiveness in Japan and the United States, 1960–1985." *Economic Studies Quarterly* 43: 313–25.

Jorgenson, Dale W., and Nishimizu, Mieko. 1987. "Japan-US Industry-level Comparison, 1960–1979." *Journal of the Japanese and International Economies* 1:1–30.

Kravis, Irving B.; Kenessy, Zoltan; Heston, Alan; and Summers, Robert. 1975. "A System of International Comparisons of Gross Product and Purchasing Power." *United Nations International Comparison Project: Phase One.* Baltimore: Johns Hopkins University Press.

Kravis, Irving B.; Heston, Alan; and Summers, Robert. 1982. "World Product and Income: International Comparisons of Real Gross Product." *United Nations International Comparison Project: Phase Three.* Baltimore: Johns Hopkins University Press.

Kravis, Irving B., and Lipsey, Robert E. 1991. "The International Comparison Program: Current Status and Problems." In Peter Hooper and J.D. Richardson, eds., *International Economic Transactions: Issues in Measurement and Empirical Research.* Chicago: University of Chicago Press, pp. 437–464.

Lachner, Josef; Tager, Uwe Chr; and Weitzel, Gunter. 1993. "The German Distribution System." OECD Working Papers, no. 137, Paris.

Lawrence, Robert Z. 1991. "Issues in Measurement and International Comparison of Output Growth in Manufacturing." In Peter Hooper and J. David Richardson, eds., *International Economic Transactions: Issues in Measurement and Empirical Research.* Chicago: University of Chicago Press, pp. 357–380.

Lichtenberg, Frank R., and Griliches, Zvi. 1989. "Errors of Measurement in Output Deflators." *Journal of Business and Economic Statistics* 7:1–9.

Maddison, Angus, and Van Ark, Bart. 1994. "The International Comparison of Real Product and Productivity." Institute of Economic Research, University of Groningen, Research Memorandum 567 (GD-6).

Maruyama, Masayoshi. 1993. "A Study of the Distribution System in Japan." OECD Working Papers, no. 136, Paris.

McKinsey & Company, Inc. 1993. *Manufacturing Productivity,* Washington, D.C.

Messerlin, Patrick A. 1993. "The French Distribution Industry and the Openness of the French Economy." OECD Working Papers, no. 138, Paris.

Meyer zu Slochtern, F.J.M., and Meyer zu Schlochtern, J.L. 1994. "An International Sectoral Data Base for Fourteen OECD Countries." OECD Economics Working Papers, no. 145, Paris.

Neef, Arthur; Kask, Christopher; and Sparks, Christopher. 1993. "International

Comparisons of Manufacturing Unit Labor Costs." *Monthly Labor Review* 116:47–58.

Nishimura, Kiyohiko. 1993. "The Distribution System of Japan and the United States: a Comparative Study From the Viewpoint of Final-goods Buyers." *Japan and the World Economy* 5:265–288.

O' Mahony, Mary. 1992. "Productivity Levels in British and German Manufacturing Industry." *National Institute Economic Review* 139:46–63.

OECD Department of Economics and Statistics. 1985. "Purchasing Power Parities and Real Expenditures" Paris.

OECD Working Paper. 1988. "An International Sectoral Database for Thirteen Countries." no. 57, pp. A–1.

OECD Statistics Directorate. 1992. "Purchasing Power Parities and Real Expenditures, 1990." vol.1, Paris.

OECD Statistics Directorate. 1993a. "Purchasing Power Parities and Real Expenditures, 1990." vol.2, Paris.

OECD Statistics Directorate. 1993b. "The International Sectoral Database." Paris, mimeo.

OECD Statistics Directorate. 1994. "National Accounts, 1980–1992." vol. 2, Paris.

Paige, D., and Bombach, G. 1959. *A Comparison of National Output and Productivity of the UK and the US,* OEEC, Paris.

Parker, Robert P. 1993. "Gross Product by Industry, 1977–90." *Survey of Current Business* 73:33–54.

Pellegrini, Luca, and Cardani, Angelo M. 1993. "The Italian Distribution System." OECD Working Papers, no. 139, Paris.

Pilat, Dirk, and Van Ark, Bart. 1994. "Competitiveness in Manufacturing: A Comparison of Germany, Japan and the United States." *BNL Quarterly Review* 47:167–186.

Prais, S.J. 1981. *Productivity and Industrial Structure: A Statistical Study of Manufacturing Industry in Britain, Germany, and the United States.* New York: Cambridge University Press.

Roy, A.D. 1982. "Labour Productivity in 1980: An International Comparison." *National Institute Economic Review* 11:26–37.

Roy, D.J. 1987. "International Comparisons of Real Value Added, Productivity and Energy Intensity in 1980." *Economic Trends* 404:87–98.

Smith, A.D.; Hitchens, D.M.W.N.; and Davies, S.W. 1982. "International Industrial Productivity: A Comparison of Britain, America, and Germany." *National Institute Economic Review* 11:13–25.

Stoneman, Paul, and Francis, Nathan Francis. 1992. "Double Deflation and the Measurement of Output and Productivity in UK Manufacturing 1979–1989." presented at a meeting of the ESRC Industrial Economics Study Group at the London Business School.

Stern, Robert M. 1962. "British and American Productivity and Comparative Costs in International Trade." *Oxford Economic Papers.*

Szirmai, Adam, and Pilat, Dirk. 1990. "Comparisons of Purchasing Power, Real Output and Labour Productivity in Manufacturing in Japan, South Korea and the U.S.A., 1975–85." *Review of Income and Wealth* 36:1–31.

Turner, Philip, and Van't dack, Jozef. 1993. "Measuring International Price and Cost Competitiveness." BIS Economic Papers, no. 39, Bank for International Settlements, Basle.

U.S. Department of Commerce, Survey of Current Business. 1994. "Benchmark Input-Output Accounts for the U.S. Economy, 1987" vol. 74, no. 4.

van Ark, Bart. 1992. "Comparative Productivity in British and American Manufacturing,." *National Institute Economic Review* 142:63–79.

van Ark, Bart. 1993. "The ICOP Approach—Its Implications and Applicability." *Explaining Economic Growth: Essays in Honour of Angus Maddison.* The Netherlands: Elsevier Science Publishers.

van Ark, Bart, and Pilat, Dirk. 1993. "Productivity Levels in Germany, Japan, and the United States: Differences and Causes." *Brookings Papers: Microeconomics 2*, pp. 1–48.

van Ark, Bart. 1995. "Productivity and Competitiveness in Manufacturing: A Comparison of Europe, Japan and the United States." *International Productivity Differences, Measurement and Explanations.* North Holland.

van Ark, Bart, and Kouwenhoven, R.D.J. 1994. "Productivity in French Manufacturing: An International Comparative Perspective." Institute of Economic Research, University of Groningen, Research Memorandum 571 (GD-10).

Wei, Shang-Jin, and Parsley, David C. 1994. "Purchasing Power Disparity During the Floating Rate Period: Exchange Rate Volatility, Trade Barriers and Other Culprits." Kennedy School, Harvard University, mimeo.

World Bank. 1993. "Purchasing Power of Currencies, Comparing National Incomes Using ICP Data, Technical Note and Sample Tables with *Stars* Diskettes." World Bank.

CHAPTER 11

Stock Market Evaluations of a European Monetary Union

Filip Abraham and Aileen Thompson

The creation of a European Monetary Union (EMU) has been at the heart of the economic policy debate in Europe. It has also generated a vast theoretical literature on the costs and benefits of further monetary integration. From a microeconomic perspective, EMU may lead to important benefits by reducing exchange rate risk. From a macroeconomic perspective, the fixing of exchange rates and the transfer of monetary policy to the European level could reinforce the credibility of low inflation policies. On the other hand, giving up national monetary and exchange rate policies represents the loss of potentially important mechanisms to cope with adverse country-specific shocks.

The Maastricht Treaty, signed in December 1991, paved the way for a full-fledged monetary union between members of the European Union (EU). The ambitious Maastricht blueprint was hailed as a major breakthrough and was greeted with considerable enthusiasm. Soon, however, it faced formidable challenges. The Danish and the French referendums indicated a deep-seated mistrust on the part of European voters; and the exchange rate crises of 1992 and 1993 led to a crisis and reform of the Exchange Rate Mechanism (ERM), ending a prolonged period of exchange rate stability. The aftermath of German reunification and the quick deterioration of economic conditions in Europe raised serious doubts about a far-reaching transfer of national sovereignty to the European level. Increasingly, member states became aware of the potential costs and questioned the potential benefits of monetary integration.

Would monetary integration generate net benefits for European economies? In this paper, we address this question by employing stock market data to investigate investors' expectations about the consequences of EMU. Stock market analysis is particularly appropriate for a study of EMU because two of its most important potential benefits depend on *perceptions*. The impact of reduced exchange rate risk and increased credibility of anti-inflationary policies cannot be measured directly, but their importance can be inferred by analyzing investors' reactions to EMU news. To evaluate investors' perceptions, we estimate the reaction of individual European stock markets to seven events that are believed to have altered the probability that the Maastricht treaty would be implemented. These events include, for example, the unexpected rejection of the Maastricht treaty in the Danish referendum.

We first perform joint significance tests of the "abnormal" stock market returns to determine whether investors perceived these events to have important implications for European economies. Implicit in this test are two hypotheses: (1) the event in question had an important impact on the perceived probability that EMU would be implemented; and (2) EMU was expected to generate significant costs or benefits for individual economies. In the second stage of our analysis, we focus on the subset of events that generated significant stock market reactions. The patterns of abnormal returns among countries are analyzed to determine whether they are consistent with economic theories about the potential costs and benefits of EMU.

The remainder of the paper is organized as follows. In the next section we provide a brief overview of the Maastricht treaty. We describe, in the ensuing section, the events and their implications for EMU. In addition, we distinguish between those countries that were directly affected by the event and those that were only indirectly affected by the event through its implications for the feasibility of EMU. For example, the Danish referendum had a primary effect on Denmark while the impact on the other EU countries depends on the perceived probability that EMU could be implemented without Denmark. In the following section, we briefly review the literature on the costs and benefits of EMU in order to derive predictions about the potential impact of EMU news on the stock markets of individual countries. In the fourth section we discuss the methodology and the data for our empirical analysis. In the following section we present the empirical results. Finally, we conclude the paper with a summary of the main findings.

Brief Background

At the outset of the paper, it is worthwhile to define precisely what we mean by EMU. We take as our benchmark the Maastricht Treaty on EMU. Maastricht foresees the irrevocable fixing of exchange rates for the participating countries in the final stage of EMU, which starts on January 1, 1997 at the earliest and on January 1, 1999 at the latest. The Treaty mentions, but does not provide, a timetable for the introduction of a single currency. At the beginning of the final stage, the European Central Bank (ECB) takes responsibility for the common monetary policy.

Not all EU countries will necessarily join the monetary union. Denmark and the United Kingdom obtained an "opt-out" which gives them the option not to participate in the final stage of EMU. At the start of the final stage potential candidates must satisfy convergence criteria for inflation, interest rates, public debt, public deficit, and exchange rate stability to be admitted. The exchange rate is of particular importance for this paper. Candidates for EMU must be part of the ERM and must have maintained a stable currency without devaluation for the two years preceding the ultimate stage of EMU.

Description of Events

This study focuses on seven events that, according to the financial press and policy-makers, had important implications for the future of EMU. An essential element of all of the events is that they were not *completely* anticipated. This suggests that they contained new information for investors. Therefore, with efficient capital markets, stock market returns on these event days should reflect expectations about EMU. The magnitude of the stock market response to a particular event depends on the impact of the event on investors' expectations as well as on the perceived consequences of EMU. In our discussion below, we draw on public opinion polls and news articles to illustrate the extent to which the events can be viewed as unanticipated.

We consider two different types of events occuring between 1991 and 1993: ratification events and currency crisis events. The former includes the treaty agreement reached during the Maastricht summit meeting as well as the ratification of the Treaty by individual member states. In particular, we assess the impact of the Danish, Irish and French referendums regarding the ratification of the Treaty and the ratification by the British parliament.

We consider two exchange rate crisis events: September 1992 and July 1993. During the first crisis, several countries either devalued their exchange rate or withdrew from the system. The second crisis led to the collapse of the ERM. Both episodes conflict with the exchange rate stability criterion for monetary union and therefore diminish the probability that EU members will satisfy the conditions for joining the final stage of EMU.

The events are discussed in more detail below and their main characteristics are summarized in table 1.

The Maastricht Treaty

The Maastricht summit meeting on December 9 and 10, 1991, completed a period of substantial, but not always smooth, progress toward monetary union that was initiated in a January 1988 Memorandum. One major hurdle concerned disagreement between Germany and France regarding the statutes and the responsibilities of the ECB and its predecessor, the European Monetary Institute. Although a growing consensus had emerged, the matter was not resolved prior to the beginning of the Maastricht summit. A second obstacle involved the acceptance of a single currency. The German Chancellor, in particular, was under pressure from his domestic constituency not to abandon the deutschemark for the ECU.

The opt-out clauses for the U.K. and Denmark were the other major difficulty facing EC ministers. On December 2, EC finance ministers decided to defer all decisions on this issue until the Maastricht summit meeting. The failure to find a solution on the first day of the summit led to uncertainty about the ultimate success of Maastricht. Negotiations continued all day on December 10. Well into the early morning hours of December 11, Britain finally obtained an opt-out for the Social Chapter in addition to the opt-out of monetary union. Denmark was given the opportunity to hold a referendum before joining EMU with the understanding that Denmark could opt-out if the referendum rejected the treaty.

As indicated in table 1, we measure stock market adjustments on

TABLE 1.   List of Events

Event Date	Description	Progress Toward EMU	Primary Effect
Referendums			
Dec. 11, 1991	Maastricht Summit	Positive	All
June 3, 1992	Danish Referendum	Negative	Denmark
June 19, 1992	Irish Referendum	Positive	Ireland
Sept. 21, 1992	French Referendum	Positive	France
July 23, 1993	British Ratification	Positive	U.K.
Currency Crises			
Sept. 17, 1992	Devaluation of Peseta	Negative	Spain
	Suspension of		U.K.
	and Lira		Italy
July 29, 30, &			
Aug. 2, 1993	ERM bands widened	Negative	Belgium
	after 2 days of		France
	speculative trading		Denmark

December 11 because this was the first day that the successful conclusion of the Maastricht Treaty was known to financial markets. Although the contents of the treaty were largely anticipated, the event contained the new information that an agreement had actually been reached. The Financial Times expressed its surprise by starting its lead article by "They did it" and by referring to the deal as "an astonishing compromise."[1] The Maastricht agreement was overwhelmingly endorsed by politicians and business alike. The Financial Times described the Treaty as "the biggest milestone in the Community's 34-year history."[2] In view of the enthusiastic reception of the agreement, we view the agreement as progress towards EMU for all nine EU countries in the sample. As all countries were directly affected by the news, we do not consider a secondary impact.

The Danish Referendum

The first test of public support for the Treaty was the Danish referendum held on June 2, 1992. Public opinion polls during the first three weeks of May indicated that a small majority of voters was opposed to the Treaty and then later, that a small majority was in favor of the Treaty. Polls released during the weekend prior to the referendum, however, indicated a strong increase in support for the Treaty. According to the Gallup Poll (Sunday, May 31), 44 percent of voters were in favor and 35 percent were opposed. Therefore, the Danish rejection of the Treaty was a surprise.

We consider June 3, the day the outcome of the referendum was learned, as the event date for our analysis. Undoubtedly, the event marked an important setback for Denmark in the progress towards EMU. In addition, this event posed a potential setback for other EC countries. It is not clear a priori, however, how important this setback was perceived to be. On the one hand, the other EC countries immediately announced that they would continue with the ratification process. On the other hand, the Danish rejection raised doubts about public support for the Treaty. Therefore, as indicated in table 1, this event is predicted to have had a primary effect on Denmark and only a secondary effect on the other EC countries.

The Irish Referendum

The Irish referendum was held less than three weeks later, on June 18. Although the public opinion polls released just prior to the referendum indicated that a strong majority of the decided voters were in favor of the Treaty, a large proportion of the voters were undecided. In addition, support had fallen since the Danish referendum. In light of the Danish experience, Irish acceptance of the Treaty could not be assumed. The Treaty was ratified on June 18 with a 69 percent majority. Our event date is the following day, when this news was learned by investors.

The ratification represented a clear endorsement by Irish voters of Irish participation in EMU. The impact on other countries depends on the perceived likelihood that EMU would have been possible after rejection by both Danish and Irish voters. It is possible that Ireland was not viewed by investors to be important enough to prevent other countries from joining a monetary union. This event is predicted to have a primary effect on Ireland and a secondary effect on the other EC countries.

The French Referendum

The French referendum was held on September 20, 1992. When the referendum was called in June, the Treaty was supported by 70 percent of voters. By the end of August, however, a strong opposition had formed. The final public opinion polls were taken one week prior to the referendum.[3] These polls indicated that only 52.4 percent of voters, on average, were in favor of the Treaty. Owing to this close margin and the fact that polls were not taken during the week before the referendum, the outcome was uncertain. The Treaty was approved by a narrow margin of 51.05. Financial markets were aware of this narrow victory when they resumed trading on the event date, September 21.

The primary impact of the referendum was on France. As indicated in table 1, this event represented progress towards EMU for this country. However, the narrow margin was disappointing in view of the strong commitment of the French government to EMU and the intensive campaign for the Maastricht Treaty. Moreover, it openly displayed the internal divisions in French politics. According to the Financial Times, "it showed that the main parties' policies on the wide range of subjects in the Maastricht Treaty are out of kilter with the views of nearly half the electorate."[4] It is therefore not surprising that former president Valery Giscard d'Estaing declared "The problem of Maastricht has been solved but the problem of France is another story."[5] Therefore, this event had implications for France that extend beyond EMU ratification.

The secondary effect of this narrow French vote on other countries is predicted to be positive but possibly small. Without French participation, the Maastricht Treaty was undoubtedly doomed. In this sense, the "yes" vote can be viewed as an event that increased the perceived probability that the Maastricht Treaty would be implemented. This point was emphasized by European Commission officials and its president Mr. J. Delors, as well as by Mr. Theo Waigel, German Finance Minister.[6] Most European Commission officials, however, also recognized that the vote was so close that it had merely removed one hurdle for the Maastricht Treaty, rather than dispelling doubt about its ratification and implementation once and for all.

The Ratification by the British Parliament

On the night of July 22, 1993—after months of sometimes acrimonious debate outside and inside the governing Tory Party—two critical issues of the Maastricht Treaty were put to vote in the House of Commons. Britain's Conservative government rejected the Labour opposition amendment on the Social Chapter with the support of a casting vote by the Speaker after a tie. The second vote endorsing the government's position on the Social Chapter was defeated by an alliance of Labour MP's and the conservative Eurosceptics. This was an unexpected and humiliating defeat for prime minister Major and a serious threat to his leadership. The next day (July 23) the Eurorebels backed their prime minister when he linked the resignation of his government to the Maastricht Treaty. The news about the ultimate ratification reached stock markets on the same day. July 23, 1993 is therefore the event day for our study.

This ratification paved the way for British participation in EMU. The other countries welcomed the British endorsement of the Treaty. In view of the British objections to monetary union, a rejection of the Treaty would not have prevented other countries from going ahead without Britain. Thus we expect this event to have a small, but positive, effect on other EC countries.

The First Currency Crisis (September 1992)

During the week before the French referendum, the Treaty faced another challenge. High German interest rates were straining the ERM, with particular pressure on the British pound and the Italian lira. Despite assertions by EC ministers in early September that currencies would not be realigned, it was announced on September 13 that the lira would be devalued by 7 percent and that Germany had agreed to reduce interest rates. As discussed in the Financial Times, this announcement may be interpreted as either good news or bad news for EMU.[7] On the one hand, it indicated that cooperation was possible and may therefore be viewed as a positive event with respect to EMU. On the other hand, the devaluation of the lira may have been viewed as an indication that the ERM was not sustainable. It should also be noted that although Germany agreed to reduce interest rates, the actual reduction was smaller than had been hoped for by other ERM members.

The pressure on the ERM continued. Following speculative attacks, the pound sterling was suspended from the ERM on the evening of September 16. Early on the next day, the peseta was devalued and the lira was (temporarily) suspended from the ERM. Stock markets were informed of these facts during the same day, September 17, which therefore becomes an event date in the study.

This event had a primary impact on Spain, the U.K. and Italy. For these countries, this event had negative implications with respect to EMU because devaluing or leaving the ERM is incompatible with the exchange rate convergence criteria of the Maastricht Treaty. The spill-over effects for other countries would be negative if the crisis of the ERM was perceived to decrease the probability of irrevocably fixed exchange rates. This view was mirrored in the Financial Times. According to bond market analysts in Paris, " . . . the ERM would take years to recover and monetary union was out of the question for the time being."[8] Yet, the secondary effect could well be negligible if the exchange rate problems in Spain, the U.K. and Italy were not perceived to diminish the scope for monetary union between the remaining countries. This would have been the case, for example, if the fundamentals of these countries were not viewed to be in line with a credible commitment to fixed exchange rates.

The Second Currency Crisis

The ERM experienced a second major currency crisis in July 1993. Belgium, France, Portugal and Denmark were forced to increase interest rates to maintain their currencies, and the value of the peseta fell substantially during the last week of July. It was hoped that the Bundesbank Council would reduce the German discount rate at its meeting on Thursday, July 29, to alleviate pressure on the weaker ERM currencies. Expectations were raised when the German repo rate was decreased by 20 basis points on the day before the meeting.[9] The decision not to reduce the discount rate was therefore unexpected and triggered two days of speculative trading. The headline of the Financial Times on Friday, July 30, read "Future of EMS in jeopardy . . . " and the values of the Belgian and French francs, the Danish krone, the escudo and the peseta were close to their ERM floors despite heavy intervention. It was clear that the current ERM system was not sustainable. On Sunday it was decided at an emergency meeting that the ERM bands would be widened to 15 percent. This decision was announced before financial markets opened on Monday, August 2.

As indicated in table 1, we focus on three event days during this exchange rate crisis. Specifically, we consider the two days of heavy speculation that followed the Bundesbank decision (Thursday, July 29 and Friday, July 30). In addition, we analyze stock markets on Monday, August 2, the day after the breakdown of the ERM. We identify Belgium, France, Denmark and Spain as the primary affected countries because their currencies were the targets of heavy speculation. But we also expect negative spill-overs for other countries because the speculation and the widening of the ERM bands raised serious doubt about the future of the ERM.

Potential Costs and Benefits of EMU

In this section we discuss three sources of potential benefits or costs of monetary union: (1) the reduction of exchange rate uncertainty; (2) increased credibility of anti-inflationary policies; and (3) the loss of macroeconomic sovereignty. We focus on these three effects because they have played a prominent role in both the academic and policy discussions concerning EMU. The implications of each of these hypotheses for individual European economies are discussed and summarized in table 2.

Reduction of Exchange Rate Uncertainty

It has been suggested that one of the primary benefits of EMU is that it will increase trade and investment by reducing risk due to exchange rate uncer-

TABLE 2.   Cost and Benefits of EMU

	Reduced Exchange Rate Uncertainty		Credible Anti-Inflation Policies	Macroeconomic Sovereignty		
	Volatility	Exposure		National Macro-economic Autonomy	Asymmetry of Shocks	High Unemployment
Predicted effect on stock prices	+	+	+	–	–	–
Belgium		s				
Denmark						
France				s		
Germany				s		
Ireland		s			s	s
Italy			s		s	
Netherlands		s				
Spain	s		s		s	s
United Kingdom	s		s	s	s	

s = domestic stock market is expected to be strongly affected tainty. A survey for the Association for the Monetary Union of Europe, for example, found that the "reduction in monetary uncertainty" was viewed as the most important benefit of a single currency.[10] This section briefly outlines some of the possible links between exchange rate uncertainty and economic efficiency. These issues are discussed in more detail in Baldwin (1991) and De Grauwe (1992).

To illustrate the relationship between exchange rate uncertainty and trade and investment, consider the following expression for the value of a firm's capital:

$$V_i = E(\pi_i) - \rho_i \tag{1}$$

where $E(\pi_i)$ represents the expected future profits to firm i, and ρ_i represents the firm's risk premium. This risk premium includes the perceived risk due to exchange rate uncertainty as well as other sources of risk. A firm's exchange rate risk is a function of both the degree of exchange rate uncertainty and the vulnerability (or "exposure") of the firm's cash flows to this uncertainty. As discussed by Bodnar and Gentry (1993), a firm's exposure to exchange rate uncertainty depends on factors such as its export activity, the importance of imported inputs, and the level of foreign-denominated assets.

Drawing on equation (1), exchange rate uncertainty reduces the value of a firm's capital and discourages investment associated with international business transactions (including, for example, foreign direct investment and investment in export-oriented firms). As discussed by Baldwin (1991), this will be particularly important when investment is irreversible. Similarly, when faced with exchange rate uncertainty, firms will have an incentive to reduce their exposure by reducing their export activities or their imports of intermediate products. By eliminating exchange rate uncertainty within Europe, EMU would therefore encourage trade and investment within Europe.

In addition to these static effects, EMU may lead to dynamic effects through encouraging investment. In the context of dynamic economies of scale, productivity increases as capital accumulates. In this case, an increase in the risk-adjusted return may lead to a permanently higher growth rate. Calibrations by Baldwin (1991) suggest that these dynamic effects may be quite important.

The predicted impact of EMU events on stock prices can be derived from the above discussion. The reduction of exchange rate uncertainty will have a direct impact on stock prices by reducing ρ and therefore increasing the value of capital reflected in stock prices. In addition, efficiency gains resulting from increased trade and investment would lead to a further increase in the value of capital and stock prices. On the other hand, however, some of these efficiency gains derive from the pro-competitive effects of trade and foreign direct investment. These effects would tend to reduce profits and stock prices. Thus, it is not clear, a priori, that the benefits of reduced exchange rate uncertainty would be reflected in positive stock price reactions. Nonetheless, it is reasonable to hypothesize that expectations about economic gains would lead to an increase in stock prices.

There are a number of caveats to the above discussion. First, as discussed by DeGrauwe (1992), price variability will, in general, increase expected profits. Thus, a reduction in exchange rate uncertainty may decrease $E(\pi_i)$, which would (at least) partially offset the positive impact of the lower risk premium. In addition, a reduction of the exchange rate risk within the European Community may result in an increase in other types of risk.[11] These factors suggest that decreasing exchange rate risk may not have the expected positive impact on European economies.

The net impact of reduced exchange rate uncertainty on stock prices is therefore theoretically ambiguous. If, however, stock markets anticipate that a reduction in exchange rate risk will have the positive impact predicted by EMU-supporters, then we would expect stock prices to respond positively to news that increased the perceived probability that EMU would be implemented. This is indicated in table 2. Furthermore, the magnitude of the stock price adjustments should be greatest for those countries that face the greatest exchange rate risk: countries with a relatively high degree of exchange rate uncertainty and/or countries with a large exposure to exchange rate fluctuations.

Exchange rate uncertainty is difficult to measure because it reflects expectations about future fluctuations. Nonetheless, it is reasonable to hypothesize that, all other things equal, exchange rate uncertainty will be greatest for those currencies that have experienced the widest fluctuations. Table 3 presents measures of intra-EC exchange rate volatility for the nine countries in our sample for the periods 1979–89 and 1989–91. In addition, because the U.K. did not join the ERM until late 1990, the period January 1991–May 1992 (ending just prior to the Danish referendum) is also included. As seen in the table, Belgium and the Netherlands have consistently experienced the lowest amount of volatility, while Spain and the U.K. have consistently experienced the greatest amount of volatility. The high volatility for these two countries prior to 1990 reflects, in part, the fact that Spain and the U.K. did not join the ERM until mid-1989 and late-1990, respectively. While volatility for these countries declined after joining the ERM, it was still notably greater than the volatility for other countries. If expectations about future volatility are related to these measures of past volatility, we would expect exchange rate uncertainty to be relatively important for these two countries. If all countries were exposed equally to exchange rate changes, the United Kingdom and Spain would be the most affected by the reduction of exchange rate uncertainty. Accordingly, the stock price response to progress towards EMU should be the strongest for Britain and Spain. In table 2 this is indicated by an "S" (for strongly affected) for those two countries. The other countries, and Belgium and the Netherlands in particular, should be less affected by reductions in exchange rate uncertainty.

The other factor determining the exchange rate risk is exposure. As discussed above, a firm's exposure depends on the importance of international business activities to its profit flows. While exposure is likely to vary among individual firms and industries within an economy, it is likely that small open economies will be more vulnerable to exchange rate uncertainty than relatively large and closed economies. To provide an indication of the degree of openness among the EC countries, table 3 reports the value of intra-EC exports relative to GDP for each country. Based on this measure, Ireland, Belgium and the Netherlands are the most open countries and would therefore be the most sensitive to intra-EC exchange rate uncertainty. According to the exchange rate exposure criterion, we expect the stock prices of those countries to react most to news about reduced exchange rate uncertainty.

The other countries, and most notably Spain, Italy and the United Kingdom, are less dependent on intra-EC trade and therefore are likely to have relatively low exposures to intra-EC exchange rate changes. It should be noted, however, that openness to international trade may not be a rele-

TABLE 3.   Intra-EC Exchange Rate Variability

| | Exchange Rate Variability | | | Openness |
	1979–89	1990–91	1/91–5/92	1990
Belgium	1.0	0.45	0.32	49.8
Denmark	1.1	0.64	0.49	13.9
France	1.1	0.61	0.45	12.5
Germany	1.1	0.58	0.43	16.1
Ireland	1.3	0.79	0.47	50.1
Italy	1.1	0.65	0.50	9.4
Netherlands	0.9	0.42	0.31	40.0
Spain	1.7	1.04	0.87	7.1
United Kingdom	2.2	1.39	0.77	9.5

Source: Exchange rate variability is measured as the weighted sum of standard deviations of monthly percentage changes of intra-EC bilateral exchange rates. Openness is measured as intra-EC exports as a share of GDP.

Note: EC Commission (1990) and DeGrauwe (1992).

vant measure for the U.K. As a major financial center, this country may be affected strongly by exchange rate uncertainty.

Summarizing, predictions about the relative importance of exchange rate uncertainty among individual countries vary depending on the indicator of exchange rate risk. Belgium and the Netherlands are the two countries with the most stable currencies, but are among the countries with the highest exchange rate exposure. On the other hand, Spain and the United Kingdom combine a relatively small degree of openness with marked exchange rate variability. One interpretation of these data is that the countries who are the most sensitive to exchange rate uncertainty have pursued policies to maintain exchange rate stability.

Monetary Union and Credible Anti-Inflationary Policies

One of the most common arguments in favour of European monetary integration is that it will provide credibility for low inflation policies [i.e. Giavazzi and Pagano (1985) and Giavazzi and Giovannini (1989)]. According to this argument, high inflation countries with weak governments can gain credibility by tying their exchange rate to a stable low inflation anchor.

This reasoning is usually explained in the framework of the Barro-Gordon model.[12] Consider the situation in figure 1 of a relatively high inflation EU country H. National policy-makers of country H face a set of convex short-run Phillips curves measuring the short-run trade-off between unemployment (U) and inflation (P) for given inflationary expectations. The long-run relation is given by the expectations-augmented vertical Phillips curve L_h. L_h is the locus of points where expected inflation equals actual inflation and where unemployment is at its natural rate U_n. Finally, government preferences for unemployment and inflation are captured by a set of concave indifference curves with curves closer to the origin yielding a higher level of utility for policy-makers of country H.

Suppose the government of H were to announce a target inflation rate of P_a, the inflation rate of the low-inflation anchor country A. This inflation rate, if realized, would bring country H to point B. This point is on the short-run Phillips curve I_0 that corresponds to an expected inflation rate P_a. Since inflationary expectations are realized, B is on the vertical Phillips curve as well and unemployment is at its natural rate, U_n. In fact, B will not be attained because the government of country H can reach a higher utility at point C by generating unanticipated inflation. This temptation to "cheat" is stronger if the government puts a heavy weight on fighting unemployment (reflected in a steep government preference func-

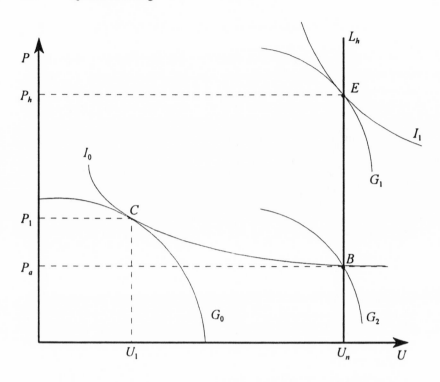

Fig. 1

tion). Cheating is also more likely with flat short-run Phillips curves because in that case substantial reductions in unemployment can be achieved with little additional inflation. A slow response of wages to falling unemployment and rising inflation would typically generate such an outcome.

The government is not able to lower permanently unemployment by generating inflation. Rational agents adjust their inflationary expectations until a sustainable equilibrium is reached at point E. This point lies on the long-run vertical Phillips curve and constitutes a tangency point between the short-run Phillips curve I_1 and the government preference curve G_1. At point E the government of H has no incentive to deviate from its announced policy. Moreover, inflationary expectations are realized so that unemployment is U_n.

In the literature on EMU, exchange rate pegging is viewed as a credible policy choice for attaining the low inflation point B. Due to purchasing power parity, fixing the exchange rate amounts to inflation convergence between the members of a currency union. The common inflation rate will be set by the low-inflation country that is not willing to participate in a currency union that would entail higher inflation. In the ERM Germany has consistently fulfilled the role of low-inflation anchor. The Maastricht Treaty shifts the anchor position to the European Central Bank (ECB), whose statutory independence guarantees price stability. The Maastricht Treaty establishes that, in the run-up to EMU, the three lowest inflation rates in the EU determine the inflation convergence criterion for participation in EMU.

Summarizing, fixed exchange rates in a monetary union may offer the prospect of low inflation for participating member countries.[13] This inspires confidence in a member country's anti-inflationary policies and therefore may be expected to raise domestic stock prices.[14] This explains the positive sign for the expected effect on stock prices in table 2. Moreover, countries whose anti-inflationary policies are the least credible without EMU should benefit the most from EMU. According to figure 1, the countries with the least credible anti-inflation policies are likely to be those with 1) a limited valuation of government for low inflation and 2) a relatively flat short-run Phillips Curve. An alternative (and complementary) measure of anti-inflationary credibility is past anti-inflationary performance.

Table 4 presents average inflation rates (measured by the CPI) for the nine EU countries of our sample during the 1985–93 and 1991–93 periods. Italy and Spain experienced the highest inflation rates throughout the entire time period. The UK can be considered as a relatively high inflation country from 1985 to 1990, while inflation was controlled from 1991 onwards. Germany, Belgium, Denmark, Ireland and the Netherlands have had a much better inflation performance although the Dutch and German inflation figures went up considerably after German reunification.

Government preferences for unemployment and inflation cannot be measured directly. A commonly used indicator is central bank independence (CBI). Independent central banks are more likely to pursue price stability as the primary objective of monetary policy. Governments that do not interfere in central bank policies implicitly reveal a greater preference for low inflation. Table 4 presents the measure of CBI proposed by Grilli et al. (1991), who base their summary statistic on the freedom of the Central Bank to choose both the final goal of monetary policy and the instruments to achieve this final goal. A higher score for the CBI indicator indicates more central bank independence. The two countries with the worst inflation performance, Italy and Spain, have the least independent central banks of the countries of our sample. Conversely, the countries with the best inflation performance, Germany and the Netherlands, have the most independent central banks. The other central banks take an intermediate position. A critical review of this classification by Eijffinger and Schaling (1993) confirms the difference in CBI between high and low inflation countries, but draws a sharper distinction between the U.K. central bank and the more independent central banks in Belgium, France and Denmark.

The slope of the short-run Phillips curve has been estimated by many authors as the short-run responsiveness of wages to unemployment. Table 4 presents Heylen and Van Poeck's (1993) weighted average of nine influential studies. A small figure points to a flat Phillips curve. Compared to countries like Japan, Switzerland, Sweden, Austria and Norway (not shown), the European Union countries are characterized by flat Phillips curves and hence have a stronger incentive to reduce short-term unemployment by generating inflation. Among EU countries, though, there is little variation in this variable.

On the whole, the various criteria identify Spain, Italy and to some degree the U.K. as the primary beneficiaries of the anti-inflationary credibility that EMU may bring. According to this hypothesis, we expect the stock markets of those countries to react the most positively to EMU events. The other countries, and in particular Germany and the Netherlands, would have less to gain from EMU. In fact, the transition from

TABLE 4.   Key Indicators for the Macroeconomic Analysis of EMU

Country	Inflation		Unemployment rate		CBI	Slope short-run Phillips-curve
	1985–1993	1991–1993	1991	1993		
Belgium	2.7	2.8	7.5	9.4	7	0.53
Denmark	3.3	1.9	8.9	10.4	8	0.25
France	3.2	2.6	9.5	10.8	7	0.61
Germany	2.3	3.9	4.2	5.6	13	0.50
Ireland	3.3	2.5	16.2	18.4	7	0.41
Italy	6.3	5.3	10.1	11.2	5	0.89
Netherlands	1.8	3.3	7.1	8.5	10	0.60
Spain	6.4	5.5	16.4	21.5	5	0.31
United Kingdom	5.2	3.7	8.9	10.5	6	0.24

Note: Inflation is the average yearly % change in the CPI. The unemployment rate measures the number of unemployed as % of the civilian labor force. Inflation and unemployment figures are from European Economy, various issues. CBI is Grilli et al's (1991) measure of Central Bank Independence. The slope of the short-run Phillips curve measures the short-run response of wages to changes in unemployment and is taken from Heylen and Van Poeck (1993).

ERM to EMU may *reduce* the anti-inflationary credibility of these low inflation countries if the ECB's policies are more inflationary than the current Bundesbank policies. EMU, however, implies an irreversible commitment to a common inflation rate. This may help even low-inflation countries to convince financial markets that their anti-inflationary policies will be permanently sustained.

Monetary Union and the Loss of Macroeconomic Sovereignty

The benefits from reduced exchange rate uncertainty and anti-inflationary credibility for a country participating in a currency union do not come without a cost. The country gives up the exchange rate as a potentially valuable policy instrument. Moreover, the country implicitly adopts the anchor inflation rate and thus loses the freedom to conduct an independent national monetary policy. The loss of macroeconomic sovereignty in monetary and exchange rate policy limits the scope for addressing country-specific problems and, as shown in table 2, is expected to depress domestic stock prices.

The macroeconomic cost of monetary union depends on factors whose importance can vary across countries (see Alesina and Grilli 1992, 1993) among others). One important element is the degree of national macroeconomic autonomy countries enjoy before monetary union. Countries with sufficient autonomy will be constrained by the transfer of macroeconomic sovereignty to the supra-national level or to another country. In the current political context of the European Union, this argument would perhaps apply to France, Germany and the United Kingdom. If financial markets perceive this to be a problem, stock prices of those countries will decline when constructive steps towards a monetary union are announced (see table 2).

Another factor concerns the (dis)similarity in economic performance of a country relative to the rest of the union. The optimum currency-area literature emphasizes the symmetry of economic shocks as a criterion for constituting a currency area. Monetary and exchange rate policies are valuable instruments for an economy experiencing adverse country-specific shocks. Such a country should not join a monetary union with countries that face different economic shocks.

Judged by the symmetry of shocks, the European Union is presumably not an optimal currency area. Using an econometric decomposition of supply and demand shocks, Bayoumi and Eichengreen (1992a) find a clear distinction between the core and other EC countries. Germany (before unification), the Benelux countries, Denmark and France experience similar shocks while disturbances in the other EC countries follow a clearly distinct pattern. Von Hagen and Neumann (1991) and De Grauwe and Heens (1991) reach a similar conclusion using real exchange rate variability as an indicator of asymmetry in economic shocks. This different pattern of shocks is prone to be a burden for the countries outside the core. Without the exchange rate instrument and with a common monetary policy primarily targeted at maintaining price stability, those countries will be constrained in addressing the country-specific problems they are likely to face. Hence, progress towards EMU is least beneficial for countries outside the core. According to this reasoning, Italy, the U.K., Ireland and Spain are the countries that are predicted to be the most strongly affected.[15]

A final factor is the actual unemployment rate. With concave policy preference curves the marginal benefit of a reduction in unemployment increases when unemployment is high. This consideration is particularly important during the transition from E to B. The required deflationary policy generally involves a temporary increase in unemployment when the high inflation country slides down the short-run Phillips curve I_1. With slow downward adjustment of inflationary expectations and hysteresis in the labor market this may result in a prolonged recession. The adjustment process will even be more painful if the anchor country conducts a restrictive monetary policy in order to achieve a very low inflation rate. A brief glance at table 4 singles out Spain and Ireland as the countries with the most severe unemployment problems. Based on this unemployment criterion, table 2 hypothesizes that stock markets in these countries would not welcome a move towards EMU.

As table 4 indicates, a marked change in the evolution of unemployment took place between the start and the end of our sample period. The signing of the Maastricht Treaty followed several years of rapid economic growth and declining (but high) unemployment. From 1992 onwards economic growth halted and unemployment went up in most EU member states. In 1993 the unemployment rate had risen in all the countries of our sample compared to 1991.

One expects countries to become more aware of the costs of monetary union when unemployment goes up. This implies that the evaluation of EMU events by financial markets can vary over time. In times of increasing unemployment the loss of macroeconomic sovereignty will be felt more strongly. This argument therefore predicts a larger drop in stock prices to positive EMU news in the later years of our sample relative to the earlier years.

EMU Events and Stock Market Adjustments

This brief overview of theoretical issues brings out the complex relationship between EMU events and predicted stock market adjustments. Progress towards EMU entails both potential costs and benefits whose importance are likely to vary among countries as well as over time. Our list of indicators does not produce a conclusive ranking of countries according to the degree by which they are affected by EMU events. Yet, Spain, Italy, Ireland and the United Kingdom are often among the countries for which theory predicts a larger stock price response (both in terms of costs and benefits). Conversely, we seldom find compelling theoretical arguments to expect significant stock market reactions in Belgium, Netherlands, Germany and Denmark.

Methodology and Data

To analyze investors' expectations about EMU, we estimate abnormal stock market returns corresponding to the seven events discussed above. These abnormal returns are estimated as the prediction errors of the market model:

$$r_{it} = a_i + B_i * r_{mt} + \sum \gamma_{ei} * d_e + \varepsilon_{it} \qquad (2)$$

where r_{it} is the return to the stock index of country i at time t, r_{mt} is the return to the global market index at time t, B_i represents the systematic risk of index i with respect to changes in global economic conditions, and ε_{it} represents a stochastic error term, assumed to have a zero mean and a variance that is constant over time. The dummy variables, d_e, are equal to one on the date of event e and zero otherwise. The coefficient, γ_{ei}, therefore represents the abnormal return for event e. For the 1993 currency crisis, which involves three event days, the three individual abnormal returns are added together to create a cumulative abnormal return for the event window.[16]

Abnormal returns are estimated for the daily stock market indices of the nine individual EC countries included in the *Financial Times* database: Belgium, Denmark, Germany, France, Ireland, Italy, the Netherlands, Spain, and the United Kingdom. All nine of these countries are potential members of EMU because they were present at the Maastricht summit, signed the agreement and proceeded afterwards with the ratification of the Treaty by their national parliaments. We use the *Financial Times* world index as our proxy for the market index. By controlling for worldwide economic shocks, the abnormal returns reflect the new information that is specific to the European countries, such as EMU-related news. The estimation periods for the Maastricht Treaty and the 1992 events are approximately one year long.[17] The estimation period for the 1993 events was shortened to ten months so that the 1992 events would not introduce unnecessary "noise" into the estimation of the market model parameters.[18]

To determine whether an EMU-related event had a significant impact on stock markets, we test the joint hypothesis that all of the abnormal returns to member countries for that event are equal to zero:

$$H_o{:}\gamma_{ei} = 0, \forall i$$

Due to the fact that European stock markets are likely to be affected by many of the same shocks, the error terms of equation (2) are likely to be contemporaneously correlated. Therefore, the joint hypothesis tests are performed within a system of seemingly unrelated regressions (SUR).[19] If the abnormal returns are jointly significant for a particular event day (or window), then we can conclude that stock market behavior was "abnormal." To evaluate whether these abnormal returns can be attributed to EMU news rather than to other economic changes learned on the event day, we also perform this test for a control group of European countries that are not members of the EU: Austria, Finland, Norway, Sweden, and Switzerland. The stock market returns to these countries are likely to reflect economic shocks that are common to European economies, but are not likely to be strongly affected by the EMU events.[20] Thus, if the abnormal returns for a particular event day are jointly significant for both the member and non-member countries, then this result would suggest that the abnormal returns may reflect news other than that related to EMU.

In the second stage of our analysis, we focus on the events for which the abnormal returns are jointly significant. First, we perform joint significance tests separately for those countries that were directly affected by the event and those that were only indirectly affected by the event. The purpose of this set of tests is to determine whether the significant reaction(s) are due solely to the countries directly affected by the event. To evaluate further the potential impact of EMU, we analyze the abnormal returns for the individual countries to assess whether the patterns are consistent with the theories discussed above.

Results

Joint Significance Tests

Table 5 presents the F-statistics for the joint significance tests for both the member and non-member countries. Of the five different votes relating to the Maastricht Treaty, the member-country abnormal returns corresponding to only the Danish and French referendums are jointly significant. For these two referendums, the hypothesis that the abnormal returns for all of the individual member countries are equal to zero can be rejected at the 1 percent level of significance. In contrast, this hypothesis cannot be rejected for the non-member countries. These results indicate that the stock market returns on these days reflect information that is specific to the member countries, such as the EMU news, rather than European-wide economic shocks.

The fact that the other three Treaty events do not give rise to significant abnormal stock returns is also an interesting result. For the Maastricht summit, in particular, this is surprising since this event marked a milestone in the creation of EMU. In addition, it is interesting to note that the Irish and British stock markets were not significantly affected by the treaty votes held in their own countries.[21]

With respect to the currency crises, the member-country abnormal returns are jointly significant for the events relating to both crises. In contrast, the abnormal returns for the non-member countries are not jointly

TABLE 5.   Joint Significance Tests

Event	F-Statistic EMU Members	F-Statistic Non-members
Treaty Ratification	1.387	0.499
	[0.188]	[0.777]
Danish Referendum	7.821**	0.314
	[0.000]	[0.905]
Irish Referendum	0.532	0.327
	[0.547]	[0.897]
French Referendum	4.458**	1.054
	[0.000]	[0.384]
British Ratification	0.471	0.379]
	[0.895]	[0.863
1992 Currency Crisis	10.076**	0.834
(Suspension of Lira and	[0.000]	[0.525]
Pound, Devaluation of		
Peseta)		
1993 Currency Crisis	4.847*	0.550
(ERM bands widened)	[0.000]	[0.738]

F-statistic corresponds to H:$\gamma_i = 0$ for all countries.
** Statistically significant at the 1% level.
P-values are in brackets.
Member countries are Belgium, Denmark, France, Germany, Ireland, Italy, the Netherlands, Spain, and the United Kingdom.
Non-member countries are Austria, Finland, Norway, Sweden, and Switzerland.

significant, suggesting that investors perceived these currency crisis events to have important implications that were specific to member countries.

Abnormal Returns to Individual Countries

We now focus on the four events for which the abnormal returns are jointly significant. Table 6 presents the abnormal returns corresponding to these events for the individual countries in our sample. Beginning with the Danish referendum, it is striking that the abnormal return to the Danish stock market is very large (–4.4 percent). The abnormal returns to the

TABLE 6. Abnormal Returns to Individual Countries (percent)

Country	Danish Referendum	French Referendum	1992 Currency Crisis	1993 Currency Crisis
F-Statistics for Joint Significance Tests				
Directly Affected	see	see	21.54**	5.10**
	Denmark below	France below	[0.000]	[0.000]
Indirectly Affected	0.67	2.85**	1.55	1.222 []
	[0.72]	[0.004]	[0.159]	[0.296]
Belgium	–0.09	0.02	1.13*	1.79
	(0.55)	(0.55)	(0.55)	(1.02)
Denmark	–4.43**	1.14	–0.17	6.08**
	(0.63)	(0.63)	(0.63)	(1.79)
France	–1.28	–2.69**	–0.9	4.87**
	(0.74)	(0.74)	(0.75)	(1.51)
Germany	0.21	–0.80	0.62	–2.08
	(0.83)	(0.83)	(0.83)	(1.29)
Ireland	–0.16	1.60*	0.95	–0.29
	(0.80)	(0.80)	(0.80)	(2.24)
Italy	–0.42	0.96	3.47**	1.29
	(0.97)	(0.97)	(0.97)	(2.65)
Netherlands	–0.23	0.01	–0.13)	0.35
	(0.53)	(0.53)	(0.53	(0.94)
Spain	–0.90	–1.78*	–0.82	2.14
	(0.86)	(0.86)	(0.87)	(1.76)
U.K.	–0.90	0.02	4.13**	1.07
	(0.69)	(0.69)	(0.69)	(1.09)
Mean	–0.91)	–0.17	0.92*	1.70*
	(0.47	(0.71)	(0.47)	(0.85)

Standard errors are in parentheses.
P-values are in brackets.
* Statistically significant at the 5% level.
** Statistically significant at the 1% level.

other countries, however, are relatively small and, with the exception of France, are less than 1 percent in absolute value.

This result is consistent with the hypothesis in table 1 that this event will have the most direct effect on Denmark and suggests that the Danish rejection represented a setback for Danish participation in EMU. Since the abnormal return is negative this setback was viewed as detrimental for the Danish economy. This implies that investors perceived EMU to be beneficial for Denmark even though the country was not singled out in the theoretical part of the paper as a main beneficiary of EMU.

We do not find any secondary spill-over effects for the other countries. As reported in table 6, the hypothesis that the abnormal returns to member countries other than Denmark are jointly equal to zero cannot be rejected at any conventional significance level. Thus, the Danish referendum had a significant impact on only the Danish stock market. One interpretation of this result is that the "market" believed that the EMU would be implemented without Denmark, if necessary. This is consistent with the fact that the ratification process did indeed continue. However, we should note that if investors perceived EMU to be very important, even a small setback should be reflected in the abnormal returns. To further evaluate whether the Danish referendum had a significant impact on countries other than Denmark, we test the joint significance of the subset of countries identified in table 2 to be the most likely to be affected by EMU: Ireland, Italy, Spain and the U.K. The hypothesis that the abnormal returns to these countries are all equal to zero cannot be rejected at any conventional level of significance.[22] Similarly, the abnormal returns to the remaining four countries are also jointly insignificant.[23]

Unlike the Danish referendum, the French referendum was essential to the fate of EMU. As seen in table 6, this event had a significant impact on a number of countries. The French stock market reacted the most strongly, resulting in a statistically significant abnormal return of –2.69 percent. Again, we find the strongest effect for the country directly affected by the event. The French stock market reacted negatively to the referendum. There are two potential interpretations of this result. One interpretation is that investors perceived the costs of EMU for France to outweigh its benefits. This is consistent with the hypothesis that the loss of macroeconomic sovereignty would be relatively costly for relatively large economies such as France. If this were the case, the "yes" vote would be bad news for the French economy. The other interpretation is that the close referendum vote was perceived to reflect a disenchantment of voters with the French government. Hence, according to this view, the stock market reacted to the internal problems in France rather than to the prospect of EMU.

The French referendum also generated significant effects for the other

EMU countries. The F-statistic reported in table 6 indicates that the abnormal returns to these countries are jointly significant at the 1 percent level. With respect to the individual countries, the Spanish, Irish, Danish and Italian stock markets all experienced abnormal returns with an absolute value greater than or approximately equal to 1 percent. The abnormal returns to the Irish and Spanish stock markets, however, are the only ones that are statistically significant at the 5 percent level.

It is interesting that three of the countries with the largest abnormal returns are among the four identified in table 2 as countries predicted to be the most strongly affected by EMU. The F-statistic for the joint significance test for the four "strongly" affected countries is 3.45 with a p-value of 0.008. Therefore, the hypothesis that the abnormal returns to these four countries are all equal to zero can be rejected at the 1 percent level of significance.

It is also interesting that the French referendum had little impact on the Belgian and Dutch stock markets and had a negative (although statistically insignificant) impact on the German stock market. As discussed above, all of these countries have maintained relatively stable currencies and low inflation rates. Thus, none of them would have a large incentive to join EMU. The cost of EMU is likely to be small for Belgium and the Netherlands due to the openness of their economies and consequent lack of autonomy in policy making. Therefore, neither country has much to gain or to lose by the transition from ERM to EMU. One could argue that EMU signals the more permanent character of their anti-inflationary policies. This hypothesis is not supported, however, by the negligible abnormal returns. For Germany, EMU would be more costly due to the loss of autonomy, which is consistent with the negative abnormal return.

The results for the currency crises are presented in the last columns of table 6. The event day for the 1992 currency crisis is September 17, the day when the pound and lira were suspended from the ERM and the peseta was devalued. As seen in table 6, the abnormal returns to the three countries directly affected by the event are jointly significant at the 1 percent level. Interestingly, the stock markets viewed the exit from the ERM as positive for the British and Italian economies. In contrast, the Spanish stock market fell in response to the devaluation of the peseta.

One interpretation of these results is that investors viewed the costs of staying in the ERM as too great, given that these currencies were under speculative attack. This is consistent with the survey of foreign exchange traders by Eichengreen and Wyplosz (1993). When asked their opinion about why Central Banks had not continued to defend certain currencies, 64.7 percent of the foreign exchange traders responding to the survey indicated that an important concern was "that further interest rate increases would worsen domestic economic conditions." Therefore, the Spanish stock market response may be a reflection of investors' disappointment that the peseta was devalued rather than withdrawn from the system. Alternatively, markets may have judged the devaluation as insufficient to correct Spain's competitiveness problems. We do not find any secondary effects from the currency crisis. The abnormal returns to the other EMU countries are not jointly significant and there do not appear to be any patterns among them. One interpretation of this result is that the crisis for the "weaker" currencies did not endanger the exchange rate system for the "stronger" currencies. In other words, it was perceived that EMU was possible without the participation of the U.K. (who already had an opt-out clause), Italy, and Spain.

Another interpretation is that some adjustment in the ERM was anticipated prior to the crisis. Therefore, although the actual outcome of the crisis may have been uncertain, it was expected that the ERM and thus the EMU would face challenges. This is consistent with the survey results of Eichengreen and Wyplosz (1993). When asked when they first anticipated that changes in the ERM parities would eventually take place, 22 percent (47 percent) of the foreign currency traders surveyed responded that they expected these changes prior to (just after) the Danish referendum.

Still another interpretation is that the weakening of the ERM and the implications for EMU were not perceived to have a significant impact on the countries that were not directly affected by the event. This interpretation is consistent with the fact that, with the exception of Ireland, the countries "indirectly" affected by the event were among the countries least likely to be affected by EMU. Turning to the second currency crisis, most of the abnormal returns are positive and the mean abnormal return is positive and statistically significant. This suggests, given the strains on many of the currencies, that the cost of maintaining the EMS bands were too high. In other words, this result can be interpreted as an indication that the market perceived the EMS to be unsustainable.

Once again, primary effects dominate, indicating that exchange rate crises have the strongest effect on the stock markets of countries whose currencies are under pressure. The two countries whose stock markets gained the most were France and Denmark, with large statistically significant abnormal returns. These countries were both forced to increase their interest rates due to pressure on their currencies during the week prior to the changes in the EMS bands. Belgium, which also increased interest rates that week, experienced a positive abnormal return that is significant at the 10 percent level. The positive abnormal returns for these three countries suggest that the costs of maintaining the narrow EMS bands were perceived to outweigh the benefits.

Conclusion

In this paper we investigate the stock market evaluations of events relating to the construction of a monetary union in Europe. Both ratification and currency crisis events are considered. In our analysis, we distinguish between those EMU member countries that were directly affected by the event and those that were only indirectly affected by the event through its implications for the progress of EMU. In addition, we distinguish between countries for whom the impact of EMU can be expected to be relatively large, based on economic theory, and those for whom the impact is likely to be small. Our results differ somewhat among events. Thus, it is difficult to draw strong conclusions. Nonetheless, some interesting points can be made.

First, it is remarkable that several events did not have a statistically significant impact on the stock market indices of European countries. This is particularly surprising for the Maastricht summit meeting, which was widely seen as a breakthrough for European monetary integration. Even if this event had a relatively small impact on the expectations of investors, one would expect it to have some discernable impact on stock markets if EMU was perceived to have important economic implications for member states.

Second, the effects of the significant events are strongest for the country or countries that are directly affected by the event. The exception is the French referendum, which had significant effects on the stock markets of a number of countries. One interpretation of this result is that the other events did not substantially alter the prospect of EMU for the indirectly affected countries. According to this view, EMU events were perceived to be country-specific except when the event concerned a key country such as France.

An alternative explanation is that the abnormal returns for the primary countries reflect more than the implications for EMU. For example, the abnormal returns corresponding to the currency crises may have been triggered by short run considerations about interest rate policies and speculative attacks rather than by the question of eligibility for EMU. The insignificance of the remaining abnormal returns would then suggest that either the currency crisis events were not perceived to have important implications for the future of EMU or that EMU was not expected to have important (net) economic consequences for these economies.

Third, our results provide little consistent evidence that EMU was perceived to lead to significant net benefits or costs to the individual countries in our sample. The significant negative reaction of the Danish stock market to the Danish referendum and some of the abnormal returns to the

French referendum suggest that EMU may have some net benefits for individual countries. In contrast, the positive reactions to the currency crises may indicate that EMU was expected to be too costly and therefore unsustainable, at least for those countries whose currencies were under speculative attack.

Finally, economic theories about monetary union provide potential insight into the differential impact of the French referendum among countries.

In sum, our analysis has provided some interesting results that are suggestive, but not conclusive. Clearly, more research is necessary. Formal theoretical modelling of the stock market effects of EMU may lead to more precise hypotheses. In addition, as discussed in Section 3, the reduction of exchange rate uncertainty may have a differential impact among individual firms and industries. Therefore, analysis of more disaggregated data may provide a clearer indication of the importance of exchange rate stability.[24] Furthermore, other financial indicators such as bond rates, forward interest rates and the spread between the theoretical and market ECU rates could be considered. Finally, the empirical analysis could be extended to include recent events in order to obtain more information about the link between monetary integration, exchange rate stability, and stock markets.

NOTES

1. See "A Heath Robinson design for Europe," *Financial Times,* December 12, 1991, p. 14, and "European business endorses move on monetary union," *Financial Times,* December 12, 1991, p. 4.

2. See "A Heath Robinson design for Europe," *Financial Times,* December 12, 1991, p. 14.

3. Polling is prohibited during the last week of campaigning.

4. "Poll reveals gulf between French leaders and voters," *Financial Times,* September 22, 1992.

5. "Poll reveals gulf between French leaders and voters," *Financial Times,* September 22, 1992.

6. See "France narrowly votes Yes," *Financial Times,* September 21.

7. "System is still under pressure despite action," *Financial Times,* September 15, 1992, p. 2.

8. "Speculators find new ERM targets after lira and peseta," *Financial Times,* September 18, 1992.

9. See, for example, *The Economist* (July 31).

10. See Emerson and Huhne (1991).

11. See DeGrauwe (1992) for a more complete discussion. Artis and Taylor

(1994), however, find that intra-ERM exchange rate volatility fell relative to the volatility of non-ERM currencies during the operation of the ERM *without* leading to an increase in interest rate volatility. This suggests that a reduction in exchange rate risk may not lead to an increase in risk elsewhere in the economy.

12. See, for example, De Grauwe (1992).

13. The inflation-reducing role of fixed exchange rates is not fully supported by empirical evidence. See, for example, Robertson and Symons (1992).

14. See Fama (1981) for evidence that inflation reduces stock returns.

15. Beyaert and Solanes (1995), however, find that purchasing power parity between Spain and the core EU countries is a reasonable approximation in the long run. This would suggest that monetary and exchange rate deviations are essentially short-run phenomena for Spain.

16. The standard error of this cumulative abnormal return incorporates both the variances and covariances of the individual abnormal returns. See Salinger (1992) for a discussion of standard errors in event studies.

17. The estimation period for the treaty event includes the trading days between December 3, 1990 and November 29, 1991 as well as the event date. It does not include the ten days prior to the event to allow for the (unlikely) possibility that anticipation of the summit led to unusual stock market behavior that may contaminate the estimates of the market model parameters. A single estimation period is used for all of the 1992 events since they are clustered close together. This estimation period includes the trading days between June 3, 1991 and May 29, 1991 as well as the individual event dates. Since a single dummy variable is used for each event date, the events will not have an impact on the estimation of the market model parameters [see Thompson (1993)]. It should be noted that the treaty event is included in this estimation period. We also re-estimated our results using a shorter estimation period that begins after the treaty event and found that our results were not substantially altered. This is not surprising since, as discussed below, the treaty event did not have a significant impact on stock markets.

18. The estimation period for these events includes the trading days between October 1, 1992 and July 16, 1993 as well as the individual event dates.

19. See, for example, the discussion by Theil (1971). Since the independent variables are identical for all of the equations, the estimated abnormal returns are identical to those that would be obtained by ordinary least squares estimation. The SUR approach, however, facilitates joint hypothesis testing.

20. Although these countries are candidates for potential membership in the European Union, their entry was far from certain at the time of the events.

21. The abnormal return for the Irish stock market on the day following the Irish referendum is 0.17 percent with a standard error of 0.82, and the British abnormal return on the day of the British vote of confidence is 1.07 percent with a standard error of 1.09.

22. The F-statistic for the joint significance of these abnormal returns is 0.658 with a p-value of 0.621.

23. The F-statistic is 1.088 with a p-value of 0.360.

24. See Van Camp (1993) for an analysis of the impact of EMU-related events on the stock market prices of individual Belgian firms.

REFERENCES

Alesina, Alberto, and Grilli, Vittorio. 1993. "On the Feasibility of a One or Multi-Speed European Monetary Union." *Economics and Politics* 5:145–65.

Alesina, Alberto, and Grilli, Vittorio. 1992. "The European Central Bank: Reshaping Monetary Politics in Europe." In Matthew B. Canzoneri, Vittorio Grilli, and Paul R. Masson, eds., *The Creation of a Central Bank.* Cambridge University Press and CEPR.

Artis, Michael J., and Taylor, Mark P. 1994. "The Stabilizing Effect of the ERM on Exchange Rates and Interest Rates." *IMF Staff Papers.* 41:123–148.

Baldwin, Richard E. 1991. "On the Microeconomics of the European Monetary Union." *European Economy.* Special Edition 1:19–35.

Bayoumi, Tamim, and Eichengreen, Barry. 1992. "Shocking Aspects of European Monetary Unification." National Bureau of Economic Research Working Paper no. 3949.

Beyaert, Arielle, and Garcia Solanes, Jose. 1995. "New Tests of Purchasing Power Parity: The Case of the Peseta Exchange Rate." International Economics Research Paper No. 133, CES, Katholieke Universiteit Leuven.

Bodnar, Gordon, and Gentry, William. 1993. "Exchange-Rate Exposure and Industry Characteristics: Evidence form Canada, Japan, and the U.S." *Journal of International Money and Finance* 12:29–45.

De Grauwe, Paul, and Heens, Hilde. 1991. "Real Exchange Rate Variability in Monetary Unions." International Economics Research Paper no. 87, CES, Katholieke Universiteit Leuven.

De Grauwe, Paul. 1992. *The Economics of Monetary Integration.* Oxford University Press.

Eichengreen, Barry, and Wyplosz, Charles. 1993. "The Unstable EMS." *Brookings Papers on Economic Activity* 1:51–124.

Eijffinger, Sylvester, and Schaling, Eric. 1993. "Central Bank Independence in Twelve Industrial Countries." *Banca Nazionale del Lavoro Quarterly Review* 184:49–89.

Emerson, M., and Huhne, Christopher. 1991. *The ECU Report.* London: Pan Books.

Fama, Eugene. 1981. "Stock Returns, Real Activity, Inflation and Money." *American Economic Review* 71:545–564.

Giavazzi, Francesco, and Giovannini, Alberto. 1989. *Limiting Exchange Rate Flexibility: The European Monetary System.* Cambridge, MA: The MIT Press.

Giavazzi, Francesco, and Pagano, Marco. 1985. "The Advantage of Tying One's Hands: EMS Discipline and Central Bank Credibility." *European Economic Review* 32:1055–82.

Grilli, Vittorio; Masciandaro, Donato; and Tabellini, Guido. 1991. "Political and Monetary Institutions and Public Financial Policies in the Industrial Countries." *Economic Policy* 13:341–392.

Heylen, Freddy, and Van Poeck, Andre. 1993. "Government Preferences and Equilibrium Inflation : A Simple Test of the Barro-Gordon Model." Seso-Rapport 93/291. UFSIA.

Robertson, Donald, and Symons, James. 1992. "Output, Inflation, and the ERM." *Oxford Economic Papers* 44:373–386.

Salinger, Michael. 1992. "Standard Errors in Event Studies." *Journal of Financial and Quantitative Analysis* 27:39–53.

Theil, Henri. 1971. *Principles of Econometrics.* New York: John Wiley & Sons, Inc.

Thompson, Aileen. 1993. "The Anticipated Sectoral Adjustment to the Canada-United States Free Trade Agreement: An Event Study Analysis." *Canadian Journal of Economics* 26:253–271.

Van Camp, Guy. 1993. "Anticipated Effects of the EMU: An event study." Unpublished M.A. Thesis. CES, Katholieke Universiteit Leuven.

Von Hagen, Jurgen, and Neumann, Manfred J.M. 1991. "Real Exchange Rates Within and Between Currency Areas: How Far Away is EMU?" International Economics Research Paper no. 81, CES, Katholieke Universiteit Leuven.

CHAPTER 12

On the Dynamic Effects of Monetary and Fiscal Policy in a Monetary Union

Jay H. Levin

Recent discussions concerning the possibility of a monetary union among the countries in the European Monetary System have received wide attention.[1] Despite the recent breakdown of the Exchange Rate Mechanism, some observers believe that a single currency in Europe is still possible.[2] The purpose of this paper is to focus on one aspect of a monetary union—the short-run effects of monetary and fiscal policy within a union on the member countries. In the analysis that follows, the money supply within a two-country union is controlled by a union central bank, but each of the member countries is permitted to conduct its own fiscal policy.[3] Capital is assumed to be perfectly mobile within the union and between the union and the outside world, and the exchange rate against the rest of the world floats freely. These assumptions guarantee that interest rates are equalized within the union and that uncovered interest parity prevails vis-à-vis the outside world. In addition, real wages (in terms of consumption goods) are assumed to be flexible in response to exchange rate movements, and therefore monetary expansion by the union central bank will have real effects.[4]

The paper is organized in the following way. The model of the monetary union is developed in the next section. Then the dynamic effects of monetary expansion by the union central bank are derived. In the third section I analyze the dynamic effects of fiscal expansion by one of the countries in the union. The results of the paper are summarized in the final section. The major findings of the paper, derived from simulations of the model, are as follows. Monetary expansion causes output in the two countries to expand temporarily by lowering real interest rates in the two countries and by causing the union's currency to depreciate, making both countries more competitive with the outside world. In contrast, fiscal expansion by one of the countries causes output in that country to expand there temporarily but only temporarily because exchange rate appreciation eventually depresses aggregate demand. The fiscal expansion has an ambiguous effect on output in the other member country. On the one hand, there is an increase in export demand coming from the first country, but on the other hand the appreciation of the union's currency and gradually rising interest rates work in the opposite direction to depress aggregate demand.[5]

The Model

The framework employed here is a modification of the variable output version of the sticky-price monetary approach developed by Dornbusch (1976, 1171–75) applied to two union countries floating against the outside world. In each country aggregate demand depends on a fiscal policy variable, the real exchange rate vis-à-vis the outside world, relative prices with respect to the other union country, the domestic real interest rate, domestic income, and partner country income. Furthermore, since policies do not operate instantaneously on real output, it is assumed that in each country real output responds only gradually to excess demand in the goods sector. In addition, a lag is introduced into the effect of the real exchange rate on aggregate demand in each country. This lag reflects the gradual response of trade flows to the exchange rate and will play a prominent role in the analysis of fiscal policy.[6] The model is as follows:

$$\dot{y}_1 = \Omega_1 [\mu_1 + \frac{\Omega_3 \delta_1 (e + p^* - p_1)}{D + \Omega_3} + \delta_2 (p_2 - p_1) - \sigma_1 (r - \dot{p}_1) - (1 - \gamma_1) y_1 + m_{21} y_2] \quad (1)$$

$$\dot{y}_2 = \Omega_2 [\mu_2 + \frac{\Omega_4 \delta_3 (e + p^* - p_2)}{D + \Omega_4} - \delta_2 (p_2 - p_1) - \sigma_2 (r - \dot{p}_2) - (1 - \gamma_2) y_2 + m_{12} y_1] \quad (2)$$

$$m - w p_1 - (1 - w) p_2 = \phi_1 y_1 + \phi_2 y_2 - \beta r \quad (3)$$

$$\dot{p}_1 = \pi_1 (y_1 - \bar{y}_1) \quad (4)$$

$$\dot{p}_2 = \pi_2 (y_2 - \bar{y}_2) \quad (5)$$

and

$$r = r^* + \dot{e} \quad (6)$$

where y_1 = log of real output in country 1; y_2 = log of real output in country 2; $_1$ = fiscal variable in country 1; μ_2 = fiscal variable in country 2; e = log of the exchange rate on the outside world currency; p_1 = log of the domestically produced goods price level in country 1; p_2 = log of the domestically produced goods price level in country 2; p^* = log of the outside world price level; r = nominal union interest rate; $\bar{y}_1$ = log of the natural level of output in country 1; $\bar{y}_2$ = log of the natural level of output in country 2; r^* = outside world interest rate; and D is the differential operator.

Equations (1) and (2) show that output adjusts gradually in each country in response to excess demand in the goods sector, where Ω_1 and Ω_2 are the speeds of output adjustment in the two countries. Furthermore, in each country there is a lag in the effect of the real exchange rate on aggregate demand. The speeds of adjustment of the effects of changes in the real exchange rate on aggregate demand in the two countries are given by Ω_3 and Ω_4. Notice also that in each country inflationary expectations are assumed to be held with perfect foresight, so that in the definition of the real interest rate $E(\dot{p})$ is replaced with actual $\dot{p}$. Equation (3) is the monetary sector equilibrium condition in the monetary union, where the real stock of money equals the demand for money. The nominal money stock is controlled by the union central bank, and the price level for calculating the real money stock is a weighted average of the domestic goods price levels of the member countries. The demand for money in the monetary union is a transactions demand that depends on real income in each country and the nominal union interest rate. Following Dornbusch, inflation in each country is represented by a simple Phillips curve, as shown by equations (4) and (5).[7] Finally, equation (6) is the usual interest parity condition, where it is assumed that asset holders are risk neutral, and exchange rate expectations are held with perfect foresight. Hence, $E(\dot{e})$ is replaced with actual $\dot{e}$. Although there is considerable empirical evidence based on survey studies that exchange rate expectations may not be rational, no consensus has been reached on an alternative mechanism. Consequently, the perfect foresight assumption is retained as a benchmark case.

Equations (1)–(6) determine the time paths of the six variables y_1, y_2, r, p_1, p_2, and e. In order to derive these paths, it is first necessary to obtain the system's characteristic roots. We can show that this system has a seventh-degree characteristic equation and that one of the roots must be positive because of the assumption that exchange rate expectations are held with perfect foresight. However, if the other six roots have negative real parts, the system will converge to a saddle point. Convergence will occur if the output adjustment lags are sufficiently short. It can then be shown, as demonstrated in the appendix, that if exchange rate expectations are held with perfect foresight, they can be described by the following exchange rate expectations scheme:

$$\dot{e} = \theta_1(\bar{e}-e) + \theta_2(y_1-\bar{y}_1) + \theta_3(y_2-\bar{y}_2) + \theta_4(p_1-\bar{p}_1) + \theta_5\dot{y}_1 + \theta_6\dot{y}_2 . \quad (7)$$

where $\bar{e}$ is the long-run equilibrium exchange rate, and $\bar{p}_1$ is the long-run equilibrium price level in country 1. Notice that this scheme contains six variables, corresponding to the six negative characteristic roots.[8] Thus, rational asset holders determine their exchange rate expectations on the basis of six pieces of information, which enable them to forecast exchange rates correctly. Substituting the solution for $\dot{e}$ in equation (7) into equation (6) then yields the equivalent interest parity condition

$$r = r^* + \theta_1(\bar{e}-e) + \theta_2(y_1-\bar{y}_1) + \theta_3(y_2-\bar{y}_2) + \theta_4(p_1-\bar{p}_1) + \theta_5\dot{y}_1 + \theta_6\dot{y}_2. \quad (8)$$

Equations (1)–(5) and (8) constitute an equivalent system that determines the time paths of the six variables. However, in order to derive the solution equations for these variables, we must first obtain the values of $\theta_1...\theta_6$. The procedure is to derive the characteristic equation of this system, which can be written in the general form

$$\theta_1 f_1(\lambda) + \theta_2 f_2(\lambda) + \theta_3 f_3(\lambda) + \theta_4 f_4(\lambda) + \theta_5 f_5(\lambda) + \theta_6 f_6(\lambda) + f_7(\lambda) = 0 \quad (9)$$

Then by substituting each of the six negative roots one at a time into equation (9), we obtain a system of six equations, which can be solved simultaneously for θ_1 through θ_6. Of course, to obtain the values of the six negative roots from the characteristic equation of the original system (1)–(6), we must impose specific values for the structural parameters of the model as specified below. The resulting values of θ_1 through θ_6, may then be used to derive the system's initial conditions, first for monetary expansion and then for fiscal expansion, and we can obtain the solution equations for y_1, y_2, r, p_1, p_2, and e.[9]

Monetary Expansion

Consider now the effects of monetary expansion by the union central bank. It will prove useful to introduce several pre-shock normalizations. Initially, r^* is set to 5% and p^*, m, $\bar{y}_1$, and $\bar{y}_2$ to 0. In addition, μ_1 is set equal to the value of $\sigma_1 r$ prior to the monetary shock; σ_2 is set equal to the value of $\sigma_2 r$ prior to the monetary shock; and p_1 is set equal to p_2 prior to the monetary shock. From (1) and (2) these assumptions guarantee that the real exchange rates, $e + p^* - p_1$ and $e + p^* - p_2$, prior to the monetary shock are normalized at zero. It follows that the values of e and p_1 prior to the monetary shock are equal, and the same is true of the values of e and p_2. From the monetary sector equilibrium condition (3) these pre-shock values of e, p_1 and p_2 must equal βr, or $.05\beta$, where the pre-shock value of r is 5 percent because interest parity holds. Notice that the pre-shock values of the real interest rates in the two countries are also 5 percent since the inflation rate in each is initially zero.

After programming the model and assigning values for the structural parameters, simulations were undertaken to determine the effect of a 1 percent monetary expansion by the union central bank.[10] The parameter values were chosen for the baseline simulation in such a way that the countries are virtually identical.[11] Figure 1a and figure 1b show the response of the system to this monetary shock. Consider first the impact effects. Since output and prices adjust sluggishly in the model, the entire impact of the monetary expansion is felt as a decline in the nominal interest rate within the union to maintain equilibrium in the monetary sector, and as a depreciation of the union's currency to maintain interest parity. The nominal interest rate falls to 4 percent, and the exchange rate on the foreign currency rises from its pre-shock level of .05 to .0589.[12] Hence, the exchange rate undershoots its new long-run equilibrium level of .06.[13] Finally, the real exchange rates of the two countries depreciate ($e + p^* - p_1$ and $e + p^* - p_2$ rise from 0 to .0089) because of the depreciation of the union currency and the initially unchanged price levels in the two countries.

Now consider the dynamic behavior of the system over time. First observe that the monetary expansion causes output in the two countries initially to expand and eventually to return to its natural level.[14] The expansion occurs because of the initial decline in the real interest rates in the two countries and the depreciation of the union currency, which makes both countries more competitive with the outside world. The eventual decline in output is the result of the return of the real interest rates and the real exchange rates to their original levels. Notice that the inflation rate in each country, which is determined by a Phillips curve relationship, rises initially because of the expansion in output above its natural level and then declines as output falls. Observe also that since inflation is virtually the same in the two countries, relative price movements between the two are extremely small, and hence competitiveness between the two countries remains essentially unchanged over time.

The behavior of the nominal interest rate in the union is determined by the behavior of the real money stock and the response of output in each country. After the initial monetary expansion, the real money stock declines over time because of the gradual rise in the union price level as the inflation rate in each country becomes positive. In addition, during the period in which output expands in each country, the demand for money rises in the union. Consequently, the nominal interest rate gradually rises and even overshoots its original level. Eventually, as output declines in

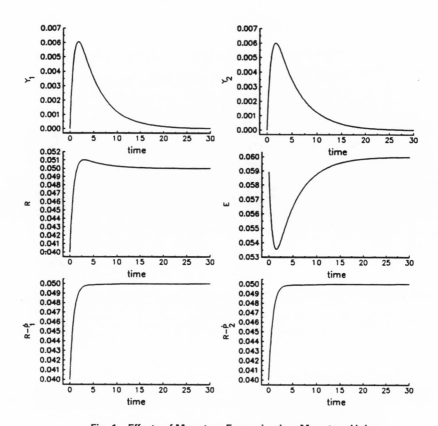

Fig. 1a. Effects of Monetary Expansion in a Monetary Union

each country toward the natural level, the demand for money falls, and interest rates return to their original level. In addition, notice that the real interest rate in each country behaves much like the union's nominal interest rate. However, real interest rates do not overshoot because after a point the inflation rate in each country continues to fall, causing the real interest rates to converge directly to their original level. Observe also that the real interest differential between the two member countries is close to zero since their inflation rates remain very nearly equal.

Next observe that after its initial depreciation, the home currency subsequently appreciates but eventually reverses direction and depreciates directly to its new long-run equilibrium level. This behavior of the union's currency is dictated by interest parity. As long as the union's interest rate

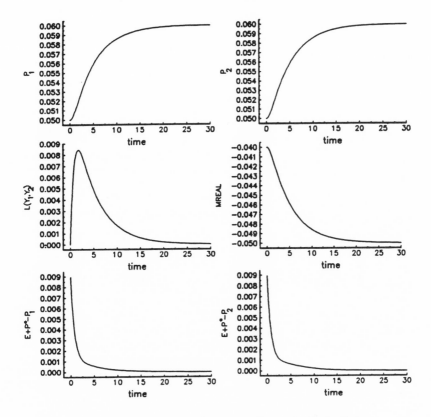

Fig. 1b. Additional Effects of Monetary Expansion in the Union

is below the world level, the union currency must be appreciating to maintain interest parity. However, once the union's interest rate eventually rises above the world level, the union currency must be depreciating to maintain interest parity. Finally, the behavior of the real exchange rates reflects the movement of the nominal exchange rate and the price level in each country. Although the exchange rate on the union currency eventually depreciates, the depreciation is outweighed by the rising price level in each country. Hence, each country's real exchange rate appreciates after the initial depreciation.

Finally, consider the effect of monetary expansion on real wages (in terms of consumption goods) and the current account in each country. Real wages in each country are defined in terms of a weighted average of domestic, partner country, and world prices:

$$rw_1 = w_1 - [u_1 p_1 + u_2 p_2 + (1 - u_1 - u_2) e] \tag{10}$$

and

$$rw_2 = w_2 - [v_1 p_1 + v_2 p_2 + (1 - v_1 - v_2) e] \tag{11}$$

where rw_1 = log of the real wage in country 1; rw_2 = log of the real wage in country 2; w_1 = log of nominal wage in country 1; and w_2 = log of nominal wage in country 2. Prior to the monetary shock, the log of real wages in each country in terms of domestic goods ($w_1 - p_1$ and $w_2 - p_2$) is normalized at 0 by setting nominal wages to the price of domestic goods.[15] Therefore, from (10) and (11) and the normalizations on p_1, p_2 and e real wages in terms of consumption goods are normalized at 0 prior to the monetary shock.

The current account surplus in each country is defined as follows:

$$CA_1 = -(e + p^* - p_1) + \frac{\Omega_3(1 + \delta_1)(e + p^* - p_1)}{D + \Omega_3} + \delta_2(p_2 - p_1) + m_{21} y_2 - m_{12} y_1 \tag{12}$$

and

$$CA_2 = -(e + p^* - p_2) + \frac{\Omega_4(1 + \delta_3)(e + p^* - p_2)}{D + \Omega_4} - \delta_2(p_2 - p_1) + m_{12} y_1 - m_{21} y_2. \tag{13}$$

Country 1's current account surplus depends on relative prices against the outside world, relative prices against country 2, and real output in countries 1 and 2. Output in the outside world is assumed to be exogenous. Notice that, because prices against the outside world affect real trade flows with a lag, the first term captures a separate price effect holding trade volumes constant, and the second term captures the lagged volume effect. In contrast, there is no lag of prices against country 2 on trade flows, and hence the third term includes both the price effect and the volume effect. An analogous treatment of country 2's current account surplus is given by equation (13). Finally, from the normalizations on p_1, p_2, e, y_1, and y_2 the current surplus of each country prior to the monetary shock is normalized at 0.

Figure 1c shows the effect of monetary expansion on real wages and the current account of each country.[16] Since monetary expansion causes the union's currency to depreciate immediately, raising the price of imported goods from the outside world, real wages drop immediately in each country. Over time, however, each country's real exchange rate appreciates, and real wages therefore rise toward their original level. With

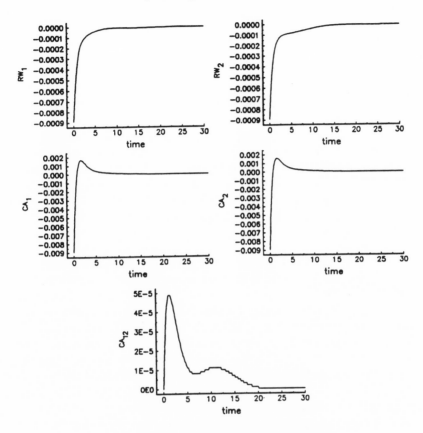

Fig. 1c. Real Wage and Current Account Effects

respect to the current account, the initial rise in import prices from the outside world caused by the depreciation of the union's currency causes the current account of each country to move immediately into deficit. Subsequently, however, the current account rises because of the lagged effect of the depreciation on trade volumes. In the new equilibrium, the current account deficits disappear as all variables affecting the current account return to their original levels. Finally, notice that country 1's current account surplus with country 2 remains essentially zero throughout the adjustment process since relative prices between the two countries remain essentially constant and real output behaves in a virtually identical way in the two countries.

These results are based on a simulation in which the two countries are virtually identical. However, once asymmetries are introduced additional patterns emerge. Output in each country can undergo temporary reversals. The exchange rate can undershoot and subsequently overshoot before converging to the long-run equilibrium. The exchange rate can also overshoot and undergo a temporary reversal before converging to the long-run equilibrium. The real interest rate can eventually overshoot its new equilibrium level, and the real exchange rate can undergo a temporary reversal before converging to its original level. Finally, the real exchange rate can eventually overshoot before converging to its original level, and relative prices between the two countries can display a humped pattern over time. These patterns introduce some complexities into the time paths of the variables, but they are essentially minor variations to the results presented in figures 1a–c.

Fiscal Expansion

Now consider the effects of fiscal expansion by one of the countries in the monetary union. It is assumed here that the union central bank is holding the union money supply constant. The pre-shock normalizations that were used in the analysis of monetary expansion will be retained here. Simulations of the model can then be undertaken to determine the effect of a 1 percent expansion in government spending in country 1 using the same parameter values as in the baseline monetary policy simulation. Figure 2a and figure 2b show the response of the system to this fiscal shock.

Consider first the impact effects. Since output and prices adjust sluggishly in the model, and since the union money supply is being held constant by the union central bank, the nominal interest rate within the union is initially unchanged. Real interest rates in the two countries also remain unchanged because their inflation rates remain at zero. Nevertheless, the union's currency appreciates (e falls from .05 to .0264) in response to a long-run appreciation of $\bar{e}$, which is required to eventually produce complete crowding out in country 1. This current appreciation is necessary to restore interest parity. However, notice also that the union's currency overshoots its new long-run equilibrium level ($\bar{e}$ falls from .05 to .03 to restore equilibrium in the goods sector in the long-run). The reason is that in the exchange rate expectations scheme (7), the expected instantaneous exchange rate movement, $\dot{e}$, depends on $\dot{y}_1$ and $p_1 - \bar{p}_1$. Fiscal expansion causes output in country 1 to expand gradually, and it raises the long-run equilibrium price level in country 1. These changes lead to expectations of a future appreciation, and so the union currency immediately overshoots to reestablish the expectation that the exchange rate will not change and thereby restore interest parity.[17] Finally, each country's real exchange rate

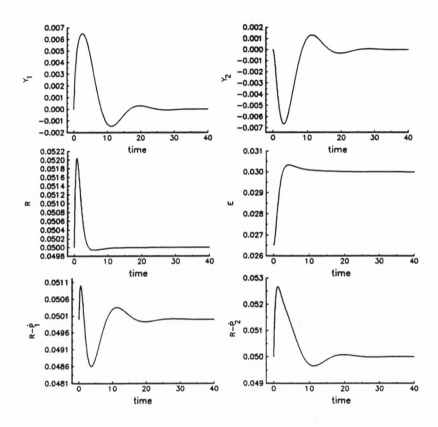

Fig. 2a. Effects of Fiscal Expansion in Country 1

immediately appreciates because of the appreciation of the union currency and the initially unchanged domestic price levels.

Now consider the dynamic behavior of the system over time. The fiscal expansion in country 1 causes output first to expand in country 1, then to decline below the natural level, and finally to converge on that level cyclically. The expansion occurs because the crowding-out effect of the appreciation of the union currency occurs only gradually. On the other hand, the fiscal expansion in country 1 causes output to decline gradually in country 2, then to rise above the natural level, and finally to converge on it cyclically. The contraction in country 2 occurs because the appreciation of the union currency gradually reduces aggregate demand there. In addi-

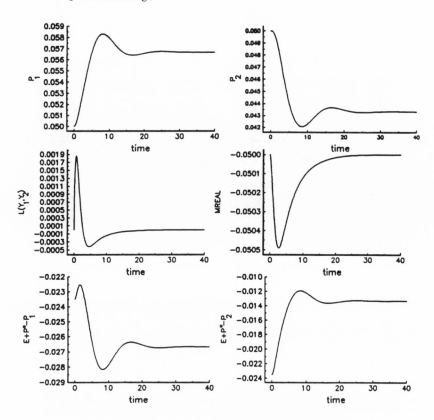

Fig. 2b. Additional Effects of Fiscal Expansion in Country 1

tion, interest rates in the union begin to rise, also reducing spending in country 2. Of course, country 2 also experiences an increase in export demand as country 1 begins to expand, but the negative exchange-rate and interest-rate effects dominate the positive export-demand effect. Thus, fiscal expansion in one country of a monetary union can produce negative international transmission on the other union members.[18] Notice also that the inflation rate in country 1, which follows the pattern of the output gap, gradually rises because of the expansion in output above its natural level and then declines as output falls, becomes negative, and finally converges to zero with cycles. The opposite happens to the inflation rate in country 2. Because of these differences in inflation behavior, country 2 becomes more competitive with country 1 over time. That is, country 1's price level rises relative to country 2's price level.

The behavior of the nominal interest rate in the union is determined once again by the behavior of the real money stock and the response of output in each country. After the fiscal expansion, the real money stock declines over time because the union price level gradually rises as the rising prices in country 1 outweigh the falling prices in country 2.[19] In addition, the demand for money in the monetary union initially expands because output rises faster in country 1 than it falls in country 2. This happens because the fiscal expansion in country 1 has an immediate effect on aggregate demand there, whereas the appreciation of the union currency has a lagged effect on aggregate demand in country 2. Consequently, the nominal interest rate gradually rises. Eventually, however, the union price level begins to fall as the rate of deflation in country 2 exceeds the rate of inflation in country 1, and the real money stock begins to expand. In addition, the demand for money eventually begins to contract because output eventually falls in country 1 and dominates the eventual rise in output in country 2. Hence, the nominal interest rate eventually falls, overshoots the world level, and ultimately converges on it.

There are important differences in the behavior of the real interest rates in the two countries in response to the fiscal expansion. In country 1 the real interest rate initially rises by less than the nominal interest rate because of the inflation that develops there. In contrast, in country 2 the real interest rate initially rises by more than the nominal interest rate because of the deflation that develops there. In both countries the real interest rate eventually declines and overshoots its original level and then converges on it cyclically. Consequently, the real interest differential between the two countries first declines and then reverses direction and finally converges cyclically to zero.

Next, observe that after the initial appreciation of the union currency, the latter subsequently depreciates and overshoots its new long-run equilibrium level and then converges upon it. This behavior of the union's currency is again dictated by the requirement of interest parity. As long as the nominal interest rate within the union is above the outside world interest rate, the union currency must be depreciating to maintain interest parity. Despite this subsequent depreciation, however, the fiscal expansion still causes the union currency to appreciate permanently above its original level. Finally, the behavior of the real exchange rates reflects the movement of the union currency and the price level in each country. In country 1 the fiscal expansion causes prolonged inflation, and the price level rises and converges cyclically to a permanently higher level. Moreover, country 1's price level initially rises at the same time as the union currency starts to depreciate; and the former effect is sufficiently strong that country 1's real exchange rate eventually appreciates and converges cyclically to a permanently higher level. Therefore, country 1 becomes less competitive with the outside world, and this crowding-out effect helps restore output in country 1 to its natural level. In country 2 the fiscal expansion causes prolonged deflation, and the price level falls and converges cyclically to a permanently lower level. Moreover, country 2's price level initially falls at the same time as the union currency starts to depreciate, and the real exchange rate of country 2 depreciates and converges cyclically to a new long-run equilibrium. Notice, however, that in the new equilibrium $e + p^* - p_2$ is below the initial level of 0. Thus, in the new equilibrium country 2 loses competitiveness with the outside world. However, since country 2 gains competitiveness with country 1, output in country 2 is eventually restored to its original level. Country 1's loss of competitiveness with country 2 is another factor that crowds out aggregate demand in country 1 and causes output to converge to its natural level there.

Finally, consider the effect of fiscal expansion on real wages and the current account in each country shown in figure 2c. Since fiscal expansion causes the union's currency to appreciate immediately, lowering the price of imported goods from the outside world, real wages rise immediately in each country. Furthermore, since country 1's real exchange rate eventually appreciates to a higher long-run equilibrium level, and country 1's price level rises relative to country 2's price level, real wages in country 1 rise over time to an even higher permanent level. In contrast, while country 2's real exchange rate appreciates permanently, country 2's price level falls relative to country 1's price level, and real wages in country 2 fall permanently below their original level.

With respect to the current account, the initial fall in import prices from the outside world induced by the appreciation of the union's currency causes the current account of each country to move immediately into surplus. Subsequently, however, the current account surplus begins to decline because of the lagged effect of the appreciation on trade volumes. In the new equilibrium, the current account in country 1 moves into deficit because country 1 becomes less competitive with respect to country 2 as well as with the outside world. To put it another way, fiscal expansion in country 1 requires crowding out through the current account to restore equilibrium in the goods sector. In country 2, the current account surplus returns to zero as country 2 becomes more competitive with country 1 but less competitive with the outside world. A zero current account surplus for country 2 is required to restore equilibrium in the goods sector there.

In the benchmark simulation, fiscal expansion in country 1 causes output to decline in country 2. However, it is also possible for positive international transmission to occur. To see this, consider another simulation with a modified set of parameter values.[20] In each country real exchange rates now have weaker effects on aggregate demand, income has

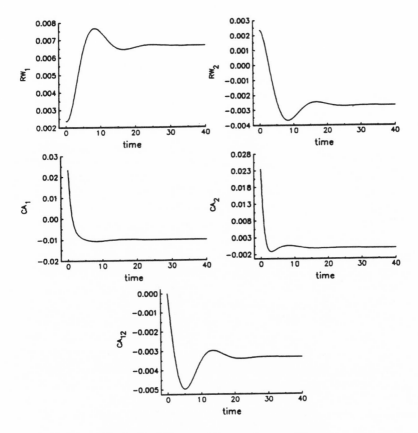

Fig. 2c. Real Wage and Current Account Effects

a stronger effect on import demand, and the real interest rate has a weaker effect on investment spending. Consequently, the expansion in income in country 1 has a stronger effect on export demand in country 2, while the appreciation of the union currency and the rising union interest rate have a weaker effect on aggregate demand there. The overall effect is that output begins to expand in country 2.

Figures 3a–3c show the response of the system to a 1 percent expansion in government spending in country 1. As before, in terms of the impact effects, the union's currency appreciates and overshoots its new long-run equilibrium level. The real exchange rates of each country again appreciate because of the appreciation of the union's currency and the initially unchanged domestic price levels. As before, all other variables

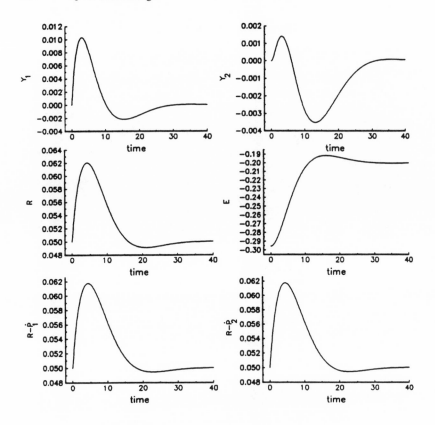

Fig. 3a. Effects of Fiscal Expansion in Country 1

remain initially unchanged. With respect to the dynamic behavior of the system, fiscal expansion in country 1 again causes output there first to expand, then to decline below the natural level, and ultimately to converge to that level. However, output now expands in country 2 also and then declines below the natural level, eventually converging upon it. The results for the other variables are for the most part broadly similar to those for the benchmark simulation.

Conclusion

The major findings of this paper, derived from simulations of a three country model of a monetary union with sticky nominal wages and prices, are as follows. First, monetary expansion in the monetary union causes out-

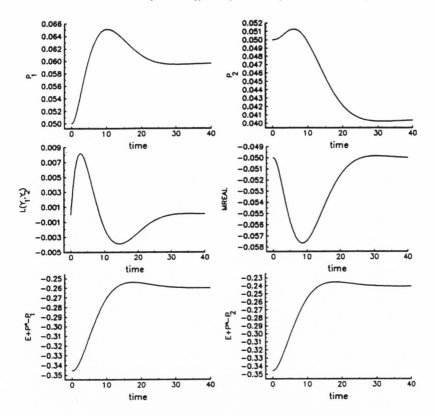

Fig. 3b. Additional Effects of Fiscal Expansion in Country 1

put in the two countries initially to expand temporarily by lowering real interest rates in the two countries and by causing the union's currency to depreciate, making both countries more competitive with the outside world. However, the expansion of output is only temporary since real interest rates and exchange rates gradually return to their original levels.

Second, fiscal expansion by one of the countries causes output in that country to expand because the resulting appreciation of the union currency does not have an immediate crowding out effect. However, the effect of fiscal expansion on output in the other country is ambiguous. The reason is that the second country experiences conflicting effects on aggregate demand. On the one hand, the second country experiences increased export demand coming from the first country, but on the other hand the appreciation of the union's currency and gradually rising interest rates

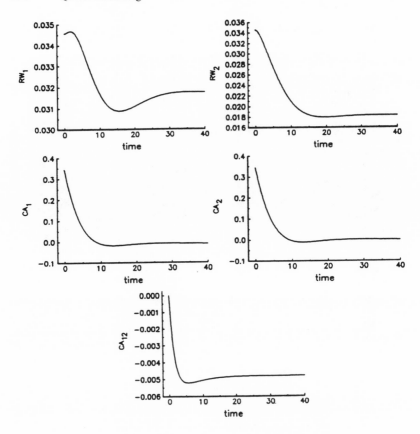

Fig. 3c. Real Wage and Current Account Effects

reduce aggregate demand. Thus, fiscal expansion in one country of a monetary union can produce either positive or negative international transmission on the other union members. In addition, both countries experience a permanent loss of competitiveness with the outside world, and country 1 loses competitiveness with country 2. Also, the union currency permanently appreciates, the price level in country 1 rises, and the price level in country 2 falls.

Third, monetary expansion causes real wages to decline initially in each country because the immediate depreciation of the union currency raises import prices from the outside world. However, the decline in real wages is only temporary, as the real exchange rates of the two countries appreciate over time. The immediate depreciation of the union's currency also causes the current account of each country to move into deficit because of the higher import prices from the outside world. Over time, however, the lagged effects of the depreciation on trade volumes eventually return the current accounts to their original levels.

Finally, in the case of fiscal expansion, real wages initially increase in both countries because the appreciation of the union currency lowers import prices from the outside world. Real wages remain permanently higher in the country undergoing fiscal expansion, but the effect on real wages in the other country is ambiguous. Finally, the current accounts of the two countries initially move into surplus because the appreciation of the union currency lowers import prices from the outside world. In the long run, however, the current account in the country undergoing the fiscal expansion shifts into deficit while that in the other country returns to its initial level.

Appendix

Derivation of the Exchange Rate Expectations Scheme

Consider the interest parity condition (8):

$$r = r^* + \theta_1(\bar{e} - e) + \theta_2(y_1 - \bar{y}_1) + \theta_3(y_2 - \bar{y}_2) + \theta_4(p_1 - \bar{p}_1) + \theta_5 \dot{y}_1 + \theta_6 \dot{y}_2 \quad (8)$$

Differentiating equation (8) with respect to time yields

$$\dot{r} = -\theta_1 \dot{e} + \theta_2 \dot{y}_1 + \theta_3 \dot{y}_2 + \theta_4 \dot{p}_1 + \theta_5 \ddot{y}_1 + \theta_6 \ddot{y}_2 \quad (A1)$$

Solving (A1) for 'e then yields

$$\dot{e} = \frac{-\dot{r} + \theta_2 \dot{y}_1 + \theta_3 \dot{y}_2 + \theta_4 \dot{p}_1 + \theta_5 \ddot{y}_1 + \theta_6 \ddot{y}_2}{\theta_1} \quad (A2)$$

Then using (1) and (2) to eliminate $\ddot{y}_1$ and $\ddot{y}_2$; (4) and (5) to eliminate $\ddot{p}_1, \ddot{p}_2$ $\dot{p}_1$, and $\dot{p}_2$; equations (3), (4), and (5) to eliminate $\dot{r}$; and equation (3) to eliminate $(p_2 - \bar{p}_2)$ yields an expectations scheme of the form

$$\dot{e} = A_1(\bar{e} - e) + A_2(y_1 - \bar{y}_1) + A_3(y_2 - \bar{y}_2) + A_4(p_1 - \bar{p}_1) + A_5 \dot{y}_1 + A_6 \dot{y}_2 \quad (A3)$$

where $A_1...A_6$ are functions of the θ's. Therefore, the perfect foresight expectations scheme (7) is consistent with the model.

NOTES

1. For a survey of European monetary unification, see Eichengreen (1993).

2. See, for example, Thygesen's (1994) recent recommendation that a European Monetary Union be established by the end of the decade. For a discussion of the options for the transition to EMU, see Eichengreen and Wyplosz (1993, 113–122).

3. For a discussion of the key issues relating to the design and implementation of monetary policy in a European Monetary Union, see Frenkel and Goldstein (1991). The Maastricht Treaty imposes restraints on the use of fiscal policy in a future EMU, but Eichengreen (1992, 29) points out potential loopholes in the effectiveness of these restraints. For further discussion of fiscal policy in the European union context see Buiter, Corsetti, and Roubini (1993), Corsetti and Roubini (1993), De Grauwe (1992), Eichengreen (1992), Frankel (1993), Kenen (1992), and Masson and Taylor (1993).

4. Eichengreen (1992, 20–21) presents evidence showing that real wages are responsive to price changes in 8 EC countries although less so than in Canada and the United States.

5. The prediction of negative international transmission from German fiscal expansion to other European countries in the context of the EMS under fixed exchange rates has been suggested by the simulations of the McKibbon-Sachs (1991) Global model, the IMFs multimod model (Masson et. al, 1990), and a model constructed by Roubini (1991).

6. It would be possible to introduce other lags into the model, such as lags in the effect of the real interest rate and of relative member country prices on aggregate demand. However, the real exchange rate lag is the crucial one here, so other lags affecting aggregate demand are ignored.

7. This implies that inflationary expectations are ignored in the wage-setting process. An alternative way to introduce inflationary expectations would be to incorporate perfect foresight (rational) expectations into an overlapping wage contract model. However, the procedure used by Dornbusch is adopted here in order to avoid further complicating the model.

8. In the Dornbusch model (1976) only the exchange rate gap ($\bar{e}$-e) appears in the exchange rate expectations scheme. The appearance of the additional variables here is the result of the output and trade flow lags as well as the Phillips curve in the second country.

9. The values of $\theta_1...\theta_6$ are required in order to determine from equation (8) the initial effect of monetary and fiscal expansion on the exchange rate.

10. The parameters were assigned the following values: γ_1=0.5, γ_2=0.5, ϕ_1=.7, ϕ_2=.7, σ_1=1.0, σ_2=1.0, β=1.0, δ_1=0.25, δ_2=0.25, δ_3=0.25, Ω_1=1.0, Ω_2=1.0, Ω_3=1.0, Ω_4=1.0, π_1=.25, π_2=.25, m_{12}=.19, m_{21}=.20, and w=0.5. These values are roughly in line with a number of empirical studies of industrial countries. However, in the case of $\Omega_1...\Omega_4$ values were chosen to ensure that the system was dynamically stable. In most cases only minor complexities were introduced into the simulation results when the values of the structural parameters were altered, as discussed later.

However, in some cases the system exhibited strong oscillatory behavior when the parameters were modified.

11. The countries are not exactly identical since m_{12} differs slightly from m_{21}. If m_{12} were set exactly equal to m_{21}, equations (9) would be inconsistent, and it would be impossible to calculate the values of $\theta_1 ... \theta_6$. The problem is that in solving equations (9) simultaneously for $\theta_1 ... \theta_6$, we must in effect use Cramer's Rule. However, the solution for each θ involves the ratio of two determinants, each of which converges to zero as the two countries become identical. In principle, one could use L'Hospital's Rule to resolve this problem, but in practice this is impossible because of the complexity of the determinants.

12. From equation (3) the fall in the nominal interest rate is given by $(-1/\beta)dm$, where β is 1.0. Hence r falls by .01.

13. The exchange rate undershoots here to compensate for movements in some of the other variables in the interest parity condition (8). In addition to causing r to decline, the monetary expansion causes an equal movement in $\bar{p}_1$, and it also causes $\dot{y}_1$ and $\dot{y}_2$ to become positive. However, with a different set of parameter values, it is also possible for the exchange rate to overshoot. See Levin (1994b) for an analysis of undershooting in the single country case.

14. For other parameter values it is also possible for the convergence to be cyclical. Hence, all variables can overshoot as they move toward their long-run equilibrium levels.

15. Note that the Phillips curve equations (4) and (5) imply that domestic goods prices in each country are a markup on wages. Therefore, real wages in terms of domestic goods remain constant throughout the adjustment process.

16. In the simulations $u_1=.6$; $u_2=.3$; $v_1=.3$; and $v_2=.6$.

17. The effect of growing output in country 1 and country 1's price level gap on exchange rate expectations presumably depends on the fact that asset holders will now expect interest rates to start rising. Hence, that would produce the expectation that the union currency would begin to appreciate. See Levin (1994a) for a demonstration that overshooting due to fiscal expansion in the single country case can be traced to the exchange rate lag on trade flows combined with exchange rate expectations held with perfect foresight.

18. Goldstein, et al. (1992, 51–52 and 55) point out some of the conflicting effects on the other members of a monetary union when one of them undertakes fiscal expansion and suggest that the transmission effect could be negative. See also Masson and Taylor (1993, 21–22).

19. The reason for this is that output in country 1 rises faster than it falls in country 2, as explained in the text. Therefore, the price effects are greater in country 1.

20. The following parameters were changed to new values: $\sigma_1=.1$, $\sigma_2=.1$, $\delta_1=.02$, $\delta_3=.02$, $\Omega_3=.25$, $\Omega_4=.25$, $m_{12}=.40$, and $m_{21}=.39$. These satisfy the following condition for an expansionary effect on country 2:

$$m_{12} > [\Omega_1 \phi_1 \sigma_2 - \beta \delta_3 \Omega_4 (de_0/d\mu_1)]/\beta\Omega_1 \ [de_0/d\mu_1 < 0\,]$$

REFERENCES

Buiter, Willem; Corsetti, Giancarlo; and Roubini, Nouriel. 1993. "Excessive Deficits: Sense and Nonsense in the Treaty of Maastricht." *Economic Policy* 8:57–100.

Corsetti, Giancarlo, and Roubini, Nouriel. "The Design of Optimal Fiscal Rules for Europe after 1992." In Francisco Torres and Francesco Giavazzi, eds., *Adjustment and Growth in the European Monetary Union.* Cambridge: Cambridge University Press.

De Grauwe, Paul. 1992. *The Economics of Monetary Integration.* Oxford: Oxford University Press.

Dornbusch, Rudiger. 1976. "Expectations and Exchange Rate Dynamics." *Journal of Political Economy* 84:1161–76.

Eichengreen, Barry. 1992. *Should the Maastricht Treaty Be Saved?* Princeton Studies in International Finance No. 74.

Eichengreen, Barry. 1993. "European Monetary Unification." *Journal of Economic Literature* 31:1321–57.

Eichengreen, Barry. 1994. "Fiscal Policy and EMU." In Barry Eichengreen and Jeffrey Frieden, eds., *The Political Economy of European Monetary Unification.* Boulder and Oxford: Westview Press.

Eichengreen, Barry, and Wyplosz, Charles. 1993. "The Unstable EMS." *Brookings Papers on Economic Activity* 0:51–124.

Frankel, Jeffrey A. 1993. "Three Comments on Exchange Rate Stabilization and European Monetary Union." Center for International and Development Economics Research Working Paper No. C93–013.

Frenkel, Jacob A., and Goldstein, Morris. 1991. "Monetary Policy in an Emerging European Economic and Monetary Union: Key Issues." *I.M.F. Staff Papers.*

Goldstein, Morris; Isard, Peter; Masson, Paul; and Taylor, Mark P. 1992. *Policy Issues in the Evolving International Monetary System.* Occasional Paper No. 96 International Monetary Fund.

Kenen, Peter B. 1992. *EMU After Maastricht.* Paris: Group of Thirty.

Levin, Jay H. 1994a. "Fiscal Policy, Expectations, and Exchange Rate Dynamics." *Review of International Economics* 2:50–61.

Levin, Jay H. 1994b. "On Sluggish Output Adjustment and Exchange Rate Dynamics." *Journal of International Money and Finance* 13:447–58.

Masson, Paul, and Taylor, Mark P. 1993. "Currency Unions: A Survey of the Issues." In Paul R. Masson and Mark P. Taylor, *Policy Issues in the Operation of Currency Unions.* Cambridge: Cambridge University Press.

Masson, Paul; Symnanski, Steven; and Meredith, Guy. 1990. "Multimod Mark II: A Revised and Extended Model." Occasional Paper No. 71 International Monetary Fund.

McKibbin, Warwick J., and Sachs, Jeffrey D. 1991. *Global Linkages: Macroeconomic Interdependence and Cooperation in the World Economy.* Washington, D.C.: Brookings Institution.

Roubini, Nouriel. 1991. "Leadership and Cooperation in the European Monetary System: A Simulation Approach." *Journal of Policy Modeling* 13:1–39.

Thygesen, Niels. 1994. "Monetary Arrangements." In C. Randall Henning, Gary Clyde Hufbauer, and Eduard Hochreiter, eds., *Reviving the European Union.* Washington, D.C.: Institute for International Economics.

Part Four:
Panel Discussion

CHAPTER 13

Panel Commentary

Gregory K. Schoepfle and Jorge F. Perez-Lopez

For more than twenty years, the U.S. Department of Labor's Bureau of International Labor Affairs (ILAB) has sponsored external research to examine the impact of international trade and investment policies on U.S. workers. Bob Stern has been a frequent and valued contributor to this research program.

Over this period, economic analysis of U.S. trade policy initiatives—and in particular the analysis of the implications of such major policy initiatives on U.S. workers—has increased exponentially. For example, a recent major Administration trade initiative, the North American Free Trade Agreement (NAFTA), generated more than two-dozen economic impact studies. Its potential effect on the U.S. workforce was one of the central issues in the intense national debate that surrounded that agreement. Needless to say, Bob and his colleagues produced a study for National Commission for Employment Policy that figured prominently in that debate.

In this tribute, we would like to highlight some of Bob's contributions to research on the employment effects of trade policies. To put these contributions in context, we first discuss briefly the evolution of U.S. trade policymaking and of economic research on such policies since the 1960s, and the work of the U.S. Department of Labor in support of the analysis of the economic impact of U.S. trade policies.

Development in U.S. Trade Policymaking

The Trade Expansion Act of 1962 made several significant changes to the way in which the United States formulated and implemented international trade policy. The Act required the President to appoint a Special Representative for Trade Negotiations, with the rank of Ambassador and subject to Senate confirmation, to be the chief representative of the United States at international trade negotiations. The Special Representative reported directly to the president. Prior to the passage of the Act, the locus for the formulation of U.S. trade policy and the conduct of international trade negotiations had been the Department of State.

The Trade Expansion Act of 1962 also required the President to create a Cabinet-level Interagency Trade Organization, headed by the Special Representative and composed of such department and agency heads as the President chose, to advise the President on international trade matters. The Secretary of Labor was one of the Cabinet officials designated to be a member of the new interagency body. Moreover, the Act required the President to request advice from various Cabinet departments, including the Department of Labor, regarding the list of items on which trade negotiations were to be proposed, and to hold public hearings for interested parties to offer their views on the same.

With these structural changes, the Department of Labor gained clearer authority and more direct responsibility in the area of U.S. international trade policy development and negotiation. In the interagency process, the Department of Labor was expected to offer analysis and advice on the implications for the domestic employment situation of the United States pursuing various international trade initiatives. On another track, the public hearings process provided an avenue for interested parties to offer their views and created further demand for economic analysis of trade policy decisions.

Partly in response to its increased trade policy responsibilities, in 1973 an Office of Foreign Economic Research (now the Division of Foreign Economic Research in the Office of International Economic Affairs) was created as part of the Bureau of International Labor Affairs at the Department of Labor. The mission of the research office is to examine the impact of international trade and investment flows on the employment and earnings of U.S. workers. The research results are intended to provide the Department of Labor's policymakers and representatives in interagency committees with information and advice on the employment effects of U.S. international economic initiatives.

Evolution of Trade Policy Research

The growing importance of international trade to the U.S. economy and the political sensitivity of the costs and benefits of international trade actions to the domestic economy and employment have spawned a demand for evaluations of international trade policy initiatives. The ever-expanding international trade policy agenda has demanded more sophisticated methods to analyze very complex and comprehensive agreements.

The Tokyo Round of Multilateral Trade Negotiations (MTN), conducted 1973–79, was the seventh round of MTN held under the auspices of the General Agreement on Tariffs and Trade (GATT). Prior to the Tokyo Round, there had been few comprehensive economic analyses of the effects of multilateral trade agreements. The focus of most studies up to that time tended to be on specific industrial sectors or commodity groups, reflecting the emphasis of trade negotiations on the reduction of tariffs on traded goods. However, the Tokyo Round was a more ambitious venture, going beyond the cutting of tariffs and extending to the developments of rules covering several areas theretofore not addressed in multilateral trade negotiations. In addition, the Tokyo Round also marked the beginning of broader participation by developing countries in multilateral trade negotiations.

It was about this time and in response to Tokyo Round needs for comprehensive analyses—across issues, sectors, and trading partners—that Bob Stern first developed his policy-friendly empirical models. For many years, academic trade economists had espoused the virtues of free trade and had explored the pure theory of international trade—deriving results for fairly simple two-country, two-good, two-factor idealized models that eventually were generalized to multi-country, multi-commodity cases. Often these theoretical results were illustrated with complex graphs and/or equations that were incomprehensible to most policymakers. Bob pioneered attempts to introduce more realism and to relax some of the idealized aspects of trade models, for instance, restrictive assumptions about how factor and goods markets actually operate (e.g., imperfectly competitive markets, unemployment, and factor mobility.)

As in many other areas of economics, empirical studies of international trade have lagged theoretical innovations. In part, this has been the result of inadequate information. Most nations rely on different valuation and classification systems for domestic output and for international trade transactions. Because most national statistical systems differ, making detailed international comparisons is extremely difficult. In addition, classification systems change over time making longitudinal studies difficult.

Before reporting of trade data, international efforts to harmonize valuation and classification systems, the availability of improved concordances to link trade and production classifications, availability of country input-output tables, and greater access to statistics and other information on international trade transactions—in conjunction with advances in low-cost computing power—led to more empirical trade research. The sophistication of analytical methods has also increased over time moving from sectoral partial equilibrium studies to more completely specific general equilibrium models.

Ironically, these data and computing improvements have come at a time when new challenges face international trade researchers, as the trade negotiations agenda expands from the more tractable trade in goods to the less visible trade in services (on which Bob has written) and from known tariff and quota barriers to trade to more institutionalized (or hidden) mechanisms, such as standards (on which Bob and his colleagues have written, too).

Stern's Contributions to ILAB's Research

With the establishment of the Office of Foreign Economic Research in the Department of Labor's Bureau of International Labor Affair, a modest research program was developed to support the agency's international economic policy development and analysis, comprised of a small staff of research economists supplemented by an external contract research program. Bob Stern has made significant contributions to each area in which ILAB has sponsored external contract research:

1. Data development, improved concordances between domestic and international trade classifications, and better measures of elasticities;
2. Modeling of the relationship between international trade and domestic production and employment;
3. The implications for U.S. workers of various international trade negotiations, whether multilateral (e.g., the Tokyo Round of MTNs), bilateral (e.g., U.S.-Canada Free Trade Agreement), or plurilateral (e.g., NAFTA).
4. The implications for U.S. workers of international developments such as flows of foreign direct investment, increased trade with developing countries, changes in technology, fluctuations in exchange rates, etc.; and
5. Labor adjustment issues related to international trade, including the magnitude of dislocations and the reemployment experiences of affected workers and international comparisons of other country's labor force adjustment experiences to increased international trade.

More recently, ILAB has also been interested in exploring the relationship between labor standards and international trade flows.

From nearly the beginning of the ILAB external research program, Bob Stern and his colleagues and students have been frequent contributors. They have written in virtually every area listed above. The ten studies completed or in process by Bob Stern for the Department of Labor confirm the breadth of the research undertaken by Stern and his collaborators for ILAB. The results from Bob's projects usually have been published in one form or another in professional journals. Several other studies done for ILAB were conducted by Bob's students and their students.

Bob's study of the elasticities of substitution between imports and home goods in the United States was completed in 1982. Done in association with Alan Deardorff and Clint Shiells, it provided some new estimates of the elasticities of substitution at a 3-digit Standard Industrial Classification level that are critical in assessing the domestic output response to changes in imports brought about by tariff reductions. They improve upon the common assumption of many studies that changes in imports translate into changes in domestic output on a dollar-for-dollar basis. This study also constructed new estimates of price elasticities of import demand and compared them with the work done earlier by Stern et al. (1976).

With Alan Deardorff Bob produced for ILAB in 1988 a batch mode computer facility, called the trade policy analysis package, that was based on a partial equilibrium model of the effects of trade policies on prices and quantities of trade. It enables the user to calculate automatically the effects of changes in trade quantities or tariffs on employment in 446 disaggregated U.S. industries.

Bob and his colleagues have done several studies for ILAB regarding trade negotiations, and two are now in progress. Stern's first study of this nature, conducted in association with Ed Leamer, was completed in 1975. Stern and Leamer examined the employment effects that would obtain if the post-Kennedy Round (1972) tariffs were reduced. Using a cross-section model with 20 industries and 18 countries for 1970, labor allocation was explained by the resource endowment for a country and resistance factors (e.g., tariffs and distance to market). First, they estimated the fraction of total employment in a given industry across countries; the determinants of industry employment shares were estimated through regression analysis. Then they simulated industry-by-industry employment effects for each country of alternative reductions in tariffs (10 percent and 50 percent across-the-board tariff cuts) using calculated tariff activities.

More recently, Bob presented a paper on the economic implications of NAFTA at an ILAB-sponsored conference on immigration. This paper was based on a larger study (in association with Drusilla Brown and Alan Deardorff) for the National Commission for Employment Policy. The latter study, alluded to at the beginning of this paper, was an ambitious analysis of the employment effects of NAFTA. The study provided information on the potential change in the industrial distribution of employment by region and state and by occupational category. Some scenarios related to labor migration were also examined as well as the potential demand for worker adjustment assistance in the United States.

Again in association with Drusilla Brown and Alan Deardorff, Bob is currently conducting research for ILAB on the economic effects of an East Asian preferential trading bloc and of the accession of Chile to NAFTA.

Two studies for ILAB were conducted by Bob Stern and Alan Deardorff in 1984. The first examined the effects that levels of protection in developing countries have on other countries in their economic "neighborhood", that is, countries whose economic circumstances are similar to themselves. The second examined input-output technologies and the effects of tariffs and exchange rates. In this study, the sensitivity of the specification of the input-output table, which characterizes the technology of a country in the Michigan Model of World Production and Trade, on the calculated effects of tariff removal and devaluation was examined, especially the size and nature of errors that might be introduced by using incorrect input-output tables to characterize the technology of a given country (e.g., using the U.S. input-output tables as a proxy for Brazil or using Brazil's input-output table for another developing country).

An ongoing study being conducted for ILAB by Bob, along with Deardorff and Brown, assesses the impact of the Government of India's market opening initiatives using the Michigan World Production and Trade Model.

Although Bob's seminal work (done in conjunction with Drusilla Brown and Alan Deardorff) in the area of standards and international trade was not conducted for ILAB, it should be mentioned as it demonstrated the breadth of Bob's interests and versatility. Brown, Deardorff, and Stern participated in a recent American Society of International Law project on "Domestic Policy Divergence in an Integrated World Economy: Fairness Claims and the Gains from Trade," under the general direction of Professor Jagdish Bhagwati of Columbia University and Professor Robert Hudec of the University of Minnesota. As part of this project, Brown, Deardorff, and Stern prepared an analysis which explored the theoretical connections between labor standards and trade, the welfare and other effects of labor standards themselves, and whether it is in a county's interest to adopt widely-recognized labor standards. This study represents one of the first analytical attempts to explore the implications of introducing labor standards into more traditional theoretical models of international trade.

Stern's Legacy

As a scholar, teacher, and policy analyst, Bob Stern's accomplishments are outstanding. The body of policy-oriented research studies generated by Bob and his colleagues and students at the University of Michigan has enriched public understanding of the effects of international trade actions. What stands out about Bob's policy studies—from a policymaker's perspective—is their empirical focus, lucidity, clarity in exposition, and readability. Stern possesses an uncanny ability to take complicated and technical modeling results and present them in a nontechnical way that is understandable to policymakers.

As noted earlier, another characteristic of Bob's is his versatility. He has been constantly exploring new issues—building upon prior work and pushing the frontier (e.g., in the areas of nontariff barriers, intellectual property rights, trade in services, free trade agreements, labor mobility, and the linkage between international labor standards and trade). One can see a constructive progression of this work: from studies using partial equilibrium commodity analysis to those done in a general equilibrium framework—the development of pieces that eventually fit together in a more general setting.

One of the crowning achievements of Bob's career has been the development of the Michigan Model of World Production and Trade. This is a short-run, static general equilibrium model that is larger than most computable general equilibrium (CGE) models in terms of sectors and numbers of countries, but not with the level of sectoral detail of some partial equilibrium models (e.g., the model developed by Robert E. Baldwin for ILAB in 1974). With the Michigan Model, Stern has been able to explore the effects of different modeling assumptions, terms of trade, competitive structure, and input-output technologies, among other things. The model is constantly evolving and being redefined. Some areas where further work is called for are in the areas of capital (investment) and labor markets.

Stern's legacy is not only in his own research and writing, but is reflected in the training of his students (and their students). We have been fortunate at the Department of Labor to have had several of Bob's students on our research staff at various points in time including Mike Aho, Clint Shiells, and Chip Bowen.

In fact, many of the graduates of the Michigan economics Ph.D. program have found their way to Washington, assuming responsible policy and research positions not only at the Department of Labor, but also at the International Trade Commission, the Federal Reserve Board, the Council of Economic Advisors, the International Monetary Fund, and the World Bank. Others have taken up teaching or other research or think-tank positions.

What distinguishes these graduates from the many that migrate to Washington each year is excellent training as economists and solid grounding in both theory and quantitative methods, and their desire and ability to apply their analytical tools to public policy issues.

What has emanated from "die Stern" is a very bright but low-profile constellation of children and grandchildren that offers a marked contrast to more highly visible and doctrinaire Chicago-Stanford-MIT-Harvard shooting stars that often blind Washington's heaven with brief, flashy displays, and then flame out. (Yes, there still is a heaven over Washington.) We in the Washington trade policy and research community thank Bob Stern for his many past contributions and look forward to many more in the future.

Geza Feketekuty

Robert Stern has had a major influence on both international economic research and trade policy over three decades, through his pioneering work on the empirical analysis of international trade and capital flows and the use of quantitative methods to estimate the economic effects of policy measures. He brought to bear an extraordinary competence in both international trade and monetary theory, and the tools of empirical analysis. None other than Harry Johnson recognized his distinction by observing that Stern is distinguished by his capacity to roam freely over the three major branches of the field: the pure theory of international trade, the theory of the international monetary system, and techniques and applications of empirical research on international trade and monetary problems.

He has deepened our understanding and strengthened the foundation of trade theory by empirically testing the factors influencing the pattern of international trade and the impact of policy changes on trade flows. In the process he developed and refined many of the tools of empirical analysis in the trade field.

He has improved trade policy through the practical application of the empirical and theoretical tools of economic analysis to the most current issues of concern to policymakers. There are many economists who will express views on the economic advantages or disadvantages of open trade policies, but few who can address themselves in as competent a manner to the empirically measured effects of trade policy measures. These are rather rare qualities, which have made Bob Stern one of the most sought-after economists for policy-related empirical work in the trade field.

Bob Stern has not only been one of the few distinguished, policy oriented international economists in the United States, but he has also trained a large proportion of the government and academic economists who have this capability. Robert Stern is one of those extraordinary teachers who have the unique capacity not only to pass on knowledge and skill, but also to inspire and challenge their students to follow their footsteps. A number of his former students noted that he had the capacity to make students feel that working on trade issues was one of the most exciting, interesting, and important things that they could do, and that all such work should be firmly grounded through empirical observation of the real world. Michael Aho, one of those former students, observed that "Bob has always been superb in motivating students to measure and estimate the consequences of trade liberalization. He made his students think that this dull stuff is interesting and important. The result has been that most of the students he has trained have been very good in quantifying economic relationships."

The same human qualities that make him a great teacher also make him a sought-after advisor in government trade policy circles. He has the patience and interest to listen to policy officials, and to try to understand policy issues as policymakers see them, so he could better relate his work to those policy issues. While policymakers are often frustrated by academics who provide answers based on theories that do not fit the policy issues at hand, or preconceived notions of what the problem is, Bob Stern made the effort to fit his work to the real issues at hand, and more often than not succeeded in advancing our understanding of them.

I have personally experienced Bob Stern's willingness to tackle new issues on many occasions. When I had the responsibility to develop an international consensus in the early 1980s on launching global trade negotiations on trade in services, Bob Stern was one of the academic economists I turned to in order to help me think through the theoretical and empirical issues that would have to be addressed. Most economists at that time were still convinced that services were not tradable, and that the term "trade in services" was an oxymoron. Stern's willingness to explore, measure, and debate trade in services was invaluable in attracting academic research interest in the subject, and in legitimizing the issue.

Bob Stern organized a number of conferences and meetings, and the intellectual testing of ideas that took place at those meetings helped this officer to clarify his thinking. Bob Stern also initiated new research into trade in services, including the empirical testing of trade theories as they might apply to trade in services. This work not only brought academic research on trade in services into the mainstream, but stimulated a number of his best graduate students to immerse themselves in the field. A number of the younger economists who work and publish on trade in services are former students of Bob Stern. Bernard Hoekman, in particular, has made substantial contributions to the economic literature in this area, and provided valuable conceptual support to the negotiators at the GATT during the negotiation of the Uruguay Round agreement on services. Stern himself wrote a number of articles on the analysis and measurement of trade in services that deepened our understanding of trade in services and the policy issues involved.

The broad appreciation for Bob Stern's contribution to the trade policy world can be glimpsed from the extensive list of his consulting contracts with government departments and international organizations. He has written for the Office of the U.S. Trade Representative, the Labor Department, the State Department, the Treasury, the Senate Finance Committee, UNCTAD, the Economic Commission for Latin America, and the Economic Council of Canada. He has also traveled widely abroad for the U.S. Information Agency to Japan, the Caribbean, India, Spain, Belgium, Switzerland, Indonesia, Hong Kong, Turkey, and Sri Lanka.

Bob Stern's leadership qualities are well demonstrated by the extraordinary vitality of the University of Michigan Research Seminar in International Economics. Under his leadership, the Research Seminar generates an extraordinary stream of Discussion Papers covering a wide range of research topics. In keeping with Stern's philosophy of stimulating interest and excitement for empirical research on trade policy and of maintaining a close link with the policy community, the Discussion papers attract wide circulation. Bob Stern himself best expressed his philosophy in the Introduction to one book he coauthored with Alan Deardorff (Deardorff and Stern 1990, 2):

Because we have always viewed the Michigan Model as a practical and useful tool for the analysis of trade policies, we have made a concerted effort over the years to maintain close and continuing contacts with staff members of those agencies in the U.S. government and the international organizations that have primary responsibility in dealing with trade matters. This has involved wide circulation of the Discussion Paper Series from the University of Michigan Research Seminar in International Economics, specially arranged meetings with pertinent officials and staff in different locations, and the periodic convening of conferences on important trade issues. At the same time, we have contributed papers based on our model to, and participated as discussants in, a number of academic conferences. Many of the papers have been published in refereed journals. Our objective accordingly has been to provide useful inputs into the policy process and simultaneously to maintain recognition and respect from our peers.

Wide Impact of the Michigan Model

Robert Stern's empirical work on trade led him, in stages, to the development and publication in 1986 of one of the most widely used reference books in the field, *The Michigan Model of World Production and Trade: Theories and Applications* (Deardorff and Stern 1986), which he coauthored with Alan Deardorff. The book brought together the important technical features of the Michigan Model of World Production and Trade and a series of applications of the model to a variety of policy issues in the multilateral trading system.

The Michigan Model, in its various stages of development, for many years was the only effective tool that could be used by policymakers to estimate the potential effects of alternative tariff cutting scenarios on trade flows and employment. The model remains one of the most frequently used trade modeling tools today. Bob Stern and his colleagues and students at Michigan applied the model, in its various stages of development, to the measurement of the economic effects of tariff cuts in the Tokyo and Uruguay rounds of multilateral trade negotiations, the U.S.-Canada Free Trade Agreement and the North American Free Trade Agreement. The evaluation of the Tokyo Round tariff cuts, which Stern and Deardorff carried out under a contract for the USTR and the Labor Department, was one of the earliest and most influential applications of computable general equilibrium models at the sectoral level. From a trade policy perspective, the empirical foundation provided by Stern and his colleagues for estimating the economic effects of tariff cuts significantly assisted the process of developing public and Congressional support for the negotiated tariff cuts.

Typically, models like the Michigan Model are used before negotiations begin to provide estimates of the potential economic welfare gains and sectoral employment effects of alternative proposals for reducing trade barriers such as tariffs or import quotas. The models are also used after the negotiations are concluded to estimate the likely economic welfare gains and sectoral employment effects of the negotiated reductions in trade barriers. Typically, these estimates play an important role in convincing the Congress and the public at large that the negotiated reductions in trade barriers will result in overall gains for the nation, and that the adjustment costs in terms of job losses in particular sectors are reasonable. During the Tokyo Round, the Michigan Model was the only really viable model of its type. In the intervening years other models have been developed, but the Michigan Model retains a prominent role and was heavily used in evaluating the results of the U.S. Canadian Free Trade and NAFTA negotiations.

Prior to the publication of the book on the Michigan Model, Bob Stern published a number of books and articles that have been widely used in classrooms and research centers as key reference works on the quantitative methods and tools of analysis in international trade. The two outstanding books in this area are *Quantitative International Economics* (Leamer and Stern 1970), and *Price Elasticities in International Trade* (Stern et al. 1976).

The latter book proved particularly useful to me at a time when I was responsible for coordinating the work of various U.S. government agencies in evaluating alternative tariff cutting scenarios. The development of coordinated positions was often hampered by interagency debates over the appropriate price elasticities that should be employed in the analysis. While those debates were usually driven by the desire of various agencies to understate or overstate the effects of proposed tariff cuts, the publication of Stern's book eliminated the subterfuge and forced the agencies to focus the debate on the real issue.

Empirical Work on Factors of Production and Comparative Advantage

One of Bob Stern's continuing research interests is to measure the relationship between a country's endowment in various factors of production and its comparative advantage as revealed in its pattern of trade. His work on the composition of U.S. trade identified the importance of human capital to U.S. comparative advantage. This finding has been helpful to U.S. policymakers in explaining why the United States could compete with goods produced by cheap labor abroad. The deeper understanding of the importance of human capital to U.S. export performance, and the resulting impact of expanded trade on raising real incomes, has persuaded recent administrations to emphasize the importance of education and training for increasing national competitiveness in world markets. In a related vein, former U.S. Trade Representative Micky Kantor has pointed to recent findings by USTR Chief Economist David Walters that services jobs associated with U.S. exports on average pay higher wages than services or manufacturing jobs in the economy as a whole.

Stern's related work highlighting the interaction between macroeconomic policy and trade policy has been particularly valuable to trade policymakers. The potential adverse impact of certain macroeconomic policies on trade policy is all too often ignored. Macroeconomic policies that result in wide swings in the external balance, for example, can generate major adjustment problems as resources are shifted from tradeable to nontradeable sectors and back again. Large shifts from tradable to nontradable sectors are often perceived by politicians and the general public as excessive import competition, and therefore tend to generate sharp increases in protectionist pressures. Moreover, these shifts are often, quite wrongly, interpreted as failures of trade policy, requiring some correction.

Suggestions for Further Work

A tribute to Robert Stern's contribution to international economic research and trade policy would not be complete without a forward look at some current challenges for policy-related research in international trade. Throughout his career, Stern has looked ahead to confront challenges. The suggestions provided here fall into two categories: improvements in the Michigan model, and new trade policy-related issues that could benefit from empirical and theoretical research.

Notwithstanding the major contributions of the Michigan model to the measurement of the economic effects of trade liberalization measures, it has a number of shortcomings. The authors of the model are well aware of many of these shortcomings, since they have been brought to their attention through peer review, and they themselves have reported on a number of these critiques. Some of the shortcomings reported by Stern and Deardorff related to difficulties in applying the model to nontariff issues such as government procurement, barriers to trade in services and the absence of adequate intellectual property protection. I would agree with those observations, but at the same time argue that these shortcomings may not be as important as the tendency of the model to understate the gains from trade liberalization.

The most serious shortcoming of the model is its inability to capture the dynamic gains from trade. As has been widely recognized, the dynamic gains from trade often far exceed the static gains that comes from the improved allocation of resources. The removal of barriers can shock producers to innovate, resulting in major efficiency gains and productivity increases within the existing allocation of resources.

Arriving at a modeling solution for the estimation of dynamic gains, in my view, should have a high priority in an empirically driven trade policy research program. There is no theoretical consensus yet on how to approach the conceptualization and measurement of such dynamic gains, and empirical modeling of dynamic gains is therefore clearly a long term proposition. In the meantime, it would be useful if estimates based on static models were accompanied by statements regarding the likely direction, and possibly the order of magnitude, of change in the estimates that could be expected by the inclusion of dynamic gains from trade.

A second reason why models like the Michigan Model tend to understate the gains from trade is that they tend to aggregate trade and production data on the basis of a small number of broadly defined sectors, thereby failing to capture the efficiency gains from resource shifts occurring within those broad sectors. Given the substantial amount of intrasectoral trade among developed countries, a high level of aggregation on the basis of broad sectors is likely to miss a significant amount of the gains resulting from tariff cuts on goods traded by industrial countries with each other.

Looking beyond the modeling of tariff cuts, one of the more interesting challenges facing empirical and theoretical research in trade is the connection with competition policy. As visible, government imposed trade barriers at the border are removed, more of the trade policy focus has shifted to discriminatory regulatory measures and anticompetitive practices by enterprises that restrain trade. The literature on anti-trust policy needs to be related in a systematic way with trade theory and empirical work on trade. One interesting area of empirical research in support of the increasing link between trade policy and competition policy would be to measure unexplained price gaps between major trading partners and to explore the potential causes of such price gaps.

Alfred Reifman

I want to bear witness to Bob Stern's role in the formulation of public policy, particularly trade policy in the Congress.

Bob has been a major player in trade policy at least since the Tokyo Round was up for congressional approval. To my personal knowledge he has had an important role in the congressional debates over the Tokyo Round, the U.S.-Canada Free Trade Agreement, the North American Free Trade Agreement (NAFTA), and the Uruguay Round. Indeed, his *Economic Analysis of the Effects of the Tokyo Round* (Deardorff and Stern 1976) is one of the earliest and most influential applications of CGE system at the sectoral level that I know.

His *Quantitative International Economics* (Leamer and Stern 1970) written while Leamer was still a graduate student, is a classic, much used by students today, a quarter of a century after its first edition. His *Price Elasticities in International Trade* (Stern et al. 1976) is still used as a source for various computations by others. These two books plus his *The Balance of Payments; Theory and Economic Policy* (Stern 1973) are durable classics in the field.

Many of us were educated by Bob. Indeed, one of my coworkers is constantly referring to one or more of Bob's books when we debate, especially about quantitative methods of analysis.

But more important to me, he has done the hard work. The easy road, which I take everyday, is to talk about general economic principles. Free trade is good for you. Trade is not a zero-sum game. All countries gain. Protection is costly. Jobs are not lost or gained by trade policy. Trade policy does not affect the balance of trade.

Such "profound" statements, even when sophisticated exceptions are noted, do not require heavy lifting. The quantitative assessments that Stern does very much require it. It is not enough to say that a trade agreement is good for the United States. At least as important are the answers to such specific questions as: How good? What jobs might be affected, positively and negatively?

Bob and his team at Michigan (and Drusilla Brown) have answered these questions in numerous papers, congressional hearings and seminars at my organization, the Congressional Research Service (CRS). He has made concrete our vague generalizations about the trade effects of various initiatives, helping law-makers understand the real effects of some poorly understood academic theories.

In the debate over NAFTA, it was very effective to have some of Bob's quantitative work at hand to answer the concerns of congressmen. There is nothing like a specific number to put concepts like "the great sucking sound" in perspective.

Another example may help to illustrate this point. While the U.S.-Canada FTA was being debated in the Congress, CRS ran a workshop on the subject. Bob's presentation was the centerpiece of the session. He described the quantitative analysis of the effects of the FTA and ended the session with an Overview and Assessment of his and the other studies. Some 112 congressional staff attended. It was generally considered one of the best seminar presentations that my organization has run. It was certainly one of the best attended.

Bob's skill in translating econometric jargon makes it possible for estimates not only to be understood by members of Congress but to be accepted by them. Congress, as you are aware, is impatient with economic theory, especially when it runs counter to what they perceive as the interest of their constituents. But give them a number, they have little choice but to stop and rethink their preconceived notions of economic policy. And Bob has plenty of numbers.

Our task in advising the Congress on the impact of various economic policies, particularly trade policies, would be much more difficult without the advice and work of Bob Stern.

W. Max Corden

It is a pleasure to be asked to comment on Bob Stern's influence on policy and research contributions. Just as Geza Feketekuty is one of Bob's most seasoned students, I am one of Bob's most seasoned colleagues. I am only 13 days older than he, and we are both part of a generation influenced strongly by Harry Johnson.

I want to focus on Bob's pathbreaking early work. Bob pioneered the empirical analysis of the cost of protection. His 1964 paper on the cost of protection in the United States was the first of his research studies that caught my attention. This is how I got to know him before I ever met him. In a survey of empirical work on the cost and consequences of protection (published in Kenen 1975), I noted that "the only comprehensive calculations of this type for a developed country, as far as I am aware, have been done by Stern (1964), who pioneered this work in the United States but assumed constant export and import prices (the small-country assumption), and then by Basevi (1968) and Magee (1972)."

A few years later, he caught my attention when he visited Oxford and stayed with us. He also caught my wife's attention. "What a nice man!" she remarked. *I* took her to mean "modest," and in fact "modest pioneering" is a nice way of describing Bob's influence ever since.

Two important contributions illustrate my point. After the Leamer-Stern book, Bob's subsequent surveys in the 1970s were immensely influential: his 1973 *Journal of Economic Literature* article on tariffs and other measures of trade control and his chapter in the same Kenen volume on testing trade theories were both authoritative treatments. Yet each survey contains only *one* reference to work by Robert M. Stern! One of Bob's most distinctive traits compared to his peers is that his modesty knows no bounds!

No tribute to Bob's policy influence is complete without mentioning his extensive externalities. Bob has trained an enormous number of professionals who made their way into the policy community and who still reflect his strength and style. And his yearly conferences are legendary for bringing together researchers, students, and policy practitioners for mutual education and stimulation.

In sum, Bob's research, his character, and his extended professional family have all shaped his significant influence on policy. It is a special privilege for me to testify to that today.

Selected Publications of Robert M. Stern

Articles and Surveys

1. 1959. "The Price Responsiveness of Egyptian Cotton Producers." *Kyklos.*

2. 1959. "Agricultural Surplus Disposal as a Means of Financing Economic Development." *Economia Internazionale.*

3. 1959. "The Regional Pattern of World Food Imports and Exports." *Weltwirtschaftliches Archiv.*

4. 1960. "Agricultural Surplus Disposal and U.S. Economic Policies." *World Politics.*

5. 1960. "A Simple Unimodal Lag Distribution." With Henri Theil. *Metroeconomica.*

6. 1962. "The Price Responsiveness of Primary Producers." *Review of Economics and Statistics.*

7. 1962. "The Theory and Measurement of Elasticity of Substitution in International Trade." With Elliott Zupnick. *Kyklos.*

8. 1962. "British and American Productivity and Comparative Costs in International Trade." *Oxford Economic Papers.*

9. 1963. "International Compensation for Fluctuations in Commodity Trade." *Quarterly Journal of Economics.*

10. 1964. "The U.S. Tariff and the Efficiency of the U.S. Economy." *American Economic Review,* Papers and Proceedings.

11. 1964. "Devaluation in a Three-Country World." With Elliott Zupnick. *Economia Internazionale.*

12. 1965. "Malayan Rubber Production, Inventory Holdings and the Elasticity of Export Supply." *Southern Economic Journal.*

13. 1965. "The Determination of the Factors Affecting American and British Exports in the Interwar and Postwar Periods." With Alan Ginsburg. *Oxford Economic Papers.*

14. 1972. "Problems in the Theory and Empirical Estimation of International Capital Movements." With Edward Leamer. In F. Machlup, et al., eds., *International Mobility and the Movement of Capital.* Columbia University Press.

15. 1973. "Tariffs and Other Measures of Trade Control: A Survey of Recent Developments." *Journal of Economic Literature.*

16. 1975. "Testing Trade Theories." In P. Kenen, ed., *International Trade and Finance: Frontiers for Research.* Cambridge University Press.

17. 1976. "Capital-Skill Complementarity and U.S. Trade in Manufactures." In H. Glejser, ed., *Quantitative Studies of International Economic Relations.* North-Holland.

18. 1976. "Some Evidence on the Factor Content of West Germany's Foreign Trade." *Journal of Political Economy.*

19. 1976. "Evaluating Alternative Tariff Formulae for Reducing Industrial Tariffs." *Journal of World Trade Law.*

20. 1976. "The Accommodation of Interests Between the Advanced Industrial Countries and the LDCs." *Journal of World Trade Law.*

21. 1977. "An Empirical Analysis of the Composition of Manufacturing Employment in the Industrialized Countries." With Edward Leamer and Christopher Baum. *European Economic Review.*

22. 1977. "A Multi-Country Simulation of the Employment and Exchange-Rate Effects of Post-Kennedy Round Tariff Reductions." With Alan Deardorff and Christopher Baum. In N. Akrasanee, et al., eds., *Trade and Employment in Asia and the Pacific.* University Press of Hawaii.

23. 1977. "The Presentation of the Balance of Payments: A Symposium." In *Essays in International Finance,* No. 123, Princeton University.

24. 1978. "The Terms-of-Trade Effect on Expenditure: Some Evidence from Econometric Models." With Alan Deardorff. *Journal of International Economics.*

25. 1979. "Evidence on Structural Change in the Demand for Aggregate U.S. Imports and Exports." With Chrisopher Baum and Mark Greene. *Journal of Political Economy.*

26. 1979. "The Sensitivity of Industrial Output and Employment to Exchange-Rate Changes in the Major Industrialized Countries." With Alan Deardorff and Mark Greene. In J. Martin and A. Smith, eds., *Trade and Payments Adjustment Under Flexible Exchange Rates,* MacMillan.

27. 1979. "What Have We Learned from Linked Econometric Models? A Comparison of Fiscal Policy Simulations." With Alan Deardorff. *Banca Nazionale del Lavoro Quarterly Review.*

28. 1981. "Determinants of the Structure of U.S. Foreign Trade, 1958–76." With Keith Maskus. *Journal of International Economics.*

29. 1981. "A Disaggregated Model of World Production and Trade Applied to the Tokyo Round." With Alan Deardorff. *Journal of Policy Modeling.*

30. 1982. "Economic Effects of the Tokyo Round." With Alan Deardorff. *Southern Economic Journal.*

31. 1983. "Tariff and Exchange-Rate Protection under Fixed and Flexible Exchange Rates in the Major Industrialized Countries." With Alan Deardorff. In J. Bhandari and B. Putnam, eds., *Economic Interdependence and Flexible Exchange Rates.* MIT Press.

32. 1983. "The Economic Effects of Complete Elimination of Post-Tokyo Round Tariffs." With Alan Deardorff. In W. Cline, ed., *Trade Policy in the 1980s.* Institute for International Economics.

33. 1984. "The Effects of the Tokyo Round on the Structure of Protection." With Alan Deardorff. In R. Baldwin and A. Krueger, eds., *The*

Structure and Evolution of Recent U.S. Trade Policy. University of Chicago Press.

34. 1985. "Structure of Tariff Protection: The Effects of Foreign Tariffs and Existing NTBs." With Alan Deardorff. *Review of Economics and Statistics.*

35. 1985. "Input-Output Technologies and the Effects of Tariff Reductions." With Alan Deardorff. *Journal of Policy Modeling.*

36. 1985. "Methods of Measurement of Nontariff Barriers." With Alan Deardorff. UNCTAD/ST/MD/28.

37. 1985. "Global Dimensions and Determinants of International Trade and Investment in Services." In R. Stern, ed., *Trade and Investment in Services: Canada/U.S. Perspectives.* University of Toronto Press.

38. 1986. "Estimates of the Elasticities of Substitution Between Imports and Home Goods for the United States." With Alan Deardorff and Clint Shiells. *Weltwirtschaftliches Archiv.*

39. 1986. "Neighborhood Effects of Developing Country Protection." With Alan Deardorff. *Journal of Development Economics.*

40. 1987. "Current Issues in Trade Policy: An Overview." With Alan Deardorff. In R. Stern, ed., *U.S. Trade Policies in a Changing World Economy.* MIT Press.

41. 1987. "The Effects of Protection on the Factor Content of Japanese and American Foreign Trade." With Robert Staiger and Alan Deardorff. *Review of Economics and Statistics.*

42. 1987. "An Evaluation of Factor Endowments and Protection as Determinants of Japanese and American Foreign Trade." With Robert Staiger and Alan Deardorff. *Canadian Journal of Economics.*

43. 1987. "What Do the Multisector Trade Models Show?" With Drusilla Brown. In R. Stern, et al., eds., *Perspectives on a U.S.-Canadian Free Trade Agreement.* Brookings Institution.

44. 1987. "Issues and Data Needs for GATT Negotiations on Services." With Bernard Hoekman. *The World Economy.*

45. 1987. "The Economic Consequences of an Import Surcharge: Theory and Empirical Evidence for the U.S. Economy." With Alan Deardorff and Filip Abraham. *Journal of Policy Modeling.*

46. 1988. "The Impact of Tariffs on Profits in the United States and Other Major Trading Countries." With Filip Abraham and Alan Deardorff. *Weltwirtschaftliches Archiv.*

47. 1989. "An Analytical Survey of Formal and Informal Barriers to Trade and Investment in the United States, Canada, and Japan." With Gary Saxonhouse. In R. Stern, ed., *Trade and Investment Relations Among the United States, Canada, and Japan.* University of Chicago Press.

48. 1989. "Computational Analysis of the U.S.-Canadian Free Trade Agreement: The Role of Product Diffferentiation and Market Structure." With Drusilla Brown. In R. Feenstra, ed., *Trade Policies for International Competitiveness.* University of Chicago Press.

49. 1989. "A Computational Analysis of Alternative Safeguards Policy Scenarios in International Trade." With Alan Deardorff. In R. Jones and A. Krueger, eds., *The Political Economy of International Trade.* Basil Blackwell.

50. 1991. "Impact of the Tokyo Round and Macroeconomic Adjustments on North American Trade." With Alan Deardoff. In C. Reynolds, et al., eds., *The Dynamics of North American Trade and Economic Relations: Canada, Mexico, and the United States.* Stanford University Press.

51. 1991. "Evolving Patterns of International Trade and Investment in Services." With Bernard Hoekman. In P. Hooper and J.D. Richardson, eds., *International Economic Transactions: Issues in Measurement and Empirical Research.* University of Chicago Press.

52. 1992. "Some Economic Effects of Unilateral and Multilateral Reductions in Military Expenditures in the Major Western Industrialized and Developing Countries." With Jon Haveman and Alan Deardorff. *Conflict Management and Peace Science.*

53. 1992. "A North American Free Trade Agreement: Analytical Issues and a Computational Assessment." With Drusilla Brown and Alan Deardorff. *The World Economy.*

54. 1992. "North American Integration." With Drusilla Brown and Alan Deardorff. *Economic Journal.*

55. 1993. "Effects of Reductions in NATO Military Expenditures on U.S. Employment by Sector/Occupation/Region." With Alan Fox. *The World Economy.*

56. 1994. "Multilateral Trade Negotiations and Preferential Trading Arrangements." With Alan Deardorff. In A. Deardorff and R. Stern, eds., *Analytical and Negotiating Issues in the Global Trading System.* University of Michigan Press.

57. 1994. "The GATT's Trade Policy Review of Japan." *The World Economy.*

58. 1995. "Expanding NAFTA: Economic Effects of Accession of Chile and Other Major South American Nations." With Drusilla Brown and Alan Deardorff. *North American Journal of Economics and Finance.*

59. 1996. "International Labor Standards and Trade: a Theoretical Analysis." With Drusilla Brown and Alan Deardorff. In J. Bhagwati and R. Hudec, eds., *Fair Trade and Harmonization: Prerequisites for Free Trade?* Cambridge: MIT Press.

60. 1996. "Modelling Multilateral Liberalization in Services." With Drusilla Brown and Alan Deardorff. *Asia-Pacific Economic Review.*

61. 1996. "The Liberalization of Services Trade: Potential Impacts in the Aftermath of the Uruguay Round." With Drusilla Brown, Alan Deardorff, and Alan Fox. In W. Martin and L.A. Winters, eds., *The Uruguay Round and Developing Countries.* Cambridge: Cambridge University Press.

62. 1996. "Conflict and Cooperation in International Economics Policy and Law." *Journal of International Economic Law.*

63. 1997. "Issues of Trade and International Labor Standards in the WTO System." In Korea Economic Institute, *The Emerging WTO System and Perspectives from East Asia,* Joint U.S.-Korea Academic Studies.

Books Written

64. 1970. *Quantitative International Economics.* With Edward Leamer. Allyn and Bacon.

65. 1973. *The Balance of Payments: Theory and Economic Policy.* Aldine Publishing.

66. 1976. *Price Elasticities in International Trade.* With Jonathan Francis and Bruce Schumacher. MacMillan.

67. 1986. *The Michigan Model of World Production and Trade: Theory and Applications.* With Alan Deardorff. MIT Press.

68. 1990. *A Computational Analysis of Global Trading Arrangements.* With Alan Deardorff. University of Michigan Press.

Books Edited

69. 1961. *Equilibrium and Growth in the World Economy: Economic Essays by Ragnar Nurkse.* With Gottfried Haberler. Harvard University Press.

70. 1987. *U.S. Trade Policies in a Changing World Economy.* MIT Press.

71. 1987. *Perspectives on a U.S.-Canadian Free Trade Agreement.* With Philip Tresize and John Whalley. The Brookings Institution.

72. 1989. *Trade and Investment Relations Among the United States, Canada, and Japan.* University of Chicago Press.

73. 1993. *The Multilateral Trading System: Analysis and Prospects for Negotiating Change.* University of Michigan Press.

74. 1994. *Analytical and Negotiating Issues in the Global Trading System.* With Alan Deardorff. University of Michigan Press.

75. 1994. *The Stolper-Samuelson Theorem: The Golden Jubilee.* With Alan Deardoff. University of Michigan Press.

76. 1995. *New Directions in Trade Theory.* With Alan Deardorff and James Levinsohn. University of Michigan Press.

Contributors

Filip Abraham
University of Leuven
Belgium

W. Max Corden
School of Advanced International Studies
Johns Hopkins University

Geza Feketekuty
Center for Trade & Commercial Diplomacy
Monterey Institute of International Studies

Joseph Francois
Trade and Development Group
Department of Applied Economics
Erasmus University of Rotterdam
Netherlands

Kishore Gawande
Department of Economics
University of New Mexico

Bernard Hoekman
International Trade Division
The World Bank

Peter M. Hooper
Division of International Finance
Board of Governors of the Federal Reserve System

Wilhelm Kohler
Department of Economics
University of Linz
Austria

Edward E. Leamer
Anderson Graduate School of Management
University of California, Los Angeles

Jay H. Levin
Department of Economics
Wayne State University

Will Martin
International Trade Division
The World Bank

Keith E. Maskus
Department of Economics
University of Colorado

Rachel McCulloch
Department of Economics
Brandeis University

John Mutti
Department of Economics
Grinnell College

Mohan Penubarti
Department of Political
   Science
University of California, Los
   Angeles

Jorge F. Perez-Lopez
Bureau of International
   Labor Affairs
U.S. Department of Labor

Peter A. Petri
Department of Economics
Brandeis University

Alfred Reifman
Formerly of the Congres-
   sional Research Service

Gregory K. Schoepfle
Bureau of International
   Labor Affairs
U.S. Department of Labor

Aileen Thompson
Department of Economics
Carleton University

Elizabeth Vrankovich
Division of International Finance
Board of Governors of the
   Federal Reserve System

Bernard Yeung
School of Business Administration
University of Michigan

Discussants

Sven Arndt
The Lowe Institute
Claremont McKenna College

Robert Baldwin
Department of Economics
University of Wisconsin

Robert Barsky
Department of Economics
University of Michigan

Jeffrey Bergstrand
College of Business
Notre Dame University

Harry Bowen
Department of Economics
University of California, Irvine

Drusilla Brown
Department of Economics
Tufts University

Alan Deardorff
Department of Economics
University of Michigan

Mitsuhiro Fukao
Faculty of Business and Commerce
Keio University
Japan

Edward Gramlich
Department of Economics
University of Michigan

Theresa Greaney
Department of Economics
Syracuse University

Jon Haveman
Department of Economics
Purdue University

David Hummels
School of Business
University of Chicago

John Jackson
School of Law
University of Michigan

Jim Levinsohn
Department of Economics
University of Michigan

J. David Richardson
Department of Economics
Syracuse University

Martin Richardson
Department of Economics
University of Otago
New Zealand

Gary Saxonhouse
Department of Economics
University of Michigan

Frank Stafford
Department of Economics
University of Michigan

Robert Staiger
Department of Economics
University of Wisconsin

Marie Thursby
Department of Economics
Purdue University

Jozef Van't dack
Bank for International Settlements
Switzerland

Hal Varian
School of Information
    Management and Systems
University of California, Berkeley

Index